Introduction to Transfer Pricing

Introduction to Transfer Pricing

Second Edition

Jérôme Monsenego

Wolters Kluwer

Published by:
Kluwer Law International B.V.
PO Box 316
2400 AH Alphen aan den Rijn
The Netherlands
E-mail: lrs-sales@wolterskluwer.com
Website: www.wolterskluwer.com/en/solutions/kluwerlawinternational

Sold and distributed by:
Wolters Kluwer Legal & Regulatory U.S.
7201 McKinney Circle
Frederick, MD 21704
United States of America
E-mail: customer.service@wolterskluwer.com

Printed on acid-free paper.

ISBN 978-94-035-1483-3

e-Book: ISBN 978-94-035-1493-2
web-PDF: ISBN 978-94-035-1503-8

Printed in the Netherlands.

To Liv, Ella and Axel

About the Author

Jérôme Monsenego is Full Professor of International Tax Law at Stockholm University (Sweden), Research Fellow at the Amsterdam Centre for Transfer Pricing and Income Allocation, and Chairman of IFA Sweden. He obtained his PhD *summa cum laude* and was awarded an honourable mention by the jury of the IFA Mitchell B. Carroll Prize for his doctoral thesis *Taxation of Foreign Business Income Within the European Internal Market* (IBFD Doctoral Series, 2012). He has published articles in English, French and Swedish on various topics of international taxation, a book on transfer pricing, and a book on fiscal State aid (*Selectivity in State Aid Law and the Methods for the Allocation of the Corporate Tax Base,* Kluwer Law International, 2018) that was shortlisted for the 2019 IBFD Frans Vanistendael Award. He has taught at several foreign universities and has been visiting professor at Université Paris 1 Panthéon-Sorbonne (France), Università degli Studi di Torino (Italy), Meiji University (Japan), as well as visiting scholar at Boston College School of Law (USA). He has intervened as an expert before courts and advised governments on legislative projects. Prior to joining academia on a full-time basis, he worked as an international tax advisor at PwC in Paris and Stockholm.

Table of Contents

List of Abbreviations

APA	Advance Pricing Arrangement
ATAD	Anti Tax Avoidance Directive
BEFIT	Business in Europe: Framework for Income Taxation
BEPS	Base Erosion and Profit Shifting
CCA	Cost Contribution Arrangement
CCCTB	Common Consolidated Corporate Tax Base
CFC	Controlled Foreign Company
CJEU	Court of Justice of the European Union
COGS	Cost of Goods Sold
CUP	Comparable Uncontrolled Price
DAC	Directive on Administrative Compliance
DAEMPE	Development, Acquisition, Enhancement, Maintenance, Protection and Exploitation
DEMPE	Development, Enhancement, Maintenance, Protection and Exploitation
EBIT	Earnings Before Interest and Taxes
EBITDA	Earnings Before Interests, Taxes, Depreciation and Amortization
EU	European Union
FCM	Full Cost Mark-Up
IP	Intangible Property
IT	Information Technology
MAP	Mutual Agreement Procedure
MLI	Multilateral Instrument
OECD	Organisation for Economic Co-operation and Development
OECD Guidelines	OECD Guidelines for Multinational Enterprises and Tax Administrations, July 2010
OPEX	Operating Expenses

R&D	Research and Development
TNMM	Transactional Net Margin Method
UN	United Nations

List of Figures

List of Tables

Foreword

Transfer pricing is an area of international tax which has become more and more important, and an increasing number of highly specialised experts are making their living by using their expertise in this area. Still, the market needs even more specialists who have sufficient skills to solve transfer pricing cases in practice. Therefore, it is extremely important for universities and similar institutions to offer courses on transfer pricing and provide students with the necessary training. The academic institutions of a large number of countries have started to offer such training. However, there has been a long gap in the literature: there are primers on European tax law and tax treaties on the one hand, and there is highly specialised literature on transfer pricing on the other hand. Nevertheless, an introductory book on transfer pricing has been missing so far.

Prof. Jérôme Monsenego has filled this gap by providing students and beginners in practice with an excellent introduction to the topic. Those of us who have been authoring or editing tax books know how tempting it is to write big books with a lot of details, and how difficult it is to write a small book which provides the basic knowledge. Jérôme has managed to deal with this challenge and resisted going into all the details (although he definitely would be the expert to do this and has shown that on several occasions). Academics who run courses in the area of transfer pricing now really have a book they can recommend to their students without feeling that they are demanding too much of them. If students read this book when they register for a transfer pricing class, they will be excellently prepared. The same is true for tax practitioners who want to become familiar with transfer pricing issues. Therefore, I am really confident that this book, which has long been awaited by the transfer pricing community, will be very well received.

For the second edition, Jérôme updated the book, included additional examples as well as court cases from various countries, and deepened certain analyses on a few controversial topics. While the material related to transfer pricing has increased with the Base Erosion and Profit Shifting (BEPS) project, he tried to keep the book short, and this is the most difficult challenge, because one always finds ideas to include in a book.

It is most important to keep such a book short; otherwise, it will not be accepted by practitioners and students. I want to congratulate Jérôme for being so disciplined!

Michael Lang
Professor, Institute for Austrian and International Tax Law, WU Vienna

Preface to the Second Edition

The international tax world has changed significantly since the publication of the first edition of this book in 2015. In the field of transfer pricing, the BEPS project resulted in amendments to the OECD Guidelines and the UN Manual, aiming mainly at reinforcing the link between the place where economic activities are carried out and the place where profits are taxed. Important changes relevant to transfer pricing also occurred in areas such as dispute resolution or transparency.

This book does not rely on the tax system of a particular country, but provides a general introduction to transfer pricing by referring mostly to the 2022 OECD Guidelines and the 2021 UN Manual. In addition, court cases as well as domestic rules from various countries illustrate different transfer pricing concepts. Bibliographical references are included to let readers deepen the topic.

As with the previous edition, I have been trying to introduce transfer pricing in a pedagogical way, using examples and explanations. However, a handbook can always be improved: comments are most welcome and may be sent to jerome.monsenego@juridicum.su.se.

I would like to thank colleagues from the international tax community as well as former students from around the globe for providing invaluable feedback on the previous edition of the book. I am also thankful to the research foundation *Stiftelsen för stöd till skatterättslig forskning vid Stockholm Centre for Commercial Law* for providing financial support to this book project.

The book takes into account legal developments up to 1 July 2022.

Jérôme Monsenego
Stockholm, 10 August 2022

Preface to the First Edition

I thought about the need for such a book when teaching transfer pricing, as I found difficult to provide reading recommendations to students, especially at an introductory level. Therefore, my primary objective when writing this book was to introduce transfer pricing in a pedagogical way, in particular through relying on examples and thorough explanations of transfer pricing principles. At the same time, I tried to provide analyses and bibliographical references so as to let readers understand the complexity of transfer pricing and be able to deepen different questions. The book does not rely on the tax system of a particular country, but instead aims to provide a general introduction to transfer pricing by relying mostly on the OECD Guidelines, the UN practical manual on transfer pricing, as well as court cases from various countries.

An earlier version of this book was originally published in 2013 by Studentlitteratur, a Swedish publishing house, before being published in a revised and updated edition by Kluwer Law International. I am thankful to Kluwer Law International and Studentlitteratur for making the transition as easy as possible. The book is published at a special time, given that many of the rules and principles of international tax law, including the OECD Guidelines, are being reviewed as part of the project on BEPS that is carried out by the OECD on behalf of the G20 countries. Therefore, where relevant, the proposals made by the OECD as part of the BEPS project are mentioned and commented upon, although these proposals were in a draft version at the time of publishing this book.

I would like to thank my colleagues, former students, and friends from the tax community for providing invaluable feedback on earlier drafts of this book. I am also thankful to the foundation TOR/Skattenytt as well as the Uppsala Center for Tax Law, a research foundation supported by Deloitte, Ernst & Young, KPMG, Mannheimer Swartling, PwC and Skeppsbron Skatt (Taxand), for the financial support provided to this book project.

This book takes into account the legal developments up to 31 May 2015. Comments are most welcome and may be sent to jerome.monsenego@jur.uu.se.

Jérôme Monsenego
Stockholm, 31 May 2015

Introduction

Transfer pricing is an area of tax law that has significantly expanded over the last few decades. This is partly explained by the globalisation of business activities: enterprises are getting more global so as to reach new markets and make their organisation more efficient. Another reason is related to the tax planning opportunities that may be available through cross-border controlled transactions and differences across the tax systems of various countries, something that States are willing to monitor through different mechanisms, including transfer pricing rules to avoid the illegitimate erosion of their tax base. The focus on transfer pricing has also amplified during recent years as States are under pressure to levy taxes and reduce their public deficits, thereby increasing the number, and sometimes the complexity, of transfer pricing disputes. Finally, despite the global reach of the OECD Transfer Pricing Guidelines for Multinational Enterprises and Tax Administrations (OECD Guidelines) and the United Nations (UN) Manual, differences still exist in how States apply transfer pricing rules and interpret the arm's length principle, thus leading to situations of double taxation that are not always eliminated. Consequently, transfer pricing has become a key question for multinational enterprises and tax administrations alike, something that is likely to increase in the future.[1]

The importance of transfer pricing rules and principles culminated with the work of the Organisation for Economic Co-operation and Development (OECD) on Base Erosion and Profit Shifting (BEPS). The OECD indeed received a mandate from the G20 countries to investigate the extent of BEPS as a phenomenon, and reflect on how to address it through fifteen work streams (so-called Actions) intended at suggesting changes to domestic laws, tax treaties, States' practices, and various principles including transfer pricing principles.[2] The combined effect of all such changes,

1. *See Spillovers in international corporate taxation*, IMF Policy Paper, 32, para. 50 (9 May 2014): 'The burden on companies of justifying, and on the authorities of verifying, that transfer prices used correspond to [arm's length pricing] is widely recognized to be substantial. And they will increase: as businesses become more knowledge-intensive and technology driven, management becomes more geographically diffuse, and intra-group operations become easier to transfer and more difficult to price.'
2. *See* OECD, *Action Plan on Base Erosion and Profit Shifting* (2013).

assuming they are consistently implemented by as many countries as possible, was to result in an international framework where both double non-taxation and double taxation are prevented while at the same time ensuring that income is taxed in the right country, i.e., the country where 'value' is deemed to be created.[3] Transfer pricing was one of the key areas under review during the BEPS project because of three main reasons: first, the incorrect application of the arm's length principle may result in double non-taxation or taxation in the wrong country, due to non-arm's length prices or misapplications of the arm's length principle. This would point to the need for a more robust guidance, ensuring taxation in line with substance or 'value creation';[4] second, the arm's length principle as such may result in outcomes that are considered incorrect, thereby pointing to the possible need to deviate from this principle; third, the guidance on the application of the arm's length principle needed clarification as the interpretation of this principle may vary from one country to another, thereby creating a risk of double taxation. For all these reasons, transfer pricing was an essential element of the BEPS project. Somewhat paradoxically, the changes made to the transfer pricing framework as part of the BEPS project stressed the need to adopt other types of provisions if countries were to tax digital activities carried out with no or low physical presence. This resulted in the so-called Pillar 1 project, endorsed by the members of the OECD/G20 inclusive framework in 2021, the objective of which is to develop rules that in certain cases apply in addition to transfer pricing rules, so as to reallocate part of the corporate tax base from the country of origin to the country of destination.

Introduction to Transfer Pricing has a twofold purpose. First, it intends to provide a general introduction to the fundamentals of transfer pricing. The book does not take the perspective of a particular country and instead focuses on the general principles and mechanisms that apply, albeit to various extents, in most countries.[5] Although most of these principles are found in the OECD Guidelines, the views of other international organisations, in particular the UN and the European Union (EU), are also taken into account in the book, especially when such views confirm or differ from the OECD Guidelines with respect to critical issues. Given the breadth and the complexity

3. This objective of the BEPS project can be described as strengthening the link between the taxes that are levied, and the substance – i.e., the reality – of a given transaction or corporate structure. Therefore, the BEPS project aimed at a strengthened application of the principle of territoriality in international tax law, by reinforcing the connection between the right to tax and the presence of a given substance in the territory of a State.
4. The notion of 'value creation' is controversial, especially given the fact that it is attributed different meanings in different contexts. It seems also to be resulting in interpretation problems with respect to the use of this concept in the OECD Guidelines as amended by the BEPS project (*see* Richard S. Collier and Ian F. Dykes, *On the Apparent Widespread Misapplication of the OECD Transfer Pricing Guidelines: Risk and Post-BEPS Problems for the Arm's Length Principle,* 20–43 (Bulletin for International Taxation, 2022-1)). For the sake of clarity, this concept is avoided in this book when other concepts are deemed more suitable. The author's analysis of the concept of 'value creation' in the context of transfer pricing is found in Jérôme Monsenego, *Transfer Pricing and Value Creation,* in Werner Haslehner and Marie Lamensch (eds), Taxation and Value Creation, 107–129 (IBFD EATLP International Tax Series, 2021).
5. Although domestic laws and the wordings of various tax treaties are outside the scope of this book, references to such sources are made occasionally. The purpose of such references is to illustrate certain differences with the recommendations of the OECD or other international organisations.

of this discipline, as well as the pedagogical aim of this book, only the key principles necessary to understand transfer pricing are dealt with. EU law is mostly taken into account with respect to secondary law that is binding on the Member States of the EU such as the dispute resolution directive or country-by-country reporting; compatibility issues between transfer pricing rules and EU primary law are out of the scope of this book.[6] Also, the connection between transfer pricing and other areas of tax law is outside the scope of this book.[7]

Second, to strengthen the pedagogical objective of this book, *Introduction to Transfer Pricing* intends to illustrate the fundamentals of transfer pricing by concrete examples and transfer pricing models frequently used by multinational enterprises.

The book is divided into the following seven chapters:

Chapter 1 The Key to Understanding Transfer Pricing: The Arm's Length Principle.
Chapter 2 Transfer Pricing Methods.
Chapter 3 Transfer Pricing Models.
Chapter 4 Cross-Border Business Restructurings.

6. In this respect *see* Jérôme Monsenego, *Transfer Pricing in the European Union*, in Raffaele Petruzzi, Giammarco Cottani and Michael Lang (eds), Fundamentals of Transfer Pricing: Industries, Regions, New Technologies, and Other Topics, 333–367 (Kluwer Law International, 2022). With respect to the compatibility of the arm's length principle, safe harbours and formula apportionment with the State aid rules *see* Jérôme Monsenego, *Selectivity in State Aid Law and the Methods for the Allocation of the Corporate Tax Base* (Kluwer Law International, 2018).
7. In particular, value-added taxation and customs duties, although connected to transfer pricing, are outside the scope of this book. With respect to value-added taxation, one issue relates to whether primary adjustments, secondary adjustments, corresponding adjustments, and voluntary prospective adjustments made for transfer pricing purposes should also imply VAT consequences; it has been suggested – although it is not the generally accepted view – that such transfer pricing adjustments do not correspond to supplies of goods or services, and thus should be outside the scope of VAT: *see* European Commission, VAT Expert Group, *Possible VAT implications of Transfer Pricing* (18 April 2018, taxud.c.1(2018)2326098 – EN). When it comes to transfer pricing and customs duties, while customs valuation and transfer pricing approaches both aim at determining an appropriate price for cross-border transactions, a conflict exists because of the different interests pursued by customs and income taxes: a high price on imported goods reduces the tax base of the importer, while increasing the customs duties payable for such goods. Therefore, a risk exists that 'While the direct tax authority would focus on overvalued import prices, the customs authority will seek to ensure that the declared customs value has not been undervalued to reduce duty liability' (*see* para. 3.6.6.1 of the 2021 UN Manual). Because of these diverging interests, no harmonisation of the systems for customs and income taxes has been reached. For recommendations on how to deal with this issue, *see* the *WCO Guide to Customs Valuation and Transfer Pricing* (2nd ed., World Customs Organization, 2018). More generally on this issue *see* the *Hamamatsu* case ruled by the CJEU (*Hamamatsu Photonics Deutschland GmbH v. Hauptzollamt München*, CJEU (20 December 2017, Case C-529/16)) where the court in para. 26 found that the customs value had to be determined primarily according to the 'transaction value' method under Art. 29 of the Customs Code; case *Refrescos y Envasados S.A. v. Administración General del Estado*, Supreme Court of Spain (*Tribunal Supremo*) (30 November 2009, case number 3582/2003); Anuschka Bakker and Belema Obuoforibo (eds), *Transfer Pricing and Customs Valuation: Two Worlds to Tax as One* (IBFD, 2009).

Chapter 5 The Substance Requirement from a Transfer Pricing Perspective.
Chapter 6 The Attribution of Profits to Permanent Establishments.
Chapter 7 Administrative Aspects: Compliance Issues and Transfer Pricing Disputes.

CHAPTER 1

The Key to Understanding Transfer Pricing: The Arm's Length Principle

'Transfer pricing is a "zero sum game" – a situation in which the "gain" of taxable profits by one jurisdiction must be matched by a "loss" by the other jurisdiction'.[1]

1.1 INTRODUCTION

When companies do business abroad, they may choose to do so by cooperating with *independent enterprises*, i.e., companies with which there are no legal or economic connections. In such cases, the prices of transactions are normally determined by *market forces*, i.e., supply and demand.[2] Although the taxable income of each party to the transaction – and thus also the corporate income tax paid by each party – will be directly influenced by the prices of the transactions, from a fiscal perspective, the tax administrations of the countries concerned have no strong reasons to worry about the prices of these transactions because the parties are independent of each other. Each party is assumed to be business minded and act in its own interest by trying to maximise its profits. Therefore, there is no need – from a fiscal perspective – to monitor the prices of such transactions. In contrast, when companies engage in cross-border business activities through dealing with *associated enterprises*,[3] it is quite possible that no such market forces apply given the legal or economic connections between the parties to the transaction.[4] As a result, the price of transactions between associated

1. UN, *Practical Manual on Transfer Pricing for Developing Countries*, para. 1.7.16 (2013).
2. For a definition of market forces, *see* the *Oxford English Dictionary* (online version): 'The economic factors affecting the price of, demand for, and availability of a commodity.'
3. The notion of associated enterprises refers broadly to companies that belong to the same group. For a presentation of this notion, *see* section 1.4.1 of this book.
4. For example, the legal or economic connections between associated enterprises may result in a company not proceeding by a call for tenders from potential business partners, in order to

enterprises may deviate from what would have been agreed between independent companies because of the lack of market forces. From a fiscal perspective, the problem is that deviations from the prices that would result from market forces affect the level of taxable income of associated enterprises, and thus the amount of corporate income tax they pay in each country.

The area of tax law that is dedicated to the tax consequences of the pricing of cross-border intercompany transactions is usually referred to as *transfer pricing*[5] since this area of tax law is concerned with the prices of goods or services that are sold, or 'transferred', between associated enterprises. Figure 1.1 gives an example of the transfer of goods from a parent company that manufactures goods to a subsidiary of the parent company that distributes such goods.[6]

Example: A parent company (company A) resident in country A manufactures goods. Its wholly owned subsidiary (company B) is resident in country B and purchases the goods to distribute them in country B.

Figure 1.1 Payment in Exchange for Goods

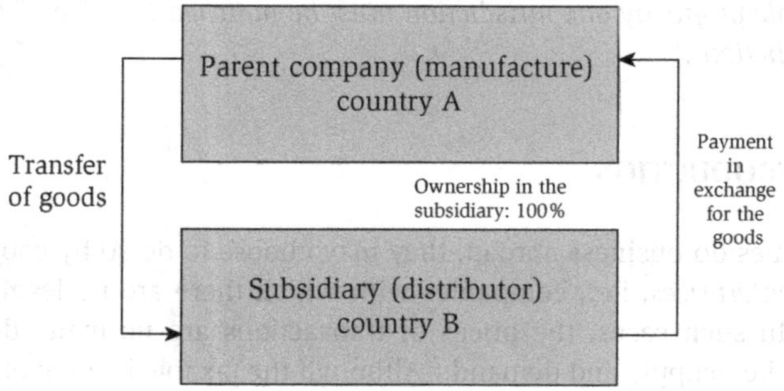

In many cases, transfer pricing may not be an issue if the parent company and the subsidiary were resident in the same country, as long as a tax equalisation mechanism applies.[7] Transfer pricing may not be an issue in a cross-border context and between

purchase a good directly from a supplier that belongs to the same group without negotiating the price of the good with the intention to maximise its own profit.

5. Transfer pricing rules and the arm's length principle have been in operation for nearly one hundred years. For a historical perspective on the genesis and the rise of the arm's length principle, *see* Richard Collier and Joseph L Andrus, *Transfer Pricing and the Arm's Length Principle after BEPS*, 6–49 (Oxford University Press, 2017). *See also* Jefferson VanderWolk, *The Arm's-Length Standard Enters Its Second Century*, 961–968 (Tax Notes International, 4 March 2019).
6. Multinational enterprises may enter into many other types of intercompany transactions, involving, e.g., R&D, financial services, or sales of assets between associated enterprises. Examples of intercompany transactions are provided in section 3.4 of this book.
7. For example, if company A and company B are residents in the same country, and assuming that this country allows the transfer of profits or losses between associated enterprises or the consolidation and taxation of profits at the level of one of the companies, it may not matter for the group and for the tax administration of this country how the tax base is allocated between

independent companies either, because the price of the goods would normally be determined by supply and demand; i.e., the price would be influenced by market forces. However, in the above example, the manufacturer owns 100% of the shares in the distributor; i.e., the enterprises are associated. Such an ownership indeed makes it possible for the shareholder to influence the decisions made by the subsidiary, so the price of the goods may be set at a higher or lower level than the market price, thanks to the relationship of dependence existing between the two companies.[8] In addition, company A and company B are residents in different countries. Accordingly, a deviation from the market price will have consequences for the taxes paid in countries A and B as compared to if market prices were applied because the taxable income of each company is influenced by the transfer prices; if the goods are sold at a price that is higher than the market price, the income of the seller (company A) will be higher than if the goods are sold to a non-related party. At the same time, the income of the buyer (company B) will be lower than if the goods are purchased from a non-related seller because the price paid will exceed the market price. Consequently, assuming that both companies are profit-making[9] and that company A sells a good to company B over the market price, country A will get more taxes than if the transaction takes place between independent parties, while country B will get less.

The impact of transfer pricing on the taxable profits (and thus on the taxes paid) in each country where a multinational enterprise enters into intercompany transactions is illustrated by the two examples below (Table 1.1 and Table 1.2). In both examples, a multinational enterprise has a total taxable profit of 150. It is also assumed that the corporate income tax rate in country A amounts to 30% (country A is described as a high-tax country), while it amounts to 10% in country B (country B is described as a low-tax country). The purpose of this example is to compute the corporate income

company A and company B. This is because the group will anyway be taxed on its net profit. Therefore, although the prices of the transactions between company A and company B will influence the profits of these companies at first sight, there is no need from a tax perspective to monitor the prices of the transactions between company A and company B. This is an illustration of the *principle of neutrality* in the area of corporate taxation, whereby a group is taxed on its net or economic income, irrespective of the transactions that take place between the group members or the way the group is structured. For a discussion on the issues of principle related to the taxation of corporate groups on their net profit, *see* Bertil Wiman, *Equalising the Tax Burden in a Group of Companies*, in Gustaf Lindencrona, Sven-Olof Lodin and Bertil Wiman (eds), International Studies in Taxation: Law and Economics, Liber Amicorum Leif Mutén, 363–378 (Kluwer Law International, 1999).

8. However, it should not be assumed that all transactions between associated enterprises are able, or intended, to depart from market forces simply because they take place between companies that are related to each other. For example, it is quite possible that associated enterprises need to negotiate with each other and maximise their own profits as independent enterprises. That would be the case when two companies belong to the same corporate group but to different business units: it is well possible that the management of each business unit needs to meet certain profitability objectives (the managers of each business unit may even be remunerated based on the profits of the business unit), which would result in each company having an incentive to maximise its own profits.
9. The levels of transfer prices are also relevant for companies that are loss-making because the pricing of an intercompany transaction affects the losses that may be carried back or carried forward.

taxes paid in country A and in country B, as well as the total tax burden of the whole group.[10]

In Table 1.1, a multinational enterprise has a total taxable profit of 150, of which 100 is attributable to a manufacturer (resident in country A) and 50 is attributable to a distributor (resident in country B). Thus, the group earns a relatively high profit in a high-tax country.

Table 1.1 High Profit in a High-Tax Country

Taxable profit in country A	100
Tax rate of country A	30%
Taxes paid in country A	100 × 30% = 30
Taxable profit in country B	50
Tax rate of country B	10%
Taxes paid in country B	50 × 10% = 5
Total taxable profits of the group	100 + 50 = 150
Total tax burden of the group	30 + 5 = 35

In the above example (Table 1.1), the total tax burden of the multinational enterprise is 35, given that corporate income taxes paid in country A amount to 30, while corporate income taxes paid in country B amount to 5. However, as countries A and B have different corporate income tax rates, the total tax burden of this multinational enterprise would not be the same with other transfer prices, as the taxable profit in each country would be higher or lower than in the first example. In other words, the group would have a different total tax burden with different transfer prices. This is illustrated by the second example below (Table 1.2), where the multinational enterprise has the same total taxable profits (150), but the taxable profit in country A is lower (50), while the taxable profit in country B is higher (100). Thus, the group earns a relatively high profit in a low-tax country.

Table 1.2 High Profit in a Low-Tax Country

Taxable profit in country A	50
Tax rate of country A	30%
Taxes paid in country A	50 × 30% = 15
Taxable profit in country B	100
Tax rate of country B	10%
Taxes paid in country B	100 × 10% = 10
Total taxable profits of the group	50 + 100 = 150
Total tax burden of the group	15 + 10 = 25

10. The total tax burden of the whole group is computed as the sum of the corporate income taxes paid in country A and in country B.

As a consequence of the group earning more profits in a country with a lower corporate income tax rate (country B) and less profits in a country with a higher corporate income tax rate (country A), the total tax burden of the group in the second example (25, Table 1.2) is lower than in the first example (35, Table 1.1), although the total profits of the group remain unchanged (150 in both cases). Since it is assumed that these two companies have entered into intercompany transactions, the issue of transfer pricing becomes relevant for the multinational enterprise and the tax administrations of countries A and B. On the one hand, the setting of transfer prices may be of interest for the multinational enterprise as it may enable tax savings at the group level. On the other hand, if the tax administration of country A or B suspects transfer prices not to have been correct, it would normally consider that its tax base has been illegitimately eroded (i.e., too little tax has been paid) and would seek to revise the transfer prices for taxation purposes, thus creating a risk of *economic double taxation*[11] for the multinational enterprise. Accordingly, it is necessary to strike a balance between the interests of multinational enterprises and tax administrations with regard to the setting of transfer prices, something that is normally done through applying the *arm's length principle* when pricing the goods or services transferred between the associated enterprises.

1.2 POSSIBLE METHODS FOR SHARING THE PROFITS OF MULTINATIONAL ENTERPRISES

1.2.1 The Objectives of a Method for Sharing the Profits of Multinational Enterprises

The aim of transfer pricing, from a tax perspective, is to share the taxable base of a group – i.e., the profits or losses – arising from cross-border intercompany transactions. This goal can hardly be reached in a satisfactory manner by countries taking individual and uncoordinated initiatives: such initiatives would probably result in different principles being applied, multinational enterprises would have no foreseeability and would be subject to double taxation or double non-taxation, and countries would have troubles ensuring that they levy the right amount of taxes. It is therefore necessary to agree at an international level on a way to share the taxable base of multinational enterprises when they enter into cross-border intercompany transactions.

11. The risk of economic double taxation exists when a tax administration rejects the transfer prices applied to a given intercompany transaction to increase the taxable profits earned by a resident company. When the taxable profits of the counterpart to the intercompany transaction remain unchanged, the group would be subject to double taxation as the same profits are subject to tax in two countries. Such economic double taxation is usually described as 'economic' (as opposed to 'juridical') because the double taxation occurs at the level of two separate legal subjects. For an example of economic double taxation created by a transfer pricing reassessment, *see* below section 7.2 of this book.

Methods for sharing the profits of multinational enterprises can pursue different objectives. The prevention of double non-taxation and the elimination of double taxation are fundamental objectives to avoid that cross-border business activities are taxed too differently from domestic business activities. Neutrality in the international allocation of taxing rights is also an important objective to ensure that the method chosen does not favour certain countries or types of companies. More recently, it has been emphasised that the international tax system should be fair[12] both to multinational enterprises and to the countries in which they are doing business: the need to achieve fairness in international taxation has been strongly advocated by countries and international organisations, especially the G20 countries and the OECD as part of the BEPS project, together with the UN, the EU,[13] the International Monetary Fund and various stakeholders such as non-governmental organisations. Hence, achieving fairness in the international allocation of taxing rights was one of the main objectives of the BEPS project.[14] It is not only a technical issue but also a political one. The aim of achieving fairness in the international allocation of taxing rights through designing tax rules is reflected in most parts of the BEPS project, including the work on transfer pricing, although it is expressed in different manners. Yet, fairness is not defined in the material published by the OECD or by other international organisations working with tax policy. Fairness should reasonably include the prevention of tax avoidance (which was also one of the objectives of the BEPS project), as a tax system that enables tax avoidance can hardly be said to be fair; fairness includes also another dimension, one of justice in the international allocation of taxing rights, which is exacerbated when it comes to digital companies.[15] Therefore, a need for reform has

12. The concept of 'fair' cannot be objectively defined. It is a dynamic concept that evolves with time and can also be perceived differently in different countries. To ensure the legitimacy and acceptability of an international tax system, policymakers would normally try to design rules that are perceived as sufficiently fair to the parties directly involved in the levy of corporate tax (taxpayers and tax administrations); however, international taxation has become a topic that triggers a broad interest, so the rules need also to be perceived as fair by persons who are not directly involved in the levy of tax on the profits of a corporation: competing enterprises, competing countries, non-governmental organisations, and even society at large. On the need to achieve fairness in the protection of the interests of tax administrations and multinational enterprises, *see* particularly paras 4 and 18 of the preface to the OECD Guidelines. *See also* OECD, *Report on the Attribution of Profits to Permanent Establishments*, Part I, para. 3 (17 July 2008). More generally, for a discussion on fairness in international tax law, *see* Alice Pirlot, *The Vagueness of Tax Fairness: A Discursive Analysis of the Commission's 'Fair Tax Agenda'*, vol. 48, issue 4, 402–415 (Intertax, 2020); Paul B.W.L. Lamberts, *Fair Taxation: Truth Is in the Eye of the Beholder*, vol. 45, issue 1, 49–53 (Intertax, 2017); João Dácio Rolim, *Proportionality and Fair Taxation* (Kluwer Law International, Series on International Taxation, 2014); *see also* Nancy H. Kaufman, *Fairness and the Taxation of International Income*, 145–203 (Law & Policy in International Business, 1998).
13. *See*, e.g., the package proposed by the European Commission in 2018 in relation to the 'fair' taxation of the digital economy: https://ec.europa.eu/taxation_customs/business/company-tax/fair-taxation-digital-economy_en.
14. *See*, e.g., OECD, *Addressing Base Erosion and Profit Shifting*, 36 (2013): 'In an era where non-resident taxpayers can derive substantial profits from transactions with customers located in another country, questions are being raised as to whether the current rules ensure a fair allocation of taxing rights on business profits.'
15. This is because the tax rules developed during the twentieth century lie largely on the physical presence as a prerequisite to allocate taxing rights. Consequently, companies with little physical

emerged as a consequence of the globalisation and the digitalisation of the world's economy so as to better achieve fairness in the international tax system.

Having regard to the above-mentioned objectives, two main methods can be contemplated to share the profits or losses incurred by the members of a group of companies and arising from cross-border intercompany transactions: formulary apportionment (section 1.2.2) and the arm's length principle (section 1.2.3).[16]

1.2.2 Formulary Apportionment

One method for sharing the profit of multinational enterprises would be to start from the income earned by each group member and consolidate such income before sharing it between the different members of the group on the basis of an *allocation key*. This method is usually referred to as *formulary apportionment* or *unitary taxation*. The income originally earned by each group member on the basis of separate accounting would have no importance, as each country would eventually be allocated a certain portion of the consolidated profits or losses for tax purposes, independently from the income recorded by each entity for accounting purposes. The apportionment would be based on the presence of the elements of a formula in the territory of each country where the group has set up a company or has a permanent establishment. Such a formula may include elements that have a tangible existence, for example, the number of persons employed by a group in a given country, the sales achieved there, the tangible assets located in the territory of this country, or elements with no such tangible existence, such as the digital presence of a foreign company. Intangible assets are usually considered as not suitable for inclusion in an allocation key, given the difficulty to value and locate them. A group's consolidated income would be shared between different countries on the basis of the proportion of the elements of the formula that are present in each country. Lastly, each country would tax the share of the consolidated income that it has been attributed with its own tax rate. For taxation purposes, the pricing of transactions between group members would ultimately play no role as taxes are levied on the basis of the portion of the consolidated profits or losses allocated to each group member. Hence, with a system of formula apportionment, the pricing of

---

presence in foreign markets (e.g., through remote sales) have largely been able to escape corporate income taxation in these markets, which raises an issue of fairness. On the need for physical presence in order to create a nexus as a prerequisite for levying tax, *see* Jérôme Monsenego, *Nexus for Transfer Pricing Purposes Before and After BEPS 2.0: From Form to Substance, and Back to Form?*, in Edoardo Traversa (ed.), Nexus and Jurisdiction in International and EU Tax Law (IBFD GREIT Series, 2022).

16. For a general discussion on the two main alternatives to sharing the taxable base of multinational enterprises, *see* Michael C. Durst, *Beyond BEPS: A Tax Policy Agenda for Developing Countries*, 12–13 (ICTD Working Paper 18, June 2014); Reuven S. Avi-Yonah, *Between Formulary Apportionment and the OECD Guidelines: A Proposal for Reconciliation*, vol. 2, issue 1, 3–18 (World Tax Journal, February 2010); Reuven S. Avi-Yonah, Kimberly A. Clausing and Michael C. Durst, *Allocating Business Profits for Tax Purposes: A Proposal to Adopt a Formulary Profit Split*, vol. 9, 497–553 (Florida Tax Review, 2009); H. David Rosenbloom, *Angels on a Pin: Arm's Length in the World*, 523–530 (Tax Notes International, 9 May 2005); Joann M. Weiner, *Using the Experience in the U.S. States to Evaluate Issues in Implementing Formula Apportionment at the International Level* (OTA Paper 83, April 1999).

cross-border intercompany transactions would not be a significant issue for governments and multinational enterprises; at the same time, other issues would arise.

The below example (Tables 1.3 and 1.4) shows how the income of a multinational enterprise could be shared between different countries on the basis of formulary apportionment. Let us first assume the following facts: a multinational group has three companies A, B, and C, that are resident in countries A, B, and C. Each company reports turnover, profits, and employs personnel as summarised below. It is also assumed that the three companies enter into intercompany transactions (Table 1.3).

Table 1.3 A Multinational Group Carries on Business Through Three Companies Set Up in Three Countries

	Company	*Country*	*Turnover*	*Number of Employees*	*Profits*
	A	A	200	25	10
	B	B	500	40	30
	C	C	300	12	60
Total	**N/A**	**N/A**	**1,000**	**77**	**100**

At first sight, from an accounting perspective, country A gets to tax 10, country B gets to tax 30, and country C gets to tax 60. However, since the companies belong to the same group and enter into intercompany transactions, there is a need to make sure that the profit initially attributed to each country is also a correct one, or a fair one. Indeed, companies A, B, and C could report different turnovers and profits by solely pricing the intercompany transactions differently. If countries A, B, and C intend to choose formulary apportionment as the method to share the total income of the group and tax the income eventually allocated to each territory, they would need to apply the following methodology: (i) agree on a certain formula, (ii) consolidate the income, (iii) compute the relative part of each element of the formula that is located in each country, and (iv) determine the share of the consolidated income that is attributable to each country. For the purpose of this example, let us assume that countries A, B, and C have chosen to use the turnover and the number of employees as the elements of the formula. It is also assumed that the turnover and the number of employees are attributed the same weight in the formula.[17] Consequently, the share of each country will be computed according to the following formula, where T stands for turnover and E stands for employees:

17. The three countries could, instead of giving the same weight to each element of the formula, decide to attribute more weight to one element of the formula and less weight to another element. For example, sales could weigh one-third of the consolidated income, whereas the number of employees could weigh two-thirds of the consolidated income. That would result in attributing more taxable income to the country where a group has its employees, which is likely to be the country of origin of the group. Conversely, a formula could attribute more taxable income to the country of destination, where sales are made; that could be achieved, for example, if the sales were attributed two-thirds of the consolidated income, while the employee factor is attributed one-third of the consolidated income.

Share for each country = consolidated profit × [(share of T/consolidated T)/2 + (share of E/total number of E)/2]

Table 1.4 illustrates the application of the formula to the facts described above.

Table 1.4 The Income of a Multinational Enterprise Is Consolidated and Apportioned Between the Three Countries in Which the Group Is Doing Business

	Turnover	*Number of Employees*	*Weighed Total Share*	*Profits Attributed to Each Country*
Share attributed to country A	200/1,000 = 20%	25/77≈32.4%	(20%/2) + (32.4%/2) = 26.2%	26.2% × 100 = 26.2
Share attributed to country B	500/1,000 = 50%	40/77 = 52%	(50%/2) + (52%/2) = 51%	51% × 100 = 51
Share attributed to country C	300/1,000 = 30%	12/77≈15.6%	(30%/2) + (15.6%/2) = 22.8%	22.8% × 100 = 22.8
Total	**100%**	**100%**	**100%**	**100**

The first column shows the share of the turnover attributable to each country and the second column shows the share of the number of employees attributable to each country. Since the formula includes two elements (i.e., the turnover and the number of employees), and given that it is assumed that these two elements are attributed the same weight, the relative presence of each element of the formula in the territory of a given country will directly determine the profits attributed to this country. In this example, the application of formulary apportionment has an influence on the profits eventually attributed to each country since such profits are different from those that were initially incurred: countries A and B, where the profits initially incurred were respectively of 10 and 30 (*see* Table 1.3), are now attributed profits that amount to 26.2 and 51 after application of the system of formulary apportionment (*see* Table 1.4). In contrast, while profits of 60 were initially incurred in country C, this country is only allocated 22.8 after apportionment of the consolidated income.

Formulary apportionment has, as any method for the cross-border allocation of the corporate tax base, certain advantages and drawbacks. On the one hand, formulary apportionment has a more mechanical operation than arm's length pricing and may be relatively foreseeable and easy to apply, which may mitigate the risks of disagreements between tax administrations and multinational enterprises. From a tax policy perspective, formulary apportionment gives also an opportunity to agree on a particular allocation of profits (e.g., whether profits should be taxed more at origin or destination, whether or not to include certain factors in the allocation key, etc.), whereas the arm's length principle is more neutral and dependent on a comparison with transactions between independent enterprises.

On the other hand, only the elements of the formula attract income that will be shared between the respective countries, which means that other aspects are wholly disregarded from the apportionment mechanism. In certain cases, a country may consider that it has a strong connection with a group of companies, whereas the formula attributes only little profits to this country. A typical example relates to intangible assets, which often contribute to a significant part of a group's profits,[18] but that are difficult to take into account as an element of an allocation key when sharing corporate profits on the basis of formulary apportionment.[19] The assumption of risks is also disregarded for the purpose of relying on formulary apportionment.[20]

Formulary apportionment is applied internally in certain federal States to divide the tax base at a national level and has been considered in the EU.[21] However, the application of formulary apportionment at an international level has so far been rejected by most countries as well as by the OECD and the UN.[22] There are several

18. *See* Toshio Miyatake, General Report, Cahiers de Droit Fiscal International, *Transfer Pricing and Intangibles*, vol. 92a, 19 (2007); *see also* Isabel Verlinden and Yoko Mondelaers, *Transfer Pricing Aspects of Intangibles: At the Crossroads Between Legal, Valuation and Transfer Pricing Issues*, vol. 17, issue 1, 49 (International Transfer Pricing Journal, January/February 2010).
19. Several reasons may explain why intangible assets are not suitable to be taken into account in an allocation key under a formulary apportionment system, such as the difficulty to locate intangible assets and determine their ownership, the ease with which intangible assets can be moved, or the controversies as to how to value intangible assets. It has nevertheless been argued that ignoring intangible assets is not an issue as such assets would be the result of the activities of the whole group, rather than the result of just certain companies that would be developing the intangibles: *see* Reuven S. Avi-Yonah, *Between Formulary Apportionment and the OECD Guidelines: A Proposal for Reconciliation*, vol. 2, issue 1, 11 (World Tax Journal, February 2010), footnote 25: 'Any formula that "ignores" intangibles in fact assigns their value to the entire MNE (divided based on the other factors used in the formula), and we believe this result more accurately reflects the nature of intangibles.'
20. *See* Wolfgang Schön, *International Taxation of Risk*, 287 (Bulletin for International Taxation, July/August 2014).
21. The European Commission has put forward a proposal to tax European companies on the basis of an apportionment of their consolidated income. This was done first as part of the project for a common consolidated corporate tax base (CCCTB): *see Proposal for a Council Directive on a Common Consolidated Corporate Tax Base (CCCTB)* (25 October 2016, COM(2016) 683 final). For a particular analysis of the apportionment mechanism of the CCCTB, *see CCCTB: possible elements of the sharing mechanism* (13 November 2007, CCCTB/WP060\ doc); *see also* Stefan Mayer, *Formulary Apportionment for the Internal Market* (IBFD, Doctoral Series, 2009). The proposal for a CCCTB did not reach consensus among the Member States. Following the work on CCCTB, the European Commission suggested another system, Business in Europe: Framework for Income Taxation (BEFIT): *see Communication from the Commission to the European Parliament and the Council – Business Taxation for the 21st Century* (18 May 2021, COM(2021) 251 final).
22. *See* paras 1.16–1.32 of the 2022 OECD Guidelines; OECD, *Action Plan on Base Erosion and Profit Shifting*, 14 (2013); Masatsugu Asakawa, *Transfer Pricing in the New Global Landscape: The OECD's Engagement Beyond Its Borders*, 213 (Tax Notes International, 17 October 2011). *See also* UN, *Practical Manual on Transfer Pricing for Developing Countries*, para. 3.2.3 (2013); the 2021 UN Manual is more nuanced with respect to formula apportionment (*see* para. 10.1.3.3 of the 2021 UN Manual). Some proposals have been made in the doctrine to replace the arm's length principle by formulary apportionment: among numerous publications, *see*, e.g., Yariv Brauner, *Formula Based Transfer Pricing*, vol. 42, issue 10, 615–631 (Intertax, 2014); Reuven S. Avi-Yonah and Ilan Benshalom, *Formulary Apportionment: Myths and Prospects – Promoting*

reasons for such a rejection, the most important one being that some countries would be 'losing' part of the tax base if important elements of the formula are lacking in their territory or if certain factors that attract the corporate tax base under the arm's length principle are not taken into account under formulary apportionment. This is, e.g., the case for countries with a significant digital market (i.e., many potential consumers that may buy products online, thereby mitigating the sales factor if remote sales are not included in the formula) or countries with a small market that invest heavily in higher education: since higher education may contribute to the creation of valuable intangible property (IP), and assuming that IP is not part of the formula, countries where IP originates would not be directly attributed taxing rights on such IP. Therefore, it would be difficult for countries to agree on applying a comprehensive system of formulary apportionment at an international level, although regional initiatives like the BEFIT project may be implemented in the future.[23]

1.2.3 The Arm's Length Principle

Instead of applying formulary apportionment, the member countries of the OECD and most non-OECD countries (as particularly emphasised in the UN Model Tax Convention) prefer sharing the profits or losses incurred by the members of a group, and arising from cross-border intercompany transactions, on the basis of the pricing of comparable transactions between independent companies. Accordingly, the international standard for sharing the income of multinational enterprises arising from intercompany transactions consists in favouring intercompany pricing that is in line with the market price, i.e., the so-called *arm's length principle.*[24] Although it was found as part of the BEPS project that transfer pricing rules had been 'vulnerable to manipulation',[25] the arm's length principle remains the standard for the cross-border allocation of the profits of associated enterprises. To prevent such manipulations, various amendments have been brought to the OECD Guidelines; as a result, transfer pricing rules have increasingly been conferred an anti-avoidance function.[26]

The arm's length principle relies on a general principle, that of transposing to associated enterprises the conditions existing between independent enterprises; as this principle is abstract, its practical implementation supposes a case-by-case analysis of cross-border intercompany transactions, with adjustments being made to the conditions of intercompany transactions if such conditions deviate from what can be observed between independent enterprises. Hence, contrary to a tax system

Better International Tax Policies by Utilizing the Misunderstood and Under-Theorized Formulary Alternative, vol. 3, issue 3, 371-398 (World Tax Journal, October 2011).

23. Some features of formulary apportionment are nevertheless found in the Pillar 1 project: *see* OECD/G20 BEPS Project, *Statement on a Two-Pillar Solution to Address the Tax Challenges Arising from the Digitalisation of the Economy* (8 October 2021).
24. *See* para. 1.32 of the 2022 OECD Guidelines.
25. *See* OECD, *Aligning Transfer Pricing Outcomes with Value Creation, Actions 8-10: 2015 Final Reports*, 9 (2015).
26. For an illustration of the increased anti-avoidance function of transfer pricing rules, *see* the example of a Spanish case: Aitor Navarro, *Spain: Contractual Allocation of Risks and Substance: The Acer Case*, vol. 28, issue 3, 203–209 (International Transfer Pricing Journal, 2021).

implementing formulary apportionment, where the income originally earned by each group company is in principle always adjusted before being shared between the group members, under the arm's length principle, the income originally earned by each group company does not need to be adjusted per se. It needs first to be tested against the arm's length principle. If it is concluded that the pricing of intercompany transactions matches the pricing of comparable transactions between independent companies, the income will remain as it was and no changes in the income earned and the taxes levied will need to take place. In contrast, if it is demonstrated that the intercompany prices differ from those applied to comparable transactions between independent companies, the multinational enterprise should adjust its transfer prices in order to implement the arm's length principle. Tax administrations may, according to most domestic tax laws and tax treaties,[27] have the right to reassess the taxable income of the company that is under scrutiny if the arm's length principle is not complied with. Given the right of tax administrations to reassess the income of members of a multinational enterprise that deviates from the arm's length principle, and the risk to face double taxation when the same item of income is taxed in two countries, multinational enterprises have an incentive to enforce the arm's length principle while entering into intercompany transactions, i.e., before the pricing of such transactions is tested by tax administrations. However, enforcing the arm's length principle is often complex, so even when a multinational enterprise tries to be as compliant with the arm's length principle as possible, a risk always exists that the pricing of intercompany transactions is deemed not to comply with the arm's length principle.

Certain key differences between arm's length pricing and formulary apportionment appear immediately: whereas formulary apportionment lies on a predetermined formula that offers foreseeability but may not be suitable to take into account the special features of different types of business activities, arm's length pricing is quite the opposite as it is a principled approach[28] that implies a case-by-case analysis that is adapted to each situation – thereby being closer to the reality of each transaction. In other words, the arm's length principle is in a better position to capture the contributions of the parties to an intercompany transaction in a more nuanced manner than formulary apportionment.[29] Put shortly, formulary apportionment is quantitative, while the arm's length principle is qualitative. At the same time, the arm's length principle is complex to apply, brings little foreseeability and may easily give rise

27. In the vast majority of tax systems, a domestic arm's length provision is necessary to make a transfer pricing adjustment. This means that in the absence of such a provision, no transfer pricing adjustment can be made, even if the tax treaty provides for a provision similar to Art. 9 of the OECD Model Tax Convention: *see* Georg Kofler and Jens Wittendorff, *Klaus Vogel on Double Taxation Conventions*, in Ekkehart Reimer and Alexander Rust (eds), (5th ed., Kluwer International Law, 2021), Art. 9 at m.no. 6: 'Article 9(1) OECD and UN MC does not create any legal basis for rewriting taxpayers' accounts.'
28. *See* Isabel Verlinden, *The Value of a Principle ... the Arm's Length Principle*, vol. 49, issue 3, 206–209 (Intertax, 2021).
29. For example, under the arm's length principle, the importance of the functions performed by different members of a group will affect their profitability. Such nuances cannot be directly captured with a system based on formula apportionment.

to controversies.[30] At the end of the day, the choice between formulary apportionment and the arm's length principle boils down to a matter of priority. Should priority be given to allocating the tax base according to certain features of a group of companies that are measurable and that may be determined in advance? Should priority be given to foreseeability and certainty, possibly to the detriment of the correctness of the allocation of income between different countries? Or should priority be given to the search for a principled, well-motivated allocation of income, at the cost of creating complexity and increasing risks of double taxation and disputes? So far, priority has been given to the arm's length principle and to the search for a theoretically correct allocation of the income of multinational enterprises.[31] Only minor deviations from the arm's length principle have been agreed as part of the Pillar 1 project, given the limited scope of this suggested set of rules.[32] However, the arm's length principle may not remain the prevailing principle for sharing the tax base of multinational enterprises in the long run.[33]

It is virtually impossible that formulary apportionment and the arm's length principle result in similar outcomes. In most cases, the results produced under formulary apportionment and the arm's length principle are likely to differ from each other, as the principles for sharing the income of multinational enterprises also differ between these two methods. In particular, while formulary apportionment may hardly take into account intangibles and risks as an element of the allocation key, the arm's length principle puts great emphasis on risks (especially who controls such risks) as well as on the contribution of associated enterprises to intangibles: for example, a group with valuable intangibles but little sales and few employees in a given country may allocate to this country only a small portion of its total profits under formulary apportionment, whereas the group would allocate a greater portion of its total profits to the same country under the arm's length principle.

30. Of course, disputes may arise and do arise in the countries that apply formulary apportionment at the domestic level. Issues would also arise between the Member States of the EU if a common tax system like BEFIT would be implemented. However, the existence of a predetermined formula limits controversies to issues relating to the application of the formula. In contrast, as the arm's length principle is only a principle, virtually any aspect of its application may give rise to controversies. Therefore, the arm's length principle seems more likely to give rise to disagreements between tax administrations and multinational enterprises than formulary apportionment.
31. Here, it can be observed that 'special measures' that deviate from the arm's length principle have been under consideration by the OECD as part of the BEPS project, to ensure that transfer pricing outcomes are in line with the creation of value: *see* OECD, *BEPS Actions 8, 9 and 10: Discussion Draft on Revisions to Chapter I of the Transfer Pricing Guidelines (Including Risk, Recharacterisation, and Special Measures)*, 38–43 (December 2014). However, no such special measures have been adopted as part of the BEPS project, except perhaps (although it was not qualified as such) the so-called hard-to-value intangibles approach; in that respect, *see* below section 3.3.
32. *See* OECD/G20 BEPS Project, *Statement on a Two-Pillar Solution to Address the Tax Challenges Arising from the Digitalisation of the Economy* (8 October 2021).
33. *See* Han Kogels, *Tax Systems Twenty-Five Years from Now*, vol. 22, issue 6, 266 (EC Tax Review, 2013), in relation to a question asked to the participants of a session at the 2013 congress of the International Fiscal Association: 'Voting on the question whether the arm's length principle, as it is typically understood today, would survive the next twenty-five years, only half of the audience replied in the affirmative.'

Since the arm's length principle is the international standard for sharing the income of multinational enterprises when they enter into intercompany transactions, the question arises as to the legal source of the arm's length principle. The domestic tax laws of numerous – albeit not all[34] – countries contain a provision allowing their tax administrations to reassess the taxable income of associated enterprises when it is demonstrated that the prices of intercompany transactions did not comply with the arm's length principle.[35] However, there are important variations among countries when it comes to the level of details provided by the domestic laws or regulations with respect to the interpretation and application of the arm's length principle: some countries provide only a general provision reflecting the arm's length standard, other countries provide more detailed guidance on different types of transfer pricing issues (e.g., the use of transfer pricing methods, or the pricing of particular intercompany transactions such as financial transactions). In any case, domestic laws and regulations would most often be completed by the guidance provided by international organisations – in particular the OECD and the UN. Reliance on interpretative guidance is, in some countries, explicitly recommended in domestic laws or regulations, whereas in other countries, it is rather the practice of taxpayers, tax administrations and courts to refer to interpretative guidance without explicit support for such recommendations in the domestic law or regulation. Except if the domestic law is very precise as to the need to interpret the domestic arm's length provision in the light of a specific interpretative source,[36] controversies are frequent as to the legal value of interpretative guidance such as the OECD Guidelines, the UN Manual, or the material published within the EU.[37]

34. Certain countries have indeed enacted transfer pricing legislations that deviate from the arm's length principle. *See*, for example, para. 1.1.2 of the 2021 UN Manual (Part D), where it is mentioned that in Brazil 'with regard to the Cost Plus Method and Resale Price Method, instead of making use of comparable transactions, the law established fixed margins for gross profits and mark-up'; *see also* João Marcus de Melo Rigoni, *A Brazilian View on Base Erosion and Profit Shifting: An Alternative Path*, vol. 42, issue 11, 735–736 (Intertax, 2014).
35. *See* Hugh J. Ault and Brian J. Arnold, *Comparative Income Taxation: A Structural Analysis*, 529 (3rd ed., Kluwer Law International, 2010). It is now estimated that 'the arm's length principle has spread to the tax laws of more than 100 countries': *see* Kristen A. Parillo, *Tax Analysts Interview: OECD's Mary Bennett*, 231 (Tax Notes International, 25 July 2011). *See also* Theresa Zinn, Nadine Riedel and Christoph Spengel, *The Increasing Importance of Transfer Pricing Regulations: A Worldwide Overview*, vol. 42, issue 6/7, 352–404 (Intertax, 2014).
36. For an overview of the reliance on the OECD Guidelines by different countries, *see* the transfer pricing country profiles published by the OECD where the two first items presented for each country are: (i) whether or not the domestic legislation or regulation makes reference to the arm's length principle, and (ii) what role is given to the OECD Guidelines under the domestic legislation: https://www.oecd.org/tax/transfer-pricing/transfer-pricing-country-profiles.htm#tpcountryprofiles (accessed 13 July 2022). For an example of country with precise reliance on the OECD Guidelines *see* the country profile of Ireland, where it is mentioned that 'Ireland's transfer pricing rules are construed in accordance with the OECD's Transfer Pricing Guidelines for Multinational Enterprises and Tax Administrations published by the OECD on 10 July 2017 ("TPG") supplemented by the Guidance for Tax Administrations on the Application of the Approach to Hard-to-Value Intangibles, the Revised Guidance on the Application of the Transactional Profit Split Method, and any additional guidance published by the OECD on or after the date of the passing of the Finance Act 2019 (i.e. 22 December 2019) as the Minister for Finance may designate by order' (accessed 13 July 2022).
37. This issue is discussed below in section 1.6.

Despite the wide reliance on the arm's length principle for the purpose of setting the prices of intercompany transactions, the practical application and interpretation of this principle may differ from one country to another, thus leading easily to situations of double taxation. The statistics[38] published by the OECD show the extent of cross-border tax disputes involving transfer pricing issues. This is mainly due to the arm's length principle being only a general principle of taxation with no precise material content,[39] hence involving judgment – and thus, room for disagreement – for its practical operation.

1.3 THE ARM'S LENGTH PRINCIPLE IN THEORY

The rationale for the arm's length principle builds on the theory of market forces: as a consequence of the supply and demand of a certain good or service, the market forces normally result in a price that is acceptable to both of them at a given point in time. Ensuring that the prices paid for intercompany transactions are acceptable to both parties contributes to also ensuring that their income (and eventually the corporate income taxes paid on their profits) is acceptable to their tax administrations. Most countries consider that the arm's length price, determined by the market forces, is the fairest way to set prices between associated enterprises and ultimately divide the tax base of multinational enterprises. Indeed, the arm's length principle does not favour one or the other counterpart to a transaction, nor does it favour one country or another per se. Rather, the arm's length principle lets the price of a good or service be determined by objective factors that are relevant not only between associated enterprises but also between independent enterprises.[40] The arm's length principle also promotes equity and fair competition between independent taxpayers and related taxpayers, since in both cases the prices paid – and the income earned – are directly influenced by the market forces. Therefore, through ensuring that all cross-border intercompany transactions abide by the arm's length principle, it could be assumed that a fair share of the profits or losses made by a multinational enterprise is attributed to each country.[41]

38. *See* the statistics published by the OECD for so-called mutual agreement procedures (*see* section 7.2.2 of this book for an explanation of mutual agreement procedures): https://www.oecd.org/tax/dispute/mutual-agreement-procedure-statistics.htm (accessed 13 July 2022).
39. However, the rationale for the arm's length principle can be precisely described, i.e., the objective to transpose to cross-border intercompany transactions the conditions that would exist between independent comparable enterprises.
40. These factors are described below in section 1.4 of this book.
41. *See* Kristen A. Parillo, *Tax Analysts Interview: OECD's Mary Bennett*, 231 (Tax Notes International, 25 July 2011), where it is submitted that the governments of the member countries of the OECD 'continue to strongly support the arm's length principle as the best available approach to follow, based on its neutrality, fairness, administrability, and broad acceptance around the world'. *See also* David D. Stewart, *Tax Analysts Interview: OECD's Caroline Silberztein*, 417 (Tax Notes International, 8 August 2011), where it has been observed that the arm's length principle is 'neutral for capital exporting countries and developing economies'. The arm's length principle seems also to achieve a balanced allocation of the taxing rights between the Member States of the EU: *see*, e.g., *Société de Gestion Industrielle v. Belgian State*, Court of Justice of the European Union (21 January 2010, case number C-311/08). *See also* Moritz Glahe,

This raises the discussion of whether or not the arm's length principle is fair to all kinds of countries, especially in the relationship between developed and developing countries. From a theoretical point of view, it could be considered that since the arm's length principle is intrinsically neutral, it favours neither the developed nor the developing countries and should, accordingly, be applied in the transactions between associated enterprises irrespective of their State of residence, so as to ensure a fair allocation of the tax base of multinational enterprises between the countries in which they carry out business activities. However, there are several arguments against the suitability of the arm's length principle - or at least its application under the OECD Guidelines - to developing countries, such as the intrinsic complexity of the arm's length principle or the recurrent lack of local comparable independent transactions.[42] In addition, even if the arm's length principle may, in itself, be considered as neutral and thus fair to both developed and developing countries, the strong reliance on factors that are more likely to be present in developed than developing countries (especially IP and risk management) may produce outcomes that are considered as unfair to developing countries.[43] For example, a multinational enterprise may have a low-risk distributor in a developing country that is attributed a low income given its low-risk profile; at the same time, this distributor may achieve sales levels that are far above those of a distributor in a developed country, thus contributing to a greater extent to the global profits. Similarly, a multinational enterprise may have a low-risk manufacturer (e.g., a toll manufacturer or a contract manufacturer) in a developing country that does not perform important functions and thus is not attributed a high income; at the same time, this manufacturer may be a key success factor for the multinational enterprise, thanks to its low production costs, thereby increasing the profit margin on each good sold.

In order to strike a balance between the interests of the developed and developing countries, the solution favoured by the UN when it comes to taxing multinational enterprises consists in relying on the arm's length principle,[44] while helping developing countries apply this principle efficiently. To that end, the UN committee of experts on international cooperation in tax matters has drafted a Manual on transfer pricing for developing countries, the purpose of which is to provide practical guidance on the application of the arm's length principle for the specific case of developing countries. According to the UN Manual, several issues are particularly problematic for developing countries: the lack of comparables, the lack of experience and requisite skill sets, the

---

Transfer Pricing and EU Fundamental Freedoms, vol. 22, issue 5, 232 (EC Tax Review, 2013), where it is concluded that 'By its Thin Cap GLO and SGI judgments, the ECJ has recognized that arm's length profit adjustments follow legitimate objectives as they contribute to taxpayer equity as well as internation equity.'

42. It may indeed be difficult, as part of a comparability analysis, to find comparable independent companies resident in developing countries, either because of the lack of such companies or because of the lack of efficient tools (in particular, databases with financial information) to perform benchmarking studies.
43. For suggestions relating to how developing countries may apply the arm's length principle, *see* Michael C. Durst, *Pragmatic Transfer Pricing for Developing Countries*, 279-285 (Tax Notes International, 23 January 2012).
44. *See* para. 2.4.1.3 of the 2021 UN Manual.

treatment of group synergies, the complexity of transfer pricing rules, and the digitalisation of the economy.[45] The 2021 UN Manual also includes a description of the transfer pricing practices in Brazil, China, India, Mexico, South Africa, and Kenya. The lawmakers, tax administrations, courts, and competent authorities of developing countries may indeed need assistance for drafting transfer pricing legislation and for managing transfer pricing issues in practice,[46] on top of other tax issues.[47] Despite the efforts of the OECD and the UN to provide a common framework for the design and the application of transfer pricing rules, in some cases, developed and developing countries may still have different views on certain issues, particularly when different rules have a clearly different impact on their respective fiscal revenues.[48] Eventually, a risk is that developed and developing countries, or other groups of countries, choose different taxation principles, or apply differently the same taxation principle, something that may lead to situations of unrelieved double taxation.[49] That would be the case, for example, if most countries apply the arm's length principle while a group of countries implement certain deviations from that principle.

Despite being accepted by the OECD, the UN, as well as many countries, the relevance of the arm's length principle to sharing the income of multinational enterprises has been criticised.[50] The arm's length principle as it was interpreted in the 2010 OECD Guidelines was found, in certain cases, to enable multinational enterprises to achieve unacceptable tax savings.[51] Moreover, relying on a comparison with the

45. *See* paras 2.5.2 and following of the 2021 UN Manual. Solutions to deal with these issues are provided both in the UN Manual and in other material developed by the UN.
46. The process of developing knowledge and tools is often described as 'capacity building'. An example of issue with which developing countries may need assistance is the ability to make risk assessments and select which intercompany transactions to audit, as well as manage cross-border tax disputes. Another example relates to the need to improve the availability of information on comparable local companies or transactions, which may be particularly necessary in order to prevent abusive transfer pricing in relation to natural resources (*see Spillovers in International Corporate Taxation*, IMF Policy Paper, 11 (box 1) and 18 (box 2) (9 May 2014)).
47. For example, developing countries may need assistance with respect to the drafting and the application of anti-avoidance provisions that may efficiently supplement transfer pricing rules with respect to the objective of preventing the erosion of the tax base.
48. *See*, e.g., Glenn DeSouza, *What the UN Manual Really Means for China?*, vol. 41, issue 5, 331–338 (Intertax, 2013), where the application of the arm's length principle from the perspective of China is described in relation to several types of transfer pricing issues.
49. *See Spillovers in International Corporate Taxation*, IMF Policy Paper, 34 (box 5) (9 May 2014). To prevent the erosion of their tax base, certain countries may choose to apply various anti-avoidance provisions, levy withholding taxes (especially since such taxes are generally levied on payments, as opposed to net income), or depart from the arm's length principle – for instance, by expecting certain levels of profitability that do not rely on comparable independent transactions (in this respect *see* above footnote 29 for the example of Brazil).
50. For discussions on some of the flaws of the arm's length principle, *see* Michael C. Durst, *It's Not Just Academic: The OECD Should Reevaluate Transfer Pricing Laws*, 247–256 (Tax Notes International, 18 January 2010); David L.P. Francescucci, *The Arm's Length Principle and Group Dynamics: Part 1 – The Conceptual Shortcomings*, vol. 11, issue 2, 55–75 (International Transfer Pricing Journal, March/April 2004).
51. An example is the attribution of income to a group company that solely provides funding to other companies, thanks to having an excess of capital. Although this issue was already addressed under the 2010 OECD Guidelines (para. 9.32 of the 2010 OECD Guidelines emphasises that 'a high level of capitalisation by itself does not mean that the highly capitalised party carries risk'),

circumstances that would be relevant between independent enterprises reveals both a strength and a weakness of the arm's length principle. On the one hand, the arm's length principle is relatively neutral, which is a strength for its survival since it does not intrinsically favour or harm any group of countries.[52] It is also neutral with respect to different industries.[53] Moreover, relying on independent comparable data ensures that the conditions applied between associated enterprises for the purpose of attributing profits are close to the concept of income, as opposed to a formula that per definition allocates profits on the basis of parameters that are chosen by the lawmaker and that do not necessarily have a strong connection to the concept of income. On the other hand, it may be argued that requiring associated enterprises to set transfer prices as independent enterprises would do is intrinsically flawed, as associated enterprises and independent enterprises are different from each other. In particular, the arm's length principle relies on the assumption that associated enterprises should deal with each other as if they were independent from each other, while the very reason for the existence of a group of companies may be the benefits from the integration between the members of the group: for example, the arm's length principle does not take into account the fact that a group may pursue a common interest without necessarily each member of the group directly benefiting from a particular transaction.

The OECD and the UN are aware of the flaws of the arm's length principle and are continuously working on improving its application.[54] On the one hand, it was included in the scope of the BEPS project to issue guidance in order to assure that transfer pricing outcomes are in line with value creation;[55] it was indeed found that 'the rules should be improved in order to put more emphasis on value creation in highly integrated groups, tackling the use of intangibles, risks, capital and other high-risk transactions to

---

the OECD still found that a source of BEPS concern is the 'over-capitalisation of lowly taxed group companies' (*see* OECD, *Action Plan on Base Erosion and Profit Shifting*, 20 (2013)). Accordingly, it restated in a 2014 discussion draft on the transfer pricing aspects of risks that 'Financial capacity to bear risk is a relevant but not determinative factor in considering whether a controlled party should be allocated a risk return' (*see* OECD, *BEPS Actions 8, 9 and 10: Discussion Draft on Revisions to Chapter I of the Transfer Pricing Guidelines (Including Risk, Recharacterisation, and Special Measures)*, 22, para. 66 (December 2014)). Nevertheless, while the OECD at some point of the BEPS work did consider 'special measures' that would deviate from the arm's length principle when the provision of capital leads to 'inappropriate returns' (*see* OECD, *BEPS Actions 8, 9 and 10: Discussion Draft on Revisions to Chapter I of the Transfer Pricing Guidelines (Including Risk, Recharacterisation, and Special Measures)*, 42–43 (December 2014)), no such 'special measures' were eventually adopted in the 2017 and 2022 updates to the OECD Guidelines.

52. However, as emphasised above in this section, this argument is not fully convincing if one takes into account the effects of the application of the arm's length principle for countries with different characteristics.
53. This argument too can be nuanced: since the parameters that are taken into account in the 2022 OECD Guidelines rely mostly on the physical presence and the importance of this physical presence, businesses with strong digital features could be considered as favoured by such parameters.
54. *See* Kristen A. Parillo, *Tax Analysts Interview: OECD's Mary Bennett*, 231 (Tax Notes International, 25 July 2011): 'no system designed to deal with the challenge of allocating profits among countries will ever be perfect'.
55. *See* OECD, *Action Plan on Base Erosion and Profit Shifting*, 20–21 (2013).

shift profits'.[56] This objective resulted in changes to the OECD Guidelines with the 2017 and 2022 updates. The 2021 UN Manual pursues a similar objective, and refers to the concept of value creation too.[57] An example of the measures suggested by the OECD to correct a shortcoming of the arm's length principle is the recommendation to take into account the effects of group synergies[58] that result from deliberate concerted group action.[59] In certain cases, the BEPS work clarified the intended application of the arm's length principle without modifying its content, i.e., the outcomes reached under the suggested amendments could also be reached under the 2010 Guidelines without being incompatible with them. In other cases, the amendments made to the OECD Guidelines had more important implications, thus potentially resulting in an evolution of the arm's length principle as such. Nevertheless, certain intrinsic features of the arm's length principle cannot be avoided or improved, and thus could not be addressed while staying within the realm of the arm's length principle: for example, although groups pursue a common interest, the arm's length principle as it is stated in the OECD Guidelines and accepted by most countries clearly expects each party to a transaction to act in its own interest.[60] While 'special measures' that go beyond the arm's length principle[61] were considered as part of the draft work on BEPS Actions 8–10,[62] no such

56. *See* OECD, *Action Plan on Base Erosion and Profit Shifting*, 14 (2013).
57. *See*, e.g., paras 1.3.3.2, 4.6.1.6, 9.1.2 and 12.2.1.3 of the 2021 UN Manual.
58. An example of synergy is the bargaining power obtained, thanks to centralising a purchasing function within one member of a group. Synergies are often seen as the reason for conducting business within groups, as opposed to between independent entities. Therefore, synergies are by essence problematic for transfer pricing purposes, since there may not be a benchmark provided by independent transactions, while the arm's length principle requires that certain synergistic benefits be shared consistently with how independent enterprises would have done.
59. *See* paras 1.177 and following of the 2022 OECD Guidelines. For a criticism of the recognition of 'contributions' to synergies made by individual group members on the basis of the argument that synergies would rather be the consequence of the interactions between the group members, *see* Yariv Brauner, *Transfer Pricing in BEPS: First Round – Business Interests Win (But, Not in Knock-Out)*, vol. 42, issue 1, 78 (Intertax, 2015).
60. This is particularly evidenced by the need to apply transfer pricing principles that take into account the options realistically available to all the parties to an intercompany transaction: *see*, e.g., paras 1.38, 6.111 and 9.27 and following of the 2022 OECD Guidelines.
61. Special measures that deviate from the arm's length principle were found as potentially necessary when this principle is deemed insufficient to prevent the erosion of the tax base: for example, although an arm's length provision is necessary to counter situations where a group creates an intercompany loan with too high an interest rate so as to decrease the tax base of the borrower and increase the tax base of the lender, the mere effect of the arm's length principle may not be sufficient to prevent the erosion of the tax base. Indeed, if the arm's length principle is seen as only allowing the correction of the interest rate, without allowing the correction of the amount of the loan as such, it may be necessary to have anti-avoidance provisions that supplement the arm's length principle in order to prevent the erosion of the tax base through the payment of interests expenses on excessive loans.
62. *See* OECD, *BEPS Actions 8, 9 and 10: Discussion Draft on Revisions to Chapter I of the Transfer Pricing Guidelines (Including Risk, Recharacterisation, and Special Measures)*, 38–45 (December 2014). It can be observed that measures that depart from the arm's length principle exist in certain countries' domestic tax laws. An example is what is often referred to as 'safe harbours'. Another example is the rule in the United States under which income received for the transfer or the licence of an intangible asset shall be regularly monitored so as to ensure that it is 'commensurate' (i.e., in proportion) with the income actually attributable to this intangible asset: for a description of this rule, *see* James R. Repetti, Diane M. Ring and Paul McDaniel, *Introduction to United States International Taxation*, 156–157 (6th ed., Kluwer Law

special measures were eventually implemented in the 2017 and 2022 updates to the OECD Guidelines,[63] although in certain cases the amendments made to the OECD Guidelines might be seen as in breach of the arm's length principle.[64] Also, despite introducing the notion of value creation and reinforcing the substance requirement, the changes made with the 2017 and 2022 updates did not imply fundamentally novel views on cross-border profit allocation, and did not address the main shortcoming of the arm's length principle that emerged from the BEPS project, namely the impossibility to tax digital business models. Therefore, several countries implemented their own special measures to tax remote sales,[65] and initiatives were taken regionally.[66] As a result, the OECD coordinated the Pillar 1 project to find a common solution for the tax challenges of the digitalisation of the economy.

1.4 THE ARM'S LENGTH PRINCIPLE IN PRACTICE

Setting intercompany prices at arm's length implies relying on the pricing that would be adopted by independent companies in comparable situations, for the pricing of controlled cross-border transactions between associated enterprises. That is, the rationale of the arm's length principle lies in a comparison of the conditions of transactions between independent enterprises, on the one hand, and controlled associated enterprises, on the other hand.[67] While this rationale may be easily described, it is not easily applied in practice: an objective and robust comparison supposes setting transfer prices according to a precise methodology. In order to compare transactions that are actually comparable and apply the arm's length principle correctly, a transfer pricing analysis is basically divided into two steps. First, the accurate delineation of the transaction (which includes especially a *functional analysis* of the controlled transaction under review) (section 1.4.2); second, based on the

International, 2014), where it is also mentioned that it has been debated whether or not this rule is in line with the arm's length principle. A comparable rule is suggested in Chapter 6 of the 2022 OECD Guidelines, the so-called hard-to-value intangibles approach (for a description *see* section 3.3 of this book).

63. This may be due to the fact that many countries adopted interest limitation deductions that would address the issue of thin and thick capitalisation, such problems being hardly addressed under the arm's length principle.
64. Two examples can be mentioned here. First, the control over a risk is a prerequisite for the recognition of the assumption of that risk, and thus for the attribution of income connected to it; here, the counterargument could be that independent parties do not always control the risks they assume (e.g., an investor willing to risk money, hoping for an important gain). Second, the hard-to-value intangibles approach enables, in certain cases, a reassessment of profits following a transfer of IP; here, the counterargument could be that independent parties may not agree on a provision according to which the transfer price of an intangible asset may be reassessed in view of future variations in the value of that asset.
65. Such taxes are levied, in most cases, on the turnover made on remote sales.
66. *See*, e.g., *Proposal for a Council Directive on the common system of a digital services tax on revenues resulting from the provision of certain digital services* (COM(2018) 148 final, 22 March 2018).
67. *See* para. 1.33 of the 2022 OECD Guidelines, which refers to 'a comparison of the conditions in a controlled transaction with the conditions that would have been made had the parties been independent and undertaking a comparable transaction under comparable circumstances'.

outcome of the first analysis, transfer prices are determined by way of a *comparability analysis* (section 1.4.3). However, a transfer pricing analysis should start by verifying that transfer pricing rules are actually applicable, which is normally the case when two companies are resident of different countries and are deemed to be *associated*. Association is indeed a prerequisite for the application of transfer pricing rules because it is the close relations between the parties that may enable a deviation from market prices and justify the need to adjust transfer prices. Therefore, before delving into the functional and comparability analyses, the notion of associated enterprises needs to be defined (section 1.4.1).

1.4.1 The Notion of Associated Enterprises

The reason for applying transfer pricing rules and potentially adjusting the prices of certain transactions lies in the bias that may result from the association between the parties to a transaction. The concept of associated enterprises is, in certain cases, problematic. It varies from one country to another,[68] and is also debated in the literature.[69] The difficulty comes from the breadth of this concept, as well as the lack of harmonised definition. Whether or not enterprises are associated is often defined in a broad manner, to cover both legal and economic relations between group companies. Indeed, the two types of relations make sense to consider: from a legal perspective, the ownership of shares over a certain threshold may give control to the subsidiary, with the possibility of influencing transfer prices. From an economic perspective, even with no formal ownership of shares, one company may influence the other, for example, by participating in its management. Defining associated enterprises broadly allows covering different types of situations where the relations between the parties may influence the price of a transaction. At the same time, a broad but vague definition of this concept makes its application unforeseeable, for example, in situations where there is no legal ownership of one party in the other but only some economic links between them.

68. For examples of definitions in several countries, *see* section 10.1.5 of the 2021 UN Manual.
69. For an overview *see* Ramon S.J. Dwarkasing, *The Concept of Associated Enterprises*, vol. 41, issue 8/9, 412–429 (Intertax, 2013). On the definition of an 'enterprise', *see* Kees van Raad, *'Enterprise' and 'Enterprise of a Contracting State': Towards a Century of Confusion Regarding the Term 'Enterprise' in the Model Double Taxation Conventions*, in Guglielmo Maisto (ed.), The Meaning of 'Enterprise', 'Business' and 'Business Profits' under Tax Treaties and EU Tax Law, vol. 7, 61–83 (IBFD, EC and International Tax Law Series, 2011); *see also* Jacques Sasseville, *'Enterprise', 'Business' and 'Business Profits': From the League of Nations to the Current OECD Model Tax Convention*, in Guglielmo Maisto (ed.), The Meaning of 'Enterprise', 'Business' and 'Business Profits' under Tax Treaties and EU Tax Law, vol. 7, 41–58 (IBFD, EC and International Tax Law Series, 2011). For a domestic illustration of the difficulty to define the notion of 'control', *see*, e.g., the legislative changes that occurred in Italy: Domenico Ponticelli and Sabrina Tronci, *The Non-unique Notion of 'Control' in Transfer Pricing: Interpretation, Legislative Developments and Problematic Aspects from an Italian and International Perspective*, vol. 28, issue 4, 291–298 (International Transfer Pricing Journal, 2021).

The notion of associated enterprises is normally defined in a country's domestic tax law.[70] Domestic definitions are often inspired by Article 9(1) of the OECD Model Tax Convention as well as Article 9(1) of the UN Model Tax Convention,[71] which put a strong emphasis on the notion of control from a factual, rather than legal, perspective. Paragraph 1 of Article 9 had the following drafting in the 2017 OECD Model Tax Convention and the 2021 UN Model Tax Convention:[72]

1. Where
   a) an enterprise of a Contracting State participates directly or indirectly in the management, control or capital [*this means that both legal and economic connections are taken into account*] of an enterprise of the other Contracting State, or
   b) the same persons participate directly or indirectly in the management, control or capital of an enterprise of a Contracting State and an enterprise of the other Contracting State [*this means that enterprises may be considered as associated in an horizontal relationship, e.g. two sister companies controlled by the same persons*], and in either case conditions are made or imposed between the two enterprises in their commercial or financial relations, which differ from those which would be made between independent enterprises [*here it is assumed that the transfer prices applied to intercompany transactions between the associated enterprises did not enforce the arm's length principle*], then any profits which would, but for those conditions, have accrued to one of the enterprises, but, by reason of those conditions, have not so accrued, may be included[73] in the profits of that enterprise and taxed accordingly [*this means that when the transfer prices between the associated enterprises did not respect the arm's length principle, article 9 of the OECD and UN Model Tax Conventions allows the correction of such transfer prices and the taxation of the associated enterprises as if the transfer prices were those applied by independent enterprises*].

70. *See* para. 10.1.5.2 of the 2021 UN Manual: 'the degree of control required to trigger the application of transfer pricing legislation has in effect been left to domestic legislation'.
71. At the time of publication of this book, the two latest updates to the OECD Model Tax Convention (2017) and the UN Model Tax Convention (2021) had the same wording for Art. 9(1).
72. The comments between square brackets have a pedagogical purpose and are not included in Art. 9 of the OECD and the UN Model Tax Conventions or in the commentaries thereof.
73. Who is allowed to correct non-arm's length prices as a result of Art. 9 of the OECD Model Tax Convention may be debated, depending on the way tax treaties are interpreted and applied domestically. Certain countries interpret this article as allowing domestic transfer pricing provisions to be enacted, i.e., a domestic law would still be necessary to levy taxes in the case of non-arm's length transactions between associated enterprises. On the other hand, other countries interpret this article as directly allowing tax administrations to correct non-arm's length prices even in the absence of domestic transfer pricing provisions, i.e., Art. 9 would have a legal value on its own. In this respect, *see* para. 2 of the commentary on Art. 9 of the 2021 UN Model Tax Convention where it is mentioned that a domestic provision is required in most countries for making an income adjustment on the basis of the arm's length principle. For an example of court case where Art. 9 was not found to entitle, by itself, a country to taxing rights on transactions between associated enterprises, *see Chevron Australia Holdings Pty Ltd v. Commissioner of Taxation*, Federal Court of Australia (23 October 2015, case number (2015) FCA 1092).

Article 9 of the OECD Model Tax Convention thus states that enterprises are associated when 'an enterprise of a Contracting State participates directly or indirectly in the management, control or capital of an enterprise of the other Contracting State' (this is typically the case when a parent company owns shares in a subsidiary), or when 'the same persons participate directly or indirectly in the management, control or capital of an enterprise of a Contracting State and an enterprise of the other Contracting State' (this is typically the case when two sister companies are owned by the same parent company).

Despite the widespread use of Article 9 of the OECD Model Tax Convention in double taxation conventions for the taxation of associated enterprises, certain countries define associated enterprises in their domestic law from a more legal perspective, e.g., by setting ownership thresholds beyond which two companies are deemed to be associated. While this option may offer the advantage of simplicity and foreseeability, it is not without shortcomings: ownership thresholds may be abused, e.g., by spreading the ownership so that several shareholders have holdings below the threshold. If the ownership threshold is relatively low, e.g., 25%, other countries may not consider the companies as associated. The lack of common definition of associated enterprises can be problematic, given that it may lead to situations where two countries disagree on the existence of association: one country could find that transfer pricing rules are applicable as a consequence of the existence of association, while the other country may consider that enterprises are not associated and, thus, that transfer pricing rules are not applicable. This latter country would most likely refuse to grant a corresponding adjustment under Article 9(2) of the OECD Model Tax Convention,[74] and, thus, discrepancies in the definition of associated enterprises may result in situations of double taxation.

1.4.2 The Accurate Delineation of the Transaction

Once it has been ascertained that a cross-border intercompany transaction has been entered into between two associated enterprises, transfer pricing rules are applicable and a transfer pricing analysis can be conducted. The accurate delineation of the transaction is the first step of any transfer pricing analysis. It comprises several steps. The general context[75] for the transaction will need to be understood with respect to the industry sector in which the multinational enterprise operates, and the value drivers or factors affecting the performance of companies active in that sector.[76] The key part of the accurate delineation of the transaction will, however, focus not on the business sector, but on the specificities of the multinational enterprise, with the main objective

74. A corresponding adjustment means that the increase of the tax base in country A is mirrored by a decrease of the tax base in country B. This results in a shift of the tax base from country B to country A, since the tax base is decreased in country B in order to let country A levy tax on a higher tax base.
75. The general context, comprising an industry analysis and an analysis of the value drivers of a multinational enterprise, is likely to be described in the so-called master file of the transfer pricing documentation: *see* section 7.1.1 of this book.
76. *See* para. 1.34 of the 2022 OECD Guidelines.

of understanding the role played by each party to the transaction. This is fundamental because the main effect of the arm's length principle will be to set prices (and thus remunerate the parties to a transaction) consistently with their role: the more important role a party plays in a given transaction, the more exposed this party should be to the profits or the losses that arise from this transaction.[77] Conversely, a party that does not play a significant role in a transaction should be less exposed to the profits or the losses derived from the same transaction. This underlying rationale of the arm's length principle corresponds to what would usually happen between independent enterprises taking part in any business activities: for example, if a person starts a company that runs a bakery with no employees, it will earn all the profits from the business activities. If, in contrast, the company pays to obtain a recipe or to employ qualified staff, it will not anymore perform all the functions and own all the relevant assets, and thus it will only earn the profits left after paying for the recipe or the staff costs.

How can an intercompany transaction be accurately delineated? This part of a transfer pricing analysis has been subject to more detailed recommendations since the BEPS project, and comprises an analysis of the contractual terms of the transaction, the functions performed by each of the parties to the transaction (i.e., the *functional analysis*), the characteristics of property transferred or services provided, the economic circumstances of the parties and of the market in which the parties operate, as well as the business strategies pursued by the parties.[78] Among these parameters, the functional analysis is absolutely central because it will reveal the conduct of the parties and the importance of their respective contributions to the generation of income earned by the multinational enterprise as a whole. It is only once the functional profile of the parties to an intercompany transaction has been determined that it is possible to investigate the prices set or the profits earned by comparable independent parties (i.e., the second part of a transfer pricing analysis).

The OECD Guidelines highlight three main elements that should be investigated in order to identify the role of an associated enterprise in an intercompany transaction: the functions performed,[79] the risks assumed,[80] and the assets used[81] by a company as

77. *See* para. 1.56 of the 2022 OECD Guidelines: 'Usually, in the open market, the assumption of increased risk would also be compensated by an increase in the expected return, although the actual return may or may not increase depending on the degree to which the risks are actually realised.'
78. These parameters are likely to be described in the so-called local file of the transfer pricing documentation: *see* section 7.1.1 of this book.
79. Examples of functions are the performance of R&D activities, the manufacturing of goods, or the provision of services.
80. Examples of risks are the credit risk (i.e., the risk that a customer does not pay its debt in time), the currency risk (i.e., the exposure to currency fluctuations), or the obsolescence risk (i.e., the risk that goods that are kept in a company's inventory become too old to be sold at their usual price).
81. Assets refer to tangible assets (such as a warehouse, a factory, or machinery), intangible assets (such as a patent, know-how, or a brand), and financial assets (such as stocks or cash). It is important to emphasise that the existence, location, and valuation of assets for transfer pricing purposes does not necessarily follow the existence, location, and valuation of such assets for legal or accounting purposes: the substance, i.e., the reality, for transfer pricing purposes takes precedence over the form, i.e., the legal or accounting treatment of assets.

part of a given controlled transaction. Accordingly, under the theoretical framework described in the OECD Guidelines, when a company enters into intercompany transactions with an associated enterprise, each party should be exposed to the economic outcome (whether a profit or a loss) of the transaction in proportion to the functions it performs, the risks it assumes, and the assets it uses for the purpose of the transaction. In other words, the more important functions are performed, the more significant risks are assumed, and the more valuable assets are used, the more exposed an associated enterprise should be to the economic outcome of an intercompany transaction. The connection between the functional analysis and the exposure to the profits or losses that are generated by an intercompany transaction is illustrated by Figure 1.2.

Figure 1.2 Exposure to Economic Outcome Depends on Functions, Risks and Assets

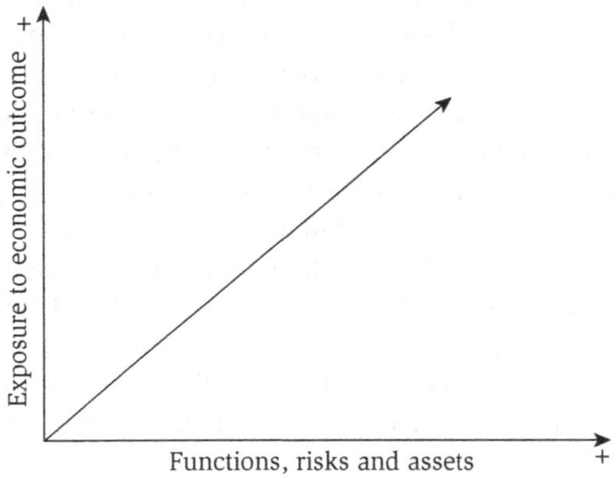

Functions, risks, and assets are closely linked to each other; for example, the assumption of certain risks may follow from the performance of certain functions, and the ownership of assets may follow from both the performance of functions and the assumption of risks. A typical example relates to IP: the legal ownership of IP (e.g., being the legal beneficiary of a patent following registration), the property of an intangible from an accounting perspective (e.g., when a patent is registered on the balance sheet of a company), or even the actual payment of royalties in exchange for the right to use IP will not necessarily be acknowledged from a transfer pricing perspective: if the functions that are needed to develop and protect the IP have not been performed by the company claiming ownership of such IP, it is likely that from a transfer pricing perspective tax administrations in other countries will claim the right to tax part of the income connected to the intangibles. In other words, the lack of functions points to the lack of substance, and thus the lack of entitlement to profits.[82]

Here, it is interesting to emphasise the growing importance of the physical performance of functions for the allocation of profits in relation to the other two main

82. This topic is studied in Chapter 5 of this book.

parameters of the functional analysis, when looking at the evolution of the OECD Guidelines. With the amendments made in 2017 following the work on BEPS Actions 8–10, the physical performance of functions has gained priority over risks and assets, which is understandable given the objective of the BEPS project to ensure taxation in line with substance, which is mainly defined in a functional manner. In other words, profit allocation will mainly follow the important functions within a multinational enterprise.[83] Therefore, when performing a functional analysis, it is critical to thoroughly understand the functions performed by the parties to an intercompany transaction, as such functions will also influence the risks and assets that are attributed to each party. This means that the assumption of risks alone (e.g., putting capital at risk by investing or paying for costs), or the ownership of assets alone (e.g., by legally owning a patent), is not likely to result in the attribution of significant income from a transfer pricing perspective. Moreover, it is often complex to identify the existence of risks and determine who assumes such risks,[84] and it may be difficult to identify, locate, and value intangible assets;[85] the identification of functions is less complex, which may also explain why priority has been given to functions.

To get the full picture of the role played by each party in an intercompany transaction, it is necessary to perform a functional analysis that takes into account the contributions of all the parties involved in such a transaction. By so doing, it is possible to understand to what extent each party contributes to the profits made by a multinational enterprise. With the vocabulary used in the amendments made to the OECD Guidelines in 2017 and 2022, the functional analysis allows identifying each group member's contribution to the 'creation of value' (which is not necessarily synonymous to the value 'added'[86] by each party) in relation to the contributions made by other parties (i.e., the total value created by all the parties to a given intercompany transaction).[87] This will enable a correct identification and understanding of the

83. Functions are especially important with respect to the control over risk, and the development of intangibles. This topic is further studied in Chapter 5 of this book.
84. To facilitate this process, the Guidelines contain an analytical framework for risks with several steps that are to be followed in order to correct the existence and the assumption of risks: *see* paras 1.60 and following of the 2022 OECD Guidelines. For an analysis of this analytical framework for risks, *see* Richard S. Collier and Ian F. Dykes, *The Virus in the ALP: Critique of the Transfer Pricing Guidance on Risk and Capital in the Light of the COVID-19 Pandemic*, 702–720 (Bulletin for International Taxation, 2020-12).
85. To facilitate this process, Chapter 6 of the Guidelines has been revised as part of the BEPS project.
86. For a definition of value added, *see* the *Oxford English Dictionary* (online version): 'The amount by which the value of an article is increased at each stage of its production, exclusive of the cost of materials and bought-in parts and services.'
87. The need to take into account the contribution of each party to the value chain of a given good or service has been emphasised by the OECD as an important aspect of the prevention of the erosion of the tax base: *see* OECD, *Action Plan on Base Erosion and Profit Shifting*, 20 (2013), where the report mentions the objective of 'ensuring that profits associated with the transfer and use of intangibles are appropriately allocated in accordance with (rather than divorced from) value creation'. As a result of the emphasis of the BEPS amendments to the OECD Guidelines, multinational enterprises tend to conduct thorough analyses of their value chains, something that may be described as a 'value chain analysis': *see* Emmanuel Llinares and Ralph Meghames, *Value Chain Analysis: An Analytical Tool to Evaluate Economic Contribution in the Overall Framework of Value Creation*, in Werner Haslehner and Marie Lamensch (eds), Taxation and

transaction, as well as how each party should be remunerated for its respective contributions. Let us illustrate the functional analysis by an example.

Example: Analysis of the functions performed, risks assumed and assets used as part of a warehousing activity

Assume that company A is resident in country A and manufactures goods. These goods are then stored in a warehouse owned by company B, resident in country B. Companies A and B are associated. Since these companies enter into a transaction (i.e., company B provides a storage service to company A by making its premises available for the storage of goods), are residents of different countries, and are associated, transfer pricing rules apply, and the arm's length principle requires that the pricing of this transaction is comparable to what would be applied between independent enterprises in a comparable situation. The first step consists in performing a functional analysis through investigating the functions performed, risks assumed and assets used by companies A and B as part of the intercompany transaction at hand. This is typically done by answering questions that are adapted to the transaction at hand, such as: Who decides upon the management of the warehouse (i.e., question related to a function)? Who assumes the obsolescence risk in case the goods become too old to be sold and have to be scrapped (i.e., question related to a risk)? Who owns the warehouse (i.e., question related to an asset)? The answers to these questions will reveal how companies A and B have organised their business activities and shared the roles; on that basis, it will be possible to conclude how to set the transfer prices so as to remunerate appropriately their respective contributions.

The outcome of the functional analysis, sometimes described as the 'characterisation' of the parties to a transaction, indicates the functional profile of each company and the expectations concerning its exposure to the economic outcome (i.e., the profits or the losses) of a given intercompany transaction. In other words, if the functional analysis reveals that one company performs important functions, takes important decisions, and/or assumes important risks, it will have an important exposure to the economic outcome of the transaction. Conversely, a company making low contributions will only be exposed to the economic outcome of the transaction to a limited extent, as independent parties would do. In the above example, if the functional analysis reveals that the manufacturer (company A) also decides on the management of the warehouse (owned by company B), company A will probably be deemed to make more important contributions than company B, thereby being exposed to the economic outcome of the transaction to a greater extent. The 'characterisation' that results from the functional analysis may point to certain typical concepts used (possibly abused)[88] in transfer pricing, such as: an entrepreneur (i.e., a company

Value Creation, 185–198 (IBFD EATLP International Tax Series, 2021). *See also* paras 1.3.3 and following of the 2021 UN Manual.

88. This precision refers to situations where the characterisation of the parties is exaggerated and does not take into consideration in a sufficiently nuanced manner the respective contributions of the parties. This would be the case, for example, if a functional analysis mechanically points to one company being the entrepreneur, and the other being a low-risk tested party, whereas the reality is more blurred. Another example is if a low-risk entity enables costs savings, thanks to

performing all important functions), a principal (i.e., a company owning valuable IP and performing certain important functions), or a routine entity (i.e., a company performing low-risk functions and not taking important decisions). The amendments made to the OECD Guidelines as a consequence of the BEPS project emphasise the need to make such a 'characterisation' cautiously and in a nuanced manner, to avoid quick conclusions pointing to a certain profit allocation.

The functional analysis alone is not enough to determine the actual transfer prices that should be applied to an intercompany transaction, or the income that should be earned by an associated enterprise when it enters into an intercompany transaction; the functional analysis reveals the reality existing between the parties. It is this reality that needs to be remunerated at arm's length, by comparison with the effect of the market forces. Therefore, the functional analysis should be supplemented by a comparability analysis.

1.4.3 The Comparability Analysis

As explained above, the functional analysis helps identify the role played by each party to a transaction. Once this role has been identified, the next step of a transfer pricing analysis consists in searching for information that will help define the conditions for the intercompany transaction, including (but not limited to)[89] the transfer price of the goods or services transferred, or the remuneration that the parties should earn upon entering in this transaction. This is when the comparability analysis comes into the picture. The prices paid to – or by – the associated enterprise will be tested against those paid to – or by – a comparable independent company, or a panel thereof; alternatively (depending on the transfer pricing method used),[90] it will be the profits earned by the associated enterprise that will be tested against those earned by a comparable independent company, or a panel thereof. Apart from the situation where a predetermined pricing or profit margin already exists in the law or regulations applicable (a so-called *safe harbour*), the comparability analysis should be made on a case-by-case basis and when necessary include comparability adjustments to improve the reliability of the comparison, which excludes the use of proxies: 'in no event can unadjusted industry average returns themselves establish arm's length prices'.[91]

The rationale of the arm's length principle implies relying on the price or profit margin that would be applied between independent companies in a comparable situation. Here, two types of independent transactions may be relied on to set the

being established in a country where costs are lower, thus pointing to the possible need to remunerate this entity for the costs savings it allows. For an example where the French Supreme Administrative Court expected a detailed and nuanced functional analysis (as opposed to mechanically distinguishing between routine and non-routine entities), *see* Pierre-Jean Douvier and Saro Gocer, *Profit Shifting and Comparability: The French Supreme Administrative Court Provides Useful Clarification on Functional Analysis and the Concept of Routine Entity*, vol. 29, issue 2, 106–110 (International Transfer Pricing Journal, 2022).

89. *See* para. 1.7 of the 2022 OECD Guidelines.
90. Transfer pricing methods are presented in Chapter 2 of this book.
91. *See* para. 1.40 of the 2022 OECD Guidelines, last sentence.

transfer price of a controlled transaction: transactions between a group company and an independent company (*internal comparables*),[92] or transactions between two independent companies that are not related to the multinational enterprise (*external comparables*).[93] The two types of comparables need to satisfy the same comparability requirements and may be equally reliable, as both are subject to the market forces. However, in practice, it is often difficult to find external comparables that are sufficiently reliable. The two types of comparables are illustrated in the below example.

Example: Internal and external comparables

Company A is resident in country A and manufactures chairs. It sells the chairs both to an external distributor (company B, resident in country B) and to its wholly owned subsidiary (company C, resident in country C). Company B also purchases chairs from another supplier (company X, resident in country X); it is assumed that companies B and X are independent from each other. The transactions between companies A and B, as well as B and X, take place between independent companies, so transfer pricing rules do not apply. The cross-border intercompany transaction that is to be priced is the sale of chairs by company A to company C since these two companies are associated and are residents of different countries. Since the transaction between companies A and C is subject to transfer pricing rules, and given that the arm's length principle relies on a comparison between controlled and uncontrolled transactions, a benchmark provided by uncontrolled transactions is needed to set the price of the sale of goods between companies A and C. For that purpose, the multinational group could rely either on an internal comparable (i.e., the sale of chairs by company A to company B) or on an external comparable (i.e., the sale of chairs by company X to company B). Since it is assumed that the same chairs are sold by company A to companies B and C, the products are comparable. However, other parameters may affect the reliability of this internal comparable. For example, the quantities, the currency, or the product responsibility may differ between the two transactions entered into by company A. For that reason, in addition to product comparability, it will need to be investigated whether other circumstances, described below in more detail as *comparability factors*,[94] point to the same conclusion, i.e., the comparability of the controlled and uncontrolled transactions. For the external transaction (i.e., the sale of chairs by company X to company B) to be comparable to the controlled transaction (i.e., the sale of chairs by company A to company C), the comparability test is more difficult to meet, since it will need to be investigated whether the products sold in the two transactions are comparable to each other, in addition to analysing the other comparability factors described below. Therefore, since it is often difficult to find external comparables that are sufficiently reliable, internal comparables are more frequently used. In any case, as

92. Such transactions are often referred to as 'internal comparables' because one of the parties to the transaction is an associated enterprise.
93. Such transactions are often referred to as 'external comparables' because the two parties to the transaction are independent and do not belong to the group of companies.
94. *See* paras 3.4 and following of the 2021 UN Manual.

mentioned above, the two types of comparables need to satisfy the same comparability requirements.

Information on independent comparable transactions may be gathered by any means,[95] the important thing being to find one or several independent transaction(s) sufficiently comparable to the controlled transaction under review. The process of looking for comparable independent transactions is usually described as a *benchmarking study*. A benchmarking study would typically lie on a given *search strategy*, which is a method for searching information on comparable independent transactions.[96] The search strategy is based on the characteristics of the associated enterprises and the controlled transaction under review (i.e., the outcome of the functional analysis); it may also be necessary to have decided which transfer pricing method to apply before performing the benchmarking study.

If there is only one independent transaction that is comparable to the intercompany transaction under review, one would either apply the value of the independent transaction directly to the intercompany transaction to be priced or correct it through *comparability adjustments*[97] if there are some differences that prevent directly using the value.[98] If there are several uncontrolled transactions that are comparable to the intercompany transaction under review, one would typically aggregate the information to arrive at an *arm's length range*.[99] An arm's length range is made up of a range (or a scale) of figures that are comparable from a transfer pricing perspective. The limits of the arm's length range (i.e., the lowest and the highest values of the comparables selected as part of the benchmarking study) are easily determined. However, the range may comprise a wide spectrum of values between the lowest and the highest values, especially if many comparables have been selected, or if important differences exist between these comparables. The breadth of the range may be problematic for setting the transfer prices because of the difficulty of choosing where in

95. In practice, it is often relied on databases that include publicly available information (*see* paras 3.30–3.34 of the 2022 OECD Guidelines).
96. The OECD Guidelines contain a description of the typical process for a benchmarking study, which is divided into nine steps: *see* para. 3.4 of the 2022 OECD Guidelines. Steps 2 and 3 of a benchmarking study will be particularly relying on the accurate delineation of the transaction. For an example of search strategy and benchmarking study, *see* Andrew Hughes, *Transfer Pricing Benchmark: North American Healthcare Distribution*, 1407–1410 (Tax Notes International, 13 June 2022). For a critical analysis of the framework provided in the OECD Guidelines for conducting a benchmarking analysis, *see* Michael C. Durst, *It's Time to Reform Transfer Pricing Benchmarking*, 1271–1278 (Tax Notes International, 6 June 2022). *See also* the typical process for a comparability analysis described in paras 3.2.1 and following of the 2021 UN Manual.
97. For a description of the need for different types of comparability adjustments, together with examples, *see* paras 3.5.3 and following of the 2021 UN Manual.
98. An example of comparability adjustment would be if the volume of an intercompany transaction is significantly higher than the volume of a comparable independent transaction. Given that higher volumes would normally entitle the buyer to a rebate, the price applied in the independent transaction may have to be decreased when being transposed to the intercompany transaction. Many other types of circumstances may require that comparability adjustments be performed.
99. *See* paras 3.55–3.66 of the 2022 OECD Guidelines.

the range to position the transfer prices and how to prevent disputes.[100] Therefore, to improve the reliability of the arm's length range and set the transfer prices in an objective manner, different types of statistical measures may be made within the range. It is, for example, frequent to divide the results of the arm's length range into the different quartiles.[101] The three quartiles are described below:

- The first quartile, or lower quartile, represents the 25% lowest values observed in the panel of comparables.
- The second quartile, or median, separates the higher half from the lower half of the results.
- The third quartile, or upper quartile, represents the 25% highest values observed in the panel of comparables.

The observations that are between the lower quartile and the upper quartile are usually described as the *interquartile range*. In addition to the quartiles, or alternatively to the quartiles, it may be relevant to use other statistical measures, such as the deciles[102] or the average of the results observed in the panel of comparables. It is important to observe that in the OECD Guidelines, it is considered that a transfer price or a profit margin that is within the arm's length range is in line with the arm's length principle: 'if the relevant condition of the controlled transaction (e.g. price or margin) is within the arm's length range, no adjustment should be made'.[103] The UN Manual adopts a similar position.[104] However, this does not tell how to set the limits of the range, and which statistical measures to use. Even if the interquartile range is frequently used, it is not necessarily the most adopted tool to determine the arm's length price or profit margin in a given case: the arm's length range may but does not need to correspond to the interquartile range.[105] Only a case-by-case analysis, taking into account in particular the functional analysis, the industry, and the comparables obtained as part of the benchmarking study, will lay the ground for the choice of the statistical measures that are the most adapted to the case at hand.

---

100. Here it is important to keep in mind that transfer pricing always involves at least two countries that would normally have diverging interests, since the tax base in each country varies in opposite directions with variations of the transfer price. If too high a price is paid for a good or a service, the seller would earn too much, while the purchaser would pay too much. Therefore, the wider the range is, the more likely it is that the two countries involved in the transaction disagree. This would especially be true if a multinational enterprise chooses a point in the range that is close to the limits of the range.
101. This method is used in statistics. For a definition of quartiles, *see* the *Oxford English Dictionary* (online version): 'The first or third of the three values of a variate which divide a frequency distribution into four groups each containing one quarter of the total population.'
102. Deciles divide a frequency distribution into ten groups.
103. *See* para. 3.60 of the 2022 OECD Guidelines. For instance, if a company produces a table and wants to sell it to its associated distributor, a transfer pricing analysis may show that three comparable independent companies sell comparable tables for 50, 55 and 60. The arm's length range would then be 50–60, which means that the table may be sold by the manufacturer to its associated distributor for a price ranging from 50 to 60.
104. *See* para. 3.5.5.1 of the 2021 UN Manual.
105. *See* para. 3.57 of the 2022 OECD Guidelines. For an example of court case in which the interquartile range was accepted, *see A Oy*, Finnish Supreme Administrative Court (13 September 2021, case number KHO:2021:127).

Consequently, transfer pricing in most cases is not about finding a 'perfect' comparable to set a 'perfect' arm's length price or profit margin; when such a 'perfect' comparable does not exist or is not available,[106] a range of comparable prices or profit margins is the only way to arrive at an acceptable basis for setting the transfer price.[107] The quality of the transfer pricing analysis will thus be decisive, given that the functional and comparability analyses have a direct influence on the final outcome, and yet require judgment. Indeed, as explained in the OECD Guidelines, 'transfer pricing is not an exact science but does require the exercise of judgment on the part of both the tax administration and taxpayer'.[108]

Table 1.5 illustrates the use of an arm's length range to set the transfer price of goods on the basis of the operating margin that should be earned by the company distributing such goods.

Assume that a group of companies sets up a subsidiary in country A. The purpose of setting up the subsidiary is to distribute goods manufactured by associated enterprises resident in other countries. Since the goods are purchased by the subsidiary from other members of the group, it is necessary to set the conditions (especially the transfer prices) applying to the goods at arm's length so that the manufacturers and the distribution subsidiary earn an arm's length income. After performing a benchmarking study through searching independent distributors performing functions comparable to those of the tested party, the following values are found based on the operating margins of the panel of independent distributors.

Table 1.5 Interquartile Range Showing the Operating Margin of Independent Distributors

Upper quartile	5%
Median	4%
Lower quartile	2%

These figures are based on a benchmarking study that aggregates the operating margins earned by comparable independent enterprises performing distribution activities. As paragraph 3.60 of the 2022 OECD Guidelines recommends reaching a profitability level that is within the range, in this example, the transfer prices should prima facie be set so that the subsidiary earns an operating margin between 2% (lower

106. A good example of such situation is when a controlled transaction is unique, and thus does not exist between independent parties. Despite the lack of comparable, the arm's length principle still requires hypothesising how independent parties would have priced the terms of a transaction. In addition, the OECD Guidelines make clear at several instances that the mere fact that a transaction may not be seen between independent parties does not mean that it does not have characteristics of an arm's length arrangement: *see* paras 1.11, 1.142, 1.143 and 9.109 of the 2022 OECD Guidelines, as well as para. 3.1.3 of the 2021 UN Manual. The UN Manual emphasises that 'where no comparables are found for a controlled transaction between associated enterprises, it may become necessary to use approaches not depending directly on comparables to find an arm's length price': *see* para. 3.1.5 of the 2021 UN Manual.
107. *See* para. 3.55 of the 2022 OECD Guidelines.
108. *See* para. 1.13 of the 2022 OECD Guidelines.

quartile) and 5% (upper quartile). A profit margin below 2% or above 5% would fall outside the range, and normally be considered in breach of the arm's length principle. A transfer pricing adjustment may, accordingly, be justified in the country of the distributor (if the distributor earns a profit margin below 2%; i.e., it earns too little) or in the country of the manufacturer (if the distributor earns a profit margin above 5%; i.e., it earns too much). Transfer pricing adjustments may also occur if the method to perform the benchmarking study was incorrect and produced wrong results.

In certain situations, it may be justified that the operating margin falls outside the interquartile range,[109] which is an area of frequent disputes. This may be the case if there are particular circumstances existing in country A that would justify earning more or less profits than comparable independent companies. For example, the market circumstances in a given country may be particular, or the performance of a company may have been influenced by certain specific factors. Consequently, in the example above, whereas company A should normally earn an operating margin that is within the range of 2% to 5%, there may be reasons justifying that it earns an operating margin that is below 2%, or above 5%. In any case, deviations from the arm's length range should be motivated by objective arguments, whether the claims to depart from the arm's length range are made by tax administrations or multinational enterprises.

For the purpose of setting transfer prices between associated enterprises and achieving a high degree of comparability between controlled and uncontrolled transactions, the OECD Guidelines and UN Manual recommend taking into account four *economically relevant characteristics* or *comparability factors*, in addition to performing the functional analysis.[110] When performing a benchmarking study, not only should the controlled and uncontrolled transactions be comparable from a functional point of view, such transactions should also be comparable from the point of view of the four following comparability factors: the characteristics of the property or the services at hand, the contractual terms of the transaction at hand, the economic circumstances that are relevant for the transaction at hand, and the business strategies of the independent and associated enterprises. It is important to take into consideration all of these comparability factors, as they may affect the transfer prices or the profit margins applied between the associated enterprises:

- The characteristics of the property or the services at hand may affect the transfer prices or the profit margins applied between associated enterprises since the price of goods or services often depends on the characteristics of such goods or services. For example, a product of particularly high quality may be sold at a higher price than a product having the same use but lower quality.
- The contractual terms of a transaction may also influence the prices applied by the parties. For example, higher volumes may result in higher discounts.[111]

109. *See* para. 3.61 of the 2022 OECD Guidelines.
110. *See* paras 1.36 and following of the 2022 OECD Guidelines. *See also* para. 3.2.4 of the 2021 UN Manual.
111. It is emphasised that the 'contractual terms' have a broad meaning here, as this expression encompasses both the written terms of the agreements that exist between the parties and the

- The economic circumstances that are relevant for the transaction at hand are of importance. For example, an economic downturn may result in lower profit margins within a given industry, as a result of the lower demand of consumers. Another example concerns local market features (i.e., the particular features of a geographic market such as the cost of labour, the cost of raw material, or subsidies) that may give rise to location savings (i.e., costs savings due to these local market features).[112] Here one should mention the COVID-19 pandemic, which had an important impact on the economy but at the same time implied certain government subsidies, and thus had to be taken into account from a transfer pricing perspective.[113]
- The business strategies of the independent and associated enterprises may influence transfer prices, for example, when prices are kept at a low level during the start-up phase of a product newly launched.

Taking into account the above-mentioned comparability factors is necessary to ensure a sufficient degree of comparability between the transaction to be priced and the comparables selected as part of the benchmarking study. If the comparability analysis reveals certain differences between the controlled and the uncontrolled transactions, the general recommendation of the OECD Guidelines is that the uncontrolled transactions are valid (i.e., sufficiently comparable to the controlled transaction) only if 'reasonably accurate adjustments can be made to eliminate the effects of such differences'.[114] If no such adjustments can be made, the transactions are not comparable, and it should not be relied on the given uncontrolled transaction(s) to set the transfer price of the intercompany transaction at hand. Comparability adjustments consist in modifying the data relating to controlled and/or uncontrolled transactions, for such transactions to become more comparable.[115] In practice, the way comparability adjustments are performed may depend on the transfer pricing method

actual terms of the relationships between the parties as emphasised by their conduct. This view, which is in line with the substance-over-form principle, is presented in Chapter 5 of this book.

112. *See* paras 1.159 and following of the 2022 OECD Guidelines. According to para. 3.4.5.6 of the 2021 UN Manual, location savings are 'the net cost savings that an MNE realizes as a result of relocation of operations from a high-cost jurisdiction to a low-cost jurisdiction'.
113. In this respect *see* OECD, *Guidance on the Transfer Pricing Implications of the COVID-19 Pandemic* (2020). This report provides interpretations of the OECD Guidelines with respect to different issues triggered by the COVID-19 pandemic. This concerns particularly the comparability analysis (*see*, e.g., Andrew Barton, Vinu Subramaniam and Paola Marino, *Impact of COVID-19 and Transfer Pricing: Approaches for Comparability Adjustments*, vol. 69, issue 3, 981–1001 (Canadian Tax Journal, 2021)), losses and the allocation of costs specific to the pandemic, government assistance programmes, and APAs. The pandemic could also have consequences on other issues, such as the residence of companies or the existence of a permanent establishment: *see* OECD, *Updated Guidance on Tax Treaties and the Impact of the COVID-19 Pandemic* (2021). On this topic *see also* Matt Andrew and Richard S. Collier, *COVID-19 Challenges for the Arm's-Length Principle*, 1363–1368 (Tax Notes International, 22 June 2020).
114. *See* para. 1.130 of the 2022 OECD Guidelines, as well as step 8 of the analysis described in para. 3.4 of the 2022 OECD Guidelines.
115. Comparability adjustments are described in detail in paras 3.47–3.54 of the 2022 OECD Guidelines. For an illustration of such adjustments, *see* Thomas Bittner and Anna-Katharina

applied to set transfer prices between associated enterprises.[116] The below example illustrates a possible method to make a comparability adjustment.

Example: Comparability adjustment

Assume that company A (resident in country A) manufactures goods and sells them to its subsidiary B (resident in country B) as well as to an independent distributor C (resident in country C). One way of setting a transfer price would be to sell the goods from company A to company B at the price applied between companies A and C if these transactions are comparable (that would be an internal comparable). If there are differences between these two transactions (e.g., the manufacturer also transports the goods sold to company B, but does not provide this service when selling goods to company C), it should be assessed whether 'reasonably accurate adjustments' can be made to eliminate the effect of such differences. If this is not the case, the price paid by company C cannot be relied on in setting the price charged to company B. In this case, there is a functional difference between the transaction under review (the sale of goods from A to B including transportation) and the comparable uncontrolled transaction (the sale of goods from A to B with no transportation). A possible method to make a comparability adjustment and arrive at an arm's length price would be to assess the transportation cost of delivering the goods to company B and add this cost to the price of the goods sold to company C, which by definition is at arm's length since company C is independent. This comparability adjustment would mitigate the functional difference between the two transactions, thus better enforcing the arm's length principle.

1.5 THE TAX ARBITRAGE RESULTING FROM INTERCOMPANY PRICING

Given the fact that corporate income tax rates vary between countries, a tax arbitrage effect may be reached by increasing the income of companies located in countries with lower tax rates or where income may be subject to a favourable regime such as a patent box,[117] and decreasing the income of companies located in countries with higher tax rates.[118] For example, a multinational enterprise may decide to locate certain strategic Research and Development (R&D) functions in a country with a low corporate income

Jann, *Capital Adjustments in Transfer Pricing Analysis: OECD Example of Working Capital Adjustments*, vol. 18, issue 1, 14-16 (International Transfer Pricing Journal, January/February 2011).

116. *See* Chapter 2 below for a description of different transfer pricing methods.

117. A patent box refers to the possibility offered in certain countries to apply a lower tax rate to income connected to an intangible asset such as a patent. In 2015, the OECD suggested a regime (the 'modified nexus approach') aimed at ensuring that income taxable in a patent box is commensurate with the proportion of qualifying expenditures necessary to develop an intangible asset and located in the country of the patent box: *see* OECD, *Countering Harmful Tax Practices More Effectively, Taking into Account Transparency and Substance, Action 5: 2015 Final Report* (2015).

118. By 'tax arbitrage effect', it is referred to the impact on the total tax burden of a multinational enterprise of variations in income earned and being subject to tax in each country where the

tax rate to ensure a low taxation of the profits expected from that R&D while manufacturing and distributing goods worldwide. Moreover, the tax accounting rules for the computation of corporate income are also different from one country to another, something that may enable a tax arbitrage effect since profits may not be taxable, and costs may not be deductible to the same extent in different countries. For example, the deduction of interest expenses is often subject to limitations, in addition to the obligation to meet the arm's length standard.[119]

That a tax arbitrage may be sought by multinational enterprises does not necessarily mean that it is not acceptable for tax purposes. The OECD Guidelines and the UN Manual recommend that as long as the arm's length principle is enforced, lowering the global tax burden of a multinational enterprise through tax planning should, under certain assumptions and for transfer pricing purposes only, be accepted by tax administrations.[120] This position is understandable: since the objective of the OECD Guidelines is to suggest a common methodology to set transfer prices in line with the arm's length principle, it would be contradictory to reject transfer prices that have been set in accordance with the same principle, for the sole reason that prices in line with the arm's length principle give rise to a tax saving. At the same time, seeking a tax arbitrage effect while enforcing the arm's length principle does not prevent countries from applying anti-avoidance rules, whether general or special, when a transaction is (partly) motivated by the objective to minimise the tax burden. In that respect, minimum taxation rules discourage tax planning strategies implying the taxation of profits below the minimum tax rate. In other words, while transfer pricing planning may not be able to be challenged on the sole basis of an arm's length provision, other rules may apply to limit tax planning, such as minimum taxation, controlled foreign company (CFC) rules, withholding taxes, the principle purposes test in tax treaties, or domestic interest limitation deductions. This tolerance for what could be described as 'acceptable transfer pricing tax planning' is, however, not recognised by all countries.

Example: Tax arbitrage and shift of profits due to moving a function

Assume that a high value-adding function such as a key executive person is moved from company A (resident in country A) to company B (resident in country B). Companies A and B are associated. The key executive is moved at the end of year 1, as illustrated by Figure 1.3.

enterprise carries on business activities. The total tax burden of a multinational enterprise would be the sum of the taxes paid in each country.

119. In this respect, *see*, e.g., Art. 4 of the Anti Tax Avoidance Directive (ATAD) (Council Directive (EU) 2016/1164 of 12 July 2016 laying down rules against tax avoidance practices that directly affect the functioning of the internal market, OJ L 193, 19.7.2016, pp. 1–14).

120. *See* para. 9.34 of the 2022 OECD Guidelines, and para. 8.1.1.4 of the 2021 UN Manual.

Figure 1.3 Key Executive Working for Company A (Year 1) and for Company B (Year 2)

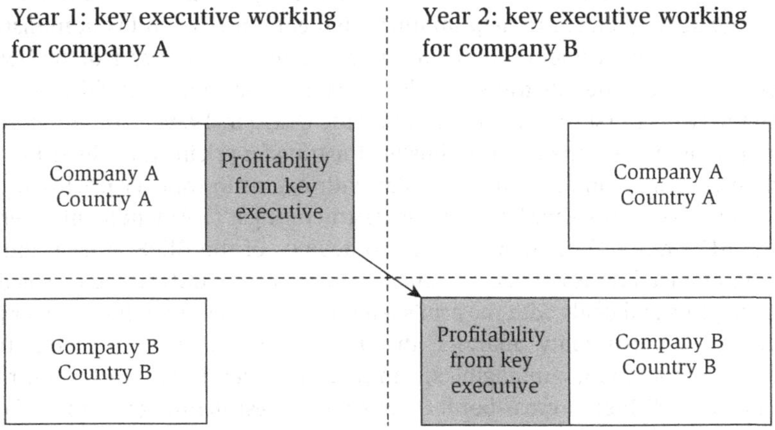

In this situation, a function was performed by company A in year 1, and by company B in year 2. According to the principles set by the OECD Guidelines, the profitability resulting from the activities of the key executive are to be attributed to the company for which this person actually works: if the key executive is moved from company A to company B, the country of origin (i.e., country A) should, in principle, recognise this move of functions and for year 2 refrain from taxing the profits resulting from the activities of the key executive after that this person has moved to company B. Instead, since the function was performed by company B in year 2, the profits connected to the function should be taxed by the country of destination (i.e., country B) from the time the person has moved to that country.[121] The move of the key executive may be motivated by operational reasons, tax reasons, or both. A lower tax rate in country B as compared to country A would decrease the global tax burden of this multinational enterprise, something that the OECD Guidelines and the UN Manual – under certain assumptions – do not refuse as multinational enterprises are normally allowed to organise their business 'as they see fit', i.e., including when such an organisation leads to tax savings.[122]

121. However, the principles relating to business restructurings have to be observed, in particular with regard to the potential levy of an exit tax upon the transfer of functions, risks and/or assets from one country to another. In that respect, *see* Chapter 4 of this book.
122. *See* para. 9.34 of the 2022 OECD Guidelines, as well as paras 8.1.1.4 and 8.2.1.4 of the 2021 UN Manual.

1.6 THE OECD GUIDELINES, THE UN MANUAL, AND THE GUIDANCE PROVIDED BY THE EU

As a result of the increasing focus put on transfer pricing, the OECD has issued recommendations intended to help multinational enterprises and tax administrations apply the arm's length principle in a coordinated manner.[123] The work of the OECD has been influenced by the US transfer pricing regulations, although differences exist between the two. A first report was issued by the OECD in 1979.[124] After the issuance of more specific studies, the OECD published the transfer pricing guidelines in 1995.[125] An update was made in 2010, in particular with regard to transfer pricing methods, comparability, and cross-border business restructurings.[126] Amendments were then made in 2017 and 2022 to implement the outcomes of the BEPS project and add a chapter on financial transactions. The 2022 version of the OECD Guidelines is divided into ten chapters and deals with the arm's length principle as such, the transfer pricing methods, the comparability analysis, dispute prevention and resolution, transfer pricing documentation, intangibles, intra-group services, cost contribution arrangements (CCAs), cross-border business restructurings, and financial transactions.[127] The OECD Guidelines are updated from time to time, to reflect the developments and best practices within the field of transfer pricing.

Given the complexity of transfer pricing and the diversity of views among multinational enterprises, tax administrations and courts, the drafting of the OECD Guidelines is a difficult task that aims at reaching a consensus that will be acceptable to most users of the Guidelines. The need to achieve consensus may, nevertheless, result in formulations that have a general character and that could be interpreted in different ways. This situation is hard to avoid and comes as a consequence of the global reach of the Guidelines, which goes beyond the OECD member countries. In addition, the OECD Guidelines are mainly based on the application of a principle - the arm's length principle - as opposed to detailed rules with a clear material content. Although the description of the arm's length principle is filled with concepts and is sometimes

123. The need for consensus among different countries is very important in the area of transfer pricing, as per definition transfer pricing is a cross-border discipline. With no consensus double taxation is hardly avoidable, thus hampering cross-border exchanges.

124. OECD, *Transfer Pricing and Multinational Enterprises* (1979).

125. OECD, *Transfer Pricing Guidelines for Multinational Enterprises and Tax Administrations* (1995).

126. For a historical perspective on the arm's length principle, *see* Hubert Hamaekers, *Arm's Length: How Long?*, in Paul Kirchhof, Moris Lehner, Kees van Raad, Arndt Raupach and Michael Rodi (eds) International and Comparative Taxation: Essays in Honour of Klaus Vogel, 29-52 (Kluwer Law International, 2002); Jens Wittendorff, *Transfer Pricing and the Arm's Length Principle in International Tax Law*, 84-111 (Kluwer Law International, 2010); Martin Lehner, *Article 9: Associated Companies*, in Thomas Ecker and Gernot Ressler (eds), History of Tax Treaties: The Relevance of the OECD Documents for the Interpretation of Tax Treaties, 389-409 (Linde, 2012). For a description of the 2010 update of the OECD Guidelines, *see* Caroline Silberztein, *The 2010 Update to the OECD Transfer Pricing Guidelines*, in Dennis Weber and Stef van Weeghel (eds), The 2010 OECD Updates, 147-160 (Kluwer Law International, 2011).

127. OECD, *Transfer Pricing Guidelines for Multinational Enterprises and Tax Administrations* (2022).

illustrated with examples, the principled nature of the OECD Guidelines makes transfer pricing an area easily subject to controversies.

The legal value of the OECD Guidelines has since long been a controversial issue. The nature of the Guidelines – a recommendation – makes them non-binding: according to Article 5 of the Convention on the Organisation for Economic Co-operation and Development of 14 December 1960, 'In order to achieve its aims, the Organisation may: (a) take decisions which, except as otherwise provided, shall be binding on all the Members; (b) make recommendations to Members; and (c) enter into agreements with Members, non-member States and international organisations.' Therefore, the OECD Guidelines are not legally binding per se.[128] They solely reflect the views of the members of the OECD when it comes to the conditions for the application of Article 9 of the OECD Model Tax Convention.[129]

The difficulty comes from the fact that despite the lack of binding effect, the OECD Guidelines – which are intended to represent 'internationally agreed principles'[130] – are widely, yet differently, relied on throughout the world.[131] Here, a distinction can be made between several situations. In certain countries, the OECD Guidelines are explicitly relied on in the domestic law in a manner that is intended to give them a binding effect. For example, in Germany, a circular made the OECD Guidelines binding on the tax administration (but not on taxpayers).[132] In such cases, although the Guidelines have no binding value as such, their implementation in a domestic legal order gives them a binding effect. Some difficulties can nevertheless arise, such as the question of which version of the Guidelines is applicable, whether a static or dynamic approach should be applied (i.e., whether or not an amended version of the Guidelines may be applied retroactively), or how to deal with potential incompatibilities between the Guidelines and certain domestic provisions.[133] In some other countries, the Guidelines may be referred to, but without granting them a binding effect. For example, the norm referring to the Guidelines may be non-binding, such as a statement of practice issued by the tax administration. Another situation where the legal value of the Guidelines arises is when they are referred to by the tax

128. *See* Jose Calderón, *The OECD Transfer Pricing Guidelines as a Source of Tax Law*, vol. 37, issue 1, 9 (Intertax, 2007). For an example of court case where the OECD Guidelines were not found to be binding – in particular with respect to the need to enforce the principle of legality – *see Toyota Argentina S.A. v. Administración Federal de Ingresos Públicos,* Federal Tax Court of Argentina (*Tribunal Fiscal de la Nación*) (28 April 2011, case number 26-860). On the legal value of the reports published by the OECD, *see* Michael Lang, *Introduction to the Law of Double Taxation Conventions*, paras 108 and following (3rd ed., Linde/IBFD, 2021).
129. *See* para. 1 of the commentary to Art. 9 of the 2017 OECD Model Tax Convention.
130. *See* para. 1 of the commentary to Art. 9 of the 2017 OECD Model Tax Convention.
131. For an overview of the reliance on the OECD Guidelines by different countries, *see* the transfer pricing country profiles published by the OECD: https://www.oecd.org/tax/transfer-pricing/transfer-pricing-country-profiles.htm#tpcountryprofiles (accessed 13 July 2022).
132. *See* Björn Heidecke, *Germany: New Circular on the Application of the Arm's Length Principle Issued by the Federal Ministry of Finance – Commitment to OECD Guidelines*, 375–380 (International Transfer Pricing Journal, 2021-6).
133. For example, certain anti-avoidance solutions suggested in the Guidelines (e.g., the hard-to-value intangibles approach) may conflict with domestic provisions of a tax system, especially when less far-reaching solutions would normally be applied according to the domestic law.

administration or by domestic courts (although courts around the globe do not always rely on the Guidelines)[134] while not having a binding value under the domestic law. The Guidelines would be considered non-binding, but they would often be deemed to provide some form of valuable guidance and thus be relied on to various extents, depending on the case at hand.[135] Such situations may be problematic, as it can be legally incorrect to apply certain paragraphs of the Guidelines in a given case, for example, when certain changes have a new material content, or when a recommendation made in the Guidelines conflicts with a provision of the domestic law.[136] This problem is exacerbated by the fact that the OECD Guidelines contain mainly principles or general recommendations, which makes it often difficult to determine whether or not the Guidelines – and if so, which version – are applicable in a given case. The OECD Guidelines may also influence the interpretation of a domestic arm's length rule, without being necessarily referred to in the domestic law or in a court case.[137]

Finally, a further issue relates to whether or not the OECD Guidelines may be used retroactively. While in certain cases, the updates made to the Guidelines merely provide a clarification, in other cases, certain changes bring a new interpretation of the arm's length principle – or even deviations from it. For example, it may be debated if

---

134. For example, *see* the case *Commissioner of Taxation v. SNF Australia Pty Ltd*, Federal Court of Australia (1 June 2011, case number (2011) FCAFC 74), where it was found that the OECD Guidelines were 'not a legitimate aid to the construction of the double taxation treaties'; for a comment on this case, *see* Michael Butler and Jessica Pengelly, *Commissioner Loses Transfer Pricing Appeal in SNF Case*, vol. 18, issue 5, 362–365 (International Transfer Pricing Journal, September/October 2011).
135. For example, it was found in the United Kingdom that a domestic law that does not refer to the OECD Guidelines may still be interpreted in their light: 'in determining the arm's length price, the approach of the OECD model is a useful aid which we should apply in the absence of any other guidance as they are the best evidence of international thinking on the topic': *see DSG Retail Ltd v. Her Majesty's Revenue and Customs*, Commissioners for Her Majesty's Revenue and Customs (31 March 2009, case number TC 00001). To take another example, although the General Court of the European Union considered the OECD Guidelines as 'merely a non-binding tool', it nevertheless found that the Guidelines 'reflect the international consensus achieved with regard to transfer pricing' and thus 'have a certain practical significance in the interpretation of issues relating to transfer pricing': *see Grand Duchy of Luxembourg, Amazon EU Sàrl and Amazon.com, Inc. v. European Commission*, General Court of the European Union (12 May 2021, case numbers T-816/17 and T-318/18), paras 122 and 154.
136. This might be the case, for example, for the non-recognition of intercompany transactions: while the 2022 OECD Guidelines allow the non-recognition of intercompany transactions in certain exceptional circumstances (*see* para. 1.142 of the 2022 OECD Guidelines), domestic law may not enable such far-reaching measures, mandating rather amendments to the prices of transactions. For that reason, certain countries may need to (or prefer to) amend their domestic tax laws to explicitly accept the non-recognition of transactions: for the example of Finland, where following the impossibility to recharacterise transactions the domestic law was amended, *see* Katriina Pankakoski, *Finland: Amendment Transfer Pricing Adjustment Provision Announcement 9 December 2021*, vol. 29, issue 3, 207–211 (International Transfer Pricing Journal, 2022) as well as Merja Raunio and Matti Urpilainen, *Finland: Case SAC 2020:35 – Supreme Administrative Court Reasserts the Prohibition to Recharacterize Transactions, Now in a Case That Deals with Group Internal Financing*, vol. 27, issue 5, 379–383 (International Transfer Pricing Journal, 2020).
137. *See*, e.g., Ryan Finley, *After Coca-Cola, Practitioners See DEMPE as Part of U.S. Law*, 1133–1134 (Tax Notes International, 24 May 2021).

the recommendations included in the 2022 OECD Guidelines with respect to the criteria for the non-recognition of certain transactions,[138] the possibility to consider *ex post* outcomes as presumptive evidence about the appropriateness of the pricing of hard-to-value intangibles,[139] or the 5% profit mark-up for low value-adding services[140] may be applied to intercompany transactions that were entered into before the relevant updates to the Guidelines were made. The answer can hardly be a general right to apply these recommendations indistinctly in a retroactive manner, unless the domestic law regulates the legal nature of the OECD Guidelines and accepts their retroactive application. An approach more in line with the principle of legality and the peculiar nature of the OECD Guidelines mandates rather a case-by-case analysis that takes into account both the domestic law and the specific recommendations of the OECD Guidelines in the case at hand. Unless the OECD Guidelines have a legally binding nature, it is only if the recommendations do not conflict with the domestic law that the Guidelines may be applied in a particular case.

Although the OECD Guidelines are formally drafted by the OECD and endorsed by the OECD member countries, since the start of the BEPS project an ambition to encourage convergence[141] in the taxation principles used by OECD and non-OECD countries has been developed, so as to avoid situations where different countries rely on different principles. This is why the work of the OECD on BEPS was not limited to the OECD members, but was supported by a larger group of countries – which would later become the so-called Inclusive Framework – in which all interested countries participated on an 'equal footing'.[142] The objective is to try to reach a compromise that as many countries as possible will find acceptable.

While the OECD Guidelines are widely relied on, transfer pricing matters still give rise to frequent differences of interpretations between multinational enterprises and tax administrations, or between the competent authorities of different countries when a cross-border tax dispute cannot be solved domestically. This is because transfer pricing is, by essence, a controversial area. Two main reasons explain why transfer pricing gives rise to disputes. First, there is no universal interpretation of the arm's length principle. Although the OECD Guidelines are intended to represent 'internationally agreed principles', not all countries agree on their (whole) content, and other interpretative sources – not necessarily consistent with the Guidelines – may be

138. *See* para. 1.139 of the 2022 OECD Guidelines.
139. *See* paras 6.186 and following of the 2022 OECD Guidelines.
140. *See* para. 7.61 of the 2022 OECD Guidelines.
141. On this point *see* Ryan Finley, *BEPS 5 Years Later: Still No Convergence on Transfer Pricing*, 26–29 (Tax Notes International, 5 October 2020).
142. *See*, e.g., OECD, *Action Plan on Base Erosion and Profit Shifting*, 20, 26 (2013): 'it is proposed that interested G20 countries that are not members of the OECD will be invited to be part of the project as Associates, i.e. on an equal footing with OECD members (including at the level of the subsidiary bodies involved in the work on BEPS), and will be expected to associate themselves with the outcome of the BEPS Project. Other non-members could be invited to participate as Invitees on an ad hoc basis'; OECD, *Tax Challenges Arising from Digitalisation: Report on Pillar One Blueprint – Inclusive Framework on BEPS*, 3 (2020): 'the OECD established the OECD/G20 Inclusive Framework on BEPS (Inclusive Framework) in 2016, bringing together all interested and committed countries and jurisdictions on an equal footing in the Committee on Fiscal Affairs and all its subsidiary bodies'.

considered equally or even more relevant. While the Guidelines may be fully relied on in certain countries, other countries have their own views on certain issues, sometimes in contradiction to the OECD Guidelines, something that may stem either from the domestic tax legislation or from the interpretation made by domestic courts. Differences of views may obviously exist between OECD member countries and non-OECD member countries, but there may also be divergences among OECD member countries. In view of these possible differences of interpretations, it cannot be taken for granted that the OECD Guidelines are fully relied on in a given country, even if it is a member of the OECD. It cannot either be taken for granted that the arm's length principle is applied by a country simply because the tax treaties concluded by this country include an article similar to Article 9 of the OECD and the UN Model Tax Conventions; in most countries there needs to be a domestic provision for the levy of tax, for Article 9 of a tax treaty to be applicable.[143] Consequently, it is necessary to have knowledge about the domestic transfer pricing rules and case law in order to properly apply the arm's length principle in a given country. Second, even when countries do agree on the relevance of the OECD Guidelines from a theoretical perspective, they may still disagree on how to interpret and apply the Guidelines. The interpretation of the OECD Guidelines is indeed not always homogeneous, which is understandable as they provide general principles, and only few concrete solutions. Transfer pricing is simply not an 'exact science';[144] rather, it is a matter of reasoning and of analysis. To mitigate risks of disputes such reasonings and analyses should preferably be conducted on the basis of similar principles (which the OECD Guidelines aim at), but even when the same principles are relied on, it cannot be avoided that disputes arise. Therefore, mechanisms to prevent and solve disputes are an important complement to transfer pricing principles.[145]

In addition to the OECD, other international organisations are active in the area of transfer pricing. In particular, the UN issued a Manual to help developing countries manage transfer pricing issues, provide practical interpretations of many transfer pricing issues, as well as (for the 2021 edition of the UN Manual) descriptions of the transfer pricing regimes applicable in Brazil, China, India, Mexico, South Africa, and Kenya.[146] Similarly to the OECD Guidelines, the UN Manual is not legally binding per se. The UN also publishes a Model Tax Convention, which has been updated in 2021. It is to be emphasised that the UN Model Tax Convention partly differs from the OECD Model Tax Convention with respect to issues that are relevant for transfer pricing, especially the wording of Articles 7, 9 and 25, and the commentaries thereof.[147]

---

143. UN, *Practical Manual on Transfer Pricing for Developing Countries*, para. 1.7.1 (2013): 'It is generally understood that Article 9 is not "self-executing" as to domestic application – it does not create a transfer pricing regime in a country where such a regime does not already exist.'
144. *See* para. 1.13 of the 2022 OECD Guidelines.
145. *See* Chapter 7 of this book on the prevention and the resolution of transfer pricing disputes.
146. *See* UN, *Practical Manual on Transfer Pricing for Developing Countries* (2021). For a comment on a previous edition of the UN Manual, *see* Jens Wittendorff, *U.N. Transfer Pricing Manual: The Choice Between International Consistency and Conflict*, 569-576 (Tax Notes International, 5 November 2012).
147. *See* Stig Sollund and Marcos Aurélio Pereira Valadão, *The Commentary on Article 9: The Changes and Their Significance and the Ongoing Work on the UN Transfer Pricing Manual,*

At the level of the EU, the European Commission has created an expert group, the Joint Transfer Pricing Forum,[148] which issues recommendations to reduce the compliance costs and the situations of double taxation that may occur in connection with transfer pricing. The recommendations of the Joint Transfer Pricing Forum are generally meant to complement the OECD Guidelines.[149] Although some of the recommendations issued by the Joint Transfer Pricing Forum have been endorsed by the European Commission[150] and the Council of the EU,[151] none of these recommendations has a binding effect. In addition, several directives adopted by the Member States of the EU have an impact on transfer pricing. Such directives are binding on the Member States, which must implement them in their domestic legislation.

In this book, the views and recommendations of the UN as well as the EU are taken into account, although the most important source remains the OECD Guidelines. The other sources are usually relevant when they are read in combination with the Guidelines, as the purpose of drafting transfer pricing recommendations by bodies other than the OECD is to either suggest interpretations of the OECD Guidelines, clarify the way the OECD Guidelines should be applied, or make a difference with the OECD Guidelines.

1.7 TRANSFER PRICING AND TAX AVOIDANCE: IS THE ARM'S LENGTH PRINCIPLE AN ANTI-AVOIDANCE RULE?

Transfer pricing rules, when they are based on the arm's length principle, can lead to a reassessment of the taxable income of a company, when such income has been too low because of non-arm's length prices. In this sense, transfer pricing rules based on the arm's length principle can be described as partly having an anti-avoidance nature, as these rules allow correcting the non-payment of tax due to non-arm's length

608–611 (Bulletin for International Taxation, November 2012). For general comments on the 2011 update to the UN Model Tax Convention, *see* Armando Lara Yaffar and Michael Lennard, *An Introduction to the Updated UN Model (2011)*, 590–597 (Bulletin for International Taxation, November 2012).

148. *See Commission decision of 26 January 2015 setting up the EU Joint Transfer Pricing Forum expert group*, 27 January 2015, COM(2015) 247 final.

149. *See*, e.g., EU Joint Transfer Pricing Forum, *The Application of the Profit Split Method Within the EU*, JTPF/002/2019/EN, Brussels (March 2019), p. 3, where it is indicated that the report issued by the Joint Transfer Pricing Forum is meant to be 'complementary to, and supportive of, the text of the OECD Revised Guidelines on the application of the Transactional Profit Split Method issued in June 2018'.

150. *See*, e.g., *Communication from the Commission to the European Parliament, the Council and the European Economic and Social Committee on the work of the EU Joint Transfer Pricing Forum in the period July 2012 to January 2014* (4 June 2014, COM(2014) 315 final).

151. *See*, e.g., the 3088th Economic and Financial Affairs Council meeting, Brussels (17 May 2011), during which the Council endorsed the following Communication from the European Commission: *Communication from the Commission to the European Parliament, the Council and the European Economic and Social Committee on the work of the EU Joint Transfer Pricing Forum in the period April 2009 to June 2010 and related proposals 1. Guidelines on low value adding intra-group services and 2. Potential approaches to non-EU triangular cases* (25 January 2011, COM(2011) 16 final).

prices.[152] However, in such cases, the reassessment of taxable income is not linked to the intention of a multinational enterprise to avoid taxes; it is rather due to the fact that transfer prices or profit margins are deemed as incorrect. Therefore, the arm's length principle may serve as an anti-avoidance rule based on objective grounds (i.e., the fact that the arm's length principle has not been enforced), not on subjective ones such as the intention to minimise the tax burden of a multinational enterprise. It is only when an associated enterprise is deemed not to act in a commercially rational manner, while an independent enterprise would, that the intention of a taxpayer might be taken into account for transfer pricing purposes and lead to the *non-recognition* of certain intercompany transaction. This possibility is, however, limited to 'exceptional circumstances':[153] a transaction may be disregarded and potentially replaced by an alternative transaction where the arrangements made in relation to a transaction, viewed in their totality, differ from those which would have been adopted by independent enterprises behaving in a commercially rational manner in comparable circumstances.[154] In other than such exceptional circumstances, e.g., when an intercompany transaction is similar to an uncontrolled transaction between independent parties, non-recognition is excluded: tax administrations must accept the existence of an intercompany transaction, and may only adjust the transfer price of that transaction.

Therefore, even in cases where intercompany transactions aim at minimising the tax burden (e.g., certain business restructurings),[155] it is on objective grounds that transfer pricing rules based on the arm's length principle may be relied on to reassess the taxable income of an associated enterprise. This assessment, however, remains a subjective exercise, especially in situations where there are no reliable comparables, as it would then be necessary to assess how independent enterprises would have behaved in a comparable situation. An example is the situation where an intercompany transaction is deemed to be supported by too little substance: finding out the right substance is a *subjective exercise* (because of the importance of judgment and the difficulty to rely on comparables), but it is carried out for an *objective purpose* (reproducing in a controlled context the conditions existing in an independent context).

Finally, it must be emphasised that the (non)application of transfer pricing rules does not preclude the application of other tax rules, including anti-avoidance rules.[156]

152. In this respect, it can be observed that the possibility for tax administrations to reassess intercompany transactions on the basis of the arm's length principle has been reinforced through several amendments to the OECD Guidelines, in particular the reinforcement of the substance-over-form principle (including the possibility to disregard certain transactions), the precision of the substance requirement (especially with regard to the need to perform certain functions in order to obtain certain benefits), and the introduction of Chapter 9 on business restructurings.
153. *See* paras 1.141 and following of the 2022 OECD Guidelines. In particular, non-recognition applies only when no similar transactions exist on the open market and that the intercompany transaction is not 'commercially rational'.
154. *See* para. 1.142 of the 2022 OECD Guidelines.
155. *See* Chapter 4 of this book.
156. *See* para. 9.34 of the 2022 OECD Guidelines.

So if transfer pricing rules based on the arm's length principle cannot be used as an anti-avoidance measure as such (e.g., because the arm's length principle has been enforced), other domestic or tax treaty-based anti-avoidance rules may apply. This goes for both general[157] and special[158] anti-avoidance rules.[159]

1.8 THE DIFFERENT STEPS OF A TYPICAL TRANSFER PRICING PROCESS

Throughout this book, the different steps of a typical transfer pricing process are presented. A transfer pricing analysis aims at determining the transfer prices of cross-border intercompany transactions consistently with the arm's length principle. Typically a transfer pricing analysis would imply the following steps: the determination of whether or not a cross-border intercompany transaction has taken place between associated enterprises (*see* section 1.4.1), a complete functional analysis (*see* section 1.4.2), the characterisation of the parties to the intercompany transaction (*see* section 1.4.2), the selection of the tested party (*see* the introduction to Chapter 2), the selection of the transfer pricing method (*see* Chapter 2), and the comparability analysis (*see* section 1.4.3). When organising their business activities, multinational enterprises may apply different types of transfer pricing models (*see* Chapter 3). They may also choose to carry out business activities through permanent establishments (*see* Chapter 6), or change their organisation (*see* Chapter 4). In any case, no matter which transfer pricing model is chosen, a central issue must be considered: the substance necessary to support a given transfer pricing model (*see* Chapter 5).

Once the different steps of a transfer pricing analysis are completed, a multinational enterprise would normally describe its transfer pricing policy in a transfer pricing documentation (*see* section 7.1.1); for certain multinational enterprises, a country-by-country report may need to be prepared (*see* section 7.1.2) and information on certain transactions may need to be disclosed to tax administrations (*see* section 7.1.3).

To prevent future disputes, taxpayers may consider applying for an advance pricing arrangement (APA) (*see* section 7.2.1). When a dispute arises, instead of

157. General anti-avoidance rules are found in domestic law (e.g., the Member States of the EU have implemented a domestic general anti-avoidance rule as a consequence of Art. 6 of the anti-tax avoidance directive) as well as tax treaties (e.g., the principal purposes test at Art. 29(9) of the 2017 OECD Model Tax Convention).
158. Examples of special anti-avoidance rules are CFC rules and limitations to the deductibility of interest expenses.
159. An example of a situation where transfer pricing rules and anti-avoidance rules may apply cumulatively is the deduction of interest expenses in relation to an intercompany loan. The arm's length principle would typically apply first and imply certain limitations, e.g., with respect to the determination of an interest rate in line with the market rates. Once the arm's length principle has been applied, the remaining interest expenses (possibly adjusted following the application of transfer pricing rules) may need to pass other tests before being deductible, such as earning-stripping rules or thin capitalisation rules.

(sometimes in addition to) domestic court proceedings, disputes may be solved through a mutual agreement procedure (MAP) (*see* section 7.2.2); when a MAP does not lead to the elimination of double taxation, an arbitration phase may, in certain cases, be initiated (*see* section 7.2.3).

CHAPTER 2
Transfer Pricing Methods

2.1 INTRODUCTION

The choice of a transfer pricing method comes after the accurate delineation of the transaction since the accurate delineation of the transaction is a prerequisite for the correct choice of a transfer pricing method. The purpose of a transfer pricing method is to find out a methodology, often based on financial figures, to *set* or to *test* the transfer price of a given intercompany transaction. The OECD Guidelines describe five transfer pricing methods, which are not intended to exhaust all possible methods, but are still 'widely accepted by national tax authorities'.[1] The transfer pricing methods recognised by the OECD Guidelines have a common objective, which is to set transfer prices in accordance with the arm's length principle.[2] However, the use of these methods is normally not compulsory to ensure compliance with the arm's length principle: what matters is that the transfer prices or the profit margins correspond to the conditions that would exist between comparable independent enterprises, not the formal compliance with a transfer pricing method recognised by the Guidelines. In other words, applying a transfer pricing method recognised by the Guidelines does not ensure, in itself, compliance with the arm's length principle. Conversely, not applying a transfer pricing method recognised by the Guidelines does not, as such, imply that the arm's length principle has been breached. At the same time, the transfer pricing methods recognised by the Guidelines build on significant experience in the field of transfer pricing; they are also widely relied on in different parts of the world, both by tax administrations and

1. UN, *Practical Manual on Transfer Pricing for Developing Countries*, para. 1.5.10 (2013).
2. It is important to emphasise that not all countries accept all the transfer pricing methods recognised by the OECD Guidelines. In addition, other transfer pricing methods, not recommended by the OECD Guidelines, may be adopted by certain countries or used by certain taxpayers. An example is the 'sixth method', developed originally by Argentina and applied particularly by certain Latin American countries, presented in section 2.4.

multinational enterprises. Therefore, while not compulsory,[3] in most cases it is a reasonable choice to at least consider these methods, since it is likely that one of the methods will be sufficiently reliable in a given case.

The choice of a transfer pricing method has also practical implications as it determines the internal processes that a multinational enterprise has to put in place to achieve arm's length pricing and be able to demonstrate compliance with the arm's length principle in various contexts.[4]

In practice, the way a multinational enterprise actually *sets* the transfer prices of its day-to-day intercompany transactions may not always follow the chosen transfer pricing method. The transfer prices may not even be at arm's length on a transaction-by-transaction basis. Instead, the prices of day-to-day intercompany transactions may be set according to a method that is practical to implement for the company in question, while the chosen transfer pricing method will help *test* whether or not the outcome is at arm's length over a certain period of time and possibly *adjust* such outcome in case the arm's length principle is not met. Ideally, both the test and the adjustments are done during one and the same financial year so that the outcome of that year is at arm's length. However, it may be too burdensome, technically impossible,[5] or even incorrect[6] to carry out this process each year. Therefore, the general recommendation expressed in the OECD Guidelines and in the UN Manual is that measurement of arm's length compliance should preferably be carried out over a certain period of time.[7] The example below illustrates the difference between setting transfer prices and testing transfer prices.

Example: The difference between setting transfer prices and testing transfer prices

Company A, resident in country A, is a member of a group that provides legal services. Company A works mostly for external clients, but it works also for a group company (company B, resident in country B) that does not include certain types of services in its offering. Company B ends up purchasing a great number of working hours from its associated enterprise company A, more than any single client purchases from company A. In other words, company B is the biggest client of company A, although company A has many clients and makes most of its turnover by selling services to other companies than company B. For the sake of convenience, company A may charge the services supplied to company B at the same hourly rate as the one applied to its external clients,

3. Of course, the domestic law of a country may go further than the recommendations of the OECD Guidelines and make the use of certain transfer pricing methods compulsory.
4. On the practical implementation of transfer pricing policies and the interaction with other areas, *see* paras 1.4.1 and following of the 2021 UN Manual. *See also* Sunny Kishore Bilaney, *Operational Transfer Pricing: Transfer Pricing, Finance, and IT Functions Converge*, 1029–1032 (Tax Notes International, 23 May 2022); Vesela Grozeva, Chris Schulman, Jessie Coleman and Pravin Ugalat, *Why Operationalizing Transfer Pricing Is More Important Than Ever*, 373–382 (Tax Notes International, 18 April 2022).
5. For example, because of the limitations of an IT system.
6. For example, when costs and revenues tend to be incurred at different periods of time, the arm's length character of intercompany transactions may have to be assessed in view of a complete economic cycle.
7. *See* para. 4.1.3.3 of the 2021 UN Manual.

which would be the way the prices are *set*. However, although this pricing mechanism may seem in line with the Comparable Uncontrolled Price (CUP) method,[8] it may not be compliant with the arm's length principle to use the same hourly rate as the one applied to external clients because the comparability factors[9] may reveal differences between the transactions with company B and the transactions with external clients. For example, the volume of working hours purchased may influence the price per hour, if independent parties would normally agree on a discount. Therefore, in addition to be *set*, the transfer prices would also need to be *tested*, e.g., by regularly investigating how many hours have been purchased and analysing whether independent parties would have agreed on discounts depending on the volumes purchased. If it is concluded that a discount should be granted, the transfer prices will have to be *adjusted* in order to meet the arm's length principle.

The choice of a transfer pricing method is, in principle, up to a company. However, the OECD Guidelines tend to limit the liberty to choose a transfer pricing method in two ways. First, the Guidelines encourage the use of the method most appropriate to the circumstances of the case: 'the selection of a transfer pricing method always aims at finding the most appropriate method for a particular case'.[10] This requires that a taxpayer performs an analysis to determine which transfer pricing method is the most suitable for a particular intercompany transaction.[11] Second, of the two categories of transfer pricing methods (i.e., the traditional transaction methods and the transactional profit methods), the Guidelines express a preference for the traditional transaction methods, particularly the CUP method.[12] The 2021 UN Manual does not express such a hierarchy: 'No preference for particular methods is advocated in this Manual. The most suitable method should be chosen taking into consideration the facts and circumstances.'[13]

The OECD Guidelines recognise and describe different transfer pricing methods, classified into two categories: traditional transaction methods and transactional profit methods.[14] These methods are often used separately, but several methods may also be combined with each other. Before getting into the details of these methods, it is important to emphasise that some of these methods are *one-sided*, while others are *two-sided*. The particularity of one-sided methods is that they apply to one party to a

8. *See* section 2.2.1 for a presentation of the CUP method.
9. With respect to comparability, *see* section 1.4.3 of this book.
10. *See* para. 2.2 of the 2022 OECD Guidelines. For a summary of the way of reasoning suggested by the OECD to determine the most appropriate transfer pricing method, *see* OECD, *Transfer Pricing Methods*, 16, para. 58 (July 2010). For a similar position, *see also* para. 4.1.2.1 of the 2021 UN Manual.
11. Such an analysis may have to take into account the respective strengths and weaknesses of different transfer pricing methods in relation to a given intercompany transaction, as well as the availability of sufficiently reliable information on comparable independent companies. Therefore, the same kind of transaction performed in different contexts may be subject to different transfer pricing methods.
12. *See* para. 2.3 of the 2022 OECD Guidelines.
13. *See* para. 4.1.3.2 of the 2021 UN Manual.
14. In addition, according to para. 2.9 of the 2022 OECD Guidelines, multinational enterprises may use methods that are not described in the Guidelines, as long as they arrive at an arm's length result.

transaction, while two-sided methods apply to two (or more) parties to a transaction. As all intercompany transactions imply at least two parties (i.e., the two counterparts to a transaction, such as a seller and a buyer), the application of a one-sided method requires choosing the party to which it is applied; remunerating this party at arm's length would ultimately ensure that the other party also receives an arm's length remuneration. This party is often referred to as the *tested party*, and is the one that has 'the less complex functional analysis'.[15] The one-sided transfer pricing methods are the resale price method, the cost-plus method, and the Transactional Net Margin Method (TNMM). The two-sided transfer pricing methods are the CUP method and the profit split method.

This chapter follows the distinction made in the OECD Guidelines between traditional transaction methods (section 2.2) and transactional profit methods (section 2.3). In addition, the so-called sixth method described in the 2021 UN Manual is presented (section 2.4). Finally, this chapter presents the combined use of several transfer pricing methods (section 2.5).

2.2 TRADITIONAL TRANSACTION METHODS

There are three traditional transaction methods: the CUP method (section 2.2.1), the resale price method (section 2.2.2), and the cost-plus method (section 2.2.3). All these transfer pricing methods imply a comparison between independent and controlled transactions of conditions that are close to the actual transactions, such as the transfer price, the cost of goods sold (COGS), or the gross margin. As opposed to profit-based methods, transactional methods normally do not imply the comparison of items that are further down in the income statement, to preserve sufficient proximity with the transactions.

2.2.1 The CUP Method

The CUP method is a two-sided transfer pricing method.[16] Under the CUP method, there is no tested party (since this method is two-sided and focuses on the price of a transaction, not on the profitability of a party), but there is a tested product or service, the transfer price of which is based on a comparison with an independent transaction: the rationale of the CUP method is to set the price of a good or a service transferred with a controlled transaction on the basis of an uncontrolled transaction. The price of this uncontrolled transaction either will be used as such for the controlled transaction or may be adjusted in order to take into account the differences in the comparability factors of the two transactions. This is the transfer pricing method for which product comparability is the most important since differences in the product (or service) will directly influence the price.

15. *See* para. 3.18 of the 2022 OECD Guidelines.
16. The characteristics of the purchaser and of the seller of a good or a service are taken into account with the CUP method, thereby making it a two-sided transfer pricing method.

Example: Application of the CUP method to an intercompany loan

The CUP method may be used to determine the interest rate applied when granting a loan between associated enterprises. The interest rate could then be set on the basis of the average interest rate used as part of uncontrolled transactions such as banks lending money to their clients. When a bank and its client are unrelated parties, the interest rate is indeed determined by the market forces. Relying on such an interest rate (or the average of interests rates applied to a combination of several loans) to determine the rate of an intercompany loan may be, in this case, the best way to enforce the arm's length principle because the source of information on market prices is as close as possible to the open market. The pricing of the intercompany loan is then done on the basis of the CUP method. The uncontrolled price (i.e., the interest rate applied between banks and their clients) may be used as such between the associated enterprises, or after having been adjusted if the comparability factors reveal certain differences between the controlled and the uncontrolled transactions.

The CUP is the transfer pricing method favoured by the OECD Guidelines, as it sets intercompany prices in the closest possible way to prices actually paid in uncontrolled transactions.[17] However, the major problem of the CUP method is the high standard of comparability that it requires to be applicable.[18] While the pricing of certain types of intercompany transactions may relatively easily rely on uncontrolled transactions (this could be the case for certain raw materials that are publicly traded and for which there is a quoted price),[19] most intercompany transactions cannot be priced directly - i.e., without adjustments - on the basis of uncontrolled transactions. Adjustments may have to be performed to improve the reliability of the CUP method, but such adjustments cannot correct all the differences between controlled and uncontrolled transactions. Some differences may be overcome, such as - depending on the circumstances of the case - the fact that the price may vary with the volume of the transactions. The intercompany price would then be determined by starting with the uncontrolled price, and adjusting it to take into account the differences that have been identified, such as the volume of different transactions. However, more substantial

17. The fact that the CUP method is to be favoured over other transfer pricing methods may be illustrated by the outcome reached in the case *Commissioner of Taxation v. SNF Australia Pty Ltd*, Federal Court of Australia (1 June 2011, case number (2011) FCAFC 74). In this case, the taxpayer successfully relied on the CUP method, while the Australian tax authorities relied on the TNMM. The fact that the use of the CUP method was accepted by the Federal Court of Australia, with no need to assess whether the TNMM produced more reliable results, illustrates the primacy of the CUP method in this case. For examples on the use of the CUP method, *see* Richard T. Ainsworth and Andrew B. Shact, *Transfer Pricing: Case Studies of the CUP Method*, 465-484 (Tax Notes International, 30 April 2012). It can also be observed that the OECD recommends that the CUP method is the preferred method for the pricing of commodity transactions: the reasoning behind this suggestion is found in OECD, *BEPS Action 10: Discussion Draft on the Transfer Pricing Aspects of Cross-Border Commodity Transactions*, 4, para. 8 (December 2014). For the final recommendation on using the CUP method for the pricing of commodity transactions, *see* paras 2.18 and following of the 2022 OECD Guidelines.
18. *See* para. 1.128 of the 2022 OECD Guidelines: 'Among the methods described at Chapter II of these Guidelines, the requirement for comparability of property or services is the strictest for the comparable uncontrolled price method.'
19. In this respect, *see* para. 2.18 of the 2022 OECD Guidelines.

differences may prevent the use of the CUP method when no reasonably accurate adjustments can be made to eliminate the effect of the differences. For example, the price used between a manufacturer and the end-consumer may not be used by a wholesaler. Indeed, the functions performed by a manufacturer selling to the end-consumer are likely to be more complex and costly than when the product is sold to a wholesaler because in the latter case part of the value chain[20] is performed by that wholesaler. As a result, the necessary adjustments may be too important to be performed in a reasonably accurate manner.

There are two types of CUPs, internal CUPs and external CUPs:

(1) Internal CUPs refer to the price of a good or a service charged between a group member and an independent party. For example, an internal CUP may exist if a manufacturer sells goods both to associated enterprises and to third parties. The transfer price used with third parties could then be relied on to set prices with associated enterprises, as long as the comparability factors described in the OECD Guidelines are fulfilled or that reasonably accurate adjustments can be made to eliminate the effect of any differences.

(2) External CUPs refer to the price of a comparable good or service between two unrelated parties. For example, an external CUP may exist if a group manufacturing and distributing goods uses the transfer price of similar goods between two independent companies. Here, it is crucial that the products are sufficiently comparable. Indeed, great differences may exist due to, for example, the intrinsic quality of the products, the volumes sold, the markets on which the products are sold, the logo, or the trade name of the products. In many situations such differences are impossible to correct through adjustments, because it would be too difficult to value these differences with sufficient accuracy, thus preventing the use of an external CUP.

According to the OECD Guidelines, whether or not a CUP may be applied should in principle be the first step of the selection of a transfer pricing method because this method is preferred to other methods. If no CUP is found, or no reasonably accurate adjustments can be made, another transfer pricing method may be used.

2.2.2 The Resale Price Method

The resale price method is a one-sided transfer pricing method.[21] It has a relatively limited scope of application, and is thus unsuitable to many types of intercompany transactions as it applies mostly to the sale of tangible property to a related party (a

20. For a definition of value chain, *see The Oxford Dictionary of Business*, 520–521 (2nd ed., Oxford University Press, 1996): 'The chain of activities by which a company buys in materials, creates a good or service, markets it, and provides services after a sale is made. Each step creates more value for the consumer.' The concept of value chain in the context of intercompany transactions is illustrated by the series of business activities described in Chapter 3 of this book.
21. It is the profitability of the tested party that is measured, thereby making the resale price method a one-sided transfer pricing method.

reseller or a distributor) that is involved in the resale of such tangible property to independent companies. The rationale of the resale price method is to set the transfer price of a certain good based on the *gross margin* that should be earned by the distributor at arm's length.[22] The distributor is thus the tested party, and the purchase price of the goods (i.e., the COGS) will have to be set so as to let the distributor earn a gross margin at arm's length. To compute the purchase price of the goods, the price on the resale of the product by the distributor to a third party (which by definition is at arm's length since the goods are sold to independent parties) is reduced by an arm's length gross margin to let the distributor cover the remaining of its costs (i.e., the costs left after the COGS, mainly the operating expenses (OPEX)) and possibly earn a profit.[23] The gross margin left after purchasing the goods is what the tested party has to cover its OPEX and earn a profit.

Example: Application of the resale price method

Assume that a group manufactures and sells computers as finished products to its distributing subsidiaries that will then resell the computers to independent retailers. The group sets the transfer prices of computers according to the resale price method, and the COGS is determined on the basis of the targeted gross margin of the distributors. Such a targeted gross margin would typically be based on a benchmarking study, to find out the gross margin earned by independent companies in a comparable situation. If the benchmarking study demonstrates that independent comparable distributors normally earn a gross margin of 25% on their sales, the transfer price of computers should be set in such a way that the related distributor also earns a 25% gross margin on computers purchased from an associated enterprise and resold to independent retailers, unless comparability adjustments would need to be performed. The determination of the COGS is the result of a two-step process, as illustrated in Table 2.1.

Table 2.1 Determination of the COGS

Step 1: The Turnover and the Targeted Gross Margin Are Identified			
	Turnover	100	Assumed sales to independent retailers
–	COGS	?	
=	Gross margin	25	25% of sales (as evidenced by benchmarking study)
Step 2: The COGS Is Computed According to the Targeted Gross Margin			
	Turnover	100	
–	COGS	75	100–25 = 75
=	Gross margin	25	25% of sales

22. The determination of a gross margin that is in line with the arm's length principle, or an arm's length range of gross margins, is normally done through performing a benchmarking study.
23. The distributor is indeed to cover its operating, financial, and exceptional expenses with the gross margin left after purchasing the goods.

In this example, the turnover of the tested party (i.e., 100) is known or at least expected, as it corresponds to the sales made by the distributor to independent third parties. This figure is by definition at arm's length, as the goods are sold to an external part. In this example, the targeted gross margin (25% of the sales, i.e., 25) is also known, as this figure corresponds to the outcome of the benchmarking study. What is lacking is the transfer price for the goods (i.e., the COGS), which is a controlled transaction between associated enterprises. As a result, the COGS should amount to the difference between the turnover and the gross margin, i.e., 75 (100–25 = 75). That is, by paying 75 to acquire a certain quantity of computers, the distributor will be able to achieve the targeted gross margin (25%), given that the distributor sells (or plans to sell) for 100. Some adjustments, for example, to take into account customs duties,[24] may be needed to determine the definitive transfer price.

Compared to the CUP method, the resale price method is less demanding with regard to product comparability, as 'minor product differences are less likely to have as material an effect on profit margins as they do on price'.[25] However, the resale price method requires that the functions, risks, and assets of the controlled and uncontrolled companies are truly comparable. Indeed, there are many costs left after purchasing the products to complete the whole value chain performed by the distributor, as the costs of the products purchased by the distributor are reflected in the gross margin, while the remaining expenses are usually considered as OPEX and are reflected in the operating margin. Therefore, with a given COGS and gross margin, differences in the functions performed, risks assumed, and assets used between different distributors may result in significant variations in their operating margin. This is illustrated by the examples below, where a distributor sells products for which there are significant differences from a competition perspective, thus resulting in varying levels of marketing expenses.

Example: A distributor sells products on a highly competitive market

Assume that a distributor purchases goods for 80 and sells them for 100. This leaves the distributor a gross margin of 20 (100–80 = 20). It is assumed that the market is highly competitive, which requires that the distributor invests massively in marketing and advertising, thus supporting OPEX amounting to 23.[26] The income statement of this distributor is presented in Table 2.2.

Table 2.2 A Distributor Sells Products on a Highly Competitive Market

	Turnover	100
–	COGS	80
=	Gross margin	20

24. *See* para. 2.27 of the 2022 OECD Guidelines.
25. *See* para. 2.29 of the 2022 OECD Guidelines.
26. It is assumed that marketing and advertising expenses are accounted as operating expenses.

–	OPEX	23
=	Operating margin	–3

In the above example, the highly competitive market requires the distributor to support significant OPEX, which results in a negative operating margin (–3). In contrast, in the below example (Table 2.3), it is assumed that there is only little competition on the market, so that the distributor supports much lower marketing and advertising expenses (10), while still purchasing the goods for 80 and selling them for 100.

Example: A distributor sells products on a market with few competitors

Table 2.3 A Distributor Sells Products on a Market with Few Competitors

	Turnover	100
–	COGS	80
=	Gross margin	20
–	OPEX	10
=	Operating margin	10

As there is only little competition on this market, the distributor does not need to invest massively in marketing and advertising. OPEX are lower than in the first example, which results in a higher operating margin (10, compared to –3 in the first example). Therefore, applying the resale price method through targeting a gross margin of 20% in both cases may not be a suitable solution: even if the distributors in principle exercise the same role in the value chains of these two products (i.e., a role as distributors selling at the same level of the value chain), the differences in the marketing function performed to sell the goods imply different levels of OPEX, thus also resulting in different levels of operating margin. Moreover, the higher marketing expenses incurred in the first example (Table 2.2) may contribute to the creation of IP, which is unlikely in the second example (Table 2.3), where it is assumed that the low competition on the market makes it unnecessary to incur important marketing expenses. Such differences could preclude the use of the resale price method, at least when no adjustments are made to the targeted gross margin.

Many other types of differences may preclude the use of the resale price method, such as differences in the quality of the products, differences in the accounting standards used, the (non)exclusivity of the right to distribute the products, or economic circumstances such as foreign exchange rates and interest rates. Consequently, it is necessary to deeply analyse the transaction at hand and the potential comparable independent transactions in order to determine whether or not the resale price method is a proper transfer pricing method, as well as if adjustments should be made to the targeted gross margin. The necessary information to perform comparability adjustments may not be available, which could preclude the use of the resale price method. Eventually, as a result of the diversity in the factors that may influence the level of comparability between controlled and uncontrolled transactions, the resale price method may be particularly suitable when the distributor does not add substantially to the value of the products,[27] and resells them within a short time of their purchase:[28] in such cases, it is indeed less likely that the functions performed or the risks assumed by the tested party or the comparable companies will significantly change their functional profile, which would undermine the use of the resale price method. Therefore, the tested party that relies on the resale price method is normally not a company performing valuable functions or using valuable intangibles as part of the transaction that is being priced, as in such a case it would most often be difficult to find independent comparable companies. In any case, even if an intercompany transaction corresponds to what is described in the OECD Guidelines as a typical case where the resale price method may be used, it would still be advisable to ensure that there is sufficient functional comparability between the tested party and the independent transactions, given that the reliability of the resale price method is very sensitive to functional differences.

Finally, it must be observed that since the resale price method targets the gross margin of an associated enterprise, the tested party may eventually – depending on its turnover and OPEX – incur operating profits or losses. The examples in Tables 2.2 and 2.3 above illustrate the different results that the resale price method may produce. Here, the question may be asked whether it is in line with the arm's length principle to apply the resale price method in situations where the tested party makes an operating loss. Generally, an independent enterprise would aim for profits and would not tolerate losses indefinitely,[29] but this does not mean that the arm's length principle always implies an obligation to be profitable, not even for low-risk entities. Independent enterprises may incur losses, even when they do not take important risks. Therefore, the OECD Guidelines do not condition the use of the resale price method to the eventual existence of an operating profit. The tested party is only expected to 'seek' to 'make an appropriate profit',[30] with no obligation to actually make a profit. This feature of the resale price method is often presented as an advantage when being compared to the TNMM: as argued in the UN Manual, a strength of the resale price method is that it can be used 'without forcing distributors to inappropriately make profits'.[31]

27. *See* para. 2.35 of the 2022 OECD Guidelines.
28. *See* para. 2.36 of the 2022 OECD Guidelines.
29. *See* para. 1.149 of the 2022 OECD Guidelines.
30. *See* para. 2.27 of the 2022 OECD Guidelines.
31. *See* para. 4.3.5.1 of the 2021 UN Manual. However, there are cases where the TNMM has been accepted in court, thus denying losses that would be incurred with other transfer pricing methods: *see*, for example, a case ruled by the Danish Supreme Court, in which the taxpayer had been loss-making while using the resale price method: Nikolaj Bjørnholm and Bodil Tolstrup, *Denmark: Danish Supreme Court Rules Against the Taxpayer in Its Third Transfer Pricing Case*, vol. 28, issue 5, 333–337 (International Transfer Pricing Journal, 2021).

2.2.3 The Cost-Plus Method

The cost-plus method is a one-sided transfer pricing method,[32] and consists in determining a transfer price based on the sum of a cost and a profit mark-up: a good or a service will thus be transferred at a price that corresponds to the costs incurred in the production of the good or the supply of the service, to which a profit mark-up is added. Consequently, the rationale of the cost-plus method is to set a transfer price that covers certain costs and lets the supplier cover other costs and earn an arm's length mark-up.[33] The cost-plus method is often suitable to set transfer prices for the sale of goods or the provision of intercompany services when the activity is performed on a low-risk basis, as this transfer pricing method can ensure that the seller will be reimbursed for certain of its costs and have the possibility to earn a profit. In practice, the cost-plus method is typically used for transactions involving intercompany services.[34]

The cost-plus method does not apply, contrary to what its name seems to imply, to all costs incurred by the service provider. The cost-plus method is based on *transactions*, as opposed to *profits*. It is the costs incurred for a specific transaction that the transfer price will need to cover. Accordingly, setting transfer prices on the basis of the cost-plus method implies that the company providing the services distinguishes between the costs that are linked with the specific transaction (typically direct costs such as the costs of production of the goods or the services),[35] and the costs that are not related to this transaction (e.g., the OPEX). The profit mark-up will correspond to the gross margin left after incurring the costs of production of the goods or the services.[36] The remaining costs such as the OPEX that are not directly linked with a specific transaction will be wholly or partly covered by the profit mark-up. As a result, a company that invoices an associated enterprise on the basis of the cost-plus method would normally incur a positive gross margin (as the costs of production of the goods

---

32. It is the profitability of the tested party that is measured, thereby making the cost-plus method a one-sided transfer pricing method.
33. The profit mark-up would typically need to be determined on the basis of a benchmarking study. However, in certain cases the profit mark-up could be determined in advance, something that would usually be seen as providing foreseeability to both companies and tax administrations. Such situations where profit mark-ups are determined in advance are referred to as *safe harbours* and may be provided by a country's domestic tax law or by a mutual agreement between the competent authorities of two countries. Several downsides are nevertheless associated with safe harbours, in particular the risk that they are at breach of the arm's length principle. For more details on safe harbours *see* section 3.1. of this book.
34. *See* para. 7.31 of the 2022 OECD Guidelines. For an example of court case in which the cost-plus method was found more suitable than the CUP method for low value-adding, *see A. A.G.*, Swiss Tribunal Federal (3 May 2021, case numbers 2C_548/2020, 2C_551/2020).
35. Typical examples of such costs are the purchase price of raw material before they are manufactured, or the wages costs of employees dedicated to a manufacturing process.
36. *See* para. 4.4.1.3 of the 2021 UN Manual: 'Like the Resale Price Method, the Cost Plus Method is a gross margin method; that is, it attempts to derive an arm's length amount of gross profit, in this case through an arm's length mark-up on COGS.' *See also* UN, *Practical Manual on Transfer Pricing for Developing Countries*, para. 1.5.6 (2013): 'The price is determined by adding to costs incurred by the supplier an appropriate gross margin so that the supplier will make an appropriate profit in the light of market conditions and functions performed.'

or the services are covered by the price charged to the purchaser), but at the same time, the company may incur a negative net margin (as the gross margin may not be sufficient to cover all remaining OPEX).

It is well possible to set transfer prices on the basis of all the costs incurred by the supplier of goods or services. In such a case, since the profit mark-up will cover both the COGS and the OPEX, it will let the supplier earn a specific net margin, as opposed to the gross margin earned on the basis of the cost-plus method. This transfer pricing method is referred to in the OECD Guidelines as the 'transactional net margin method'.[37] Since the profit mark-up earned on the basis of the cost-plus method corresponds to the gross margin of a company, such a mark-up will normally be higher than the one earned on the basis of the TNMM given that in this last case the OPEX have already been covered.

The application of the cost-plus method is illustrated by the example below.

Example: Application of the cost-plus method

Company A is resident in country A and manufactures pens on behalf of its associated enterprise company B, resident in country B. Company B designs the pens and provides quantitative and qualitative instructions to company A in relation to the production of the pens. Once the pens have been manufactured, they are sold by company A to company B. The group decides to set the transfer price of this intercompany transaction on the basis of the cost-plus method. It is assumed that a benchmarking study reveals than an arm's length profit mark-up on the costs directly linked with the production of pens ranges from 20% (lower quartile) to 30% (upper quartile), with a median of 25%. The group chooses to target the median and applies a profit mark-up on the costs directly linked with the production of pens (defined here as the COGS) of 25%. If it is assumed that the COGS amount to 100, company A will need to charge 125 (100 + (100 × 25%) = 125) to company B. The remaining gross margin amounts to what is left after covering the COGS, i.e., 25 (125–100 = 25). This gross margin will, in its turn, serve to cover the OPEX and, if possible, let the manufacturer earn a profit. If it is assumed that the OPEX amount to 20, the net margin will be positive and amount to 5 (25–20 = 5). These calculations are presented in Table 2.4.

Table 2.4 Application of the Cost-Plus Method

	Turnover	125	100 + (100 × 25%) = 125
–	COGS	100	
=	Gross margin	25	125–100 = 25
–	OPEX	20	
=	Operating margin	5	25–20 = 5

The level of mark-up is dependent on the functions performed, the risks assumed and the assets used by the company selling goods or providing services. Consequently,

37. This transfer pricing method is described in section 2.3.1 of this book.

product comparability is less important than with the CUP method. It is likely that low value-adding functions are associated with a lower mark-up than high value-adding functions, but in any case it is necessary that the mark-up is determined on the basis of independent transactions. As with the CUP and the resale price method, both internal and external transactions may be used as a benchmark. An internal comparable exists if an associated enterprise sells goods or services both to associated enterprises and to independent parties, and an external comparable exists if a similar good or service is sold between two independent companies.

Either way it is particularly important that there is sufficient comparability with regard to the functions performed (together with the risks assumed and the assets used) as well as the accounting standards used. Differences in the functions performed by the related entity and the comparable transactions (whether internal or external) may affect their profitability, especially if intangibles are used or developed.[38] For example, a manufacturer receiving technical instructions on the production of a certain good is not likely to achieve the same results as a manufacturer producing similar goods on the basis of its own know-how because the latter is likely to be exposed to higher costs (due to the development of manufacturing intangibles) and higher gains (due to the ownership of valuable manufacturing intangibles). Differences in the accounting standards used may also disrupt the application of the cost-plus method, for example, when it comes to classifying costs between the COGS and OPEX. Adjustments may be made to correct such differences, but it should be emphasised that the OECD Guidelines do not always recommend making adjustments to take into account certain OPEX.[39]

Many other differences may also need to be considered, such as the level of market at which the product or the service is sold, the determination of the cost basis, the terms of the engagement between the parties, whether all costs should be subject to a mark-up, etc. While in certain cases adjustments may be possible to make, too important differences may prevent the use of the cost-plus method, as adjustments may not be made with sufficient accuracy.

2.3 TRANSACTIONAL PROFIT METHODS

There are two transactional profit methods: the transactional net margin method (section 2.3.1), and the transactional profit split method (section 2.3.2). There has previously been some reluctance to use these transfer pricing methods, as they focus on profits, not on transactions. This would imply a less precise, and potentially incorrect application of the arm's length principle, since the pricing would be more distant from the transactions. Indeed, independent parties would normally not do business and set prices on the basis of an analysis of profits, especially net – as opposed to gross – profits. They would rather do so on a transactional basis. Also, transactional profit methods may result in aggregating the profits of different transactions, when they

38. *See* section 3.3 of this book for a description of intercompany transactions involving intangibles.
39. *See* para. 2.51 of the 2022 OECD Guidelines.

are assessed together for transfer pricing purposes. The problem with aggregating transactions is the loss of traceability on the profitability of each transaction, as different transactions (possibly involving different levels of functions, risks and assets) may trigger different profitability levels, and thus different prices; indeed, when possible, a transfer pricing analysis should preferably be made on a transaction-by-transaction basis.[40] Consequently, the OECD has been cautious with recommending the use of transactional profit methods, which, until the 2010 update of the OECD Guidelines, were considered as methods of 'last resort'.[41] By last resort, it was meant that transactional profit methods could be used only when traditional transaction methods could not be applied reliably.

However, due to the practical difficulties of using the traditional transaction methods and the experience and best practices accumulated since the edition of the OECD Guidelines in 1995, as well as in view of the move of the US towards a more frequent use of income-based methods, the last resort status of the transactional profit methods was abandoned in the 2010 update of the OECD Guidelines.[42] It is still considered, though, that where a traditional transaction method and a transactional profit method 'can be applied in an equally reliable manner, the traditional transaction method is preferable to the transactional profit method'.[43]

2.3.1 The Transactional Net Margin Method

The TNMM is a one-sided transfer pricing method. It focuses not on the gross margin (as the resale price method and the cost-plus method do) but on the net margin of the tested party; i.e., it includes the OPEX in the margin that is measured. The rationale of the TNMM is to set the transfer price of a certain good or service based on the net margin that should be earned by the tested party at arm's length, in relation to a particular item of the financial statements of the tested party. This method may be applied to a wide range of activities and be a 'practical solution to otherwise insoluble transfer pricing problems',[44] as the TNMM is less sensitive to product and functional differences than the traditional transaction methods.[45] However, the TNMM should be

40. *See* para. 3.9 of the 2022 OECD Guidelines, and para. 3.3.3.2 of the 2021 UN Manual.
41. *See* para. 3.50 of the OECD Guidelines before the 2010 update (OECD, *Transfer Pricing Guidelines for Multinational Enterprises and Tax Administrations* (2009)): 'There are [...] cases where traditional transaction methods cannot be reliably applied [...]. In such cases of last resort, practical considerations may suggest application of a transactional profit method either in conjunction with traditional transaction methods or on its own.'
42. It may also be argued that the transactional profit methods are consistent with the language of Art. 9 of the OECD Model Tax Convention, which uses the term 'profits': *see* especially the sentence in Art. 9(1) where it is indicated that 'any *profits* which would, but for those conditions, have accrued to one of the enterprises, but, by reason of those conditions, have not so accrued, may be included in the *profits* of that enterprise and taxed accordingly' (my emphasis).
43. *See* para. 2.3 of the 2022 OECD Guidelines.
44. *See* para. 2.80 of the 2022 OECD Guidelines.
45. *See* para. 2.75 of the 2022 OECD Guidelines. *See also* para. 4 of Annex I to Chapter II of the 2022 OECD Guidelines (Sensitivity of gross and net profit indicators): 'enterprises performing different functions may have a wide range of gross profit margins while still earning broadly similar levels of net profits'.

applied only if the tested party does not make unique and valuable contributions as part of the transaction that is being priced. Indeed, the profitability of the tested party would then be much more difficult to assess, and it may be impossible to find relevant comparable companies, so in such a situation the profit split method may have to be favoured.[46]

Given the fact that the TNMM takes into account the OPEX of the tested party, it is necessary to carefully monitor such expenses. Indeed, the net margin is by definition sensitive to variations in OPEX, something that prices and gross margins are not.[47] Also, it is crucial to make sure that financial and exceptional expenses, as well as income taxes, are not included in either the income statement of the tested party or the income statement of the comparable companies.

The TNMM, in most cases, assesses the operating margin of the tested party in relation to its sales, costs, or assets. In other words, it is a ratio between two different items in the financial statements of the tested party. Such ratios are often referred to as a 'financial indicator' or a 'profit level indicator'. The choice of the financial indicator is normally made depending on the type of activity that is carried on by the tested party.[48] The most common financial indicators applying the TNMM are the return on sales (i.e., the operating margin),[49] the full cost mark-up (FCM) (i.e., the return on total costs),[50] and the return on capital employed.[51] In addition, a ratio that relates the gross margin to the OPEX (the Berry ratio)[52] may be applied in cases such as intermediary activities, when other transfer pricing methods (especially the resale price method or the cost-plus method) cannot be relied on because the sales or the COGS are related to transactions with associated enterprises.[53] Indeed, in order to rely on the TNMM, the denominator 'should be reasonably independent from controlled transactions'.[54] As with the other transfer pricing methods, adjustments may be necessary to take into

46. *See* paras 2.65 and 2.126 of the 2022 OECD Guidelines.
47. *See* paras 2.68, 2.71 and 2.76 of the 2022 OECD Guidelines.
48. *See* para. 2.93 of the 2022 OECD Guidelines where it is observed that 'Typically, and subject to a review of the facts and circumstances of the case, sales or distribution operating expenses may be an appropriate base for distribution activities, full costs or operating expenses may be an appropriate base for a service or manufacturing activity, and operating assets may be an appropriate base for capital-intensive activities such as certain manufacturing activities or utilities.'
49. The return on sales may be computed according to the following formula: operating margin/sales. It is typically used for marketing, sales and distribution activities.
50. The full cost mark-up may be computed according to the following formula: operating margin/relevant full costs.
51. The return on capital employed may be computed according to the following formula: operating margin/capital employed. It is typically used for manufacturing activities.
52. The Berry ratio is computed according to the following formula: gross profits/operating expenses. It may be used – subject to certain prerequisites for being an appropriate transfer pricing method – in certain cases for service or distribution activities. On the prerequisites for the use of the Berry ratio, *see* paras 4.5.6.3 and 4.5.6.5 of the 2021 UN Manual, including the recommendations in footnote 41.
53. *See* para. 2.108 of the 2022 OECD Guidelines.
54. *See* para. 2.94 of the 2022 OECD Guidelines. For example, if the chosen financial indicator is the return on sales, it is necessary that the denominator (i.e., the sales) is the result of uncontrolled transactions, for the return (i.e., the operating margin) to be assessed in relation to a figure that is at arm's length.

consideration differences between the tested party and the comparable independent companies.[55] The application of the TNMM in combination with the return on sales is illustrated by the example below, where a comparison is also made to the resale price method.

Example: Use of the TNMM with the return on sales as a financial indicator and comparison to the resale price method

Assume that a company has the following income statement (Table 2.5).

Table 2.5 Comparison of TNMM and Resale Price Method

	Turnover	100
–	COGS	80
=	Gross margin	20
–	OPEX	15
=	Operating margin	5

The resale price method would assess the gross margin of the company, which in the above example is 20% (20/100 = 20%). The application of the TNMM, in combination with the return on sales, reveals a net margin of 5% (5/100 = 5%). Focusing on the net margin instead of the gross margin by including the OPEX in the measurement of the profitability of a tested party implies several consequences, three of which are detailed below:

(1) By focusing on the net margin, i.e., a lower level of the income statement, some differences in accounting standards are mitigated. Indeed, it is possible that the same cost is recorded as COGS in one country or by one company, while it is recorded as an OPEX in another country or by another company. This makes it difficult to compare different companies at the gross margin level. Consequently, the TNMM eases the comparison of companies that apply different accounting standards, which may be beneficial both when setting prices for different group companies and when performing benchmarking analyses.

(2) Focusing on the net margin reduces the need for product comparability and tolerates some functional differences, as differences in the functions performed 'are often reflected in variations in operating expenses'.[56] For example, a distributor buying products from a manufacturer at a certain price may invest more or less in the marketing and advertising of these products, something that would be reflected in its OPEX. Depending on the level of

55. For example, if the levels of inventory of the tested party and the independent comparable companies are not similar, a working capital adjustment may be necessary to reflect the financial consequence of such a difference. Indeed, different levels of inventory imply different levels of costs and, ultimately, different levels of profits.

56. *See* para. 2.68 of the 2022 OECD Guidelines.

involvement and risk of the distributor, its functional profile may vary. Using the resale price method to assess the profitability of such a distributor would suppose knowing its functional profile as well as the functional profile of the companies that are found in the benchmarking study, in order to compare companies that are actually comparable. In contrast, the TNMM does not require such a level of precision in the assessment of the functional profile of the tested party and the comparable companies, since the focus on the net margin tolerates some functional differences.

(3) Information on the net margin of comparable companies is more easily available and reliable than information on their gross margin, since publicly available financial information may not report gross margins.

Despite these advantages and the frequent application of the TNMM in practice, a major problem raised by the TNMM is the risk that different transactions are aggregated and remunerated together according to a single transfer pricing methodology, whereas in an independent context, the different transactions might generate different profitability. The OECD Guidelines are cautious with the aggregation of transactions and recommend that, as a rule, the arm's length principle be applied on a 'transaction-by-transaction basis'.[57] However, particular recommendations are provided in the Guidelines when transactions nevertheless need to be aggregated, in particular when separate transactions are so closely linked or continuous that they cannot be evaluated adequately on a separate basis.[58]

The risks associated with the aggregation of different transactions can be illustrated with the case of a company distributing machinery that also sells spare parts, performs services, and leases machinery. In this case, it may not be possible to remunerate all the activities of this company on the basis of a single application of the TNMM; this is because the aggregation of the remuneration of different transactions would make it impossible to assess the profitability of each transaction with sufficient accuracy, although there might be a need to assess the profitability of each transaction separately.[59] The aggregation of transactions may result in improperly transferring profits to or from the companies with which the transactions are entered into if they are all assessed in an aggregated manner. In addition, it would be difficult to find independent enterprises that perform a comparable combination of activities. Therefore, in this example (i.e., as assumed above, a company distributes machinery, sells spare parts, performs services, and leases machinery), it would be advisable to *segment* the income statement of the tested party in its different activities, to be able to set the transfer prices so that each transaction receives a net margin in accordance with the arm's length principle. This is illustrated by the examples below. In the first example (Table 2.6), the company's income statement is aggregated for the distribution of machinery, the sale of spare parts, the performance of services and the

57. *See* para. 3.9 of the 2022 OECD Guidelines.
58. *See* paras 3.9–3.12 of the 2022 OECD Guidelines.
59. Several reasons motivate this need, such as diverging functional analyses for different types of products, or differences in the comparability factors for various types of products.

leasing of machinery. On an aggregated level, the company shows a 10% return on sales. In the second example (Table 2.7), the same company's income statement is now segmented for each of the four activities, which reveals significant differences in the profitability of the different transactions, although the aggregation of the transactions still shows a 10% return on sales.

Table 2.6 Aggregated Income Statement and Use of TNMM

	Turnover	100
–	COGS	80
=	Gross margin	20
–	OPEX	10
=	Operating margin	10
	Return on sales %	10%

Because of the aggregation of the different transactions in a single income statement, the actual profitability of each transaction cannot be identified. Only the aggregated return on sales (10%) is apparent. The income statement of the same company is segmented in Table 2.7.

Table 2.7 Segmented Income Statement and Use of TNMM

		Distribution	*Spare Parts*	*Services*	*Leasing*	*Total*
	Turnover	45	10	20	25	100
–	COGS	75	5	0	0	80
=	Gross margin	–30	5	20	25	20
–	OPEX	1.5	0.5	3	5	10
=	Operating margin	–31.5	4.5	17	20	10
	Return on sales %	–70%	45%	85%	80%	10%

Although the aggregated return on sales is the same in both examples (10% of the turnover), the profitability of each transaction varies considerably. As evidenced in Table 2.7, the distribution activity is clearly loss-making (the return on sales of this activity amounts to –70%, and even the gross margin is negative), as the turnover (i.e., the sale of machinery to end-customers) does not suffice to cover the COGS and the OPEX related to the distribution activity. The purchase price (i.e., the COGS) may be too high and be challenged by the tax administration of the country of the distributor if the goods are purchased from an associated enterprise. On the other hand, the other activities are clearly more profitable, even though the return on sales may not be a suitable financial indicator to assess the arm's length character of the remuneration of such activities, nor may the TNMM be the most appropriate method. If the spare parts, services, and leasing activities are actually over-remunerated, there would be a risk of tax reassessment in the countries of the counterparts to the intercompany transactions involving the sale of spare parts, services and leasing, since the transactions would leave too high profits in the country of the tested party and too low profits in the other countries. As a result, the tested party should not aggregate its transactions and have them remunerated on the basis of a single application of the TNMM, as such a transfer pricing methodology makes it impossible to assess the actual profitability of each transaction.

The OECD Guidelines would recommend, in this situation, segmenting the income statement and remunerating each transaction at arm's length.[60] For example, the following approach may be followed:

- The distribution activity, given its focus on marketing and sales, could be remunerated on the basis of the return on sales. However, it may be necessary to differentiate between the sale of machinery and the sale of spare parts, as these two distribution activities may deserve different levels of profitability. Thus, two transfer pricing analyses, including two functional analyses and two comparability analyses may be necessary to assess what independent parties would earn at arm's length. Such a method could result in a lower remuneration for the distribution of machinery (e.g., a return on sales of 5%) and a higher remuneration for the distribution of spare parts (e.g., a return on sales of 10%), which may be the case if the sale of spare parts is more profitable an activity than the sale of machinery. The return on sales would have to cover the COGS, the OPEX related to the distribution activity, and leave a low but stable profit to the tested party.
- The service activity could be priced on the basis of a targeted FCM (e.g., by applying a profit mark-up of 10% to the sum of all the costs incurred for the purpose of the service activity). The amount charged to the recipients of the services would have to cover all the costs that are necessary to perform the service activity (i.e., including part of the OPEX), and let the service provider earn a profit.
- The leasing activity may be remunerated on the basis of the return on capital employed if the machinery is owned by the tested party (e.g., a return on capital employed of 10%).

The outcome of this approach may be totally different from the initial aggregated return on sales of 10%. Such an approach is more complex than merely measuring the aggregated net margin of the tested party. However, not performing such a detailed analysis carries the risk of breaching the arm's length principle for the remuneration of each type of transaction, something that would trigger risks of income adjustments and double taxation.

Another reason for isolating transactions and remunerating them separately is related to the necessity to prevent counterparts established in different countries, but performing the same function, from being remunerated (too) differently. One may indeed be tempted to set transfer prices so that the net margin of the tested party is at

60. *See* para. 2.84 of the 2022 OECD Guidelines.

arm's length, although the tested party enters into several – but similar – transactions with different group companies. However, although it is ensured that the aggregated net margin of the tested party is at arm's length, it is only the remuneration of the tested party that is tested, whereas the remuneration of the counterparts is not tested. If the tested party enters into transactions only with one foreign group company, such as a foreign entrepreneur, no such issue arises since the arm's length character of the intercompany transaction is valid on the two sides of the transaction; in contrast, when the tested party enters into intercompany transactions with several counterparts, it is necessary to ensure that each transaction with each counterpart is at arm's length.

The need to isolate transactions and price them separately for the purpose of ensuring that each counterpart is remunerated appropriately is illustrated by the following example. Let us assume that a company distributes drugs manufactured by several related manufacturers that are resident in countries A, B and C (manufacturers A, B and C). The tested party is characterised as a buy/sell distributor,[61] and a benchmarking study shows that the distribution of drugs by comparable independent companies may be remunerated on the basis of a return on sales of 3 %. The income statement of the tested party (i.e., the distributor) when aggregating the sales of drugs purchased from the three manufacturers is as follows (Table 2.8).

Table 2.8 Aggregation of Goods Purchased from Different Suppliers

	Turnover	100
–	COGS	80
=	Gross margin	20
–	OPEX	17
=	Operating margin	3
	Return on sales %	3 %

Apparently, the transfer pricing policy is in line with the arm's length principle, as the distributor earns a return that corresponds to what independent comparable distributors would earn at arm's length (i.e., a return on sales of 3 %). However, as the distributor purchases the drugs from three different manufacturers resident in three different countries (i.e., countries A, B, and C), this income statement does not show whether or not each transaction is in line with the arm's length principle. It just shows the accumulated sales, costs, and profits. To illustrate this issue, it is assumed that the purchase prices (i.e., the COGS of the distributor) are as follows, when one segments the income statement of the distributor depending on the manufacturer from which the drugs are purchased (Table 2.9). It is also assumed that the OPEX are borne in proportion to the turnover made for the sale of the drugs purchased from each manufacturer, and that the drugs purchased from manufacturer A account for 50 % of the distributor's turnover, the drugs purchased from manufacturer B account for 30 %

61. For the characterisation of transactions as part of distribution activities, *see* section 3.4.3 of this book.

of the distributor's turnover, and the drugs purchased from manufacturer C account for 20% of the distributor's turnover. That is, out of the total OPEX (17), 50% are attributed to the drugs purchased from manufacturer A (17 × 50% = 8.5), 30% are attributed to the drugs purchased from manufacturer B (17 × 30% = 5.1), and 20% are attributed to the drugs purchased from manufacturer C (17 × 20% = 3.4). Therefore, variations in the operating margin of the distributor are due not to differences in the OPEX, but to differences in the COGS. It is assumed that the products bought from manufacturer A were purchased for 55, whereas for those purchased from manufacturers B and C, the distributor paid 20 and 5, respectively. In total, the COGS of the distributor amounts to 80.

Table 2.9 Isolation of Goods Purchased from Different Suppliers

		Manufacturer A	*Manufacturer B*	*Manufacturer C*	*Total*
	Turnover	50	30	20	100
–	COGS	55	20	5	80
=	Gross margin	–5	10	15	20
–	OPEX	8.5	5.1	3.4	17
=	Operating margin	–13.5	4.9	11.6	3
	Return on sales %	–27%	16.3%	58%	3%

The above example shows that, although the aggregated return on sales earned by the distributor is in line with the benchmarking study (i.e., the distributor, in total, earns a 3% return on sales), the operating margin actually earned for each transaction is far from the targeted 3% of the turnover. The distributor in total earns a profit in line with the transfer pricing policy, but each of the three transactions is wrongly priced. Indeed, transactions with manufacturer A are loss-making (i.e., the COGS is too high given the sales and the OPEX), while the two other transactions are too profitable since the return on sales on products purchased from manufacturers B and C is well above 3%. This situation, which may not have been sought by the multinational enterprise, may be the result of too simplistic a transfer pricing policy; alternatively, this outcome may have been looked for, as part of an aggressive tax planning policy. Indeed, thanks to different COGS, income may be shifted between jurisdictions. In the above example, income is shifted from the country of the distributor to country A (because too little income is earned by the distributor on the drugs purchased from manufacturer A), and from countries B and C to the country of the distributor (because too high an income is earned by the distributor on the drugs purchased from manufacturers B and C). It can also be considered that income is shifted between the manufacturers, namely from manufacturers B and C to manufacturer A.

In contrast to the example of Table 2.9, by ensuring that each transaction is remunerated in accordance with the arm's length principle (i.e., in this example, a return on sales of 3% for the products purchased from each manufacturer), the profits or losses on each transaction are shared between the parties to the transactions according to the same methodology, which ensures an arm's length outcome for each transaction, and thus an arm's length taxable income in all the countries involved. To achieve such an outcome, it is necessary to adjust the COGS, which is the only intercompany transaction entered into by the distributor.[62] In this example, a correct income statement would attribute a 3% return on sales to the distributor for each transaction, as illustrated in Table 2.10. The COGS will, therefore, need to be adjusted to each transaction in order to ensure, eventually, a return on sales of 3% for each transaction.

Table 2.10 Isolation of Goods Purchased from Different Suppliers with Same Targeted Operating Margin per Transaction

		Manufacturer A	*Manufacturer B*	*Manufacturer C*	*Total*
	Turnover	50	30	20	100
–	COGS (after adjustment)	40	24	16	80
=	Gross margin	10	6	4	20
–	OPEX	8.5	5.1	3.4	17
=	Operating margin	1.5	0.9	0.6	3
	Return on sales %	3%	3%	3%	3%

The correct COGS is computed according to a formula where the operating margin is set at 3% of the turnover:

COGS = Turnover – OPEX – Operating margin

A comparison of the COGS before and after adjusting the income statement of the tested party shows the profits that could have been transferred and taxed in the wrong country (Table 2.11).

Table 2.11 Comparison of the COGS Before and After Adjusting the Income Statement of the Tested Party

	Manufacturer A	*Manufacturer B*	*Manufacturer C*
Initial COGS	55	20	5
Adjusted COGS	40	24	16
Difference	15	–4	–11

62. In contrast, the turnover is an external factor as the distributor sells to third parties. It is assumed that the operating expenses are not either the result of an intercompany transaction. In this example, another option could also have been to use the resale price method, and measure the profitability on each product at the gross margin level.

Two observations are made on the basis of the differences observed in Table 2.11:

(1) When the difference is positive (column with manufacturer A), it means that the COGS has decreased by ensuring that the intercompany transaction was at arm's length. The decrease in the COGS corresponds to an increase in the operating margin, and thus also an increase in the taxable income in the country of the distributor. The country of the distributor should no longer be willing to reassess the income of the distributor for the drugs purchased from manufacturer A, as this transaction now produces an arm's length return on sales. In theory, the tax administration of country A (where manufacturer A is resident) should also accept the price of this transaction, even after the adjustment in the COGS, as it is assumed that the transaction is now at arm's length. However, in practice, it is possible that the tax administration of country A, which has been taxing too high profits until the adjustment in the COGS, refuses such an adjustment, which would lead to double taxation.[63] Therefore, it would be advisable for the group to be able to demonstrate that the adjustment was commanded by the arm's length principle.
(2) When the difference between the initial COGS and the adjusted COGS is negative (columns with manufacturers B and C), it means that the COGS has increased by ensuring that the intercompany transactions were at arm's length. The increase in the COGS corresponds to a decrease in the operating margin, and thus also a decrease in the taxable income in the country of the distributor. The country of the distributor should theoretically not object to such a decrease in the taxable base for the transactions with manufacturers B and C because the transaction has simply been adjusted to an arm's length level. However, as mentioned above, in practice, it is possible that the tax administration of this country is reluctant to accept the new transfer prices, although such prices are meant to enforce the arm's length principle.

2.3.2 The Transactional Profit Split Method

The profit split method is a two-sided transfer pricing method, as it consists in splitting profits or losses on the basis of a formula between at least two parties. This transfer pricing method may be complex to apply, and often gives rise to controversies between taxpayers and tax administrations.[64]

From a pure operational perspective, relying on the profit split method is needed more often as multinational enterprises tend to fragment their value chain and extend

63. *See* section 7.2 of this book for a presentation of the phenomenon of double taxation and the means to prevent it, or to eliminate it.
64. *See* EU Joint Transfer Pricing Forum, *The Application of the Profit Split Method Within the EU*, JTPF/002/2019/EN, Brussels (March 2019), p. 15.

it across the borders, in a phenomenon that may be described as highly integrated[65] business models or *global value chains*.[66] This does not mean that profit split is necessary in all cases of global value chains; profit split will be particularly needed when important functions are shared so that the most important contributions to a group's profits are performed by group companies in different countries. In such situations it is unlikely that the different parties performing important functions can qualify as tested parties and be compared to independent companies, and thus be remunerated on the basis of a transactional method or the TNMM. Therefore, one may end up using the profit split method by elimination.

Since the 2010 update of the OECD Guidelines, the profit split method is not anymore a method of 'last resort'.[67] The revised guidance on the application of the transactional profit split method, which was issued in June 2018[68] and integrated to the OECD Guidelines with the 2022 update, has brought important precisions about when the profit split method may be relied on. It is especially mentioned that the profit split method may be used if it is the most appropriate method in case of unique (and thus, non-benchmarkable) and valuable contributions by each party,[69] for highly integrated operations, or if economically significant risks are shared[70] by the parties to the arrangement.[71] The 2021 UN Manual adopts a similar view.[72] It has also been clarified that the lack of comparables may, in certain cases, justify the use of the profit split method,[73] although this does not automatically imply that the profit split method

65. For an example of definition of 'highly integrated' business models, *see* EU Joint Transfer Pricing Forum, *The Application of the Profit Split Method Within the EU*, JTPF/002/2019/EN, Brussels (March 2019), p. 11: 'In practical terms, the operations would be "highly integrated" when two or more legal entities share and/ or combine functions, assets and risks, while jointly achieve a common objective (e.g. a project whereby the parties jointly contribute to each part of the process towards a common outcome).'
66. *See* OECD, *Interconnected Economies: Benefiting from Global Value Chains*, 14 (2013), where it is observed that 'the term "global value chains" was coined to reflect a strong trend towards the dispersion of value chain activities across the world. Many companies have broken up their value chains and distributed production stages across many countries; at the same time, they have outsourced parts of their value chains to external partners'. *See also* para. 1.2.6 of the 2021 UN Manual.
67. *See* para. 3.50 of the 1995 OECD Guidelines.
68. *See* OECD, *Revised Guidance on the Application of the Transactional Profit Split Method: Inclusive Framework on BEPS: Action 10* (2018).
69. This means also that if a profit split arrangement is unlikely between independent parties, the profit split method may still be applicable between associated enterprises: 'transfer pricing methods are not necessarily intended to replicate arm's length behaviour, but rather to serve as a means of establishing and/or verifying arm's length outcomes for controlled transactions' (*see* para. 2.124 of the 2022 OECD Guidelines).
70. *See* paras 2.121, 2.126, 2.134 and 2.137 of the 2022 OECD Guidelines. *See also* para. 1.105 of the 2022 OECD Guidelines: 'In circumstances where a party contributes to the control of risk, but does not assume the risk, compensation which takes the form of a sharing in the potential upside and downside, commensurate with that contribution to control, may be appropriate'; such a compensation will most likely be computed on the basis of the profit split method.
71. These are alternative, not cumulative criteria according to which the profit split method may be applied.
72. *See* paras 4.6.1.4 and 6.5.1.3 of the 2021 UN Manual.
73. *See* para. 6.209 of the 2022 OECD Guidelines for situations where no reliable comparables exist for the sale of goods or the provision of services involving the use of intangibles. It can be mentioned that the profit split method is likely to be appropriate to remunerate location savings

should be used.[74] On the other hand, when comparables do exist, the profit split method is unlikely to be the most reliable transfer pricing method.[75] Therefore, associated enterprises performing simple or routine functions, and thus being potentially tested parties, would normally not be a party to a profit split arrangement because more direct transfer pricing methods would be applicable.

Moreover, the changes brought to the OECD Guidelines in relation to the functional analysis, which since 2017 supposes to accurately delineate the intercompany transactions, tend to result in a more nuanced analysis where the relative contributions of the parties will need to be precisely identified and remunerated. For example, the incentive given to precisely measure the relative contributions of group members to the different steps of a value chain prevents too automatic applications of the TNMM or too quick characterisations as low-risk entities. Hence, although the theoretical framework remains unchanged (it is still the arm's length principle that is being applied), this revised guidance has led to an increase in the use of the profit split method.[76]

The example below illustrates the need for relying on the profit split method.

Example: The need for a profit split method in situations where other transfer pricing methods are not applicable

Assume that companies A, B, and C, resident in countries A, B, and C, participate in the development and the sales of pharmaceutical products. Each company has expertise in a specific area, and the combination of the three types of expertise enables the group to manufacture and successfully sell pharmaceutical products. In other words, the functions of companies A, B, and C are valuable, potentially unique, and complementary. Here, the transactions between the associated enterprises, i.e., the contributions of each party to the common project, are unlikely to be able to be priced on the basis of the CUP method; perhaps that similar types of arrangements may exist as part of joint-venture arrangements, but even so the comparability in the functions and in the activities would normally be too low. Since all the three companies act in an entrepreneurial manner, as opposed to acting on behalf of other companies, there is normally no company that qualifies as a tested party, something that would exclude the resale price method, the cost-plus method, and the TNMM. In the end, there is a need for a transfer pricing method that is applicable to this combined effort despite the lack of comparables. The only way to share the profits resulting from the contributions of the three associated enterprises consists in splitting the fruits of their efforts, as would

in the lack of comparables: *see* para. 3.8.3 of the 2021 UN Manual (Part D), where it is mentioned that 'It is possible to use the Profit Split Method to determine the arm's length allocation of location savings and rents in cases where comparable uncontrolled transactions are not available'.

74. *See* para. 2.128 of the 2022 OECD Guidelines, and para. 4.6.3.5 of the 2021 UN Manual.
75. *See* para. 2.143 of the 2022 OECD Guidelines, and para. 4.6.3.6 of the 2021 UN Manual.
76. For a discussion with respect to R&D functions, *see* Eyal Gonen, Leonid Karasik and Michael McDonald, *Control over Risk, DEMPE Functions, and the Remuneration of R&D Service Providers*, 1615–1630 (Tax Notes International, 21 June 2021).

independent companies do as part of joint-venture arrangements. This is what the profit split method aims at.

After presenting when to use the profit split method, focus is now on how to use this method. The OECD Guidelines emphasise that the split must be done on an 'economically valid basis';[77] profits must be split in a reliable manner.[78] The split must be consistent with the functional analysis, and especially reflect the assumption of the economically significant risks, since it is a basic transfer pricing principle that risks and returns should match: the split of profits will need to follow the parties' respective assumptions of risks, which in its turn should be in line with the performance of functions related to the control of risks. In other words, the split of profits needs to be in line with the effective control over risks, as evidenced by the performance of the relevant functions related to risks. For instance, if in the above example, companies A, B, and C all perform important functions for the development of pharmaceutical products, but that only company A assumes and controls certain important risks (e.g., the product risk in case the pharmaceutical products have defects), then the profit split arrangement will have to acknowledge this and attribute a greater share of the profits (or the losses) to company A than to companies B and C.

The profit split methodology chosen should be applied consistently over the lifetime of the arrangement; it should in particular be maintained by multinational enterprises and accepted by tax administrations if the profits that are shared vary over time. Indeed, the profit split method applies equally to profits and losses. The split concerns profits, not turnover, since it is eventually income (and not turnover) that is taxed. It is generally operating profits that are split,[79] although in certain cases the method may apply to gross profits.[80] In any case, it is the profits that result from a given business activity that are shared between the participants to a profit split arrangement, as opposed to other kinds of income such as financial income or capital gains.

Once the profits from the business activities of the participants to a profit split arrangement have been identified, such profits would be shared between the participants (and taxed in their respective State of residence) on the basis of an allocation key (also referred to as 'profit splitting factors').[81] However, to that purpose, there is no unique profit split methodology or allocation key recommended by the OECD Guidelines, as long as one approximates 'as closely as possible the split of profits that would have been realised had the parties been independent enterprises'.[82] The most reliable method to split profits is to rely on a comparison with independent transactions since this would be the method relying the most directly on independent

77. *See* paras 2.114, 2.147 and 2.166 of the 2022 OECD Guidelines.
78. *See* para. 2.147 (last point) of the 2022 OECD Guidelines.
79. *See* para. 2.162 of the 2022 OECD Guidelines.
80. In this respect, the Guidelines indicate that the split of gross profits may be appropriate for integrated functions of production or acquisition of goods: *see* para. 2.163 of the 2022 OECD Guidelines.
81. The Guidelines use the expression 'profit splitting factors': *see* paras 2.169 and following of the 2022 OECD Guidelines.
82. *See* para. 2.146 of the 2022 OECD Guidelines.

comparables.[83] It is only in the absence of reliable information on divisions of profits between independent enterprises that a less direct method can be used: profits may then be split based on 'internal' information[84] (i.e., not on independent comparables), as long as this is done in an objective manner.[85] Information internal to the MNE may comprise external sales, costs, employee compensation, headcount, time spent, assets, or capital.[86] Several allocation keys may be combined, after weighing them against each other.

In any case, the analysis starts with understanding the facts and circumstances surrounding the business activities of the associated enterprises (i.e., a two-sided functional analysis to understand the roles and respective contributions of each party), so as to choose a profit split methodology that matches reality and could be adopted by independent parties. However, as long as the relative value of the contributions by the parties can be measured, there is no need to estimate the actual market value of each party's contribution; this is a welcome precision since in certain cases there may be no objective ways of estimating the market value of the contributions of the parties.[87]

The profits to be split can be determined according to either a *contribution analysis* or a *residual analysis*. The contribution analysis aims at splitting the total profits from certain controlled transactions based on comparable data or, if comparables are not available, on the relative value of each party's contribution to such transactions.[88] Therefore, the contribution analysis is to be applied when all the profits are to be split according to the profit split method, i.e., if none of the total profits is connected to routine functions. If the total profits include routine profits connected to routine functions,[89] one would normally first remunerate such routine functions on the basis of transfer pricing methods that rely on a closer comparison with independent transactions (i.e., not the profit split method)[90] before splitting the remaining profits between the parties making non-routine contributions to the total profits. This last analysis is usually referred to as the residual analysis since it aims at splitting the residual profits that are left after remunerating the relevant routine functions. Therefore, there is no difference of principle between the contribution and residual analyses: both aim at implementing the arm's length principle. Compared to the contribution analysis, the residual analysis contains an additional step consisting in

83. *See* para. 2.167 of the 2022 OECD Guidelines for examples of industries in which divisions of profits can be observed.
84. *See* paras 2.150 and 2.174 of the 2022 OECD Guidelines. *See also* para. 4.6.5.11 of the 2021 UN Manual.
85. For an example of court case in which different allocation keys were considered, *see TMC Italia spa*, Italian Supreme Administrative Court (13 April 2021, case number 18436/2021).
86. *See* paras 2.174 and following of the 2022 OECD Guidelines. For a presentation of different profit splitting factors, together with their pros and cons, *see also* EU Joint Transfer Pricing Forum, *The Application of the Profit Split Method Within the EU*, JTPF/002/2019/EN, Brussels (March 2019), 18–21, Annex 3. *See also* para. 4.6.5.16 of the 2021 UN Manual.
87. *See* paras 2.114 and 2.150 of the 2022 OECD Guidelines.
88. *See* para. 2.150 of the 2022 OECD Guidelines.
89. By 'routine functions' it is referred to functions that do not significantly contribute to the creation of value. Such functions usually do not result in the creation of IP for the entity performing them.
90. Indeed, routine functions are likely to be benchmarkable, and should thus be remunerated on the basis of transactional transfer pricing methods or the TNMM.

remunerating the routine functions; when this is done, the residual profits are split according to the same methodology as under the contribution analysis.[91] The application of the residual profit split method is illustrated by the example below.[92]

Example: Illustration of a possible application of the residual profit split method

Assume that a multinational enterprise has three associated enterprises: A (developer), B (manufacturer), and C (distributor). These enterprises are established in three different countries, A, B, and C. It is assumed that companies A and B own valuable product intangibles and manufacturing intangibles, while C performs routine distribution functions. The multinational enterprise sells goods for 100 to its end-customers through its distributor, and on a consolidated level, the global net margin is 30% (i.e., the total operational costs amount to 70 while the sales to end-customers amount to 100). From a transfer pricing perspective, the distributor (C) is considered as a tested party and it is remunerated based on the TNMM; it is assumed that company C should earn a 5% return on sales, i.e., 5 (100 × 5% = 5). Out of the total net margin (30), this leaves 25 to be shared between the developer and the manufacturer. As the developer and the manufacturer both own valuable intangibles, companies A and B make unique and valuable contributions to the value chain and cannot be remunerated on the basis of the CUP method, the resale price method, the cost-plus method, or the TNMM given the impossibility to find comparable independent transactions. Therefore, the multinational enterprise needs to split the remaining profits between companies A and B. To that end, the group chooses the residual analysis to split between companies A and B the remaining operating margin that is left after remunerating company C. Here, the residual profits (i.e., the operating margin that is left after deducting the operating margin of the distributor from the global net margin) amount to 25 (30–5 = 25). It is assumed that independent comparable enterprises would split profits in similar joint ventures so that the developer gets 60% of these profits, and the manufacturer 40% of the profits. This 60/40 split could be obtained, for example, by evaluating to what extent the product and manufacturing intangibles (owned respectively by the developer and the manufacturer) contribute to the decision to purchase products made by the end-customers. Other allocation keys could be based, for example, on the number of people employed or the costs incurred by companies A and B. Accordingly, under the method described above the developer should be attributed 60% of the residual profits (25 × 60% = 15), while the manufacturer should earn 40% of these profits (25 × 40% = 10).

An important clarification made in the OECD Guidelines is that there should be no use of hindsight.[93] This means that the split of profits should be based on information known or reasonably foreseeable at the time of the transactions, except if

91. *See* para. 2.152, last sentence, of the 2022 OECD Guidelines.
92. For a flow chart tree presenting how the profit split method may be applied, *see* EU Joint Transfer Pricing Forum, *The Application of the Profit Split Method Within the EU*, JTPF/002/2019/EN, Brussels (March 2019), p. 17, Annex 2.
93. *See* para. 2.161 of the 2022 OECD Guidelines.

independent parties would have renegotiated the agreement in a comparable situation.[94] This is coherent with the need to apply a profit split methodology consistently over the lifetime of an arrangement. Nevertheless, the OECD Guidelines recommend a mechanism to address the information asymmetry existing between multinational enterprises and tax administrations, the so-called hard-to-value intangibles approach, which allows taking into account elements posterior to the time of a transaction.[95]

The profit split method seems to remind of formulary apportionment, described above in section 1.2.2 of this book. Indeed, both methods imply that income is shared between two or more associated enterprises on the basis of an allocation key. However, there are two fundamental differences between formulary apportionment and the profit split method. The first difference relates to the objective of the two methods: while the profit split method aims at applying the arm's length principle, formulary apportionment has no such objective. The allocation key used under formulary apportionment does not even need to abide by a certain principle, it is just about the choice of a formula. The second difference relates to the profits to be split, and the method to design an allocation key. Formulary apportionment implies that all profits are split, while the profit split method implies that only profits in relation to one (or several) transaction(s) are split, after remunerating the relevant routine functions. While formulary apportionment is normally based on a predetermined formula applicable to all companies, the profit split method implies the determination of an allocation key as a result of a case-by-case analysis.[96] On the one hand, the lawmaker that is faced with the design of an allocation key for the purpose of formulary apportionment needs to find a formula that is suitable on a macro level to as many cases as possible, something that would necessarily result in the approximation of the parameters that trigger taxable income. The general and predetermined character of an allocation key under formulary apportionment is also likely to exclude IP from the elements of the formula since IP is difficult to identify, value, and locate.[97] On the other hand, the profit split method is applied on a case-by-case basis, which enables the associated enterprises – and possibly the tax administrations – to tailor the allocation key as they see fit on a micro level, thereby making it possible to measure the relative contributions of each party to a transaction and share profits in an individualised manner. Given that in the relations between independent parties the functions, risks, and assets attributable to each party are influencing the level of prices, the same reasoning will be applied as part of a profit split analysis. Therefore, the allocation key used under the profit split method will vary depending on the functions performed, the risks assumed, and the assets owned by the parties. The IP owned or used by each party is likely to play an important role in the profit split method, whereas IP can

94. *See* para. 3.73 of the 2022 OECD Guidelines.
95. The hard-to-value intangibles approach is presented in section 3.3 of this book.
96. The fact that, contrary to formulary apportionment, the profit split method lies on individual allocation keys is both a strength (as it allows measuring the relative contributions of the parties in an individual manner) and a weakness (as the determination of the allocation key can easily lead to disagreements).
97. In this respect, *see* section 1.2.2 of this book.

normally not be taken into account with an allocation key used under formulary apportionment. Consequently, there are fundamental differences between formulary apportionment and the profit split method.

2.4 THE SIXTH METHOD

The so-called sixth method[98] starts from the premise that tax authorities may have difficulties making a reliable comparability analysis, for example, because of a lack of comparables, or because a company provides insufficient information on the pricing of its cross-border intercompany transactions. The 2021 UN Manual emphasises that 'for developing countries this concern may be even more pressing than for developed countries, as the former countries may not have data on companies doing business in their countries to perform a comparability analysis in addition to potentially having limited know-how and resources to conduct transfer pricing studies'.[99] There is also a risk of erosion of the tax base if commodities for which a quoted price exist are exported below that price. Therefore, to simplify the process of performing a reliable comparability analysis, and to avoid that commodity export prices are set below international market prices, certain developing countries rely on quoted prices as a starting point of a transfer pricing analysis for commodities for which a quoted price is available, such as coffee, grains, oil, gas, mining or fishing products.

By relying on quoted prices, the sixth method seems at first sight to resemble the CUP method.[100] Yet certain differences exist, in particular when it comes to the characteristics of the products subject to commodity price listing and the possible lack of adjustments made to take into account such differences.[101] Therefore, both the OECD Guidelines and the UN Manual are cautious when it comes to the use of quoted prices, and emphasise the need for sufficient comparability.[102]

Considering its particular operation, the sixth method has particular advantages and drawbacks. On the one hand, it provides some certainty and ease of application; on the other hand, the direct reliance on quoted prices with no comparability adjustments on a case-by-case basis may deviate from the arm's length principle and result in double taxation if this method is not recognised by the country of the counterpart to the

98. For an explanation of this method, *see* Fernando Velayos and Alberto Barreix, *Towards a New Form of International Taxation: The View from Latin America and the Caribbean*, vol. 41, issue 3, 132–133 (Intertax, 2013); *see also* Amparo Mercader and Horacio Peña, *'Sixth Method' Raises Transfer Pricing Concerns in Developing Countries*, vol. 69, 691–693 (Tax Notes International, 18 February 2013); OECD, *BEPS Action 10: Discussion Draft on the Transfer Pricing Aspects of Cross-Border Commodity Transactions*, 3, para. 3 (December 2014).

99. *See* para. 4.7.1.2 of the 2021 UN Manual.

100. *See* paras 2.18 and following of the 2022 OECD Guidelines for a description of the application of the CUP method to commodities.

101. *See* para. 4.7.1.4 of the 2021 UN Manual.

102. *See* para. 2.20 of the 2022 OECD Guidelines: 'For the CUP method to be reliably applied to commodity transactions, the economically relevant characteristics of the controlled transaction and the uncontrolled transactions or the uncontrolled arrangements represented by the quoted price need to be comparable.' As with any transfer pricing method, the OECD Guidelines recommend that reasonably accurate adjustments be considered in case of differences between controlled and uncontrolled transactions. *See also* para. 4.7.5.3 of the 2021 UN Manual.

transaction.[103] Because of its simplified operation and in certain cases its objective to prevent that commodities be exported below quoted prices, the UN Manual mentions that 'the sixth method - depending on how it is applied - could be considered as an anti-abuse rule, an abuse-deeming rule or even presumed to be a form of safe harbour'.[104] The UN Manual nevertheless does not reject the sixth method, as long as two conditions are fulfilled: (i) the taxpayer is given the opportunity to provide evidence that the intra-group transactions are not abusive and the prices are at arm's length, and (ii) the method allows comparability adjustments.[105]

2.5 THE COMBINED USE OF SEVERAL TRANSFER PRICING METHODS

The OECD Guidelines do not require that several transfer pricing methods be used together,[106] as this would be quite burdensome. In addition, there is no reason, from the point of view of principle, to require the use of several methods, as the sole objective of a transfer pricing analysis is to set transfer prices so that the arm's length principle is met. Therefore, it is enough that the most appropriate method be relied on[107] since this method should be the most suitable to achieve arm's length pricing.

Yet, the combined use of several transfer pricing methods may allow strengthening, or testing the reliability of a transfer pricing analysis. For example, the transfer prices applied with an associated enterprise performing distribution functions and qualifying as a tested party may be set on the basis of the resale price method or the TNMM. Although the OECD Guidelines do not require using both methods (as it is sufficient to apply the most appropriate method), a multinational enterprise or a tax administration may want to get certainty as to the arm's length character of the transfer prices by combining several transfer pricing methods. Indeed, if the gross margin is tested based on the resale price method and the net margin is tested with the TNMM, and assuming that in both cases the targeted margin is within the arm's length range, there are good reasons to believe that the transfer prices are at arm's length. Such a combination could be used by a multinational enterprise when it seeks certainty,[108] or by a tax administration when it seeks to test the transfer prices applied between associated enterprises as part of a tax audit.

103. For further descriptions of the advantages and drawbacks of the sixth method, *see* paras 4.7.1.5 and 4.7.5.1 of the 2021 UN Manual. For a court case in which the sixth method was deemed applicable to increase the tax base, with no need to apply it symmetrically to decrease the tax base, *see Nidera SA v. Direccion General Impositiva s. recurso directo de organismo externo*, Argentinian Supreme Court (24 June 2021, case number CAF 38801/2013/CA2-CS2).
104. *See* para. 4.7.1.4 of the 2021 UN Manual.
105. *See* paras 4.7.2.5 and 4.7.5.6 of the 2021 UN Manual.
106. *See* para. 2.12 of the 2022 OECD Guidelines.
107. *See* para. 2.2 of the 2022 OECD Guidelines.
108. That could, for example, be the case when a multinational enterprise applies for an advance pricing arrangement, and wants to convince the competent authorities that the transfer prices are at arm's length. For a presentation of advance pricing arrangements, *see* section 7.2 of this book.

It may also be convenient for a multinational enterprise to combine several methods, one for setting transfer prices (e.g., on a transaction-by-transaction basis), the other for testing transfer prices and possibly making adjustments (e.g., before a financial year is close). For instance, a company may purchase goods from an associated seller on the basis of the prices usually applied towards independent companies by relying on an internal CUP. The arm's length character of such transfer prices may then be tested (e.g., each quarter or at the end of the financial year) by computing the gross margin (i.e., through relying on the resale price method) or the net margin (i.e., through relying on the TNMM) of the tested party. If the gross or net margin is not in line with the comparability analysis, a multinational enterprise may consider making an adjustment, for the gross or net margin to eventually be at arm's length.

Last, it should be observed that combining several transfer pricing methods is recommended by the OECD Guidelines for 'difficult cases, where no one approach is conclusive'.[109] Indeed, where complex transactions are to be priced, combining several methods may provide more accurate results, although this may require more analysis and documentation.

109. *See* para. 2.12 of the 2022 OECD Guidelines.

CHAPTER 3

Transfer Pricing Models

3.1 INTRODUCTION

The purpose of this chapter is to present certain transfer pricing models. Transfer pricing models should be distinguished from business models, which would normally refer to frequent ways chosen by multinational enterprises to organise their business activities across borders. A transfer pricing model can be described as a methodology (rather than actual transfer prices or profit margins) relating to the transfer pricing aspects of a given business model.

Before delving into transfer pricing models, it is important to emphasise that there are several perspectives taken into account by each group before deciding upon a certain business organisation. Taxes are one parameter among many that may come into play for each decision. In the board room, it is not infrequent that taxes point to a certain business model, while other considerations point to another type of organisation. Therefore, business models may not always be the most efficient from a tax point of view, and transfer pricing models may not always be the most effective from an operational point of view. In certain cases, taxes and operations may be well in line with each other, while in other cases, the two may be difficult to reconcile. The transfer pricing models found in this chapter, together with their advantages and drawbacks, are presented only from a transfer pricing perspective.

As soon as a company involves a foreign associated enterprise in its business activities, transfer pricing rules become applicable, and the intercompany transactions will normally need to be priced according to the arm's length principle. Therefore, different ways of organising the business activities of a multinational enterprise may have different transfer pricing implications, and thus different tax outcomes. Indeed, as explained above in sections 1.4.2 and 1.4.3 of this book, the pricing of intercompany transactions should result mainly from the combination of the functional analysis and the comparability analysis: accordingly, depending on the way the functions, risks, and assets have been distributed between the parties to an intercompany transaction, the functional analysis will reveal different functional profiles of the associated enterprises, and the comparability analysis will point to different transfer prices or profit margins that will need to be applied to a given intercompany transaction.

Given that transfer prices - and, in the end, the corporate income taxes paid in each country - are directly influenced by the functional analysis, multinational enterprises may be willing to distribute the functions, risks, and assets needed for an intercompany transaction in one way or another. In other words, there may be different ways to organise the value chain, with different transfer pricing and tax implications. The way chosen by a multinational enterprise to distribute the functions, risks, and assets across the value chain, together with the transfer pricing and tax consequences of such a distribution, is often referred to as a *transfer pricing model*. Transfer pricing models are not legal concepts, and they are not subject to particular recommendations in the OECD Guidelines. Transfer pricing models would normally not be part of a country's domestic law, at least not from a general perspective.[1] Transfer pricing models refer simply to frequent combinations of functions, risks, and assets attributable to the parties to an intercompany transaction, to which certain types of remuneration may be associated.

Among a virtually indefinite number of possible transfer pricing models, certain are frequently applied by multinational enterprises or claimed by tax administrations. It is, therefore, useful to have knowledge of these frequent transfer pricing models. When considering a transfer pricing model, as mentioned above, multinational enterprises may face a conflict between concerns relating to the operations, on the one hand, and taxes, on the other hand.[2] Therefore, multinational enterprises must strike a balance between the needs of the operations and the needs of their corporate tax departments when considering the organisation of their operations. In certain cases, it may be possible to organise the value chain in a way that is found efficient both from an operational perspective and from a tax perspective. Multinational enterprises that do not have such a synchronised value chain may wish to amend it in order to bring more consistency to the operational and tax concerns within the group; such reorganisations, when they imply that functions, risks, or assets are redistributed between the members of the group, are often referred to in the transfer pricing context as *business restructurings*.[3]

This chapter of the book presents certain types of intercompany transactions and transfer pricing models that are frequently applied by multinational enterprises or

1. There are exceptions, for example, with respect to certain safe harbour rules: a country's domestic tax law or a tax treaty may contain a predetermined profitability level applicable to certain transfer pricing models.
2. For example, the managing staff responsible for the operations may suggest an organisation of the value chain that they believe will produce the best outcome from a business perspective, something that the managing staff responsible for taxes may not find suitable if it triggers tax risks or increases the global effective tax rate. Conversely, the managing staff responsible for taxes may favour a tax and transfer pricing model that in theory mitigates tax risks or decreases the global effective tax rate, but that the managing staff responsible for the operations may find not appropriate from a business perspective, unrealistic, or too costly to implement.
3. *See* Chapter 4 of this book for a detailed presentation of business restructurings from a transfer pricing perspective.

claimed by tax administrations. This is done through following a typical series of steps throughout the value chain of a multinational enterprise (section 3.4). However, before presenting these transfer pricing models, some introductory remarks are useful. These remarks touch upon two issues that are important to discuss before considering transfer pricing models: the advantages and drawbacks of applying standardised transfer pricing models (section 3.2), and transfer pricing considerations relating to IP (section 3.3).

3.2 STANDARDISED TRANSFER PRICING MODELS

Although each multinational enterprise's business model has unique features, the value chain of multinational enterprises often includes intercompany transactions related to certain typical activities such as R&D, manufacturing, financing, or distribution. Accordingly, groups of companies and tax administrations tend to apply, or claim the application of, certain typical or standardised transfer pricing models for setting the prices of intercompany transactions depending on how they are structured, i.e., with regard to the way functions, risks and assets are distributed between the parties to each transaction. The expression 'standardised transfer pricing models' does not per se refer to standardised transfer prices or profit margins, but rather to frequent ways of structuring intercompany transactions, something that is likely to result in a standardised characterisation of the parties. However, a given transfer price, profit margin, or a range thereof may also be determined in advance by domestic laws, tax treaties, or soft laws,[4] thus potentially constituting a *safe harbour*.[5]

Applying standardised transfer pricing models has both advantages and drawbacks. Standardised models may enhance the legal certainty, for tax administrations and multinational enterprises. That is, both tax administrations and multinational enterprises may be used to working with certain transfer pricing models, something that may mitigate tax controversies and thereby risks of double taxation or risks of an illegitimate erosion of the tax base. Also, standardised transfer pricing

4. *See*, e.g., the 5% profit mark-up for low value-adding services in para. 7.61 of the 2022 OECD Guidelines, as we as in the *Communication from the Commission to the European Parliament, the Council and the European Economic and Social Committee on the work of the EU Joint Transfer Pricing Forum in the period April 2009 to June 2010 and related proposals 1. Guidelines on low value adding intra-group services and 2. Potential approaches to non- EU triangular cases* (25 January 2011, COM(2011) 16 final), para. 65. It can be observed that this Communication from the European Commission has been endorsed by the Council of the European Union: *see* 3088th Economic and Financial Affairs Council meeting, Brussels (17 May 2011).
5. *See* paras 4.95 and following of the 2022 OECD Guidelines. In the transfer pricing context, safe harbours refer to the possibility of knowing in advance the way a given intercompany transaction should be priced. By meeting the requirements of a safe harbour, taxpayers may benefit from the certainty that intercompany prices should not be challenged by tax administrations. In addition, under a safe harbour, taxpayers and tax administrations do not need to perform a benchmarking study, something that may save resources on both sides and be helpful for tax administrations (especially in developing countries) that lack information on comparable independent transactions. Safe harbours may be granted on a unilateral, bilateral, or multilateral basis. On the relevance of bilateral safe harbours, *see* Joseph Andrus and Stig Sollund, *Improving the Transfer Pricing System: Simpler, Clearer, Faster*, 79–85, at 80 (Tax Notes International, 1 October 2012).

models may be useful to mitigate the administrative burden put on tax administrations and multinational enterprises. On the other hand, a shortcoming of standardised transfer pricing models is the more or less automatic way according to which transfer prices are set. This tends to associate intercompany transactions with certain transfer pricing models without necessarily performing sufficiently thorough functional and comparative analyses, something that may leave little room for dividing the profits (or the losses) of a multinational enterprise as closely as possible to the way independent enterprises would. However, despite the drawbacks of standardising the setting of transfer prices according to commonly used transfer pricing models, this approach is still connected to the business reality of a multinational enterprise, thanks to relying on a functional analysis. Also, the arm's length principle inherently implies some level of approximation, especially when the transactional profit methods are being used. This is why such standardised transfer pricing models are commonly applied in practice.

Consequently, although it is important to be cautious when using standardised transfer pricing models, the advantages of this approach may, in certain situations, outweigh its drawbacks.

3.3 INTERCOMPANY TRANSACTIONS INVOLVING IP

It is fundamental to emphasise the role of IP for transfer pricing purposes to understand the differences between various transfer pricing models, especially those involving different functional profiles but similar steps of the value chain. IP is, in many cases, one of the most valuable aspects of a business.[6] This is true no matter if business activities are carried out by independent or associated enterprises, domestically or cross-border. Indeed, an end-customer often purchases a product or service due to aspects connected to IP, such as a product's or service's intrinsic qualities, name, design or logo. Since intangibles are key to the earning of income (and thus to the payment of income taxes), they play a central role in the area of transfer pricing (especially with respect to preventing structures where residual profits are found to be abusively allocated to entities deemed to own valuable IP), whether such intangibles are part of a transaction involving the transfer of goods or services,[7] or are subject to a specific intercompany transaction.[8]

What is an intangible from a transfer pricing perspective? The OECD Guidelines and the UN Manual contain a relatively broad definition of intangibles that is particular to the field of transfer pricing: intangibles are defined as 'something which is not a physical asset or a financial asset, which is capable of being owned or controlled for use

6. *See*, e.g., Toshio Miyatake, General Report, Cahiers de Droit Fiscal International, *Transfer Pricing and Intangibles*, vol. 92a, 19 (2007). *See also* Isabel Verlinden and Yoko Mondelaers, *Transfer Pricing Aspects of Intangibles: At the Crossroads Between Legal, Valuation and Transfer Pricing Issues*, vol. 17, issue 1, 49 (International Transfer Pricing Journal, January/February, 2010); Neil Pereira, *Intangibles: The New Frontier*, 45–53 (Tax Notes International, 3 January 2022).
7. For example, the price of the goods sold by a fully fledged manufacturer to its distributor includes a part that is related to the manufacturing intangibles or the rights in manufacturing intangibles that are owned by the manufacturer.
8. That would be the case when an intangible is sold or licensed to an associated enterprise.

in commercial activities, and whose use or transfer would be compensated had it occurred in a transaction between independent parties in comparable circumstances'.[9] It is important to emphasise the requirement of ownership or control contained in this definition, as it distinguishes intangibles from other circumstances that may influence transfer prices without being owned or controlled by a company (e.g., the presence of competitors on a market, or group synergies that do not derive from specific actions of associated enterprises): only the former may have a major impact from a transfer pricing perspective. This definition implies also that although there may be definitions of intangibles for legal or accounting purposes,[10] it is first and foremost the transfer pricing definition that should be used.[11] Here it should nevertheless be emphasised that countries may enact their own definitions of intangibles for transfer pricing purposes, which are not necessarily in line with the OECD Guidelines. This may have important consequences in practice: a broad definition of IP may tend to increase the value of assets transferred between two associated enterprises, for example, if features such as workforce[12] or goodwill are considered to be part of an intangible asset and thus should be valued for the purpose of a transfer of asset. Conversely, a narrow definition of IP would tend to exclude certain features, and thus result in a lower value of an asset transferred.[13]

Once the existence of an intangible for transfer pricing purposes has been ascertained, the next step consists in identifying the parties entitled to the

9. *See* para. 6.6 of the 2022 OECD Guidelines, and para. 6.2.1.3 of the 2021 UN Manual. On the definition of intangibles, and especially with respect to the uncertainty that results from defining intangibles too broadly, *see* Caroline Silberztein, Mary C. Bennett and Gregg D. Lemein, *The OECD Discussion Draft on the Transfer of Intangibles (Revision of Chapter VI of the OECD Transfer Pricing Guidelines): Detailed Comments*, vol. 41, issue 2, 66 (Intertax, 2013).
10. For example, an intangible asset may be recorded on the balance sheet of a company. Another example is the situation where a company has registered a patent. These examples are only indicative: an intangible asset for legal or accounting purposes does not necessarily result in an intangible for transfer pricing purposes, and, conversely, an intangible for transfer pricing purposes is not necessarily recognised for legal or accounting purposes.
11. This is consistent with the *substance-over-form principle*, i.e., irrespective of the form (in this case legal agreements, patent registrations, assets being registered – or not – on the balance sheet and being attributed a certain value, etc.), the substance will prevail (in this case identifying the parties owning or using an intangible for transfer pricing purposes).
12. As indicated in para. 6.2.5.15 of the 2021 UN Manual, 'Generally, the existence of the workforce does not need to be remunerated separately for transfer pricing purposes. This is because the value provided by a workforce is typically reflected in the arm's length consideration to be paid for the goods produced or the services performed by the workforce.'
13. *See*, e.g., the US *Amazon* case, which related to a dispute on a transfer of IP between a US company and a Luxembourg associated enterprise as part of a CCA. Since the US company contributed to the arrangement with IP, the Luxembourg company had to make a buy-in payment (*see* section 3.4.6 of this book for a presentation of CCAs; *see also* paras 8.24 and 8.34 of the 2022 OECD Guidelines). The US tax administration argued that the valuation of the IP transferred needed to take into account different features such as goodwill or the culture of innovation, something that would increase the value of the transfer. Given the then applicable domestic law (which defined IP in a relatively narrow manner), the court rejected that claim: *see Amazon.Com, Inc & Subsidiaries v. Commissioner of Internal Revenue*, U.S. Tax Court (23 March 2017, case number 148 T.C. No. 8, Docket No. 31197-12). This view was later confirmed in *Amazon.Com, Inc & Subsidiaries v. Commissioner of Internal Revenue*, US Court of Appeals for the Ninth Circuit (16 August 2019, case number 17-72922). It can be observed that the 2017 US tax reform broadened the definition of intangible asset.

intangible-related returns and how to share such intangible-related returns. As with other transfer pricing issues, the starting point consists in analysing the legal registrations and contractual arrangements;[14] this analysis will then be completed by investigating the *substance* supporting the transactions involving intangibles, to determine how to share the intangible-related returns. Here, three main situations should be distinguished: a company may be fully entitled to intangible-related returns (e.g., an entrepreneur performing all the important functions), not entitled to intangible-related returns at all (e.g., a low-risk entity performing only routine functions), or entitled solely to some – but not all – intangible-related returns (e.g., a risk entity performing certain non-routine functions). The extent of the entitlement to intangible-related returns will be mainly dependent on the functions performed by the parties: the more important functions are performed, the more likely it is that a company is recognised as the owner or user of IP, and thus is entitled to intangible-related returns. It is often asked in practice which functions should be performed for a company to be entitled to intangible-related returns. Here the OECD Guidelines and the UN Manual provide similar guidance, despite a cosmetic difference. The 2022 OECD Guidelines emphasise the need to perform functions related to the DEMPE functions of the intangibles, to be entitled to intangible-related returns. The 2021 UN Manual adds[15] to these functions the acquisition of intangibles as an alternative to their development, hence the 'DAEMPE (development, acquisition, enhancement, maintenance, protection and exploitation)' functions.[16] Another nuance is brought by the UN Manual, which states that 'while DAEMPE activities might seem to be limited to functions, in fact they often reflect contributions of assets and the assumption of risks as well'.[17] In any case, since most activities connected to intangibles imply some risk-taking, eventually, it is the control over the risks connected to intangibles that will largely determine the profit allocation.

After presenting the role of IP in the field of transfer pricing, it is now emphasised how intangibles impact transfer pricing models. There is no unique way of taking into account intangibles for transfer pricing purposes, but in all situations the methodology will be the same: understanding the reality through the functional analysis, so as to eventually set transfer prices or profit margins as closely as possible to comparable independent transactions. The way a transaction involving intangibles is priced may vary widely depending on the type of transfer pricing model and intercompany transaction. In cases where a transaction does not exclusively concern IP but a good or

14. On the recommendations of the OECD to start a transfer pricing analysis by examining the existing contractual arrangements (i.e., the legal form), *see* paras 1.42, 1.140 and 9.17 of the 2022 OECD Guidelines.
15. This addition is not meant to diverge from the OECD Guidelines, solely to clarify that intangibles can be acquired either through development activities or by an acquisition from a third party (*see* para. 6.3.3.4 of the 2021 UN Manual).
16. *See* para. 6.3.3.1 of the 2021 UN Manual.
17. *See* para. 6.3.3.3 of the 2021 UN Manual, where this statement is supported by an illustration: 'For example, a pharmaceutical company might commit to undertaking R&D in order to develop a potential blockbuster drug. This "D" reflects, in addition to the development functions (R&D), a commitment to contribute assets to fund the development and the assumption of potentially significant risks.'

a service, the transfer price of such goods or services already includes a part corresponding to the return attributable to the intangible, if any. In such cases, the intangible would normally not need to be priced separately or be subject to an additional remuneration, as the transfer price or profit margin indicated by the comparability analysis would already reflect the impact of the relevant intangibles. Let us illustrate this by an example.

Example: The transfer price of goods or services already includes a part corresponding to the return attributable to the intangibles

A parent company acts as an entrepreneur and performs R&D, manufacturing, as well as key management functions, while selling goods to a buy/sell distributor (i.e., a company performing low value-adding distribution functions). The buy/sell distributor will normally be considered as the tested party (i.e., the party that has the less complex functional analysis). In such a situation, the most valuable IP is likely to be owned by the entrepreneur, although it cannot be excluded that the buy/sell distributor owns some less valuable intangibles (e.g., those developed as a consequence of its distribution activities). Irrespective of the transfer pricing method applied (e.g., the CUP, the resale price method, or the TNMM), the price paid by the buy/sell distributor is likely to include a return on the intangibles owned by the other party to the transaction (the entrepreneur) as well as – if relevant – a return on its own intangibles. The remuneration of the owner of the valuable intangibles will not be subject to a particular transaction, but will result from the relatively low margins earned by the tested party: as a consequence of such relatively low margins, the remainder of the profits made on the whole transaction will be earned by the entrepreneur. This means that the profits earned by the entrepreneur after selling the goods to the distributor (and remunerating that tested party with an arm's length return) will include a part that is related to the intangibles. This is because in independent transactions the price of goods sold to distributors performing low value-adding functions would normally include a return on the intangibles developed by the supplier. Accordingly, an independent distributor(s) would typically pay a relatively high price (because most of the value of the goods or services sold to end-customers stems from the IP developed by the supplier), and thus earn a low profit, while the supplier that sold the goods to the independent distributor(s) would earn the return on intangibles. Since the arm's length principle commands that a similar outcome is reached in controlled transactions, the transfer prices between associated enterprises would, in this example, often include a part corresponding to the return attributable to the intangibles. Eventually, no matter what transfer pricing method is used, the transfer price paid by the buy/sell distributor (i.e., the major part of the COGS of the distributor) will need to be adjusted so that the buy/sell distributor pays an arm's length price (if the CUP is used) or makes an arm's length margin (if the resale price method or the TNMM is used). The same transfer price is accounted for as turnover at the level of the entrepreneur who sells the goods to the distributor; the entrepreneur will cover all its expenses with this turnover, and may[18] make a profit. The final profit (or loss) will not be capped by the transfer pricing model: the final profits (often called the *residual profits*) will be earned by the entrepreneur as a result of owning the most valuable intangibles, but with no separate pricing or valuation for such intangibles. The profits that are left after paying all necessary expenses (including an arm's length remuneration paid to the various associated enterprises) will automatically include the returns created by the intangibles developed by the entrepreneur since it is assumed that no other associated enterprise is entitled to such returns.[19] Therefore, there is no particular pricing for the IP involved in this transfer pricing model; the routine remuneration of the tested parties will automatically attribute the intangible-related returns (if any) to the entity entitled to the residual profits.

In the above example, there is no separate pricing for the intangibles, as the entrepreneur receives the return attributable to the intangibles through the profits made on the sale of goods to the related buy/sell distributor. In other cases, a transaction may relate specifically to an intangible, thus requiring a particular pricing of this transaction. This is illustrated with the example below.

Example: An intercompany transaction involves the transfer of an intangible through a parent company licensing a patent to its manufacturing subsidiary

A parent company owns a patent that its manufacturing subsidiary needs to use. The parent company does not want to sell the patent because it is needed in other areas of the business. Therefore, the parent company lets its manufacturing subsidiary use the patent in exchange for the payment of a licence fee. This is a transaction involving solely an intangible asset and needs to be priced as such.

When setting a transfer price for a transaction involving intangibles, any of the transfer pricing methods recognised by the OECD Guidelines may be applicable. In practice, the methods used most frequently in relation to the transfer of intangibles are the CUP method (e.g., for determining licence fees charged by the owner of an intangible through a comparison with licence fees charged in independent transactions) and the profit split method (e.g., in order to share the return attributable to an intangible when several parties together own such an intangible). In certain

18. An entrepreneur does not need to make a profit since it is not a tested party earning a routine profit. An entrepreneur's profits will depend on the profitability of its business activities. Therefore, if the whole business is loss-making and the other associated enterprises perform routine functions, most of the losses are likely to have to be supported by the entrepreneur.
19. Residual profits have been described as 'the central difficulty in transfer pricing': *see* Stanley I. Langbein, *U.S. Transfer Pricing and the Outsourcing Problem*, 1065–1092, at 1070 (Tax Notes International, 21 March 2005). The automatic attribution of residual profits to the entrepreneur may lead to profit shifting issues. This is mainly due to the fact that residual profits may be attributed to a company owning valuable IP, the location of which may be relatively easily chosen. To mitigate illegitimate profit shifting, different types of recommendations have been made, especially with respect to the functions necessary to justify the ownership of IP and the conditions necessary for the attribution of intangible-related returns.

cases, it may be useful to perform a valuation of intangibles or rights in intangibles, for example, when an intangible is sold between two associated enterprises.[20]

Finally, a mechanism applicable to *hard-to-value intangibles* needs to be presented. This mechanism was introduced in the OECD Guidelines (but not fully in the UN Manual) with the BEPS project in view of the information asymmetry between tax administrations and taxpayers when it comes to the value of certain intangibles. This mechanism supposes the lack of reliable comparables, and that future cash flows, income, or valuation assumptions were highly uncertain at the time of the transfer. The problem arises when an intangible is transferred, and the value of that intangible after the transfer (referred to as *ex post* value) appears to be well above the value at the time of the transfer (referred to as *ex ante* value). For example, if an intangible is valued at 100 and transferred for that price, but that the value of this intangible appears to be 300 after the transfer, it may be wondered if the initial valuation was correct. Here, it is not the increase in value that is problematic, but the fact that this increase, although it was foreseeable, could not be anticipated by a tax administration because of a lack of information: in other words, *ex post* evidence should be 'necessary',[21] i.e., not just useful, to assess *ex ante* pricing.

The objective of the hard-to-value intangibles approach is to enable tax administrations use *ex post* information[22] as presumptive evidence to the existence of uncertainties at the time of the transaction. In the example above, the tax administration of the country from which an intangible was sold may argue (based on *ex post* evidence, not on comparables)[23] that the value of that intangible turned out to be 300 instead of 100. This would influence the size of a capital gain in the country of departure, and thus the tax paid upon the transfer of intangible. However, the hard-to-value intangibles approach may be rebutted by the taxpayer if it is proven – among other parameters – that the difference in value was unforeseeable or that the *ex post* value was not greater than 20% of the *ex ante* value.[24] The OECD Guidelines insist on the arm's length character of this approach,[25] and on the distinction with *hindsight*, whereby *ex post* results are used for assessment purposes without considering whether the higher value could have been anticipated.[26] This approach is not fully endorsed in

20. *See* paras 6.145 and following of the 2022 OECD Guidelines. For an example in relation to the CUP method, *see* Jens Wittendorff, *Denmark's Supreme Court Accepts CUP in Royalty Case*, 911–915 (Tax Notes International, 17 August 2020).
21. *See* the use of the word 'necessary' in para. 6.192 of the 2022 OECD Guidelines.
22. By 'information' it is meant *ex post* outcomes, or 'any relevant information' that becomes available to a tax administration and should have been considered by the taxpayer: *see* para. 8 of the Annex II to Chapter VI of the 2022 OECD Guidelines – Guidance for tax administrations on the application of the approach to hard-to-value intangibles.
23. *See* para. 16 of the Annex II to Chapter VI of the 2022 OECD Guidelines – Guidance for tax administrations on the application of the approach to hard-to-value intangibles.
24. The details of this safe harbour measure are found in para. 6.193 of the 2022 OECD Guidelines.
25. It has been debated in the doctrine whether such an approach is in line with the arm's length principle. In this respect, the hard-to-value intangibles approach is inspired by a US provision that has been considered as 'a major deviation from the arm's length standard': *see* Yariv Brauner, *Value in the Eye of the Beholder: The Valuation of Intangibles for Transfer Pricing Purposes*, vol. 28, 100–101 (Virginia Tax Review, 2008).
26. *See* para. 6.188 of the 2022 OECD Guidelines.

the 2021 UN Manual, which limits *ex post* adjustments to cases where the parties would have required a price adjustment clause or renegotiated the terms of the agreement.[27]

After introducing the importance of IP for transfer pricing purposes, the transfer pricing models frequently applied by multinational enterprises or claimed by tax administrations are described below.

3.4 COMMON TYPES OF INTERCOMPANY TRANSACTIONS AND TRANSFER PRICING MODELS

The most common types of intercompany transactions and transfer pricing models are described hereunder. This is done through following a typical series of steps throughout the value chain of a multinational enterprise involving research and development (section 3.4.1), manufacturing (section 3.4.2), and distribution (section 3.4.3). In addition, intercompany services (section 3.4.4), financial transactions (section 3.4.5), and cost contribution arrangements (section 3.4.6) are also touched upon, followed by a description of the centralised entrepreneur model frequently used in practice to centralise functions, risks, and assets (section 3.4.7). In any case, as a consequence of the substance-over-form principle, it is important to underline that transfer prices should not be determined on the basis of the terminology describing a certain transfer pricing model, but on the basis of the outcome of a comprehensive analysis including especially a functional analysis and a comparability analysis.

3.4.1 Research and Development

From a transfer pricing perspective, there are two main transfer pricing models involving R&D, depending on which party is considered as the owner of the intangibles for transfer pricing purposes. Other models are of course conceivable, for example, those where different parties share the important R&D functions. However, the focus of this section is on two typical types of organisations where the roles are either cumulated or clearly separated: on the one hand, the same company may cumulate all functions and assume all risks relating to R&D; on the other hand, a group may choose an organisation whereby the routine R&D functions are separated from the strategic ones. These two types of transfer pricing models are described subsequently.

If the same company cumulates all functions relating to R&D, including the performance of both the strategic and the more routine R&D functions as well as the control and assumption of the relevant risks[28] associated with the intangibles, the company would often be described for transfer pricing purposes as a *fully fledged researcher* as it is responsible for all the steps of the R&D. As a consequence of performing such functions and assuming such risks, the intangible that may result from the R&D activities will – for transfer pricing purposes – be owned by this entity,

27. *See* para. 3.6.2.7 of the 2021 UN Manual.

28. The relevant risks could, for example, consist in supporting the full costs of a R&D project, assuming the consequences if the project fails, and being liable to the end-customers if the product is flawed.

something that entitles it to the return attributable to the intangible:[29] the whole profit generated by the R&D activities would then be attributable to that company since it is assumed that no other group company has performed R&D functions.

Instead of cumulating all functions and risks relating to R&D at the level of a fully fledged researcher, a multinational enterprise may organise its activities so that the routine R&D functions are separated from the strategic ones. One may do so for operational purposes (e.g., in order to concentrate the important R&D functions and risks at one location), and/or for tax reasons (e.g., in order to maximise the profits taxable in a low-tax jurisdiction). Typically one would describe the two parties to such a transaction as a *contract R&D* (for the party performing the routine R&D functions) and a *principal* (for the party performing the strategic R&D functions and assuming the important risks). For this transfer pricing model to be in line with the arm's length principle, the principal would typically need to decide over the strategic parts of the R&D activities as well as control and assume the most significant risks, so that the routine R&D functions are performed by the contract R&D on behalf of the principal and at the latter's risks. For example, in certain cases, day-to-day experiences carried out in a laboratory upon the instructions provided by the principal may be deemed as contract R&D activities. From a transfer pricing perspective, the contract R&D would act as a service provider[30] on behalf of the principal. A contract R&D is not deemed as the owner of the IP created by the R&D activities, precisely because the most strategic parts are not the responsibility of the contract R&D but of the principal.[31] The IP would, instead, normally be owned by the principal. When a company acts as a principal without performing the routine R&D activities,[32] such a company would still be entitled to the return on intangibles, but not to the routine profit on the R&D activities. On the other hand, the contract R&D would normally be deemed as a tested party and be entitled to a remuneration that takes into account the routine nature of its functions, without being entitled to the returns that are in excess of such routine remuneration.[33] In frequent cases, if the CUP method is not applicable, it is the cost-plus method[34] or the TNMM (especially when it is combined to a financial indicator that measures the net

29. If several companies share the performance of functions and/or the assumption of risks, the intangibles that may result from the R&D activities will also be shared between these companies, together with the return attributable to such intangibles.
30. The services consist in the R&D that is carried out on behalf of the principal.
31. It is important to emphasise that a contract R&D may own other intangibles than the ones connected to the outcome of the R&D activities. That would, for example, be the case of a contract R&D that develops valuable know-how by providing services to the company acting as principal.
32. That is, the routine R&D activities have been outsourced, either to an associated enterprise or to a third party.
33. The remuneration takes into account the fact that the contract R&D normally supports limited risks, while more significant risks are supported by the principal. Therefore, the transfer prices applied between the principal and the contract R&D should limit the exposure of the contract R&D to the profits or losses of the R&D activities, unlike the principal which should be exposed to the economic outcome (whether positive or negative) of these activities. However, it is important to emphasise that even if an entity is characterised as a contract R&D, the transfer prices will still depend on the functions it performs, the risks it assumes, and the assets it owns or uses.
34. *See* para. 2.61 of the 2022 OECD Guidelines.

margin earned for all the costs incurred by the R&D activities)[35] that is applied to remunerate the contributions of a contract R&D through covering its costs and attributing to it a profit margin that corresponds to the profit that an independent comparable enterprise would earn. Since the IP is owned by the principal, it is also the principal that will be attributed the remaining profit (if any) generated by the IP. On the other hand, if the provider of R&D services is deemed to perform important functions (especially DEMPE functions), it may need to be remunerated on the basis of a transfer pricing method that enables taking into account such important functions; in many cases, the profit split method will be deemed to be an appropriate transfer pricing method for that purpose.[36]

From a tax planning perspective, a frequent question is whether or not, and if so under what circumstances, the return on intangibles may be separated from certain R&D activities. Indeed, multinational enterprises may be tempted not to have the return attributable to intangibles subject to a high corporate income tax rate, particularly when the intangibles give rise to significant profits. At the same time, a multinational enterprise may wish to carry out its R&D activities in a country with qualified labour force, or a country close to the targeted market(s) with a good understanding for the needs of the end-customers, which may be a high-tax jurisdiction. In principle and as explained above, under certain conditions – especially in terms of substance – outsourcing may be possible: a separation between the performance of the very R&D activities and the taxation of the return attributable to the intangibles may be achieved.[37] That is, a principal may outsource the R&D activities to a contract R&D, similarly to the models that independent companies may implement. However, the substance supporting this transfer pricing model is central for it to be acceptable to the tax administrations of the countries involved. It can especially be emphasised that if certain DEMPE functions are performed by the party to which R&D functions have been outsourced, a transfer pricing model based on the parallel existence of a principal and a contract R&D earning a routine profit will be hardly sustainable; as mentioned above, in such situations the profit split method may be the most appropriate transfer pricing method when DEMPE functions are being shared.

The example below illustrates the possible outcome of a structure where the R&D activities are carried out on a contract R&D basis, thus having only a relatively small share of the total profits subject to tax in the country where these activities are carried out. At the same time, the principal performs the important functions and assumes, as well as controls, the relevant risks.

35. In practice, this method is often described as a 'full cost mark-up'.
36. *See* Eyal Gonen, Leonid Karasik and Michael McDonald, *Control over Risk, DEMPE Functions, And the Remuneration of R&D Service Providers*, 1615–1630 (Tax Notes International, 21 June 2021).
37. The substance requirement was reinforced with the 2017 update to Chapter 6 of the OECD Guidelines, on the basis of a need to ensure 'that profits associated with the transfer and use of intangibles are appropriately allocated in accordance with (rather than divorced from) value creation' (*see* OECD, *Action Plan on Base Erosion and Profit Shifting*, 20 (2013)). The substance requirement from a transfer pricing perspective is presented in Chapter 5 of this book.

Example: A parent company sets up a contract R&D to perform R&D services in another country

Assume that a parent company, resident in State A, has a subsidiary resident in State B. The subsidiary acts as a contract R&D and performs routine R&D services on behalf of the parent company. In exchange for these services, the parent company pays a fee to the subsidiary. The extent of the fee depends on the functions performed, risks assumed and assets used by the subsidiary; in this example, it is assumed that the applicable transfer pricing method is the cost-plus method and that the arm's length mark-up on costs corresponds to 10% of the relevant costs incurred by the subsidiary, as illustrated in Figure 3.1. By limiting the functions, risks, and assets of the subsidiary, while having sufficient substance at the level of the parent company, the group may be able to separate the entitlement to the intangible-related returns (attributable to the parent company and taxed in State A) from the remuneration of the routine R&D activities (attributable to the contract R&D and taxed in State B).

Figure 3.1 Fee in Exchange for R&D Services

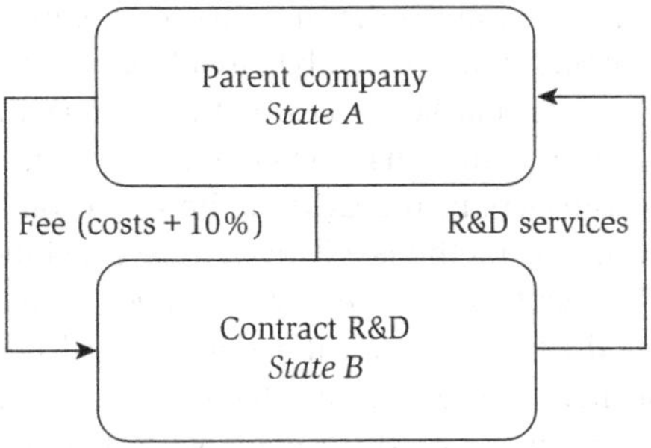

3.4.2 Manufacturing

There are different types of transfer pricing models applying to manufacturers, depending on the functions performed, the risks assumed, and the assets used by each party, i.e., as for any transfer pricing model, there is a direct connection between the functional analysis and the exposure to the economic outcome of intercompany transactions involving the manufacturing of goods. Apart from the tax aspects that come into play when deciding how to organise manufacturing activities, many other factors are taken into account by multinational enterprises such as the countries where a group needs to manufacture,[38] the cost and the qualification of labour, or the need to manufacture goods in a given strategic location.

In the transfer pricing jargon, it is often distinguished between 'toll manufacturers', 'contract manufacturers', 'licensed manufacturers', and 'fully fledged manufacturers'. These manufacturers have different functional profiles, and thus also

38. For instance, groups that extract and/or convert raw materials may have little choice about where to conduct such activities.

different entitlements to the profits or the losses resulting from the manufacturing activities. The different transfer pricing models commonly applied to intercompany transactions involving manufacturing are described below.

A *fully fledged manufacturer* is responsible for all the important parts of the manufacturing process; i.e., it performs the very production functions, manages the manufacturing process, and takes on all the risks[39] related to these activities. Accordingly, a fully fledged manufacturer will own the intangibles connected to both the manufacturing process[40] and the products manufactured,[41] when such intangibles exist. The ownership of process and product intangibles normally entitles a fully fledged manufacturer to the return on such intangibles, be it positive or negative.

A typical example of fully fledged manufacturer is the situation where a company has carried out R&D at its own risks, found an innovative product that has an economic potential, starts manufacturing the product, and then sells the finished goods to a distributor. In such a case, no other group company than the manufacturer has performed important functions or assumed important risks in relation to the manufacturing activity, and thus no other group company will be entitled to the return on intangibles.

The fact that a fully fledged manufacturer is responsible for the whole manufacturing process does not mean that no other company can be involved in that process. Independent contractors may be involved, but they will receive a remuneration that is based on market forces, without impacting the transfer pricing model. A fully fledged manufacturer may also enter into transactions with associated enterprises. As for any transaction, the CUP method is to be favoured. If no CUP is available, other transfer pricing methods will need to be considered. Because of its high level of complexity and possible uniqueness, a fully fledged manufacturer is normally not considered as a tested party. Instead, if a fully fledged manufacturer enters into transactions with associated enterprises that have a less complex functional profile (e.g., a buy/sell distributor) and if no CUP is available,[42] these last entities may be more suitable to be considered as a tested party. As a result, the transfer pricing methodology applied to such intercompany transactions will remunerate the tested party(ies) at arm's length through attributing them a routine profit for their routine functions, so that the residual income (whether positive or negative) after remunerating the tested parties with their routine profit is attributed to the fully fledged manufacturer. If, on the other hand, a fully fledged manufacturer enters into intercompany transactions with

39. Examples of risks supported by a fully fledged manufacturer are the risks that are related to the sourcing of raw materials, production planning, or quality control.
40. Intangibles connected to the manufacturing process are sometimes referred to as process intangibles and may, e.g., include the technical know-how that is developed by a manufacturer about how to carry out certain manufacturing activities.
41. Intangibles connected to the products manufactured are sometimes referred to as product intangibles and may, e.g., include the knowledge about the characteristics of a product.
42. Under the CUP method, there is no tested party (since the focus of this method is on the price of a transaction, not on the profitability of a party) but there is a tested product or service, the transfer price of which is based on a comparison with an independent transaction.

complex entities that may not be considered as tested parties,[43] a more sophisticated transfer pricing methodology may have to be put in place. The profit split method may be particularly relevant in such a case.

A *licensed manufacturer* is comparable to a fully fledged manufacturer in all respects, except when it comes to the ownership of certain intangibles that are licensed from another company (often described as an *IP company*)[44] instead of being owned by the manufacturer. That is, a licensed manufacturer purchases the right to use certain intangibles by paying a licence fee to another company that owns such intangibles. The licensed manufacturer still performs and supervises the manufacturing process at its own risk; it may develop and own intangibles in parallel to those that are used in exchange for a fee paid to the licensors.

A typical example involving a licensed manufacturer is the situation where a company (company A) performs manufacturing functions on an entrepreneurial (as opposed to routine) basis, but lacks an intangible (e.g., a patent) for being able to perform the whole manufacturing process. This intangible may be owned by company B. Accordingly, company A may want to gain access to the patent developed and owned by company B, while still performing the manufacturing functions at its own risk. To that end, company A could license the use of the patent from company B in exchange for a licence fee, while retaining the entitlement to the economic outcome of the manufacturing process after paying the licence fee. In such a case, company B would be a licensor, and company A would be characterised as a licensed manufacturer.

From a transfer pricing perspective, the same reasoning applies to licensed manufacturers and to fully fledged manufacturers, except for the need to pay a licence fee at arm's length to the owner of the intangibles used by the licensed manufacturer.[45] The determination of the licence fee will mainly build on the value of the intangible licensed, and their relevance for the manufacturing process. A licensed manufacturer will earn the residual income related to the manufacturing activity, after paying the licence fee to the owner of the IP and remunerating other companies that may be involved in the manufacturing process.[46] In the end, the final profit of a licensed manufacturer will necessarily be lower than that of a fully fledged manufacturer since it is lacking some intangibles that are necessary to the manufacturing process and for

43. An example of such a situation is when the entrepreneurial role throughout a value chain is shared by several entities, one of which is a fully fledged manufacturer.
44. An IP company owns intangibles and may let other companies use such intangibles, e.g., as part of a licence agreement.
45. For example, the arm's length nature of a licence fee paid by a licensed manufacturer has been discussed in a Canadian case where a drug manufacturer paid a fee to an associated enterprise for an ingredient necessary to manufacture a drug. While the tax administration argued that the level of the licence fee should, at most, be equal to what a generic company would pay for a generic ingredient, the Supreme Court of Canada found that the licence fee could exceed the price of a generic ingredient if other benefits were obtained by the licensee: *see GlaxoSmithKline Inc. v. Her Majesty the Queen*, Supreme Court of Canada (18 October 2012, case number 33874).
46. If such companies are associated enterprises and perform low value-adding functions, they would typically be characterised as tested parties and be entitled to a routine profit. If the associated enterprises involved in the manufacturing process may not be characterised as tested parties, a more sophisticated transfer pricing methodology will have to be used.

which it needs to pay a licence fee; the difference between the two profitability levels will depend on the value of the licensed intangibles and their importance to the manufacturing process.

A *contract manufacturer* has a significantly different role compared to a fully fledged manufacturer or a licensed manufacturer. Indeed, a contract manufacturer does not manufacture products at its own initiative and risk, but mostly at the initiative and risk of another party - the *principal* - which outsources the very manufacturing function to the contract manufacturer in exchange for a service fee. A contract manufacturer acts as a service provider and performs the very manufacturing functions and assumes certain risks,[47] but most of the risks associated with the manufacturing process are supported by the principal.[48] Important functions relating to the manufacturing process are also performed by the principal.[49] Since the main functions and risks connected with the manufacturing process are within the principal, the principal has a higher exposure to the profits or losses incurred during the manufacturing process than the contract manufacturer. The principal may even be entitled to the return attributable to the intangibles, if it owns or uses any. The contract manufacturer may own certain process intangibles,[50] but not product intangibles.[51] By not owning the product intangibles and by performing limited functions and assuming limited risks, the contract manufacturer is normally considered as being the tested party. Accordingly, the contract manufacturer is often entitled to a small but stable profit, i.e., a routine profit. If there is no reliable CUP, in many cases, the cost-plus method or the TNMM combined with a full-cost mark-up will be considered as the most appropriate transfer pricing method to remunerate a contract manufacturer, as these methods enable the contract manufacturer to have (part of) its expenses covered and earn a profit in relation to its contribution to the overall income earned by the multinational enterprise.

A typical example of transfer pricing model involving a contract manufacturer is the situation where a company (company A) through its own R&D activities finds a product that it decides to manufacture through an associated enterprise (company B) resident in another country, possibly given the lower labour costs in this other country or the geographical relevance of that country. Company A may want to keep control over the manufacturing process and own the product intangibles, thereby deciding to

47. A contract manufacturer assumes risks particularly related to investing in its own production plants and labour force. Also, a contract manufacturer normally purchases the raw materials and owns them until the (semi-) finished goods are sold to the principal.
48. A principal assumes, e.g., the obsolescence risk as well as the product risk.
49. A principal may, for example, perform strategic functions related to the decision to manufacture certain goods. The decisions made by a principal may also relate to the quality or the quantity of the goods.
50. The contract manufacturer may, indeed, develop its own know-how by performing the very manufacturing functions.
51. Product intangibles are owned either by the principal (if the principal has performed the R&D necessary to develop the product intangibles) or by another company of the group.

set up a contract manufacturing arrangement with company B. Company B would be manufacturing products on behalf of company A, with company A deciding which products to manufacture, setting the quality standards as well as the volumes, and assuming the most important risks. Company B would be responsible for its own production process, including its production plant, buying raw materials, as well as employing its own staff. From a transfer pricing perspective, company A would act as a fully fledged researcher and as a principal towards the contract manufacturer (in certain cases company A may even act as an entrepreneur),[52] thus being entitled to the residual income relating to the manufacturing process. Company B would typically be characterised as a tested party and be attributed a routine profit.

A *toll manufacturer* is comparable to a contract manufacturer as it acts on behalf of a principal while performing limited manufacturing functions and assuming limited risks related to the manufacturing process. However, unlike a contract manufacturer, a toll manufacturer does not own the raw materials or the (semi) finished products, which are owned by the principal during the whole manufacturing process. Consequently, as a result of the risks related to the raw materials and the (semi) finished products being borne by the principal, a toll manufacturer is normally entitled to a lower remuneration than a contract manufacturer.[53] In the lack of sufficiently comparable data for applying the CUP method, the cost-plus method or the TNMM combined with a full-cost mark-up are likely to be the most suitable transfer pricing methods to remunerate a toll manufacturer.[54]

The four manufacturing transfer pricing models are illustrated in Figure 3.2.

52. For a description of the centralised entrepreneur model, *see* section 3.4.7 of this book.
53. The remuneration of a toll manufacturer may still be described as a routine profit, as the functions performed by a toll manufacturer also have a routine character.
54. Given the lower risks borne by a toll manufacturer than by a contract manufacturer, the arm's length mark-up earned by a toll manufacturer should normally (i.e., all other things being equal) be lower than the one earned by a contract manufacturer. However, it is important to stress that the arm's length mark-up (or the range of mark-up) should be the result of the comparability analysis. Therefore, the arm's length mark-up earned by toll manufacturers is not by definition lower than the one earned by contract manufacturers. For example, there may be situations where a toll manufacturer within a given industry or within a certain geographical location earns a higher mark-up than a contract manufacturer within another industry or a different location.

Figure 3.2 Functional Profile and Profit Potential of Different Manufacturers

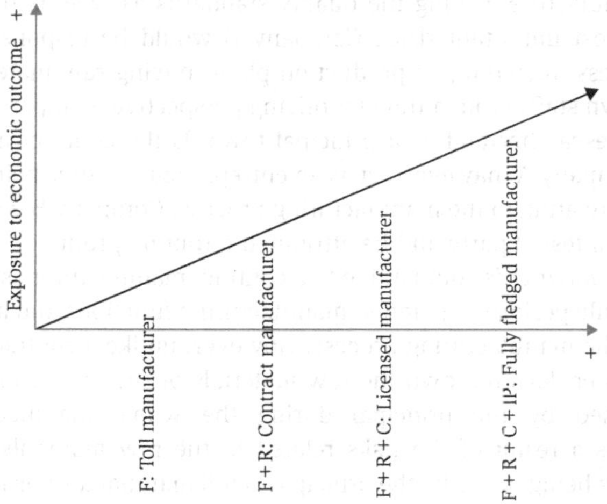

Figure 3.2 shows the growing profit potential of different manufacturers. On the lowest end, a toll manufacturer performs only the manufacturing function (indicated as 'F' in Figure 3.2), and thus is entitled to the lowest profit potential. Next, a contract manufacturer performs the manufacturing function and assumes certain risks (indicated as 'F + R' in Figure 3.2). Then comes a licensed manufacturer, who in addition to functions and risks also invests capital in the manufacturing process by supervising and financing it (indicated as 'F + R + C' in Figure 3.2). Finally, a fully fledged manufacturer intervenes at all stages of the manufacturing process, including the ownership of the valuable intangibles (indicated as 'F + R + C + IP' in Figure 3.2), and therefore is entitled to the highest profit potential.

From a tax planning perspective, these four alternatives have different implications. The choice of a particular transfer pricing model may be influenced by the level of profits that a group wishes the manufacturer, a principal or an IP company to earn, in addition to all other parameters that are taken into consideration when deciding how to organise the manufacturing activities within a group.[55] Accordingly, multinational enterprises willing to decrease the taxes paid as a result of the income generated by the manufacturing activities may consider locating a fully fledged manufacturer in a country that the group considers sufficiently attractive for its corporate income tax rate, as the functional profile of the fully fledged manufacturer will attract all the residual profits triggered by the manufacturing activity. Alternatively, a group may consider dividing the performance of functions and the

55. It is important to emphasise that taxes are only one of many factors that are taken into account when deciding where, and how to manufacture. External factors may command a particular organisation of the manufacturing activities, such as the price pressure resulting in the competition for producing at low costs, or the need to produce goods close to the end-customers in order to understand their needs and be able to deliver the products quickly.

assumption of risks – and therefore, also the ownership of IP – between several group companies located in different countries, with the aim of reducing the global effective tax rate paid on the profits generated by the manufacturing activity. A multinational enterprise could also consider separating the strategic from the routine manufacturing functions, so as to separate the place where intangible-related returns are taxed from the place where routine manufacturing functions are performed: indeed, similarly to what was indicated above for R&D, it may be possible to separate the performance of the very manufacturing activities from the taxation of the return connected to the intangibles – similarly to what independent companies may wish to implement – as long as certain conditions are fulfilled. In particular, the substance supporting such an arrangement will be critical for it to be acceptable by tax administrations.[56] The location of the manufacturer would not significantly influence the global effective tax rate paid on the profits generated by the manufacturing activity because most of the income would be attracted by the principal or the IP company.

The example below illustrates the possible outcome of a structure where the manufacturing activities are performed on a contract manufacturing basis. At the same time, the residual profits are attributable to the principal, except for the return connected to the manufacturing intangibles that is attributable to an IP company.

Example: A principal licenses a manufacturing intangible from an IP company and hires a contract manufacturer to manufacture goods on its behalf

Assume that a principal is resident in State A, and licenses from an IP company resident in State B the right to use a manufacturing intangible. The principal pays a licence fee to the IP company, which is assumed to amount to 3 % of the turnover of the principal for the sales of goods that are produced, thanks to the manufacturing intangible owned by the IP company. At the same time, the principal hires a contract manufacturer resident in State C to manufacture the goods on its behalf. In exchange for these manufacturing services, the principal pays a fee to the contract manufacturer. It is assumed that the applicable transfer pricing method is the TNMM, and that the manufacturer is remunerated on the basis of a full-costs mark-up of 5 %. By limiting the functions, risks, and assets of the contract manufacturer, while having the right substance at the level of the principal and of the IP company, the group may be able to isolate the entitlement to the return connected to the intangible (attributable to the IP company and taxed in State B), the residual profits resulting from the manufacturing activities (attributable to the principal and taxed in State A after deducting the licence fee paid to the IP company and the service fee paid to the contract manufacturer), and the remuneration of the manufacturing activities (attributable to the contract manufacturer and taxed in State C). This transfer pricing model is illustrated in Figure 3.3.

56. The substance requirement from a transfer pricing perspective is described in Chapter 5 of this book.

Figure 3.3 IP Licensed by Principal Company from IP Company

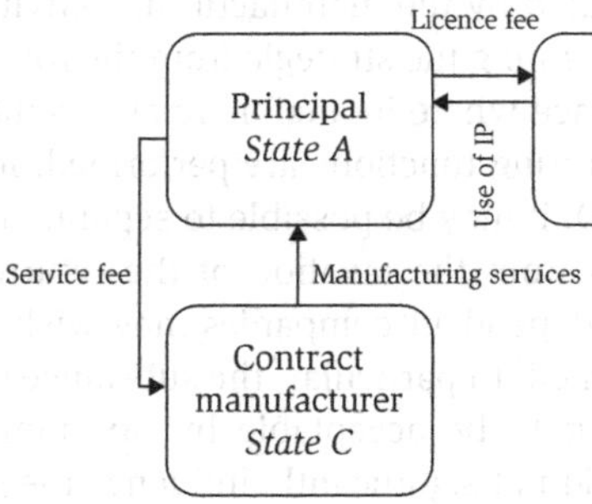

3.4.3 Distribution

The different transfer pricing models applied to distribution activities vary depending on the way multinational enterprises choose to distribute the functions, risks, and assets that are used as part of intercompany transactions involving distribution. As with any intercompany transaction, the arm's length principle commands a connection between the importance of the involvement in the value chain of a distributing entity, and the exposure to the economic outcome of transactions related to the sale of goods and goods-related services. Therefore, similarly to what was described above for R&D as well as manufacturing, groups may face several options as to how to structure their intercompany transactions involving distribution activities. And similarly to other types of intercompany transactions, taxes are one of several factors that may motivate the choice for a given transfer pricing model: for instance, multinational enterprises may need more or less presence, and the assumption of more or less responsibilities, to perform distributing functions in various countries depending on their sales objectives and the specificities of these countries.

Multinational enterprises often structure their distribution activities in such a way that it is distinguished between 'fully fledged distributors', 'buy/sell distributors', and 'commissionaires'. Since such distributors have different functional profiles, they also have different entitlements to the profits or the losses resulting from the distribution activities. The different transfer pricing models commonly applying to distributors are described below.

A *fully fledged distributor* performs, or is responsible for the performance, of all the important functions related to the distribution activity (e.g., from buying the products to marketing them and selling them to the end-customer), supports most of the related risks (e.g., the obsolescence risk in case products are not sold, or the foreign exchange risk for purchases and sales in different currencies), and owns or uses the valuable intangibles necessary to perform such functions.[57] In other words, a fully

57. The intangibles owned or used by a fully fledged distributor are often related to brands (e.g., trade names or logos) or clients (e.g., clientele). Such intangibles are sometimes referred to as marketing intangibles.

fledged distributor is autonomous in the management of the distribution activities. In certain cases, a fully fledged distributor may not own or use valuable intangibles if its activities are the result of the performance of functions and the assumption of risks that do not trigger the existence of, or require the use of, IP. In such cases, a fully fledged distributor may be characterised as a tested party, something that could allow the use of transfer pricing methods such as the resale price method or the TNMM, if the CUP method is not applicable. If the fully fledged distributor does own or use valuable intangibles, it may hardly be characterised as a tested party. The pricing of intercompany transactions with associated enterprises will then often depend on the characterisation of the counterpart to such transactions. If the counterpart may be characterised as a tested party (e.g., if a fully fledged distributor purchases products from a contract manufacturer), transfer prices could be set in such a way that the fully fledged distributor earns the profits left after remunerating the tested party at arm's length. If, in contrast, the counterpart may not be characterised as a tested party (e.g., if the fully fledged distributor purchases products from a fully fledged manufacturer), setting the prices of the transactions may raise more difficulties. The CUP or the profit split method would probably be the only transfer pricing methods applicable, as these methods do not rely on the remuneration of a tested party.

A *buy/sell distributor* focuses on buying and selling goods on behalf of a supplier that performs the strategic marketing and sales functions, assumes the important risks, and thus also owns the valuable intangible assets that may result from such distribution activities. Accordingly, a buy/sell distributor performs some of the functions and assumes some of the risks necessary to carry out the distribution activity – especially in relation to the ownership of the products – but in contrast to a fully fledged distributor, the more important functions and risks necessary to the distribution activity are attributable to another party. This relates primarily to key functions such as marketing strategy and important risks such as market risks,[58] but may also extend to other functions and risks.[59] The lack of important functions and risks is likely to characterise a buy/sell distributor as a tested party, given the relatively low complexity of such an entity.[60] The most suitable transfer pricing methods used to remunerate a buy/sell distributor are, in the absence of a CUP, the resale price method and the TNMM.

A typical example where a multinational enterprise may wish to set up a transfer pricing model involving buy/sell distributors is the situation where a group wishes to: (i) design a worldwide marketing strategy by centralising the decisions on marketing campaigns, pricing towards end-customers, brochures presenting the products, or selling techniques; and (ii) control the supply chain of the products through a centralised logistics function that also assumes the inventory and product risks across the whole supply chain. As the important functions and risks related to the distribution

58. By market risk is meant the risk that end-customers do not purchase the products as expected.
59. For example, logistics, quality control, after-sales service, inventory risks, bad debt risks, foreign exchange risks or warranty risks may be attributable to a party other than a buy/sell distributor.
60. However, the less complex functional profile of a buy/sell distributor does not mean that it may not own or use intangibles. A buy/sell distributor may, for example, develop valuable knowledge of the market or of the way to approach clients.

activity are centralised - and thus, not attributed to the buy/sell distributor, the remaining distribution activities performed in each country are rather limited and relate primarily to purchasing products that are resold without performing additional important functions or assuming significant risks.

A *commissionaire* acts as an intermediary between a principal (who owns the products sold) and the end-customer (who buys the products sold by the principal, but through being in contact with the commissionaire). That is, a commissionaire provides services to the principal (e.g., meetings with clients, promotion of the products during sales event, etc.), but the goods are owned and sold by the principal to the end-customer, unlike a buy/sell distributor who takes title to the goods. The strategic functions and important risks will not be either performed or assumed by the commissionaire because it is only a final intermediary between the principal and the client; the most important functions of the value chain have already been performed by other entities before products are sold to end-customers with the help of the commissionaire. A typical example of transfer pricing model whereby the sales are achieved with commissionaires is the situation where a group needs physical presence in or market knowledge of the countries in which it performs some sales, while centrally owning the goods until they are sold and keeping all control and risks in relation to the sales activities. A commissionaire will indeed be bound by strict instructions provided by the principal (e.g., with regard to the marketing of the products or the discounts that may be granted to clients), will not own the goods, and will thus be exposed to limited risks (mainly the commissionaire's own costs such as its own marketing expenses; all risks related to distribution are borne by another entity since the commissionaire does not perform distribution functions). Since a commissionaire performs limited functions and assumes low risks, its remuneration is also limited and will most often be determined on the basis of the CUP method, for example, through a commission based on a percentage of the sales achieved by the principal thanks to the intervention of the commissionaire.

Finally, an important aspect of the commissionaire model should be mentioned: when the commissionaire acts on behalf of a foreign principal and is involved in the latter's sales, a risk exists that the activities of the commissionaire create a permanent establishment of the principal in the country of the commissionaire. The extent of this risk depends largely on the definition of an agent permanent establishment in the applicable domestic law and tax treaty. If the definition of an agent permanent establishment is based on the pre-2017 OECD Model Tax Convention, this risk is rather low.[61] In contrast, if the definition of an agent permanent establishment is based on

61. This is due to the fact that Art. 5(5) of the OECD Model Tax Convention required, until the 2014 update to the model, that a person 'has, and habitually exercises, in a Contracting State an authority to conclude contracts in the name of the enterprise', for the foreign enterprise to have a permanent establishment in the country of the agent. In most countries, this formulation of the agent permanent establishment led domestic courts to the conclusion that a commissionaire that did participate in negotiations, but without concluding contracts in the name of the principal, could not be qualified as a dependent agent of the principal, thus precluding the existence of a permanent establishment: *see*, e.g., *Zimmer*, French Supreme Administrative Court (*Conseil d'État*) (31 March 2010, case number 304715; for a comment *see* Bruno Gouthière, *Zimmer: 'Commissionaire' Agent Is Not a Permanent Establishment*, vol. 50, issue 8, 350–358 (European

Article 5(5) and 5(6) of the 2017 OECD Model Tax Convention, this risk is higher.[62] If a principal has a permanent establishment as a consequence of the intermediary activities of the commissionaire, the commissionaire model will be less attractive as the foreign principal will have a tax liability in the country of the sales,[63] in addition to remunerating the commissionaire.

From a tax planning perspective, the level of profitability of a distributor has to match the functions performed, the risks assumed, and the assets used. As with the other transfer pricing models described above, it is in principle possible to achieve a separation between the remuneration of the distribution activities as such, and the returns connected to more profitable functions (particularly the return attributable to the marketing intangibles): the main condition for such a separation to be in line with the arm's length principle as it is described in the OECD Guidelines, is that each entity has sufficient substance and is remunerated as an independent party would.

It is also important to emphasise that the transfer pricing model used for distribution activities may be highly dependent on the conditions existing on the market at hand, and such conditions may evolve with the penetration of the actual market: for example, a distribution activity recently started in a new market may consist in understanding that market and advertising for the brand, rather than actually selling products. The transfer pricing model may have to be adapted accordingly. One way of doing so may be to view the distributor as providing services to the principal (rather than acting as a distributor who buys and sells products) and remunerate it on a cost-plus basis, as little sales may be achieved on this market during the start-up phase. When sales volumes increase, the cost-plus method may be replaced by another transfer pricing method that is more in line with the actual functions of the distributor, for example, a commission based on a percentage of the sales (if the goods are legally sold by the principal), a transfer price of the goods based on the CUP method (if the goods are legally sold by the distributor), the resale price method, or the TNMM.

Taxation, August 2010)); *Dell products*, Norwegian Supreme Court (2 December 2011, case number 2011-1581; for a comment, *see* Rainer Zielke, *Commissionaire Structure as an Agency Permanent Establishment (PE): Low Risk for Foreign Principals Constituting a PE in Norway – Dell Products v. Government of Norway, Decision of the Norwegian Supreme Court of 2 December 2011*, vol. 40, issue 8/9, 494–496 (Intertax, 2012)); *Boston Scientifics*, Italian Supreme Court (9 March 2012, case number 3769). Different conclusions have nevertheless been reached by certain courts, for example, in Spain: *see* Francisco Antonio Vaquer Ferrer, *The Concept of 'Permanent Establishment' at the Spanish Courts: Special Reference to the Roche and Dell Cases*, vol. 44, issue 8&9, 673–683 (Intertax, 2016).

62. This is due to two main reasons. On the one hand, Art. 5(5) of the OECD Model Tax Convention contains a lower threshold for the characterisation of an agent permanent establishment since the 2017 update to the model: it is now enough that a person 'habitually plays the principal role leading to the conclusion of contracts that are routinely concluded without material modification by the enterprise'. On the other hand, according to Art. 5(6) of the 2017 OECD Model Tax Convention, if the commissionaire acts 'exclusively or almost exclusively' on behalf of a foreign principal to which it is 'closely related', the exception for independent agents will not be applicable, thus increasing the chances that a foreign principal has a permanent establishment: on this theme *see* Jérôme Monsenego, *The Independent Agent Exception and Group Membership*, vol 46, issue 12, 944–959 (Intertax, 2018).
63. That tax liability will depend on the profits attributable to the permanent establishment. In this respect, *see* Chapter 6 of this book.

3.4.4 Intercompany Services

It is common that companies belonging to the same group provide services to each other. Certain categories of intercompany services have already been touched upon above, but services may also be provided in many other areas such as management, finance, law, human resources, Information technology (IT), etc. Intercompany services may be provided by various companies, or be centralised by choosing a group company that provides services to several other members of the group. Multinational enterprises often choose to centralise certain services, something that may help achieve synergies or regroup different kinds of expertise.[64] This section focuses not on the type of service provided, but on the general transfer pricing aspects of the provision of intercompany services.

There are several issues that are particularly challenging from a transfer pricing perspective in relation to intercompany services. These issues may be divided into four categories: (i) the determination of whether or not a service has been provided by one company to another; (ii) the determination of whether such a service may, at all, be charged to the recipient; (iii) the determination of the methodology according to which the services are charged to the recipients; and (iv) the determination of a transfer pricing method with which to charge the services between the provider and the recipient(s), which includes the question of the application (or not) of a profit mark-up.

First, it has to be determined whether or not a service has been provided by one company to another. While there may not be doubts about the existence of certain intercompany transactions such as the sale of goods, intercompany transactions involving services are not always obvious to identify. This is the case, for example, where an employee of one company performs certain tasks that benefit both the employer and another company. Also, in certain cases, it may not be easy to determine whether an intercompany transaction should be characterised as the provision of a service or if it should be characterised differently, for example, as an intangible.[65] Accordingly, the OECD Guidelines recommend investigating whether or not an intercompany service has been provided for transfer pricing purposes. This would

---

64. Companies providing services to several other group companies are sometimes referred to as 'shared service centres' when the services performed by the provider are shared by several recipients. Certain countries offer attractive tax conditions for setting up a shared service centre, some of which are under review as part of the work of the OECD on harmful tax competition (*see*, e.g., OECD, *Harmful Tax Practices: 2018 Progress Report on Preferential Regimes: Inclusive Framework on BEPS: Action 5* (2019); OECD, *Countering Harmful Tax Practices More Effectively, Taking into Account Transparency and Substance, Action 5: 2015 Final Report* (2015)). Within the EU, the Member States that enact attractive tax conditions need to be compliant with the rules on State aid provided in Art. 107(1) of the Treaty on the Functioning of the European Union. Moreover, the Member States of the EU have agreed on a code of conduct in order to prevent harmful tax competition for business taxation: *see Council Conclusions of the ECOFIN Council Meeting on 1 December 1997 Concerning Taxation Policy*, Official Journal of the European Communities, 98/C 2/01 (6 January 1998).
65. The characterisation of an intercompany payment as a service fee or as a royalty for the use of IP may have other consequences, such as the levy of a withholding tax. For an overview of withholding taxes on service and royalty payments, *see* Pinakin Desai and Shefali Goradia, Cahiers de Droit Fiscal International, *Cross-Border Outsourcing: Issues, Strategies and Solutions*, vol. 99A, 56–57 (2014).

notably exclude incidental benefits, in case a service is performed for certain group members but incidentally provides benefits to other group members. Such incidental benefits are not a chargeable intercompany service.[66] The same goes for benefits that result from passive association,[67] as the sole group membership is not deemed to result in a chargeable service.[68]

Second, after it is established that a company provides a service to another group company, what has to be determined is whether such a service may, at all, be charged to the recipient. In that respect, the OECD Guidelines indicate that services may be charged to their recipients only when they provide them a benefit, which is usually called the benefit test.[69] Indeed, independent companies would not purchase services if they do not need such services. This excludes, for example, services that are charged when the recipient itself already performs services that are similar, services that are performed in the interest of another group company,[70] or services that are performed in the interest of the provider. An important example of services that may not be allocated to various group members is what is sometimes referred to as *shareholder costs*. Shareholder costs are incurred by the shareholder for activities performed in its own interest or in the interest of the group as a whole. Illustrations of activities performed by the shareholder that may be characterised as shareholder costs are the preparation of consolidated accounts, the introduction of a company on the stock exchange, or the organisation of shareholders' meetings.[71] Shareholder costs should, in principle, be borne by the shareholder, i.e., they should not be allocated to the subsidiaries of the parent company.[72]

Third, there is the question of the methodology according to which services may be allocated to the recipients, when it has been ascertained that services have been provided and should be charged to their recipients. Two methods may be considered to

66. *See* para. 7.12 of the 2022 OECD Guidelines, and para. 5.2.6.18 of the 2021 UN Manual.
67. Benefits that result from passive association occur as a consequence of the sole membership in a group of companies. An example is a better credit rating, which may imply a lower cost of borrowing and thus a cost saving.
68. *See* para. 7.13 of the 2022 OECD Guidelines, and paras 5.2.6.15 and following of the 2021 UN Manual.
69. *See* paras 7.6 and following of the 2022 OECD Guidelines, and para. 5.2.2.1 of the 2021 UN Manual.
70. For example, if services are performed by a parent company in the interest of subsidiary A but are charged to subsidiary B, the latter company would have no need for such services. Therefore, the arm's length principle precludes that such services are charged to subsidiary B. In practice, deduction for tax purposes is likely to be denied by the tax administration of the country of residence of subsidiary B.
71. *See* para. 7.10 of the 2022 OECD Guidelines and para. 5.2.6.3 of the 2021 UN Manual for a non-exhaustive list of possible shareholder activities. A non-exhaustive list of shareholder costs is also provided in a Communication from the European Commission: *Communication from the Commission to the European Parliament, the Council and the European Economic and Social Committee on the work of the EU Joint Transfer Pricing Forum in the period April 2009 to June 2010 and related proposals 1. Guidelines on low value adding intra-group services and 2. Potential approaches to non-EU triangular cases* (25 January 2011, COM(2011) 16 final), at Annex 2. This document has been endorsed by the Council of the European Union (*see* 3088th Economic and Financial Affairs Council meeting, Brussels (17 May 2011)).
72. *See* para. 7.9 of the 2022 OECD Guidelines and para. 5.2.6.2 of the 2021 UN Manual.

allocate the costs to the recipients: the direct method and the indirect method.[73] Under the direct method, the cost of a service is charged directly to the recipient if the recipient can be clearly identified. The direct method may be applicable, for example, when a parent company has one subsidiary and provides services that benefit only the subsidiary. When it is applicable, the direct method is favoured by the OECD Guidelines.[74] If, in contrast, several companies benefit from the same service and the precise extent to which each recipient benefits from the service cannot be identified, the OECD Guidelines recommend applying the indirect method. The indirect method consists in sharing the costs between the recipients according to an allocation key on a pro rata basis. The allocation key will aim at allocating costs in a manner that is as close as possible to the benefits enjoyed by the recipients so that each recipient pays as much as possible for its own benefits. The allocation key will usually be determined depending on the services at hand and may rely, for example, on the turnover or the number of employees of the recipients of the services.[75]

Fourth, a transfer pricing method, with which to charge the services between the provider and the recipient(s), has to be determined. As with any other intercompany transaction, the OECD Guidelines favour the CUP method since this method is the closest to prices applied between independent parties.[76] When the CUP method is not applicable, intercompany services are often priced on the basis of the costs incurred by the service provider. This raises the question of which costs should be charged to the recipient(s), as well as whether or not the costs should be supplemented by a profit mark-up, usually in the form of a percentage of the costs incurred. As emphasised above in section 2.2.3 of this book, if the transfer pricing method chosen is the cost-plus method, the costs of production of the goods or the services will be charged to the recipient(s), excluding the costs that are not directly linked with a specific transaction such as the OPEX; in contrast, if it is the TNMM that is chosen, all the costs that are necessary to perform the service activity (i.e., including part of the OPEX) will be charged to the recipient(s). A profit mark-up enables the service provider to earn a profit on the services it provides and may have to be applied as a consequence of the arm's length principle since an independent service provider may not provide services for free. The profit mark-up added to the costs of a service provider has to be at arm's length, which often implies that a higher profit mark-up will be applied to high value-adding services (e.g., management consulting), whereas a lower profit mark-up will be applied to low value-adding services (e.g., accounting services).[77] In certain cases, safe harbours may provide predetermined profit mark-ups; it should especially be emphasised the safe harbour for low value-adding services (for which the OECD

73. *See* paras 7.21 and following of the 2022 OECD Guidelines.
74. *See* para. 7.22 of the 2022 OECD Guidelines.
75. *See* paras 5.4.8.5 and 5.4.8.6 of the 2021 UN Manual for examples of allocation keys. *See also* para. 7.25 of the 2022 OECD Guidelines.
76. *See* para. 7.31 of the 2022 OECD Guidelines. In practice, the CUP method may be particularly relevant to apply where the service provider also provides services to third parties (i.e., an internal CUP). However, it may be necessary to perform comparability adjustments to take into account differences between the two transactions.
77. *See* para. 7.49, first indent, of the 2022 OECD Guidelines.

Guidelines suggest a 5% profit mark-up on total costs),[78] and bilateral safe harbours agreed between tax treaty partners for certain low-risk functions.[79]

While in most cases services are to be charged above their costs, there are situations where services may be provided without adding a profit mark-up, for example, when the provision of a service without a profit element may be beneficial in the long run. Also, when an associated enterprise acts as an intermediary and actually purchases services from another company, in principle, no profit mark-up should be added to these costs because the price paid to the company performing the services already includes a profit element;[80] an independent purchaser would indeed not be willing to pay more than the arm's length profit made on the services.[81] However, the time and resources spent by the associated enterprise acting as an intermediary to administer the provision of services actually performed by a third party may be charged to the service recipient(s), depending on the circumstances at hand.

The issues described above relating to the transfer pricing aspects of intercompany services are illustrated by the example below.

Example: Provision of administrative services by a parent company to its subsidiaries

Assume that a parent company P incurs the following costs in relation to administrative services (Table 3.1).

Table 3.1 Types of Services and Costs Incurred by the Service Provider

Type of Service	*Costs Incurred by the Service Provider*
Accounting	30
IT	20
Legal	40
Human resources	10
Total	**100**

78. *See* para. 7.61 of the 2022 OECD Guidelines. Low value-adding intra-group services are defined in paras 7.44 and following of the 2022 OECD Guidelines. The 2021 UN Manual recognises the benefits of safe harbours for low value-adding services; however, no predetermined profit mark-up is suggested (*see* paras 5.5.2.1 and following of the 2021 UN Manual). Also, certain countries do not endorse the OECD recommendations on low value-adding intra-group services: *see*, e.g., para. 3.18.2 of the 2021 UN Manual (Part D): 'India has not endorsed the guidance in the BEPS report pertaining to Low Value-Adding Intra Group Services (LVAIGS) under Action 10 and has not opted for the simplified approach.'
79. Here it is referred to bilateral safe harbours agreed by the competent authorities of countries having concluded a tax treaty containing an article similar to Art. 25(3) of the OECD Model Tax Convention: *see* Annex I to Chapter IV of the 2022 OECD Guidelines for examples of memoranda of understanding for use by competent authorities in negotiating bilateral safe harbours for low-risk distribution, manufacturing, and R&D functions. These examples do not contain a profit mark-up, which is to be negotiated by the competent authorities.
80. *See* para. 7.61 of the 2022 OECD Guidelines. These costs are often referred to as pass-through costs: *see* para. 2.99 of the 2022 OECD Guidelines, and para. 5.4.7.1 of the 2021 UN Manual.
81. If the associated enterprise acting as an intermediary adds a profit mark-up to the price paid to the third party, it may be more rational for the service recipient(s) to purchase the service directly from the party performing it, rather than from the company acting as an intermediary.

Assume also that the parent company has two subsidiaries A and B, and that accounting, IT as well as human resources services are performed internally by the parent company and benefit all three companies (i.e., the parent company and the two subsidiaries), while the legal services benefit only subsidiary A.[82] Consequently, the costs incurred in relation to the legal services (40) will have to be charged in their entirety to subsidiary A in accordance with the direct method, which is preferred to the indirect method under paragraph 7.21 of the 2022 OECD Guidelines. Whether or not a profit mark-up has to be added would normally depend on the origin of the costs. If it is assumed that half of the legal costs (40/2 = 20) corresponds to lawyer fees invoiced by a third party to the parent company but related to subsidiary A, no mark-up should be added to avoid charging twice a profit element relating to these costs. For the remaining legal costs (20), if they are incurred by the legal department of the parent company, a profit mark-up should be added to the cost base, so that the parent company is remunerated for the services it provides. The other costs (i.e., accounting, IT and human resources, amounting to 30 + 20 + 10 = 60) benefit the three companies and are to be charged to the two subsidiaries on the basis of an allocation key (i.e., the indirect method) since the direct method cannot be applied. The costs incurred by the parent company and benefiting the parent company are not subject to a cost allocation since they are to be kept by the parent company. Assume that the turnover is chosen as an allocation key, and that the three companies have the following turnover (Table 3.2).

Table 3.2 Turnover per Company and Percentage of Total Turnover

Company	*Turnover*	*Percentage of Turnover*
Parent company B	100	50%
Subsidiary A	60	30%
Subsidiary B	40	20%
Total	**200**	**100%**

Assume also that the costs are invoiced based on the TNMM combined with the financial indicator FCM, and that a benchmarking study or a safe harbour[83] indicates that an arm's length profit mark-up of 5% should be applied to the total costs for the accounting, IT, and human resources services. As a result of the relative turnover of each company, the costs remaining after deduction of the legal costs should be allocated as follows (Table 3.3).

82. It may be assumed that the legal services relate to court proceedings concerning only subsidiary A.
83. It is assumed that such a safe harbour is consistent with the arm's length principle.

Table 3.3 Costs Allocated to Each Company with Profit Mark-Up

Type of Service	*Cost Base*	*Cost Base for Subsidiary A*	*Costs + 5% Mark-Up Charged to Subsidiary A*	*Cost Base for Subsidiary B*	*Costs + 5% Mark-Up Charged to Subsidiary B*
Accounting	30	$30 \times 30\% = 9$	9.45	$30 \times 20\% = 6$	6.3
IT	20	$20 \times 30\% = 6$	6.3	$20 \times 20\% = 4$	4.2
Human resources	10	$10 \times 30\% = 3$	3.15	$10 \times 20\% = 2$	2.1
Total	**60**	**18**	**18.9**	**12**	**12.6**

This calculation applies a 5% profit mark-up to each type of cost and allocates the costs including the mark-up to each subsidiary on the basis of its turnover. Accordingly, since subsidiary A's turnover corresponds to 30% of the total turnover, it should be allocated 30% of each type of costs, together with a 5% profit mark-up. The same goes for subsidiary B, but only 20% of the costs should be invoiced since subsidiary B's turnover corresponds to 20% of the total turnover. By so doing, the part of the costs that should be charged by the parent company to its subsidiaries is subject to a 5% profit mark-up, thus enabling the parent company to earn an arm's length profit on the services provided to its subsidiaries. In total, the parent company incurs costs amounting to 60, only half of which is to be allocated to the subsidiaries (the subsidiaries make together 100 out of 200, i.e., 50% of the total turnover). On this cost base amounting to 30 ($60/2 = 30$), the parent company should earn a 5% mark-up, thus making a profit of $30 \times 5\% = 1.5$. Indeed, the sum of the costs charged to subsidiary A and subsidiary B amounts to 31.5 ($18.9 + 12.6 = 31.5$), of which 30 covers the cost base and 1.5 is a profit. The remaining costs borne by the parent company will correspond to the benefits enjoyed by the parent company itself for the accounting, IT, and human resources services. Consequently, in the end, each company has purchased services in proportion to its needs.

The above example illustrates the potential complexity of pricing intercompany transactions involving services. Given such a complexity, certain multinational enterprises prefer not to have a particular transfer pricing model for intercompany services and, instead, include in the transfer price of other transactions a part corresponding to intercompany services. For example, instead of charging an associated enterprise separately for both goods and services, it may be considered to increase the price of the goods and refrain from charging the recipient for the services. In the end, the result should be the same if each transaction is priced correctly. However, the administrative burden saved in the first place by aggregating transactions may result in disputes at a later stage relating to the correctness of such an aggregated approach, given the potential difficulties to demonstrate that each intercompany transaction is priced at arm's length.[84] It is only if independent companies would aggregate several transactions (and that the information provided by a benchmarking study evidences such an aggregation) that it may be beneficial to also aggregate transactions in the context of an intercompany transaction. That may be the case, for example, if the sale of goods between independent parties also includes some marketing services: if information about transaction prices between independent parties concerns the sale of goods together with the provision of certain marketing services, a similar approach might be applied between associated enterprises.

3.4.5 Financial Transactions

It is frequent that multinational enterprises enter into intercompany financial transactions, without necessarily being active in the financial sector.[85] Associated enterprises may have financial needs (e.g., the need for cash in order to finance the acquisition of an asset) or financial capacities (e.g., an excess of cash following the sale of an asset) that they may want to remedy without involving a third party such as a bank, i.e., through intercompany transactions. Several types of financial transactions may take place between associated enterprises, the most frequent being intercompany loans, cash pooling and hedging.[86] Different motives may encourage associated enterprises to enter into intercompany financial transactions, such as the potentially better bargaining conditions that may be obtained when concentrating the loans of a group at the level of a single borrowing entity, the possibility of optimising cash

84. On the risks implied by aggregating different intercompany transactions, *see* above section 2.3.1 of this book.
85. This section of the book is written only from a general transfer pricing perspective; i.e., it does not take into account the special features of the financial sector. On the particularities of transfer pricing within the financial sector, *see*, e.g., Anuschka J. Bakker, *Transfer Pricing and Intragroup Financing: Low-Hanging Fruit?*, vol. 15, issue 2, 27–33 (Derivatives and Financial Instruments, March/April 2013); Irina Diakonova, Steef Huibregtse and Gesa Körner, *Where Do Financial Services Meet Transfer Pricing?*, vol. 2, issue 2, 55–73 (Derivatives and Financial Instruments, March/April 2000); Norma Kraay and Leon Bloom, *The Missing Link: Transfer Pricing and Regulatory Capital Compliance for Global Financial Institutions*, 527–531 (Tax Notes International, 13 February 2012). In the context of permanent establishments, *see* OECD, *Report on the Attribution of Profits to Permanent Establishments*, Parts II and III (22 July 2010).
86. Other financial intercompany transactions may take place between associated enterprises, such as intercompany guarantees whereby one company guarantees the solvency of an associated enterprise that takes on a loan. The guarantor will bear a risk in case of insolvency of the borrower, who will enjoy a benefit as the guarantee will decrease the cost of borrowing given the decreased risk borne by the lender. For example, in the Canadian *GE Capital* case, a group member borrowed from external parts and paid a guarantee fee to its parent company, which guaranteed the subsidiary's debt to the external lenders: *see General Electric Capital Canada Inc. v. Her Majesty the Queen*, Canadian Federal Court of Appeal (15 December 2010, case number 2010 FCA 344). Given the introductory purpose of this book, this section is limited to providing an overview of the transfer pricing aspects of the most frequent types of intercompany financial transactions.

management within a group of companies thanks to a cash pooling mechanism,[87] or the impossibility of a group member to obtain a loan from an external bank.

Before delving into certain of the transfer pricing aspects of intercompany financial transactions, it is important to emphasise that capital movements may easily be used for tax planning purposes by taxpayers,[88] thus constituting a risk for tax administrations. This is mainly due to the high mobility of capital, which can easily be shifted from one country to another. Therefore, capital has received particular attention as part of the BEPS projects, both within and outside the field of transfer pricing.[89]

Intercompany loans are particularly challenging from a tax and transfer pricing perspective. On the one hand, financial transactions may very well take place between associated enterprises for a genuine reason, something that advocates for acknowledging their existence from a tax perspective and granting them a tax treatment similar to other transactions, in particular the deduction of interest expenses. On the other hand, financial transactions may relatively easily enable the avoidance of taxes, for example, by creating intercompany loans that have no business purpose or by choosing a relatively high or low interest rate applicable to an intercompany loan. In addition, the qualification of financial flows for taxation purposes varies from one country to another, something that may give rise to situations of recharacterisation of an intercompany loan into equity, thereby disallowing the deduction of the interest expenses.[90] From a tax perspective, differences in the qualification of financial flows may also give rise to *hybrid mismatches*, thus leading to double non-taxation or double

87. By cash pooling mechanism is meant the situation where a group member (sometimes referred to as an internal bank) collects the cash of group members that do not need it at a certain time. The deposits are then lent to other group members that are in need of cash at the same moment.
88. For example, a multinational enterprise may easily decide to move capital to a low-tax jurisdiction to lend money from there and have the interest income taxed at a low rate. Capital may also be moved for structuring purposes (i.e., with respect to the ownership of shares), so as to achieve low taxation of dividends and capital gains.
89. Within the field of transfer pricing, financial transactions were mainly impacted by the revision of Chapter 1 and the addition of a new Chapter 10 in the OECD Guidelines. Outside the field of transfer pricing, interest limitation rules have been enacted and tax treaty benefits have been subjected to certain conditions.
90. For an example of court case about the possible right of the tax administration to recharacterise an intercompany loan into equity, *see* the case issued by the Supreme Administrative Court of Finland (3 July 2014, case number KHO 2014:119); in this case, the court refused the recharacterisation, partly due to the fact that a recharacterisation would imply a complete denial of deduction of the interest expenses, something that would require being provided by a domestic provision in addition to the arm's length principle. For a comment on this case, *see* Merja Raunio, *Landmark Case on the Ability of Tax Authorities to Disregard and Recharacterize Transactions*, vol. 22, issue 1, 28–32 (International Transfer Pricing Journal, January/February 2015). For an opposite example, *see* the case issued by the Full Federal Court of Australia (*Chevron Australia Holdings Pty Ltd v. Commissioner of Taxation*, Full Federal Court of Australia (21 April 2017, case number (2017) FCAFC 62)), especially in para. 55 of the judgment where the court considered the consequences of not being able to depart from the agreed terms of intercompany transactions: 'All one would have to do would be to constrain internally the transaction to give the highest price and include or omit terms of the agreement that would never be included or omitted in an arm's length transaction and which are not driven or dictated by commercial or operational imperatives, as the foundation for assessing an hypothesised arm's length consideration.'

deductions.[91] Accordingly, it is difficult for legislators and policymakers to design rules that strike an acceptable balance between the importance of preventing tax avoidance, and the needs of multinational enterprises to be able to conduct their business activities. In an attempt to protect their tax base, certain countries have enacted domestic rules that limit the amount of interest expenses deductible from a tax perspective, i.e., rules on the maximum amount of debt-financing that may give rise to deductible interest expenses. Indeed, debt-financing is often more attractive than equity-financing because interest expenses are in many cases deductible while the return on equity (i.e., dividends distributed to shareholders) is normally not deductible for tax purposes.[92] Debt is also more flexible than equity. This difference is likely to encourage debt-financing over equity-financing within groups, something that breaches the idea of neutrality between different financing forms.[93] Two types of rules on the limitation to the deduction of interest expenses[94] can be mentioned here: thin capitalisation rules (providing, e.g., that interests may be deductible only up to a ratio of debt not exceeding three times the size of the equity)[95] and rules that introduce a

91. For example, the same financial flow may be qualified as an interest expense in country A, and at the same time as a dividend in country B, as a consequence of the diverging domestic laws of these two countries. If the domestic tax law of country A allows the deduction of interest expenses while the domestic tax law of country B applies a system of exemption of dividends (a so-called participation exemption), the combination of these two domestic laws will lead to a situation of double non-taxation, as the expense that has been deducted in one country is not matched by the inclusion of the same item of income in the taxable base in the other country. Such situations, often described as hybrid mismatch arrangements, are subject to anti-avoidance rules in certain countries, especially following the work of the OECD on BEPS Action 2 (*see* OECD, *Neutralising the Effects of Hybrid Mismatch Arrangements, Action 2: 2015 Final Report* (2015)). For example, within the EU hybrid mismatches are prevented by the mechanism in Art. 9 of the ATAD: *see Council Directive (EU) 2016/1164 of 12 July 2016 laying down rules against tax avoidance practices that directly affect the functioning of the internal market*, OJ L 193, 19.7.2016, pp. 1–14 as well as the 'ATAD 2' Directive (*see Council Directive (EU) 2017/952 of 29 May 2017 amending Directive (EU) 2016/1164 as regards hybrid mismatches with third countries*, OJ L 144, 7.6.2017, pp. 1–11). It can also be observed that the Member States of the EU have amended the parent-subsidiary directive in order to tackle the issue of tax avoidance through certain hybrid mismatch arrangements (*see Council Directive 2014/86/ EU of 8 July 2014 amending Directive 2011/96/ EU on the common system of taxation applicable in the case of parent companies and subsidiaries of different Member States*, Official Journal of the European Union, L 219/40 (25 July 2014)).
92. However, equity (and thus dividends that remunerate contributions in capital) may also open certain tax planning opportunities: *see*, e.g., Peter Mason, *The Greatest Profit Shifter: The Dividend*, 693–697 (Tax Notes International, 7 February 2022).
93. In this respect, *see* Chris Finnerty, Paulus Merks, Mario Petriccione and Raffaele Russo, *Fundamentals of International Tax Planning*, 107–111 (IBFD, 2007).
94. It can be observed that such rules may raise compatibility issues with EU law, if they imply limitations to the deduction of interest expenses that are nevertheless at arm's length (*see* especially *Lexel AB v. Skatteverket*, Court of Justice of the European Union (20 January 2021, case number C-484/19)); however, this issue is not in the scope of this book.
95. Such rules target companies that are 'thinly' capitalised, i.e., companies that have too little equity in relation to their debts. In certain countries, excessive debt in relation to equity may be corrected with transfer pricing rules, on the basis of the assumption that an independent company would not, or may not, take on too high loans; in other countries transfer pricing rules are limited to the correction of the conditions for intercompany loans (mainly the interest rate), i.e., without allowing to challenge the amount of the loan as such. For an overview of thin capitalisation rules and the application of transfer pricing rules to thin capitalisation, *see* Luis Coronado, Patrick Cheung and Justin Kyle, *An Overview of Arm's Length Approaches to Thin*

ratio that links a company's right to deduct interest expenses to its profits (providing, e.g., that interests that are deductible for a given tax year cannot exceed 30% of a company's EBITDA (Earnings Before Interests, Taxes, Depreciation and Amortization)).[96] Interest limitation rules such as the one included in the ATAD, whereby net interest expenses are deductible only up to a certain percentage of the taxpayer's profits, are illustrated with the example below.

Example: Adjustment of deductible interest expenses

Revenues		**100**		
COGS	–	70		
Gross margin	=	**30**		
OPEX	–	10		
EBITDA	=	**20**	30% EBITDA =	6
Depreciation	–	10		
Interests	–	10	Adjusted interests	6
Taxable income	=	**0**	Adjusted income	4
Tax (20%)		0	Tax (20%)	0.8
			Interest not deducted	4

In the above example, it is assumed that a company has an EBITDA of 20, and net interest expenses of 10 (it is assumed that this company has no interest income). Without application of the interest limitation rule, the company would have zero taxable income, partly as a consequence of the deduction of interest expenses amounting to 10. The application of the interest limitation rule caps the interests deductible to 30% of the company's EBITDA, in this example, 30% of 20, i.e., 6. The net interest expenses in excess of 6 (10–6 = 4) will not be deducted, thereby increasing the taxable income. Domestic rules would normally entitle the taxpayer to carry forward the net interest expenses for which deduction has been denied.

From a transfer pricing perspective, the OECD Guidelines do not encroach on specific anti-avoidance rules relating to the debt-equity ratio.[97] This means that the OECD Guidelines acknowledge, among others, that the balance between debt and

Capitalization, vol. 17, issue 4, 270–275 (International Transfer Pricing Journal, July/August 2010). *See also*, for an analysis of debt and equity from a tax perspective, Patricia Brown, General Report, Cahiers de Droit Fiscal International, *The Debt: Equity Conundrum*, vol. 97b (2012); Wolfgang Schön, *The Distinct Equity of the Debt-Equity Distinction*, 490–502 (Bulletin for International Taxation, September 2012).

96. *See* OECD, *Limiting Base Erosion Involving Interest Deductions and Other Financial Payments, Action 4: 2016 Update* (2017); *see also* Art. 4 of the ATAD (*Council Directive (EU) 2016/1164 of 12 July 2016 laying down rules against tax avoidance practices that directly affect the functioning of the internal market*, OJ L 193, 19.7.2016, pp. 1–14).

97. *See* para. 10.9 of the 2022 OECD Guidelines. For a critical analysis of Chapter 10 of the 2022 OECD Guidelines (in particular the fact that it may not solve all issues and may thus result in situations of double taxation), *see* Jens Wittendorff, *Transfer Pricing Oddity: The OECD's New Guidelines on Financial Transactions*, 723-739 (Tax Notes International, 10 August 2020).

equity be addressed under domestic rules such as thin capitalisation rules. The new Chapter 10 of the OECD Guidelines emphasises the need for intercompany financial transactions to abide by the arm's length principle[98] and generally follow the recommendation in Chapters 1–3 of the Guidelines.[99] No 'special measures' that deviate from the arm's length principle are recommended in the 2022 Guidelines, although such measures have been envisaged as part of the BEPS project.[100] How one labels an intercompany financial transaction has no bearing for a transfer pricing analysis, as what matters is the substance of that transaction. In order to reveal that substance and accurately delineate an 'advance of funds' (and especially determine whether or not it should be regarded as a loan), one needs to consider several economically relevant characteristics, in particular the existence of obligations to pay interests and repay the funds.[101] Consistently with the general principles contained in the OECD Guidelines since the update with the BEPS project, it would be expected from the parties that they perform the right functions: a lender should perform certain key functions (e.g., whether and under which terms to advance funds),[102] control the risks associated to an advance of funds, and have the financial capacity to assume the risks, in order to be recognised as lender and be entitled to the profitability of the relevant transactions.[103] The same goes for the borrower, as the perspective of each of the parties must be considered. For corporate treasury activities, a key function would be to optimise liquidity across the group to ensure that the business has liquidities available in the right place and currency.[104]

With respect to intercompany loans according to the OECD Guidelines and the UN Manual, both the taking up[105] of a loan and the interest rate applied to the loan have to be at arm's length;[106] other terms and conditions would normally also have to be taken into account, e.g., the existence of a security, the currency of the loan, and implicit credit support. However, as previously mentioned, certain countries do not accept that the balance between debt and equity be addressed on the basis of transfer pricing rules. Paragraph 10.8 of the 2022 OECD Guidelines accepts that countries address this issue on the basis of domestic rules. Although the conditions for

98. *See* para. 10.1 of the 2022 OECD Guidelines.
99. *See* para. 10.14 of the 2022 OECD Guidelines. However, the recommendations included in Chapter 1 as to the accurate delineation of the transaction are not deemed as 'the only approach for determining whether purported debt should be respected as debt' (*see* para. 10.9).
100. *See* OECD, *BEPS Actions 8, 9 and 10: Discussion Draft on Revisions to Chapter I of the Transfer Pricing Guidelines (Including Risk, Recharacterisation, and Special Measures)*, 38–43 (December 2014).
101. *See* para. 10.12 of the 2022 OECD Guidelines.
102. *See* para. 10.24 of the 2022 OECD Guidelines.
103. *See* para. 10.25 of the 2022 OECD Guidelines.
104. *See* para. 10.41 of the 2022 OECD Guidelines.
105. For an example of court case in which the granting of a loan was deemed as abusive (thus implying that the interests related to the loan were not deductible), *see X. B.V.*, Gerechtshof Amsterdam (17 March 2021, case number 2021:724).
106. *See also* para. 3(a) of the commentary to Art. 9 of the 2017 OECD Model Tax Convention, where it is considered that the arm's length principle 'is relevant not only in determining whether the rate of interest provided for in a loan contract is an arm's length rate, but also whether a prima facie loan can be regarded as a loan or should be regarded as some other kind of payment, in particular a contribution to equity capital'.

intercompany loans must correspond to those of independent transactions, it is acknowledged in the OECD Guidelines that certain differences exist between these two situations. Such differences must be understood and placed in their context in order not to reach wrong conclusions from a transfer pricing perspective. For example, when a parent company has control and ownership of its subsidiary, the granting of security (i.e., contractual rights over the assets of the borrowing entity) is found to become less relevant to the risk analysis of the lender. Chapter 10 of the 2022 OECD Guidelines recommends understanding these differences before making conclusions from a transfer pricing perspective: the absence of security does not necessarily reflect the risk inherent in the loan, as the control and ownership of the subsidiary may enable the lender to have assets available as collaterals to secure the loan, and thus mitigate the risks it assumes.[107] In other words, the pricing of the loan must go beyond the form (here, the lack of security) to take into account the whole substance of the transaction (here, the control on the assets of the borrower).

With regard to the determination of the interest rate, and as with any intercompany transaction, the starting point is the functional analysis that will emphasise the functions performed, risks assumed, and assets owned by the parties in relation to the intercompany loan. Among the elements of the transfer pricing analysis that are particularly relevant for the pricing of intercompany loans, the credit rating[108] of the borrower is of fundamental importance as it directly influences the level of risk taken by the creditor when lending money to the borrower, similarly to transactions between independent enterprises. A lower credit rating indicates a greater risk of default and a higher rate of return for the lender, and conversely.[109] Therefore, the credit rating of the borrower is closely connected to its cost of funding. Consistently with the general guidance on synergies,[110] passive incidental benefits that result from the sole association with other group members should not require any payment or comparability adjustment.[111] This means that group membership may imply an 'implicit support'[112]

107. *See* para. 10.56 of the 2022 OECD Guidelines.
108. The credit rating is an opinion about a company's (or a group's) general creditworthiness, which is based on its capacity and willingness to meet its financial obligations: *see* para. 10.64 of the 2022 OECD Guidelines. In certain cases, the credit rating of a company may be obtained through rating agencies (para. 10.71); in other situations a rating can be computed through relying on financial information relating to the borrower. Courts in different countries have adopted different views on the relevance of information provided by credit rating agencies for the purposes of pricing intercompany loans and guarantees: this practice was accepted in the *General Electric* case (*General Electric Capital Canada Inc. v. Her Majesty the Queen*, Canadian Federal Court of Appeal (15 December 2010, case number 2010 FCA 344)), but not in the *Chevron* case (*Chevron Australia Holdings Pty Ltd v. Commissioner of Taxation*, Federal Court of Australia (23 October 2015, case number (2015) FCA 1092)). In the *Chevron* case, a group member borrowed from third parties and lent to its parent company at a higher interest rate, while the ultimate parent company provided a guarantee. The court found that these circumstances could be taken into account for the arm's length assessment of the intercompany loan.
109. *See* para. 10.64 of the 2022 OECD Guidelines.
110. *See* para. 1.178 of the 2022 OECD Guidelines.
111. *See* para. 10.77 of the 2022 OECD Guidelines.
112. *See* para. 10.77 of the 2022 OECD Guidelines. It may be wondered whether recognising the potential effect of implicit support can be reconciled with the arm's length principle, given that this principle supposes that the effects of association are not taken into account.

and affect the credit rating of the borrower, and thus the pricing of a loan,[113] which might make the payment of a guarantee fee superfluous.[114] This is consistent with the idea that all relevant facts and circumstances must be taken into account,[115] since between independent parties any facts and circumstances may influence the conditions of uncontrolled transactions. Moreover, as mentioned above, depending on the circumstances several other elements need to be taken into account, such as the volatility and perspectives of the borrower's business, the currency of the loan, or its length.

The transfer pricing method most commonly used to set the interest rate of an intercompany loan is the CUP method[116] (including internal CUPs),[117] although other methods like the cost-plus method can also be applicable.[118] Indeed, since the lending of money is not a transaction that is unique to associated enterprises, it may be possible to find comparable independent transactions, e.g., interbank loans, or loans between banks and their clients. The purpose of the comparability analysis is to identify the interest rates applied to loans between independent parties that are sufficiently comparable to the loan between the associated enterprises, regard being had to the elements of the functional analysis and the comparability factors described above such as the credit rating of the borrower, the existence of securities, the currency and length of the loan, or the characteristics of the business of the borrower. The outcome of the comparability analysis consists most frequently in an arm's length range of interest rates applied as part of independent transactions, as opposed to a single market rate.[119] Eventually, the interest rate applied to the intercompany loan is determined on the basis of the arm's length range of interest rates, possibly after making certain

113. For a similar view, *see General Electric Capital Canada Inc. v. Her Majesty the Queen*, Canadian Federal Court of Appeal (15 December 2010, case number 2010 FCA 344), in para. 59: 'there is no doubt that the existence of the implicit guarantee is relevant to the inquiry and must be considered in identifying the arm's length price'. *See also Chevron Australia Holdings Pty Ltd v. Commissioner of Taxation*, Federal Court of Australia (23 October 2015, case number (2015) FCA 1092); however, in this case implicit support was not found to affect the outcome of the case.
114. *See* para. 9.8.8 of the 2021 UN Manual, last sentence. This argument was raised by the Canadian tax administration in the *GE Capital* case, in support of the denial of deduction for the payment of a guarantee fee to the borrower's parent company: *see General Electric Capital Canada Inc. v. Her Majesty the Queen*, Canadian Federal Court of Appeal (15 December 2010, case number 2010 FCA 344).
115. *See* para. 1.130 of the 2022 OECD Guidelines, and para. 9.8.6 of the 2021 UN Manual.
116. *See* para. 10.90 of the 2022 OECD Guidelines. A similar position has been reached by the German Federal Tax Court: *see* Sven-Eric Bärsch and Christian Engelen, *German Federal Tax Court Rules in Favour of Taxpayer in Transfer Pricing Cases on Intercompany Financing Transactions*, vol. 29, issue 1, 19–23 (International Transfer Pricing Journal, 2022). However, *see also* Oscar Montero, *Forecasting Interest Rates for Future Intercompany Loan Planning: An Alternative Approach*, vol. 49, 313–317 (International Transfer Pricing Journal, September/October 2009).
117. *See* para. 10.95 of the 2022 OECD Guidelines.
118. *See*, for example, a case ruled by the Finnish Supreme Administrative Court where the cost-plus method was found appropriate in the context of certain financial transactions: Merja Raunio and Matti Urpilainen, *Case SAC 2021:66 on Group Internal Financing: Supreme Administrative Court Provides Lessons on How the OECD Transfer Pricing Guidelines Should and Should Not Be Used*, vol. 28, issue 5, 338–341 (International Transfer Pricing Journal, 2021).
119. *See* para. 10.91 of the 2022 OECD Guidelines. The arm's length range of interest rates determined as part of the comparability analysis may be described as the 'credit spread'.

comparability adjustments to eliminate the material effects of differences with respect to, e.g., liquidity, maturity, existence of collateral, or currency.[120]

The determination of the arm's length interest rate applicable to an intercompany loan is illustrated with the example below.

Example: Determination of an arm's length interest rate on an intercompany loan

Assume that company A (resident in country A) grants a loan to its subsidiary B (resident in country B). Assume also that countries A and B are members of the Eurozone. To determine the interest rate paid by company B to company A, the group may decide to apply the CUP method and rely on the average interest rate applicable to interbank deposits within the Eurozone, i.e., the Euro Interbank Offered Rate (Euribor). It is assumed that the risk level of lending money to company B is higher than between banks. Consequently, the group considers, based on a transfer pricing study, that an arm's length interest rate for the intercompany loan between companies A and B would be the Euribor increased by one percentage point, i.e., Euribor + 1%, in order to take into account the higher risk borne by company A.[121]

As already mentioned above, the application of the arm's length principle to intercompany loans may give rise to controversies with respect to group membership. In particular, it may be debated whether the interest paid or received by each group company should be assessed on a separate basis or if the situation of the group as a whole should be taken into account to set the interest rate applying to an intercompany loan. This issue is illustrated by the example below.

Example: A parent company takes up a loan with a bank and lends the money borrowed to its subsidiaries

Assume that the parent company of a group obtains a loan from a bank to finance certain activities of the group. The money borrowed from the bank by the parent company is then lent to other group companies. Since the parent company borrows a sum of money that may exceed its own needs, its own repayment possibilities, and its own potential securities, the bank may see a high risk in this transaction and apply a high interest rate of, e.g., 6%. The money is then lent to group companies, including company A, at the same interest rate, i.e., 6%. However, group company A is in a good financial position and borrows only a small amount that could be borrowed from a bank at a lower rate, e.g., 3%. The question is whether the portion of the loan that is lent to company A should be associated with a 3% or a 6% interest rate, or any other interest rate. A strict application of the arm's length principle from the sole perspective of the borrower points to setting the interest rate on the basis of the borrower's own situation, i.e., 3% in this example.[122] The guidance in Chapter 10 of the 2022 OECD

120. *See* para. 10.93 of the 2022 OECD Guidelines.

121. In practice, other parameters may need to be taken into account. For example, the duration of intercompany loans and interbank loans with fixed interest rates may not be similar, thus requiring comparability adjustments.

122. This view has, for example, been adopted by the Supreme Administrative Court of Finland (3 November 2010, case number KHO 2010/3092 (73)). For comments on this case, *see* Marjaana Helminen, *Determining the Arm's Length Interest Rate of an Intra-group Loan*, 153–155

Guidelines points to the same conclusion: although a company may take advantage of belonging to a group with a higher credit rating with no necessary compensation[123] (and thus *a contrario* it could be argued that a company may be affected by the lower credit rating of the group), one would need to take into account the borrower's options realistically available, in this case, the lower rate offered by an independent bank. In the opposite situation, for example, if company A is in a difficult financial position and can only borrow from a bank at a 6% rate, while the credit rating of the whole group would enable it to borrow at lower rates, group membership may be taken into account, i.e., a lower rate than 6% might be applied to the loan to company A, assuming that the benefit from that lower rate is incidental; i.e., it does not result from deliberate concerted group actions.

After presenting the transfer pricing aspects of intercompany loans, attention is now put on cash pooling transactions. Here, a difficulty comes from the fact that such transactions are unlikely to be undertaken by independent enterprises,[124] and yet the arm's length principle needs to be applied.[125] For example, a cash pooling mechanism may enable certain savings thanks to deliberate concerted action; such group synergy benefits would need to be shared on the basis of the arm's length principle.[126] The determination of the price of cash pooling transactions follows the general principle of Chapter 1 of the OECD Guidelines, a distinction being made between the cash pool leader and the cash pool members. When the cash pool leader performs only coordination functions (and thus does not assume the financial risks such as credit risks, liquidity risks, or currency risks), it is likely to be characterised as a service provider and receive a limited remuneration,[127] but if the financial risk is controlled and assumed by the cash pool leader, it will also be entitled to part or all of the spread between the borrowing and lending rates.[128] The determination of the interests paid by cash pool members is complex since there may not be reliable comparable transactions to use as a benchmark. Since one should take into account the options realistically available to determine the price of cash pooling transactions, and given that such

---

(European Taxation, April 2011); Merja Raunio, *Supreme Administrative Court Ruling on Interest Rate Reflecting Creditworthiness of Individual Companies*, vol. 18, issue 4, 296–301 (International Transfer Pricing Journal, July/August 2011).

123. *See* para. 7.13 of the 2022 OECD Guidelines ('an intra-group service would usually exist where the higher credit rating were due to a guarantee by another group member'), as well as paras 10.76 and 10.77. This view has, for example, been adopted in the case *General Electric Capital Canada Inc. v. Her Majesty the Queen*, Canadian Federal Court of Appeal (15 December 2010, case number 2010 FCA 344). In this case, the Canadian Federal Court of Appeal found it necessary to take into account the fact that a Canadian company belonged to a US group, thereby implicitly benefiting from its credit rating. For a comment on this case, *see* Christopher J. Steeves, *General Electric Capital Canada Inc. v. The Queen: Guarantee Fees and the Arm's Length Standard*, 131–136 (Derivatives & Financial Instruments, May/June 2011).
124. *See* para. 10.115 of the 2022 OECD Guidelines.
125. For an example of court case relating to a cash pooling arrangement, *see* French Supreme Administrative Court (*Conseil d'État*), case numbers 461639 and 461642 (20 September 2022).
126. That may be the case when netting the excesses and needs of cash results in a reduction of the interests paid, or an increase of the interests received, at the level of a group: *see* para. 10.121 of the 2022 OECD Guidelines.
127. *See* para. 10.130 of the 2022 OECD Guidelines.
128. *See* para. 10.141 of the 2022 OECD Guidelines.

transactions normally imply a benefit on a group level, it is generally expected that all cash pool participants will be better off than in the absence of cash pool arrangement.[129]

3.4.6 Cost Contribution Arrangements

The intercompany transactions presented above have been described under the basic assumption that two associated enterprises enter into a transaction, one party generally being the provider and the other party being the recipient of a good or a service, although in certain transactions several parties may act as provider and/or as recipient.[130] These different roles imply that the parties normally do not share functions, risks, and/or assets, something that facilitates finding comparable independent transactions where functions, risks, and/or assets are also clearly separated.

In parallel to such intercompany transactions, multinational enterprises may also carry out a business activity by sharing between several associated enterprises the functions, risks, and assets connected with a given activity, instead of fully performing them at the level of a given group company. As a result, if associated enterprises share certain functions, they will share costs or profits resulting from the shared activities. When multinational enterprises perform complementary functions and share the risks – including the costs – related to a common activity together with the benefits (or losses) connected to such an activity, they may enter – or be deemed by tax administrations to have entered – into a transfer pricing model described in the OECD Guidelines as a 'cost contribution arrangement'.[131] The 2022 OECD Guidelines define a CCA as 'a contractual arrangement among business enterprises to share the contributions and risks involved in the joint development, production or the obtaining of intangibles, tangible assets or services with the understanding that such intangibles, tangible assets or services are expected to create direct benefits for the businesses of each of the participants'.[132] Accordingly, a CCA does not necessarily relate to intangibles.[133]

There may be various reasons for entering into a CCA, e.g., the objective of reducing costs, take advantage of economies of scale, or share skills, intangibles or

129. *See* para. 10.146 of the 2022 OECD Guidelines.
130. For example, services may be performed by one company on behalf of several recipients.
131. The fact that functions, risks, assets, and benefits (potentially including returns on intangibles) are shared between the members of a group does not necessarily imply that the associated enterprises have entered into a CCA. The companies may, for example, be responsible for different parts of the value chain (i.e., different activities) without entering into a CCA. It is only when it is the same activity, for which the functions, the risks (especially the costs), and/or the assets are shared between different companies, that the OECD Guidelines describe this transfer pricing model as a CCA.
132. *See* para. 8.3 of the 2022 OECD Guidelines.
133. One can also emphasise a difference that is made in the Guidelines with respect to two types of CCAs: those relating to the development of tangible or intangible assets (which create ongoing and future benefits), and those for obtaining services (which create current benefits only): *see* para. 8.10 of the 2022 OECD Guidelines. The former are generally considered as more complex than the latter.

resources. CCAs may also be used as a tax planning tool, e.g., through letting foreign group companies contribute to the development of IP and earn the income connected to such IP.[134]

The conditions according to which functions, costs, risks, and benefits (or losses) are shared between the participants in a CCA should, according to Chapter 8 of the 2022 OECD Guidelines, comply with the arm's length principle as for any intercompany transaction.[135] Each participant makes contributions to the arrangement and is entitled to a proportionate share of benefits (or losses). The 2021 UN Manual adopts the same view.[136] Contributions must be valued at arm's length[137] (as opposed to being valued at cost),[138] and – consistently with general transfer pricing principles – each participant must exercise control over the risks it assumes and have the financial capacity to assume these risks.[139]

From a transfer pricing perspective, the starting point is the application of the arm's length principle and the delineation of the actual transaction undertaken on the basis of the contractual agreement.[140] That is, the conditions for the attribution of costs and/or benefits to the participants to a CCA have to correspond to what independent parties would have agreed to. In practice, this may prove difficult, especially as there are few independent comparable transactions that may be used as a benchmark. Accordingly, the main challenge consists in matching the contributions to a CCA and the benefits (or losses) derived by the participants in such an arrangement, as each participant's proportionate share of the overall contributions must be consistent with its proportionate share of the overall expected benefits.[141] Indeed, since a CCA implies that two or more associated enterprises share the functions, risks, costs, and benefits (or losses) related to a common activity, there may be a mismatch between the contributions and the benefits (or losses) derived by the participants in a CCA. For example, a risk of mismatch exists when a country expects a company to charge costs both directly and indirectly incurred to other parties, while the other countries only allow the deduction of direct costs.[142]

---

134. *See*, e.g., James R. Repetti, Diane M. Ring and Paul McDaniel, *Introduction to United States International Taxation*, 158–159 (6th ed., Kluwer Law International, 2014), for a presentation of the motives for enacting cost sharing regulations in the United States.
135. *See* para. 8.12 of the 2022 OECD Guidelines.
136. *See* para. 7.1.2 of the 2021 UN Manual.
137. *See* para. 8.24 of the 2022 OECD Guidelines: 'all contributions of current or pre-existing value must be identified and accounted for appropriately in accordance with the arm's length principle'. *See also* para. 7.4.1 of the 2021 UN Manual.
138. *See*, however, the recommendations in paras 8.27 and following of the 2022 OECD Guidelines, with respect to situations where it is more administrable to value contributions at cost, or when the difference between the value and costs is insignificant. *See also* para. 7.4.6 of the 2021 UN Manual for a similar view.
139. *See* para. 8.15 of the 2022 OECD Guidelines.
140. *See* paras 8.4 and 8.9 of the 2022 OECD Guidelines.
141. *See* para. 8.5 of the 2022 OECD Guidelines.
142. In this respect, it is interesting to emphasise a court case in the United States where the court found that only the expenses that were relevant for the purpose of a CCA had to be charged to the parties taking part in this arrangement. That is, there was no requirement that other expenses (in this case the expenses related to the issuance of stock options to the company's employees) be invoiced to the parties taking part in the CCA: *see Xilinx, Inc., and Consolidated*

To prevent such mismatches, the OECD Guidelines mention that so-called balancing payments may need to be paid or received to ensure consistency between the value of each participant's contributions and its share of expected benefits, when the value of a contribution or a proportionate share of benefits has been incorrectly determined.[143] No single method is recommended by the OECD Guidelines to link the contributions and proportionate share of expected benefits or losses of each participant in the arrangement. However, one method that is often used in practice consists in sharing benefits or losses according to an allocation key. The Guidelines mention as possible allocation keys the sales (turnover), profits, units used, units produced, units sold, and the number of employees.[144] The use of an allocation key is illustrated by the example below.

Example: CCA applied to the conduct of a R&D project

Assume that companies A (resident in country A), B (resident in country B), and C (resident in country C) are all members of the same group. They wish to share the costs of an R&D project, as well as the benefits (in case the project results in a successful intangible) or losses (in case the project is not successful). It is assumed that 50% of the research has been conducted and financed by company A, 30% by company B, and 20% by company C. It is also assumed that all the contributions imply comparable functions and risks, thus having similar values.[145] Accordingly, in this case, the benefits or losses of the CCA could be shared on a pro rata basis of the total costs incurred for the project by the participants to the arrangement. For example, if the R&D project results in a successful intangible and that a royalty of 100 is paid by users of such an intangible, an amount of 50 should be allocated to company A, company B should be allocated 30, and company C should be allocated 20. In contrast, if the contributions of the participants to the CCA have different values, the OECD Guidelines suggest to compensate for such differences in values by making balancing payments between the parties. That is, if one party contributes to a CCA with something more valuable than the other participants to the arrangement, the other parties should make a payment to the contributor so that it receives an arm's length payment for its

Subsidiaries v. Commissioner of Internal Revenue, United States Court of Appeals for the Ninth Circuit (22 March 2010, case numbers 06-74246 and 06-74269). For a comment on this case, *see* Anton Joseph, *Xilinx: The Unfinished Business*, vol. 17, issue 4, 283–286 (International Transfer Pricing Journal, July/August 2010).

143. Balancing payments increase the value of the contributions of the payor and decrease that of the payee: *see* para. 8.34 of the 2022 OECD Guidelines.
144. *See* para. 8.19 of the 2022 OECD Guidelines.
145. It is indeed important to emphasise that the costs incurred by the members of a CCA may not be a relevant basis for sharing the benefits or losses incurred by the arrangement if the functions and/or risks attributable to each party are not comparable. In such cases, the contributions of the participants to the arrangement may have different values. For example, if the employees of company A perform more strategic functions while the employees of companies B and C perform less strategic functions, the costs incurred by each company in relation to the total costs of the project may not be an appropriate basis for sharing the benefits or losses generated by the common R&D project (although the levels of the wages may, to some extent, mirror the importance of the functions performed).

contributions. The market value of the contribution will have to be measured, so that the balancing payment is in line with the arm's length principle.

3.4.7 The Centralised Entrepreneur Model

The centralised entrepreneur model is not an intercompany transaction on its own, but rather the combination of several intercompany transactions that are structured with the aim of centralising the important functions, risks, and assets of a group - or of a business area of a group - at the level of one company, the 'entrepreneur' (sometimes also referred to as the 'principal').[146] The centralised entrepreneur model builds on two main assumptions. First, the entrepreneur has to perform the most important functions, assume the most significant risks, and own or use the most valuable assets that are relevant for the group (or a business area within the group). This would normally entitle the entrepreneur to the economic ownership of (most of) the valuable IP that is used as part of a given value chain. Second, the other group companies that are involved in the same value chain have to perform less important functions, assume more limited risks, and should not own or use valuable assets that are relevant for the value chain, something that typically characterises these other group companies as tested parties. It is the combination of these two features that lays the ground for the centralised entrepreneur model, which from a transfer pricing perspective implies that the entrepreneur will be exposed to most of the profits or losses incurred by the value chain, whereas the other group companies will be entitled to a lower but more stable remuneration.[147] Which company(ies) act(s) as entrepreneur(s) and as tested party(ies) within a group of companies is determined by the functional analysis.

Two main effects are achieved for transfer pricing purposes, thanks to implementing a centralised entrepreneur model. The first effect is the accumulation of the residual profits incurred by the value chain in a single location, which is the State of residence of the entrepreneur. This is due to the fact that the other entities involved in this transfer pricing model are tested parties that are normally not entitled to the residual profits, which makes it possible to reduce the taxation of the residual profits incurred by the value chain through choosing a favourable location for the entrepreneur. However, countries no longer have strong incentives to provide particularly low effective tax rates, given the political[148] and legal[149] limitations to

146. For a presentation of this transfer pricing model, together with its rationale and limitations, *see* Joseph Andrus and Michael Durst, *Standing on 'Principal': Risk-Limiting Transfer Pricing Structures*, 959-963 (Tax Notes International, 18 December 2006).

147. In the transfer pricing vocabulary, an entrepreneur is close to a principal, as both perform important functions and assume important risks. However, a principal is often more limited in the scope of its activities as it would normally not be responsible for the whole value chain; a principal would typically only be involved with specific intercompany transactions (e.g., through providing instructions to a contract manufacturer or a contract R&D), whereas an entrepreneur takes responsibility for the whole value chain and is involved with most of the transactions that are part of the same value chain.

148. Many countries have committed to respect the criteria defined as part of the report on BEPS Action 5: *see* OECD, *Countering Harmful Tax Practices More Effectively, Taking into Account Transparency and Substance, Action 5: 2015 Final Report* (2015).

harmful tax regimes, as well as the introduction of anti-avoidance rules such as CFC rules[150] or minimum taxation rules.[151] Therefore, the tax arbitrage effect of the centralised entrepreneur model tends to be more limited than in the past if the value chain is globally profitable. If, in contrast, the value chain is globally loss-making, the losses will also be accumulated in a single location. The provisions on the tax treatment of losses in the country of the entrepreneur will be of particular importance, especially with respect to the possibility to carry back or carry forward losses, and the length of such possibilities. Here the arbitrage effect might be significant depending on which country is chosen, as rules on the deduction of losses vary greatly between different countries.

The second effect achieved by the implementation of the centralised entrepreneur model is related to the consolidation of the profits and losses incurred by the value chain. Since the entrepreneur enters into intercompany transactions with several other group companies that are often characterised as tested parties, the entrepreneur will usually have to ensure through the transfer prices of intercompany transactions a low but stable remuneration to these group companies. As a result, a consolidation effect is achieved at the level of the value chain controlled by the entrepreneur given that the residual income will be concentrated at the level of the entrepreneur after remunerating at arm's length each associated enterprise participating in the value chain. If certain group companies make higher profits than they are entitled to under the arm's length principle (e.g., if a group company has made higher sales or has incurred lower costs than expected), such excess profits will be repatriated to the entrepreneur,[152] something that results in accumulating profits at the level of the entrepreneur. On the other hand, the entrepreneur will have to compensate group companies that make lower profits than they are entitled to by increasing their remuneration,[153] something that results in accumulating losses at the level of the entrepreneur. Consequently, the profits of certain group companies will, in the end,

149. Attractive tax measures offered by the Member States of the EU are to abide by the rules on State aid (*see* Art. 107(1) of the Treaty on the Functioning of the European Union). For an example of court case in which attractive tax rules have been found in breach of the State aid rules, *see Kingdom of Belgium (C-182/03) and Forum 187 ASBL (C-217/03) v. Commission of the European Communities*, CJEU (22 June 2006, joined cases C-182/03 and C-217/03).

150. CFC rules are not part of the BEPS minimum standards; yet, for countries that wish to introduce such rules, recommendations in the form of building blocks were made as part of the BEPS project: *see* OECD, *Designing Effective Controlled Foreign Company Rules, Action 3: 2015 Final Report* (2015). In the EU, the introduction of CFC rules is compulsory under Arts 7 and 8 of the ATAD.

151. *See*, e.g., the GILTI (for Global Intangible Low-Taxed Income) rules in the US under section 951A of the Internal Revenue Code; *see also* OECD, *Tax Challenges Arising from the Digitalisation of the Economy: Global Anti-base Erosion Model Rules (Pillar Two) – Inclusive Framework on BEPS* (2021).

152. This is because the arm's length principle precludes that a company earns more profits than what an independent comparable company would earn. The transfer pricing model should ensure that excess returns are attributable to the entrepreneur.

153. This is because the arm's length principle precludes that a company earns less profits than what an independent comparable company would earn. The transfer pricing model should normally ensure that losses are attributable to the entrepreneur, so as to protect the tested party from risks that it does not control.

compensate for the losses incurred by other group companies, which may be described as a consolidation effect for taxation purposes.

The way the centralised entrepreneur model is implemented in practice varies from one case to another, depending on how a group wishes to structure its value chain. In any case, the issue of substance is central for such a model to be acceptable to the tax administrations of the countries involved: the entrepreneur will have to be actually performing the functions, assuming the risks, and owning the assets that are necessary to exercise the role of the entrepreneur in the value chain.[154] The example below illustrates the centralised entrepreneur model by concentrating the important functions, risks, and assets at the level of the entrepreneur (Figure 3.4). The group companies involved in intercompany transactions with the entrepreneur do so on a limited-risk basis, through being characterised as contract R&D, contract manufacturer, and buy/sell distributor.

Example: An entrepreneur centralises important functions, risks, and assets, while other companies are characterised as contract R&D, contract manufacturer, and buy/sell distributor

Figure 3.4 Centralised Entrepreneur Model

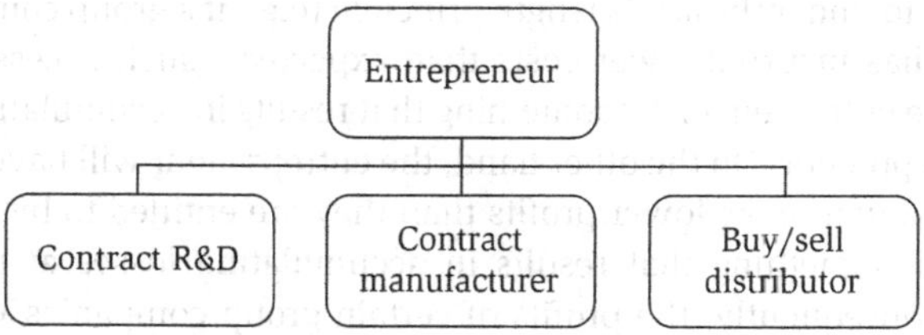

In this example, the entrepreneur concentrates important functions, risks, and assets with regard to R&D, manufacturing, as well as marketing and sales. At the same time, the three other companies are also involved in R&D, manufacturing, as well as marketing and sales, but to a much lower extent in terms of importance. That is, these companies perform less important functions, assume more limited risks, and do not own or use valuable assets that are used as part of the value chain. Consequently, the residual profits or losses incurred by this group are likely to be attributable to the entrepreneur, while the other group companies, characterised as tested parties, will receive a lower, but more stable, remuneration. The transfer pricing methods used to determine transfer prices will depend on the facts and circumstances of the case, bearing in mind that whatever transfer pricing method is chosen, it will take into account the low-risk functional profile of the contract R&D, the contract manufacturer, and the buy/sell distributor.

154. On the requirement of having sufficient substance from a transfer pricing perspective, *see* Chapter 5 of this book.

To conclude this section on the centralised entrepreneur model, the consequences of this business model from a transfer pricing perspective are illustrated below with an example containing three scenarios. In this example, the entrepreneur earns the residual profits after remunerating the tested parties. It is assumed in the three scenarios that no CUP is available, and that the tested parties perform routine functions for which they earn routine income. Under the first scenario, the group is in a start-up phase and applies low prices to end-customers, to encourage the demand of their products. Under the second and third scenarios, the prices of the goods are gradually increased. The transfer pricing model is the same as in the previous example, i.e., the entrepreneur concentrates important functions, risks, and assets, while the three companies characterised as tested parties perform R&D, manufacturing, as well as marketing and sales on a limited risks basis. It is assumed that the researcher is characterised as a contract R&D that should earn a FCM of 10%, the full costs being OPEX amounting to 20. It is also assumed that the manufacturer is characterised as a contract manufacturer that should earn a FCM of 5% and that the full costs are made of the raw material (COGS of 60) as well as OPEX (10). Last, it is assumed that the distributor is characterised as a buy/sell distributor and that the transfer pricing method chosen is the resale price method under which the distributor should earn a gross margin of 25%, having remaining OPEX amounting to 20. To operate the whole value chain, the entrepreneur needs to support OPEX amounting to 50.

The value chain is the following: the contract R&D provides R&D services to the entrepreneur, upon the entrepreneur's instructions and technical recommendations. Once the products have been designed, they are produced by the contract manufacturer who buys the raw materials and transforms them into finished products based on the qualitative and quantitative instructions provided by the entrepreneur who, eventually, purchases all the finished products. The products are then sold to the distributor who sells them to end-customers. The management of the supply chain, including all logistics, is entirely supervised by the entrepreneur.

In the first scenario (Table 3.4), it is assumed that the group is in a start-up phase and sells its goods at very low prices. Its output to end-customers amounts to 100 (i.e., the distributor sells for 100 to end-customers), but the costs incurred across the value chain exceed 100, which means that the group is globally loss-making during this start-up phase. Yet each of the tested parties is remunerated according to the transfer pricing policy, something that results in the tested parties receiving the remuneration described above, and the entrepreneur accumulating losses. The outcome of this first scenario is illustrated in Table 3.4. Table 3.4 may be read in the following way: the output of the value chain corresponds to the sales made by the distributor. Such sales amount to 100. Since the transfer pricing policy commands that the distributor is remunerated on the basis of the resale price method and earns a gross margin of 25%, the COGS needs to amount to 75 in order to let the distributor earn the targeted gross margin of 25% of the sales. Since the distributor buys the goods from the entrepreneur, the same figure (75) is observed for the COGS of the distributor and for the turnover of the entrepreneur. Next, it is assumed that the contract manufacturer purchases raw materials for 60 and assumes OPEX amounting to 10; that is, the full costs of the contract manufacturer amount to 70 (60 + 10 = 70). Since the transfer pricing policy targets a FCM of 5%, the contract manufacturer needs to sell the finished goods to the entrepreneur for 73.5 (70 + 5% = 73.5). The turnover of the contract manufacturer corresponds to the COGS of the entrepreneur. Since both the turnover and the COGS of the entrepreneur are now known, it is possible to compute the gross margin of the entrepreneur. This gross margin amounts to 1.5 (75–73.5 = 1.5), which is an indication that the entrepreneur will be loss-making since it still has to support its OPEX as well as other (e.g., financial) expenses. When it comes to the contract R&D, the transfer pricing policy targets a FCM of 10%. The contract R&D supports only OPEX; i.e., it has no COGS. Since the total costs of the contract R&D amount to 20, it will charge 22 to the entrepreneur in order to achieve a FCM of 10% (20 + 10% = 22). As indicated above, it is assumed that the entrepreneur needs to support OPEX amounting to 50 to operate the whole value chain. Therefore, the R&D services purchased from the contract R&D add to the entrepreneur's own OPEX, which eventually amount to 72 (22 + 50 = 72). Under the first scenario, the group is in a start-up phase. The simplified income statement of the companies participating in the value chain is found below.

Table 3.4 Centralised Entrepreneur Model and Start-Up Phase

Post in the Income Statement	*Buy/Sell Distributor*	*Contract Manufacturer*	*Contract R&D*	*Entrepreneur*
Turnover	100	73.5	22	75
COGS	75	60	0	73.5
Gross margin	**25**	**13.5**	**22**	**1.5**
Gross margin %	25.0%	Not relevant	Not relevant	2.0%
OPEX	20	10	20	72
Net margin	**5**	**3.5**	**2**	**–70.5**
Net margin %	5%	Not relevant	Not relevant	–94%
FCM	Not relevant	5.0%	10.0%	Not relevant
Assumptions				
External sales: 100				
Targeted gross margin of the distributor: 25%				
Cost of production of the goods: 60				
OPEX contract manufacturer: 10				
Targeted FCM of contract manufacturer: 5%				
OPEX contract R&D: 20				
Targeted FCM of contract R&D: 10%				

Table 3.4 shows that each of the tested parties is remunerated according to the transfer pricing policy. The combined effect of the transfer pricing principles applied to all the intercompany transactions results in an accumulated loss of –70.5 that is supported by the entrepreneur, which is in line with the centralised entrepreneur model. Indeed, the group is in a start-up phase and does not cover all its costs by solely having an output of 100 (i.e., the sales made by the distributor – and thus, the group – to the end-customers). It is the entrepreneur that should support the losses incurred during this start-up phase since it is also the entrepreneur that provides capital, assumes and controls the relevant risks, and is responsible for the value chain by performing the key functions and making strategic decisions, such as the decision to start selling the products at very low prices in order to kick off the sales.

In the second scenario (Table 3.5), it is assumed that the group sells the same volume of products, but at higher prices as the market reacts positively to the products. Accordingly, the sales have increased to 200, all other parameters being the same.[155] The outcome of this second scenario is shown below.

Table 3.5 Centralised Entrepreneur Model with Higher Sales Prices

Post in the Income Statement	*Buy/Sell Distributor*	*Contract Manufacturer*	*Contract R&D*	*Entrepreneur*
Turnover	200	73.5	22	150
COGS	150	60	0	73.5
Gross margin	**50**	**13.5**	**22**	**76.5**
Gross margin %	25.0%	Not relevant	Not relevant	51.0%
OPEX	20	10	20	72
Net margin	**30**	**3.5**	**2**	**4.5**
Net margin %	15%	Not relevant	Not relevant	3.0%
FCM	Not relevant	5.0%	10.0%	Not relevant
Assumptions				
External sales: 200				
Targeted gross margin of the distributor: 25%				
Cost of production of the goods: 60				

155. This example is simplified in order to emphasise the effects of the transfer pricing model on the profits earned – and thus also the taxes paid – by the participants to the value chain. The increase in sales to end-customers may also require higher costs, especially if higher volumes are produced and sold. However, for the sake of simplicity it is assumed in this example that the costs remain the same.

Post in the Income Statement	Buy/Sell Distributor	Contract Manufacturer	Contract R&D	Entrepreneur
OPEX contract manufacturer: 10				
Targeted FCM of contract manufacturer: 5%				
OPEX contract R&D: 20				
Targeted FCM of contract R&D: 10%				

Table 3.5 shows that when the sales to end-customers have increased to 200, the transfer prices of the goods will need to be increased in order to reach the targeted gross margin of the distributor (25%); if the transfer prices were not increased, the distributor would earn too high profits, and the entrepreneur would not benefit from the higher sales prices. This results in an increase of the COGS of the distributor and of the turnover of the entrepreneur (150 in Table 3.5, as opposed to 75 in Table 3.4). The income statements of the contract R&D and of the contract manufacturer are unchanged, and the break-even point (i.e., the profitability of the whole value chain) has been reached as the entrepreneur earns a profit of 4.5.

In the third scenario (Table 3.6), it is assumed that the prices of the goods have increased and reached maturity. The group's sales amount now to 300, all other parameters (especially volumes and costs) being the same. The outcome of the third scenario is shown below.

Table 3.6 Centralised Entrepreneur Model with Sales Prices at Maturity

Post in the Income Statement	*Buy/Sell Distributor*	*Contract Manufacturer*	*Contract R&D*	*Entrepreneur*
Turnover	300	73.5	22	225
COGS	225	60	0	73.5
Gross margin	**75**	**13.5**	**22**	**151.5**
Gross margin %	25.0%	Not relevant	Not relevant	67.3%
OPEX	20	10	20	72
Net margin	**55**	**3.5**	**2**	**79.5**
Net margin %	18,3%	Not relevant	Not relevant	35.3%
FCM	Not relevant	5.0%	10.0%	Not relevant
Assumptions				
External sales: 300				
Targeted gross margin of the distributor: 25%				

Post in the Income Statement	*Buy/Sell Distributor*	*Contract Manufacturer*	*Contract R&D*	*Entrepreneur*
Cost of production of the goods: 60				
OPEX contract manufacturer: 10				
Targeted FCM of contract manufacturer: 5%				
OPEX contract R&D: 20				
Targeted FCM of contract R&D: 10%				

Table 3.6 shows that the great increase in the sales benefits essentially the entrepreneur, who now earns a net margin of 79.5. The manufacturer and the researcher are not impacted by this increase, as they support the same costs and earn the same profits as in the past. The distributor earns a higher gross margin in absolute terms as the sales have increased; however, the gross margin in relative terms remains unchanged and in line with the transfer pricing policy (i.e., a 25% gross margin). The net margin of the distributor has increased throughout the three scenarios, as the distributor is remunerated on the basis of a targeted gross margin and supports similar OPEX.[156]

This example shows that it is the entrepreneur that accumulated losses in the start-up phase and excess profits when the sales increased. On the other hand, the tested parties earned stable profits when the value chain was both loss-making and profitable. The volatility of the profits of the entrepreneur and the stable profits earned by the tested parties are in line with the functional profile of the parties since the entrepreneur is entitled to the residual profits (but also to risks of losses) while the tested parties are only entitled to routine profits that match their routine functions.

156. As indicated above, this example is simplified; the distributor would often incur higher operating expenses as the sales increase.

CHAPTER 4
Cross-Border Business Restructurings

This chapter provides an introduction to the topic of cross-border business restructurings from a transfer pricing perspective (section 4.1), a presentation of some frequent types of restructurings implying a centralisation of functions, risks and/or assets (section 4.2), and a discussion about situations where a business restructuring may give rise to the payment of compensation between the restructured entities (section 4.3).

4.1 INTRODUCTION

Transfer pricing issues often arise when multinational enterprises modify their value chain across borders, i.e., when functions, risks, and/or assets are moved from one group company situated in one country to another group company situated in another country. Such modifications of the value chain are described, for transfer pricing purposes, as 'business restructurings'.

A cross-border business restructuring is defined in the OECD Guidelines as a 'cross-border reorganisation of the commercial or financial relations between associated enterprises, including the termination or substantial renegotiation of existing arrangements'.[1] In many cases, business restructurings imply the centralisation of intangibles, risks, or functions with the profit potential attached to them,[2] but other types of business restructurings exist. As with any intercompany transaction, cross-border business restructurings must be priced in accordance with the arm's length principle. This supposes that a restructuring transaction is priced at arm's length, and that it is the best option realistically available to each party.[3] In

1. *See* para. 9.1 of the 2022 OECD Guidelines.
2. *See* para. 9.2 of the 2022 OECD Guidelines.
3. Indeed, associated enterprises are expected to enter into a transaction only 'if it does not make them worse off than their next best option' (*see* para. 9.27 of the 2022 OECD Guidelines). This requirement applies to each company, as opposed to several companies taken together. For an analysis of the concept 'options realistically available' *see* Danny Oosterhoff and Bo Wingerter,

addition, as with any transfer pricing issue, restructuring transactions have to be supported by sufficient substance,[4] documented in accordance with the applicable transfer pricing documentation requirements, and they are subject in certain cases to reporting obligations.[5] Even if all business restructurings do not necessarily lead to complex transfer pricing issues, in many cases, business restructurings lead to disputes, something that is at least partly due to the twofold types of transfer pricing considerations that may be triggered by a business restructuring. On the one hand, the very restructuring transaction may need to be priced at arm's length; on the other hand, the responsibilities within a group might be reallocated as a consequence of the restructuring, something that may affect the transfer prices of future transactions. Therefore, since there are several transfer pricing aspects related to business restructurings and that such aspects may lead to disputes, business restructurings are often subject to dispute prevention mechanisms such as APAs.[6]

Let us illustrate the definition of a cross-border business restructuring according to the OECD Guidelines by an example where a group outsources a manufacturing function to a subsidiary in a country where the cost of labour is lower. This example illustrates also the need for the countries concerned by the restructuring to ensure that it has been carried out at arm's length.

Example: A group outsources a manufacturing function to a subsidiary in a country where the cost of labour is lower

Company A (resident in State A) manufactures trucks in State A. To decrease its manufacturing costs, the group decides to outsource the manufacturing of trucks to subsidiary B (resident in State B), where the cost of labour is lower. The fact that the manufacturing function is no longer performed by company A but by company B is a business restructuring, as at least one function (i.e., the manufacturing of trucks) has been transferred from company A to company B. In addition, other functions, risks, and/or assets may also have been transferred, such as the production risk or the manufacturing intangibles necessary to this production process. As a consequence of this business restructuring, the transfer prices of future intercompany transactions and the profit margins of the companies concerned may be affected, especially given the lower risks and lower profit potential of company A (who stops manufacturing trucks), and the corresponding higher risks and higher profit potential of company B (who starts manufacturing trucks). As a result, States A and B need to ensure that the restructuring as such has been carried out at arm's length and that the future transfer prices or profit margins are in line with the arm's length principle, so that the business restructuring does not illegitimately erode their tax base.

The New OECD Guidelines: The Good, the Bad and the Ugly, vol. 18, issue 2, 110 (International Transfer Pricing Journal, March/April 2011).

4. On the application of the substance requirement to cross-border business restructurings, *see* section 5.3 of this book.
5. On transfer pricing documentation requirements, *see* section 7.1.1 of this book. On mandatory disclosure, *see* section 7.1.3 of this book.
6. *See* section 7.2.1 of this book for a presentation of advance pricing arrangements.

Multinational enterprises need to constantly adapt to the international context of their business activities. Accordingly, a business restructuring implying the transformation of the value chain may have different purposes[7] and be driven, e.g., by cost reductions,[8] tax savings,[9] the willingness to reach new markets,[10] or the need to centralise the control of the value chain.[11] A reorganisation or a reconsideration of the value chain may also be relevant following a merger or acquisition process since two different business models may have to be adapted to one another.[12]

Cross-border business restructurings often give rise to complex transfer pricing issues, as such transactions do not imply the sole sale of a good or a service but rather the transfer of an activity: a business restructuring may imply the transfer of a combination of goods (e.g., an inventory), intangible assets (e.g., patents and know-how), functions (e.g., the right to make strategic decisions), risks (e.g., the assumption of responsibilities or the need to provide funding), and persons (e.g., people qualified for a certain task). Although in most cases it will be virtually impossible to find a comparable uncontrolled transaction, business restructurings still need to abide by the arm's length principle. Therefore, multinational enterprises and tax administrations need to analyse the restructuring at hand and figure out a methodology to arrive at the terms (often including the payment of compensation) that independent parties would have agreed on for a comparable uncontrolled transaction.

It should also be emphasised that the transfer pricing issues raised by business restructurings have a strong connection with the operations within multinational enterprises, something that may result in a conflict between tax and operational considerations.[13] Changes to the value chain may happen as a consequence of a management decision that intends to modify the operations, in which case the transfer pricing policy within the group will have to adapt to the operational changes. In such situations, the tax and transfer pricing issues triggered by the business restructuring

7. *See* Heinz-Klaus Kroppen and José Carlos Silva, General Report, Cahiers de Droit Fiscal International, *Cross-Border Business Restructuring*, vol. 96a (2011).
8. In particular, it should be emphasised that competition often presses prices down. This creates a need to face competition through different means such as reducing costs.
9. A business restructuring is often accompanied by a reallocation of profits within a group, thus potentially implying a reallocation of the corporate income taxes paid by a multinational enterprise.
10. For example, a group may be willing to move its manufacturing or warehousing activities closer to the new markets it wishes to reach.
11. For example, a group may wish to concentrate control over its worldwide manufacturing at the level of a single entity, to achieve similar standards of quality.
12. Such a restructuring may be relevant if, for example, a multinational enterprise acquires an independent manufacturer that has developed and owns valuable product and process intangibles. Given the development and the ownership of such product and process intangibles, the manufacturer may be qualified as a fully fledged manufacturer. However, after the acquisition, the multinational enterprise may be willing to integrate the acquired manufacturer to its value chain and convert it to a contract manufacturer, for example, if the group has implemented a centralised entrepreneur model. Also, the group may wish to let other group companies use the product and process intangibles; therefore, the group may consider moving the intangibles owned by the acquired company to a central location in the group, for example, the entrepreneur or an IP company.
13. *See* section 3.1. of this book for a presentation of the interactions between taxes and the operations within a multinational enterprise.

may be perceived as secondary by the management of the group, whereas the tax administrations of the countries concerned will be keen on ensuring that the operational changes have been carried out at arm's length. In other cases, a business restructuring may be tax driven, which would require that the operations are amended accordingly in order for the restructuring supported by the right substance.[14] In certain cases, a change to the value chain may be considered together from a tax and operational perspective; however, it may be difficult to fully satisfy the two perspectives, as what is optimal from an operational point of view may trigger transfer pricing risks,[15] tax risks[16] or an increased tax burden, whereas what mitigates tax risks and decreases the tax burden may be inefficient, difficult to implement in practice, or too costly. Therefore, a conflict may appear between the tax and operational considerations relating to changes to the value chain.

Last, a key question when it comes to cross-border business restructurings is the tax savings that may be achieved. Business restructurings may indeed result in the tax base being moved as a consequence of the shift of functions, risks, and/or assets; when functions, risks, and/or assets are moved to a country with a lower corporate income tax rate, or a country where a favourable tax regime is available, the total tax burden may decrease. Conversely, moving functions, risks or assets to a country where the corporate income tax rate is higher may increase the total tax burden. Also, operational changes such as the implementation of the centralised entrepreneur model may decrease the total tax burden, for example, by letting the group be taxed on the net income incurred throughout the value chain, thanks to the consolidation effect of the centralised entrepreneur model.[17] The OECD Guidelines consider this issue in a twofold manner.[18] On the one hand, it is clearly stated that tax savings may be achieved and should be accepted by tax administrations, even if decreasing the tax burden is the purpose of a business restructuring; on the other hand, tax savings should be accepted only when a business restructuring has been carried out at arm's length, something that supposes that the restructuring is supported by the right substance.[19]

14. *See* Chapter 5 of this book for a presentation of the notion of substance.
15. For example, the payment of a compensation upon the transfer of an intangible asset may give rise to a transfer pricing reassessment, either in the country of the transferor (if the price is deemed too low) or in the country of the transferee (if the price is deemed too high).
16. For example, the operational changes following a cross-border business restructuring may imply a risk for CFC taxation or minimum taxation (e.g., if operations are moved to a low-tax jurisdiction), withholding taxes (e.g., if payments are subject to taxes at source), or the existence of a permanent establishment (e.g., if a group company starts playing an important role in the conclusion of contracts by another company).
17. For a description of the centralised entrepreneur model, *see* above section 3.4.7 of this book.
18. For a discussion on the tax arbitrage effect that may result from transfer pricing, *see* above section 1.5 of this book.
19. *See* para. 9.34 of the 2022 OECD Guidelines, and para. 8.1.1.4 of the 2021 UN Manual.

4.2 FREQUENT TYPES OF CROSS-BORDER BUSINESS RESTRUCTURINGS

As transfer pricing issues may arise upon any modification of the value chain across the borders implying a redeployment by a multinational enterprise of functions, assets, and/or risks, each business restructuring is unique and has to be considered according to the facts and circumstances of the case. There may be different types of business restructurings; for example, certain groups may consider centralising functions, risks, and/or assets in order to achieve the effects of the centralised entrepreneur model or make synergies from an operational point of view, while other groups may be willing to spread important functions in order to move decision centres close to their customers. Another example is the case where there is a need to open or close a factory, or to move a warehouse to a strategic region. Certain business restructurings are more business-driven, while others may be more tax driven.

The very existence of a business restructuring, i.e., the recognition of the restructuring as a transaction that may have transfer pricing consequences, is not always obvious. For example, there may be cases where the functions performed by one company are taken over by another company, cases where risks are being shifted from one company to the other, or cases where an employee keeps being employed by a company but moves to another country from where he/she continues to work, which could easily trigger disagreements between multinational enterprises and tax administrations, the former arguing that no restructuring has taken place and the latter stating the opposite. On the other hand, there may be situations where a restructuring is claimed, without this being necessarily true; an example would be the situation where a group claims the shift of a group company from being highly exposed to risks to having only a limited risk exposure,[20] whereas the functions necessary for the management and control of the risks have not been moved accordingly.

Despite the potential diversity of cross-border business restructurings, certain types of restructurings are frequently carried out by multinational enterprises, in particular in order to implement the centralised entrepreneur model. Such a business restructuring may be motivated not only by tax savings but also by purely operational reasons such as the need to concentrate the most important activities in a central location.[21] Such restructurings may also occur as a consequence of the acquisition of shares in a group of companies: the acquired group is organised in a certain manner, which the buyer may need to adapt to its own organisation.[22]

Below is an example where three important elements of the value chain of numerous multinational enterprises (R&D, manufacturing, and distribution) are subject to business restructurings carried out with the objective of implementing the centralised entrepreneur model. It is assumed that a fully fledged researcher is

20. This claim may be motivated by the lower profit potential of a company with a lower risk profile.
21. In this respect, *see* above section 3.4.7 for a presentation of the centralised entrepreneur model.
22. A typical example of such restructurings is when the IP of the acquired group is transferred to the headquarters of the acquiring group. As a consequence, the functional profile of certain acquired high-risk entities would need to be amended to let the acquiring headquarters take over certain important functions and risks.

converted to a contract R&D, a fully fledged manufacturer is converted to a contract manufacturer or a toll manufacturer, and a fully fledged distributor is converted to a buy/sell distributor or a commissionaire. With respect to these three functions, it is assumed that the entrepreneur takes over the important functions and risks. These three types of cross-border business restructurings are discussed in the following paragraphs, together with some of the difficulties that these reorganisations may imply.

The conversion of a fully fledged researcher to a contract R&D implies that IP will, in most cases, not be developed by the converted company after the business restructuring, but by the company that took over the strategic functions and risk assumptions, i.e., the entrepreneur. An example of conversion of a fully fledged researcher to a contract R&D is the situation where a company, active only in one country, has developed a successful IP that has the potential to sell in other countries. The management of the company may not have expected such a success and may, accordingly, be willing to locate the principal role – and thus also the residual profits – in another jurisdiction. In such a case, it will be utterly important to ensure that the company that takes over the principal role has the right substance. This may become a complex issue if no people have moved from the former fully fledged researcher to the entrepreneur: the multinational enterprise may argue that the strategic functions are performed by the entrepreneur, whereas the tax administration of the country of departure may argue that since no people moved, the functions are in reality still performed in this country. Therefore, the competence relating to the actual R&D of the personnel employed by the entrepreneur (whether people have moved, have been hired, or if the proper competence already existed before taking over the principal role) will be key for this reorganisation to be in line with the arm's length principle.

In order to convert a fully fledged manufacturer to a contract manufacturer or a toll manufacturer, the important functions and risks formerly assumed by the fully fledged manufacturer will be taken over by the entrepreneur, who will also be attributed the residual income generated by the manufacturing function. In addition to the functions and risks being moved to the entrepreneur, the ownership of the inventory of raw material, semi-finished goods and finished products may also need to be moved to the entrepreneur, which would typically be the case upon the conversion to a toll manufacturer.[23] An example of such a conversion is the case where a multinational enterprise has acquired a competitor that owns a manufacturing intangible that would be useful to the products manufactured by the buyer: the IP owned by the former fully fledged manufacturer would typically be transferred to the entrepreneur who would then own the old IP and the newly developed IP, the combination of which could be used in other parts of the buyer's business activities. Together with the IP, the functions, risks, and tangible assets that should not be attributed to the contract manufacturer or a toll manufacturer would also be transferred

23. This is because a toll manufacturer shall not own raw materials or stocks of (semi-) finished goods. The transfer of the ownership of raw material, semi-finished and finished goods, which does not need to imply a physical transfer of goods as the legal transfer of ownership implies a shift in risks and costs, consists in a sale of tangible assets that needs to be carried out at market value.

to the entrepreneur. The substance supporting the functions performed and risks assumed by the entrepreneur will be a critical issue, e.g., with respect to the technical competence of the personnel employed by the entrepreneur with matters such as the purchase of raw materials, manufacturing know-how, production and stock planning, or logistics.

The conversion of a fully fledged distributor to a buy/sell distributor or a commissionaire implies, similarly to the examples above, a significant change to the functional profile of the distributor through a shift in the exposure to the economic outcome of the distribution activity to the entrepreneur. Here it may be particularly critical to analyse the possible existence of marketing intangibles such as trade names or lists of clients (which will need to be sold to the entrepreneur, thereby possibly giving rise to capital gains taxation in the country of the former fully fledged distributor), and the transfer of risks such as inventory risk or credit risk, especially if a former distributor is restructured to a commissionaire that no longer sells goods to clients and owns inventory. As with other types of business restructurings, the right substance will be expected from the entity taking over certain risks and functions.

The business restructurings described above, as other types of business restructurings, may imply operational changes that affect positively or negatively the profitability of a multinational enterprise as a whole. For example, *synergies* may be achieved, thanks to the increased purchasing power of a centralised purchasing function, or *location savings* may be derived, thanks to, e.g., moving manufacturing activities to a place where labour costs are lower. In both cases, the operational changes (i.e., centralising the purchasing function or moving the manufacturing activities) may have an impact on the global profitability of the group. This raises the question of whether or not the positive or negative effects of a business restructuring such as synergies or locations savings should be shared among the members of a group, and if so, how and to what extent. No single answer to this question is provided by the OECD Guidelines, the recommendation being to apply the arm's length principle to business restructurings in the same way as for other types of intercompany transactions.[24] The revisions to the Guidelines made as part of the BEPS project provide a similar answer, with some specific guidance with respect to both location savings[25]

---

24. *See* para. 9.9 of the 2022 OECD Guidelines.
25. *See* para. 1.161 of the 2022 OECD Guidelines: 'in determining how location savings are to be shared between two or more associated enterprises, it is necessary to consider (i) whether location savings exist; (ii) the amount of any location savings; (iii) the extent to which location savings are either retained by a member or members of the MNE group or are passed on to independent customers or suppliers; and (iv) where location savings are not fully passed on to independent customers or suppliers, the manner in which independent enterprises operating under similar circumstances would allocate any retained net location savings'. When location savings exist and are not fully passed on to customers, such location savings should be primarily taken into account based on the comparability analysis; when the comparability analysis has identified comparable companies or transactions in the local market, no specific adjustments for location savings would be needed as the financial information for the comparables already takes into account the existence of the location savings (para. 1.162 of the 2022 OECD Guidelines).

and group synergies.[26] The guidance with respect to synergies is illustrated with the example below.

Example: Corporate synergies achieved thanks to a centralised purchasing function

As mentioned above, synergies may be achieved thanks to the increased purchasing power of a centralised purchasing function. Here it is assumed that company X is the central purchaser of products for the members of a multinational enterprise. It is also assumed that the list price of the products is 100, and that thanks to the high volumes ordered by company X on behalf of its associated enterprises, it manages to buy the products for 70. In other words, the bargaining power of company X enables a cost saving of 30 (100–70 = 30). It is assumed that the central purchasing function is remunerated on a cost-plus basis, and that an arm's length profit mark-up of 5 is charged by company X for each product purchased on behalf of its associated enterprises. This leaves a synergy amounting to 25 (30–5 = 25) to share among the associated enterprises. How to share this saving? The OECD Guidelines recommend taking into account synergistic benefits that arise because of deliberate concerted group actions. In this case, there is a deliberate concerted group action since the associated enterprises decided to centralise their purchasing function and delegate it to company X. Therefore, the synergy benefit must be taken into account and shared among the associated enterprises. The OECD Guidelines further recommend sharing such benefits in proportion to the contributions of the group members to the achievement of the synergies. In this case, the only contribution of the associated enterprises was the volume purchased. Therefore, the saving per product should be spread in proportion to the products purchased by each associated enterprise.

The issue of the positive or negative effects achieved, thanks to operational changes, is also important from the perspective of developing countries. Indeed, developing countries may provide the opportunity to increase the global profitability (e.g., thanks to lower production costs) without being able to tax such an increased profitability; this is because the OECD Guidelines tend to allocate the gains to the high-risk-taking entities that have developed intangibles such as entrepreneurs, which may not be located in a developing country.[27] Therefore, location savings are an issue where there may typically be differences of views between developed and developing countries.[28]

26. *See* para. 1.182 of the 2022 OECD Guidelines, where it is recommended to take into account for transfer pricing purposes certain synergistic benefits that arise because of deliberate concerted group actions, by sharing the benefits of the synergies in proportion to the contributions of the group members to the achievement of the synergies. This means that synergies are not, per se, considered as IP for transfer pricing purposes, since they may not be owned or controlled by a given company (*see* para. 6.30 of the 2022 OECD Guidelines). In this respect, it has been argued that 'Synergies are *consequences* which may (or may not) be derived from the use of several assets in combination' (*see* Caroline Silberztein, Mary C. Bennett and Gregg D. Lemein, *The OECD Discussion Draft on the Transfer of Intangibles (Revision of Chapter VI of the OECD Transfer Pricing Guidelines): Main Comments*, vol. 41, issue 2, 60–65, 61 (Intertax, 2013)).
27. *See Spillovers in International Corporate Taxation*, IMF Policy Paper, 33, para. 52 (9 May 2014).
28. *See*, e.g., para. 2.20.8 of the 2021 UN Manual (Part D): 'certain issues such as location savings and market premium arise more frequently in China and other developing economies, rather than in established and developed economies'. For a concrete example of how location savings

Last, it should be emphasised that cross-border business restructurings may raise other issues than transfer pricing ones, in particular with regard to the possible existence of a permanent establishment of a principal in the country of the converted entity. The risk indeed exists that the functions performed and risks assumed by the converted entity are considered as creating a permanent establishment for the principal, when the converted entity acts on behalf of the principal. This issue is not specific to business restructurings; i.e., it may also arise when an entity is given a certain functional profile as from its setup, but the issue may be exacerbated by business restructurings that are driven by tax planning considerations that rely on an extensive interpretation of the permanent establishment concept.[29]

Whether or not a cross-border business restructuring may give rise to the payment of compensation between the restructured entities is discussed below.

4.3 SHOULD A CROSS-BORDER BUSINESS RESTRUCTURING GIVE RISE TO THE PAYMENT OF COMPENSATION BETWEEN THE RESTRUCTURED ENTITIES?

Cross-border business restructurings is a complex topic since a balance has to be reached between two diverging interests: on the one hand, multinational enterprises should be free to organise their business activities and achieve tax savings, as long as certain conditions are fulfilled. On the other hand, the tax administrations of the countries involved should be able to make sure that their tax base is not illegitimately eroded and prevent situations of tax avoidance.[30]

In order to strike that balance, a whole chapter in the OECD Guidelines is dedicated to the issue of business restructurings. Chapter 9 of the OECD Guidelines contains recommendations as to how to address certain forms of tax avoidance while still remaining within the realm of the arm's length principle. However, not all countries fully follow the recommendations in Chapter 9, and some may apply anti-avoidance rules to business restructurings that are deemed abusive.

The recommendation in the OECD Guidelines is to apply the arm's length principle to cross-border business restructurings in the same way as it applies to other types of intercompany transactions.[31] This means that a business restructuring does not constitute, as such, an act of tax avoidance (even if a business restructuring implies

may be taken into consideration, *see* para. 2.20.15 of the 2021 UN Manual (Part D); *see also* the description of the computation of the profit mark-up for a contract R&D in China in Glenn DeSouza, *What the UN Manual Really Means for China?*, vol. 41, issue 5, 331 (Intertax, 2013), where it is explained that the median full cost mark-up might be increased by 50% in order to account for a location saving of 50%. For the perspective of India *see* Pankaj Jain and Vikram Chand, *Location Savings: International and Indian Perspective*, vol. 43, issue 2, 192–198 (Intertax, 2015).

29. For example, the permanent establishment threshold may be avoided by relying on the list of exceptions provided by tax treaties drafted on the basis of Art. 5(4) of the former versions of the OECD and UN Model Tax Conventions.
30. In this respect, *see* Michael C. Durst, *Fixing Double Nontaxation under the Transfer Pricing Guidelines*, 839–842 (Tax Notes International, 28 May 2012).
31. *See* para. 9.9 of the 2022 OECD Guidelines.

lower profits in a given country), and that a restructuring should not trigger – from a transfer pricing perspective – other reactions than a normal application of the arm's length principle. Accordingly, a transfer of functions, risks and/or assets implied by a business restructuring between associated enterprises has to be carried out under the same conditions as between independent enterprises. This may require compensation to be paid from one party to the other. Indeed, in certain cases, independent enterprises may not accept significant changes in their business operations without being appropriately compensated.[32] Therefore, from a transfer pricing perspective, one of the core issues connected to cross-border business restructurings consists in assessing whether or not compensation has to be paid to the entities negatively affected by the restructuring.[33] Such compensation may be taxed in the country of the recipient and deducted in the country of the payor, depending on the domestic tax law that applies.

According to the OECD Guidelines, the payment of compensation between associated enterprises may be expected in two situations: the transfer of something of value between the parties (section 4.3.1), and the termination or substantial renegotiation of existing arrangements (section 4.3.2).

4.3.1 Has Something of Value Been Transferred from One Company to Another Company?

The OECD Guidelines indicate that the arm's length principle may require the payment of compensation (and thus the potential taxation of such compensation in the country of the recipient) when 'something of value' has been transferred from one company to another. Indeed, an independent company would not accept getting rid of something valuable without receiving appropriate compensation.

The definition of 'something of value' in the OECD Guidelines is, on purpose, quite vague, so as to cover different situations where compensation should be paid under the arm's length principle as a consequence of a business restructuring. By 'something of value', the OECD Guidelines refer to tangible assets (e.g., inventory or a machine), intangible assets (e.g., a patent, a brand or a secret formula) and ongoing concerns (which are defined as 'a functioning, economically integrated business unit').[34,35] The definition of something of value may be a complex matter, and a deep

32. For example, assume that an independent company has successfully developed an IT platform that generates high profits. This company may sell the IT platform to another company that will pursue the development of the platform and earn the corresponding profits, in exchange for the payment of a given price. The same goes between associated enterprises, and in this case the transferor will be expected to have sold to the transferee the assets connected to the IT platform at an arm's length price.
33. Other transfer pricing issues may arise as a consequence of a business restructuring, particularly the remuneration of the entities post-restructuring, the valuation of assets (both tangible and intangible), and the recognition of the business restructuring for taxation purposes. In addition to transfer pricing aspects, cross-border business restructurings give rise to other issues within areas such as corporate income tax (e.g., CFC taxation, withholding taxes, the possible existence of a permanent establishment, etc.), value-added taxation, or customs duties. Such issues are outside the scope of this book.
34. *See* para. 9.68 of the 2022 OECD Guidelines.
35. *See* paras 9.48 and following of the 2022 OECD Guidelines.

analysis of this concept is outside the scope of this book.[36] However, it is important to emphasise that in principle the sole transfer of functions and/or risks does not, as such, give rise to the payment of compensation, as the OECD Guidelines exclude the taxation of deemed compensation for the decrease in the expected profits of a company due to the transfer of a profitable function or the transfer of some risks.[37] Indeed, a profit potential is normally associated with a certain level of risk and volatility: although the transfer of a function may imply a lower remuneration, at the same time, a lower level of risk may be expected from the restructured entity. Therefore, in most cases, no exit tax on a deemed compensation will be levied by the country of the transferor upon a mere transfer of functions and/or risks. The example below illustrates the situation where a function and the risks related to the function are transferred, with no need – according solely to the OECD Guidelines – for the transferee to pay compensation to the transferor.

Example: The transfer of functions and risks for foreign exchange activities does not give rise to a taxable event

Assume that the part of the treasury function of a multinational enterprise relating to foreign exchange activities is moved from company A (resident in country A) to company B (resident in country B), together with the assumption of certain risks connected with this function (e.g., the risk of currency losses). After the business restructuring, the profits (foreign exchange gains) and losses (foreign exchange losses) related to that part of the treasury function will no longer be attributable to company A and be taxable (in case of profits) in country A, as both the functions and the risks have been moved to company B. But since nothing in addition to the functions and risks have been transferred – in particular nothing of value such as an asset, nor the whole treasury department – the application of the OECD Guidelines would normally result in no compensation being paid by the transferee to the transferor. Conversely, a compensation might be needed in case of transfer of ongoing concern, i.e., a 'functioning, economically integrated business unit', especially if it includes assets and liabilities.[38]

In contrast to the example above, if something of value is attached to the functions and/or the risks transferred, compensation may have to be paid and taxes may be levied on such compensation. This may be the case if the function that is transferred (e.g., a person responsible for R&D within a group) has resulted in the creation of an intangible such as know-how that would follow the person transferred through being used by the transferee. Something of value is also at hand when an

36. For a deeper analysis, *see* Heinz-Klaus Kroppen and José Carlos Silva, General Report, Cahiers de Droit Fiscal International, *Cross-Border Business Restructuring*, vol. 96a, 32–49 (2011); Anuschka J. Bakker (ed.), *Transfer Pricing and Business Restructurings: Streamlining All the Way*, 66–74 (IBFD, 2009).
37. *See* particularly para. 9.39 of the 2022 OECD Guidelines. However, some countries are of the opinion that the transfer of functions or risks may give rise to a taxable event: *see* Heinz-Klaus Kroppen and José Carlos Silva, General Report, Cahiers de Droit Fiscal International, *Cross-Border Business Restructuring*, vol. 96a, 32–49 (2011).
38. *See* para. 9.68 of the 2022 OECD Guidelines.

employee is transferred to a company that would, if it were independent, have to support costs such as recruitment or training costs in order to recruit a person with similar competence; something of value would then be transferred, namely the costs savings achieved, thanks to recruiting personnel already trained. To identify whether or not something of value has been transferred as part of a business restructuring, the OECD Guidelines recommend performing two functional analyses: one reflecting the situation pre-restructuring, and the other reflecting the situation post-restructuring.[39] This approach will indeed allow identification of what exactly has changed through the restructuring, as illustrated by the example below.

Example: A parent company sets up an IP company to manage a group's intangibles

Assume that a parent company resident in State A has a subsidiary resident in State B. The parent company acts as a principal, and the subsidiary acts as contract R&D. The principal purchases R&D services from the subsidiary and remunerates the contract R&D on the basis of a FCM. Assume that the intangibles developed by the group are highly profitable and that the group decides to set up an IP company in a country with a lower tax rate (State C) to manage future R&D activities and future intangibles from that country, and have intangible-related returns connected to future R&D activities taxed in State C. Figure 4.1 shows the transfer pricing model before the business restructuring ('setup pre-restructuring'), and Figure 4.2 shows the transfer pricing model after the business restructuring ('setup post-restructuring').

Figure 4.1 Setup Pre-restructuring

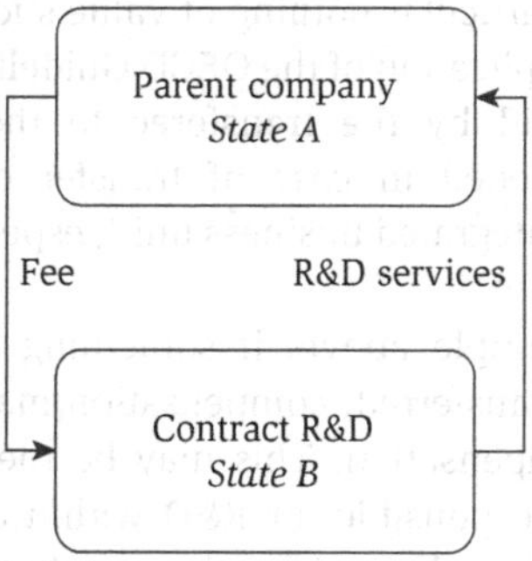

39. *See* paras 9.18, 9.21, 9.103 and 9.121 of the 2022 OECD Guidelines.

Figure 4.2 Setup Post-restructuring

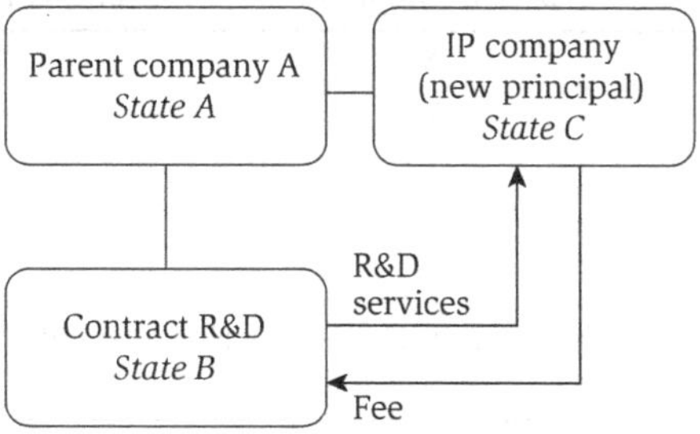

In the above example, the restructuring needs a transfer of the supervision of future R&D activities together with the control of risks related to such activities, from the parent company to the IP company, for such a restructuring to be recognised by the tax administration of State A. The new IP that will be developed from the business restructuring (which may be referred to as the 'new intangible') should be owned by the IP company, assuming that this company has the proper substance and effectively exercises the role of a principal; in this respect, the IP company should especially perform the DEMPE functions and risk control functions related to the new intangible. At the same time, the restructuring does not imply the transfer of the intangibles developed before the restructuring (which may be referred to as the 'old intangible'). Therefore, at first sight, no compensation should be paid by the IP company to the parent company upon the business restructuring, as solely certain functions and risks have been transferred, with no transfer of assets or ongoing concern. The intangibles developed after the transfer of functions and risks (i.e., the 'new intangible') will be owned by the IP company, while the 'old intangible' will still be owned by the parent company. This means that the profits connected to the 'old intangible' will still be earned and taxed in State A, while the profits connected to the 'new intangible' will be earned and taxed in State C. This situation may give rise to complex issues when attempting to distinguish the 'new intangible' from the 'old intangible', especially if the 'old intangible' and the 'new intangible' are used together. Issues may also arise for distinguishing DEMPE and risk control functions related to the old and the new intangible: for example, has the IP company the right competence, experience, and power to make independent decisions in relation to the new intangible? Are the DEMPE and risk control functions of the parent company involved in the supervision of the new intangible? If functions performed by the parent company are in reality used for the supervision of the development of the new intangible, the parent company will likely be deemed to have rights in the new intangible, and the business restructuring will probably lead to a dispute.

The business restructuring described above, implying the sole transfer of functions and risks (i.e., excluding the old intangible), is illustrated below by two functional analyses, i.e., one functional analysis performed pre-restructuring (Table 4.1) and one functional analysis performed post-restructuring (Table 4.2).[40]

40. A cross ('X') indicates that a function, risk, or asset is attributable to a given company.

Table 4.1 Functional Analysis Pre-restructuring

Functions/Risks/Assets	*Parent Company*	*Contract R&D*	*IP Company*
General management	X		
Supervision R&D	X		
Contract R&D activities		X	
R&D risk	X		
'old intangible'	X		
'new intangible'	Not relevant	Not relevant	Not relevant

Table 4.1 illustrates the functional analysis pre-restructuring. The IP company has no functions, risk, or assets, and the contract R&D performs only the routine R&D functions. No 'new intangible' exists yet. Table 4.2 shows that after the restructuring, the IP company has taken over the supervision of the R&D functions and assumes the risks thereof in relation to the new intangible, something that results in owning the 'new intangible'. However, the parent company still owns the 'old intangible'.

Table 4.2 Functional Analysis Post-restructuring

Functions/Risks/Assets	*Parent Company*	*Contract R&D*	*IP Company*
General management	X		
Supervision R&D old intangible	X		
Supervision R&D new intangible			X
Contract R&D activities		X	
R&D risk old intangible	X		
R&D risk new intangible			X
'old intangible'	X		
'new intangible'			X

In contrast to the alternative described above, the restructuring may imply, in addition to functions and risks, the transfer of the 'old intangible' from the parent company to the IP company. This is likely to be characterised as something of value, in which case compensation should be paid, after valuation,[41] by the IP company to the

41. It is indeed necessary to determine the value of what is transferred, to establish the price that should be paid upon the transfer. Such a valuation is complex and has to be sufficiently realistic. In that respect, the OECD makes it clear that a profit potential is not, as such, an asset. Therefore, the tax administration of the State of departure (if something of value is transferred from one group company to another) should not expect the transferor to receive a payment corresponding to all the future profits that may have been earned in the absence of a transfer. Instead, compensation is normally limited to the value of what is transferred at the time of the transfer. On valuation techniques for IP, *see* paras 6.153 and following of the 2022 OECD Guidelines. There may be numerous types of disagreements on the valuation upon a transfer. This may

parent company. The parent company may then be taxed on a capital gain, if the compensation received upon the transfer exceeds the acquisition cost of the 'old intangible', depending on the domestic law rules of the State of departure. The transfer of the 'old intangible' may enable an optimised taxation of the future profits attributable to the intangibles since both the 'old intangible' and the 'new intangible' will be owned by the IP company. This does not mean, however, that the business restructuring will necessarily be tax-efficient: an exit tax should be levied in State A for the transfer of the old intangible, and it is only if the tax savings on future intangible-related returns are higher than the exit tax that the business restructuring will be tax-efficient. Moreover, risks of disputes and double taxation exist, both for the valuation of the old intangible and the issue of substance: the IP company will especially need to perform all DEMPE and risk control functions related to both the old and the new intangible, with no involvement of the parent company in strategic matters. If the IP company does not have the proper competence and independence in decision-making, State A (where a profit drop will be observed since the old intangible has moved) may deem the parent company to still have rights in the intangibles, or even disregard the whole business restructuring.

A business restructuring implying the transfer of functions, risks, and the 'old intangible' may be illustrated by the following functional analyses pre-restructuring (Table 4.3) and post-restructuring (Table 4.4).

Table 4.3 Functional Analysis Pre-restructuring

Functions/Risks/Assets	*Parent Company*	*Contract R&D*	*IP Company*
General management	X		
Supervision R&D	X		
Contract R&D activities		X	
R&D risk	X		
'old intangible'	X		
'new intangible'	Not relevant	Not relevant	Not relevant

In Table 4.3, the IP company has no functions, risk, or assets, as the functional analysis is done pre-restructuring. If functions, risks, and the old intangible are transferred to the IP company, both the old and the new intangible will be concentrated post-restructuring in the hands of the IP company, which also supervises the R&D, and assumes the risks thereof (Table 4.4).

concern, for example, the profitability of future operations, or the period of time for which future cash flows need to be taken into account for valuation purposes. For example, in certain cases there may not be clear limitations to that period of time, potentially resulting in expectations of perpetual future profits: *see* Andreas Riedl and Tyll Stechmann, *Germany: Valuation of Business Restructurings in Germany – Part I – Economic Life of Businesses*, vol. 29, issue 3, 161–172 (International Transfer Pricing Journal, 2022); Andreas Riedl and Tyll Stechmann, *Germany: Valuation of Business Restructurings in Germany – Part II – Economic Life of Intangible Assets*, vol. 29, issue 4, 247–252 (International Transfer Pricing Journal, 2022).

Table 4.4 Functional Analysis Post-restructuring Including Transfer of 'Old Intangible'

Functions/Risks/Assets	*Parent Company*	*Contract R&D*	*IP Company*
General management	X		
Supervision R&D old intangible			X
Supervision R&D new intangible			X
Contract R&D activities		X	
R&D risk old intangible			X
R&D risk new intangible			X
'old intangible'			X
'new intangible'			X

In addition to identifying whether something of value has been transferred from one entity to another, the payment of compensation to restructured associated enterprises may be triggered by the termination or the substantial renegotiation of existing arrangements.

4.3.2 Does the Business Restructuring Involve the Termination or the Substantial Renegotiation of Existing Arrangements?

The renegotiation or the termination of an agreement between independent parties may be accompanied by the payment of compensation. For example, if the duration of a ten-year-long agreement is to be shortened, one of the parties may be disadvantaged by such an amendment and claim compensation to accept the new terms. Reasons for claiming compensation may be, e.g., the profits that were expected under the remaining duration of the agreement, the investments made by one of the parties in view of its legitimate expectations, or a particular clause of the agreement.

As a consequence of the arm's length principle, the same goes for associated enterprises. Therefore, the OECD Guidelines recommend considering whether compensation may have to be paid following the termination or the substantial renegotiation of existing arrangements. To this end, the 2022 OECD Guidelines encourage tax administrations and taxpayers to consider: (i) whether commercial law supports rights to indemnification for the restructured entity under the facts of the case, (ii) whether the existence or absence of an indemnification clause under the terms of the arrangement is arm's length, and (iii) which party should ultimately bear the costs related to the indemnification of the party that suffers from the termination or renegotiation of the agreement.[42]

42. *See* paras 9.75 and following of the 2022 OECD Guidelines.

CHAPTER 5
The Substance Requirement from a Transfer Pricing Perspective

In the field of tax law, it is often established a connection between, on the one hand, the existence of a given reality (which is sometimes described as 'substance') and, on the other hand, the application of certain rules.[1] This link between reality and taxation is sometimes reinforced in order to prevent tax avoidance, through conditioning either the grant of certain tax benefits or the non-application of a tax avoidance mechanism, to the fulfilment of certain requirements. For example, whether or not a company is resident[2] or has a permanent establishment[3] in a given country may depend on its actual presence there, despite what could result from the legal appearances, i.e., the 'form'. A connection between 'substance' and the application of certain rules for taxation purposes also exists in the field of transfer pricing, where the substance requirement generally has a twofold meaning: the rather traditional substance-over-form principle (whereby legal form can be disregarded to ensure taxation in line with the reality), and the determination of the appropriate functions, risks, and assets necessary to support a given intercompany transaction. These two aspects are presented below in sections 5.1 (the substance-over-form principle) and 5.2 (the determination of the appropriate substance to support intercompany transactions).

1. Generally, on the notion of substance in tax law, *see* Fredrik Zimmer, General Report, Cahiers de Droit Fiscal International, *Form and Substance in Tax Law*, vol. 87a (2002).
2. The fact that a company is incorporated in a certain country does not necessarily mean that it cannot be deemed to be resident of another country for taxation purposes (*see* Art. 4(3) of the OECD and UN Model Tax Conventions).
3. The lack of registration of a branch in a foreign country does not necessarily mean that a non-resident company has no permanent establishment for taxation purposes (*see* Art. 5 of the OECD and UN Model Tax Conventions).

5.1 THE PRINCIPLE OF SUBSTANCE-OVER-FORM IN TRANSFER PRICING

The first implication of the substance requirement in the field of transfer pricing consists in the principle of substance-over-form. This principle implies that when the legal form and the actual substance of a transfer pricing model do not match, the consequences of the actual substance prevail over the consequences of the legal form. In the field of transfer pricing, the process consisting in considering whether intercompany transactions should be accepted as such (i.e., as they are legally structured) or disregarded is often described as 'recognition' (when intercompany transactions are accepted) or 'non-recognition' (when intercompany transactions are disregarded).[4] As a first step, written contracts (when such contracts exist) normally constitute the starting point of a transfer pricing analysis.[5] At the same time, there is a need for tax administrations to be able to prioritise the conduct of the parties so as to levy taxes on the basis of the reality existing between associated enterprises: tax administrations should not be bound by the legal form of intercompany transactions (e.g., intercompany agreements) or even the apparent lack of transaction.[6] To that end, the substance-over-form principle as it is expressed in the OECD Guidelines enables tax administrations, in situations where contracts and conduct do not match, to depart from written contracts so as to prioritise the conduct of the parties for the determination of the reality of an intercompany transaction, in such manner that the reality[7] eventually lays the ground for setting the transfer prices. Given that it is the conduct of the parties that, eventually, is relied on to enforce the principle of substance-over-form and identify the contribution of each party to an intercompany transaction, the content

4. On this topic, *see* Andreas Bullen, *Arm's Length Transaction Structures: Recognizing and Restructuring Controlled Transactions in Transfer Pricing* (IBFD, Doctoral Series, 2011).
5. *See* paras 1.42, 6.35, 8.4 and 9.17 of the 2022 OECD Guidelines. It may appear surprising that the OECD Guidelines emphasise the need to start a transfer pricing analysis by the examination of the agreements between the parties, but this has to be considered together with the priority given to the conduct of the parties, which will eventually reveal the actual terms of the contractual relationships. By investigating the conduct of the parties, tax administrations may ensure that substance prevails over form. At the same time, legal relations are taken into account and not disregarded from the first place, which is a reasonable approach to contribute to a foreseeable and equitable process for the levy of tax. Tax certainty is also, to some extent, reinforced with respect to the burden of proof, as in most countries it will be up to the tax administration to argue that substance differs from legal form, although in the end it is typically up to taxpayers to bring the relevant factual evidence.
6. *See* para. 1.49 of the 2022 OECD Guidelines: 'Where no written terms exist, the actual transaction would need to be deduced from the evidence of actual conduct provided by identifying the economically relevant characteristics of the transaction. In some circumstances the actual outcome of commercial or financial relations may not have been identified as a transaction by the MNE, but nevertheless may result in a transfer of material value.'
7. The reality is determined with respect to the actual functions, risks and assets: para. 1.46 of the 2022 OECD Guidelines mentions that 'Where there are material differences between contractual terms and the conduct of the associated enterprises in their relations with one another, the functions they actually perform, the assets they actually use, and the risks they actually assume, considered in the context of the contractual terms, should ultimately determine the factual substance and accurately delineate the actual transaction.'

of written agreements plays a minor role.[8] If agreements exist, they will be the starting point of the analysis, but even so the OECD Guidelines are clear about the fact that it is anyway necessary to supplement the conclusions drawn from an analysis of the contracts by an investigation of the conduct of the parties.[9] Hence, the BEPS changes tend to reinforce the anti-avoidance dimension of the arm's length principle.[10]

The possibility of departing from written contracts concerns obviously the terms of a transaction.[11] However, any feature of an intercompany agreement having a potential influence on the transfer prices - and thus on the tax base - may be disregarded so as to take into account and prioritise the conduct of the parties. This may concern, for example, the rights of the parties (and thus their functions and risks)[12] or the ownership of an asset.[13]

The way priority is given to the actual substance over the legal form is by analysing the conduct of the parties in order to accurately delineate the controlled transaction: in other words, a thorough analysis of the conduct of the parties will reveal the reality of a transaction and how roles and responsibilities are shared between the parties. In this respect, the amendments brought to the OECD Guidelines with the 2010, 2017, and 2022 updates have reinforced the substance requirement by giving the highest priority to functions (over risks and assets) for the purpose of delineating

8. In the past, the notion of substance played a less important role: *see*, e.g., the analysis in Joseph Andrus and Michael Durst, *Standing on 'Principal': Risk-Limiting Transfer Pricing Structures*, 959–963, especially at 961 (Tax Notes International, 18 December 2006).
9. *See* Jérôme Monsenego, *The Substance Requirement in the OECD Transfer Pricing Guidelines: What Is the Substance of the Substance Requirement?*, vol. 21, issue 1, 9–23 (International Transfer Pricing Journal, January/February 2014).
10. Giving a central role to the exercise of functions have made the arm's length principle more robust to tax avoidance, since the contractual allocation of profits is not anymore possible.
11. For example, if an intercompany loan contains a provision according to which the interest rate is set to 5% and that the market rate in comparable circumstances would be 2%, it is a basic function of transfer pricing rules based on the arm's length principle to enable tax administrations to deny the deduction of interests corresponding to what is in excess of the 2% market rate. In other words, the determination of the tax base is not bound by the terms of a written agreement. This basic function of the arm's length principle is embedded in the formulation of Art. 9 of the OECD Model Tax Convention.
12. For instance, an intercompany agreement may prevent a party from the right to make certain decisions. This would tend to attribute certain functions and risks to another party, the one that has the legal right to make the decisions. However, a contractual attribution of functions and risks would let the legal form prevail over the substance: here, the substance-over-form principle enables tax administrations to depart from the contractual allocation of functions and risks, to ensure that taxation and substance (i.e., the real exercise of functions and thus the correct assumption of risks) match: *see* paras 1.60 and following of the 2022 OECD Guidelines for the framework applicable to the analysis of risks. For example, if a manufacturer is characterised in a written agreement or in the transfer pricing documentation of a multinational enterprise as a contract manufacturer, but that in reality this manufacturer acts as a fully fledged manufacturer, tax administrations are not bound by the characterisation as a contract manufacturer and are allowed to recharacterise it as a fully fledged manufacturer.
13. The legal ownership of an asset as it results from written agreements (e.g., in case an asset is acquired from another company) or from accounting measures (e.g., the inscription of an asset on the balance sheet of a company) will need to be supplemented by an analysis of the conduct of the parties, to make sure that the ownership or the use of assets for transfer pricing purposes is based on substance, not on form: *see* para. 1.85 as well as paras 6.35 and following of the 2022 OECD Guidelines.

intercompany transactions and defining the functional profile of associated enterprises: eventually, profit allocation will mostly follow the functions performed by different parties and how important these functions are for the generation of 'value'[14] by a multinational enterprise. This is evidenced by the fact that the attribution of both IP and risks rely on the performance of certain functions. In particular, the attribution of IP (and thus of intangible-related returns) follows mainly the performance of functions related to the development, enhancement, maintenance, protection and exploitation of intangibles (i.e., the DEMPE functions);[15] similarly, the attribution of risks (and thus the reward corresponding to the assumption of risks) supposes control over risks, which is also based largely on the performance of functions.[16] The recognition of the performance of DEMPE functions will, in its turn, lie on the performance of risk control functions in relation to the risks relevant to intangibles: since the value of IP is in many cases connected to the risks taken by the party who develops such IP, the key functions for the assumption of risks – especially control over risks – are central for the allocation of profits.[17]

The perspective taken in the UN Manual should be mentioned here, as the 2021 UN Manual brings some interesting nuances to Chapter 6 of the 2022 OECD Guidelines. As mentioned above in section 3.3 of this book, the 2021 UN Manual takes also into consideration the acquisition of intangibles (hence the 'DAEMPE' functions concept)[18] as an alternative to their development. This mention is, however, not meant to diverge from the OECD Guidelines: the objective is solely to clarify that intangibles can be acquired by a multinational enterprise either through development activities or by an acquisition from a third party.[19] Moreover, another nuance is brought by the UN Manual, as it is stated that 'while DAEMPE activities might seem to be limited to

14. While the notion of 'value creation' has been debated (on this topic, *see* Jérôme Monsenego, *Transfer Pricing and Value Creation*, in Werner Haslehner and Marie Lamensch (eds), Taxation and Value Creation, 107–129 (IBFD EATLP International Tax Series, 2021), where it is suggested not to use the value creation concept in the tax policy debate), this notion is nevertheless referred to in the Guidelines as an objective of the functional analysis: *see* paras 1.51 and 1.73 of the 2022 OECD Guidelines.
15. *See* paras 6.32 and following of the 2022 OECD Guidelines.
16. *See* para. 1.65 of the 2022 OECD Guidelines, according to which control over risks supposes '(i) the capability to make decisions to take on, lay off, or decline a risk-bearing opportunity, together with the actual performance of that decision-making function and (ii) the capability to make decisions on whether and how to respond to the risks associated with the opportunity, together with the actual performance of that decision-making function'. If a company lacks control over certain risks, these risks will be assigned partly or wholly to another company, together with income connected to such risks. Control over risk can also be shared between several companies, in which case the profit split method might be the most appropriate transfer pricing method: *see* paras 2.121, 2.126, 2.134 and 2.137 of the 2022 OECD Guidelines. It is beyond the purpose of this book to assess the suitability of different concepts developed in the OECD Guidelines; for an evaluation of the control over risk concept, *see* Richard Collier and Joseph L Andrus, *Transfer Pricing and the Arm's Length Principle after BEPS*, 228–232 (Oxford University Press, 2017).
17. *See* Richard S. Collier and Ian F. Dykes, *The Virus in the ALP: Critique of the Transfer Pricing Guidance on Risk and Capital in the Light of the COVID-19 Pandemic*, 702–720, at 704–705 (Bulletin for International Taxation, 2020-12).
18. *See* para. 6.3.3.1 of the 2021 UN Manual.
19. *See* para. 6.3.3.4 of the 2021 UN Manual.

functions, in fact they often reflect contributions of assets and the assumption of risks as well'.[20] This nuance is not a divergence, rather a confirmation that functions, risks and assets are linked, and that functions are the central parameter for profit allocation: this is because risks and assets follow functions when the relevant functions are performed. In other words, with no performance of the relevant functions (especially the control over risks and DEMPE/DAEMPE functions), risks and assets are unlikely to be attributable to a group company, thus depriving it also of the profits connected to such risks and assets.

The fact that the conduct of the parties takes precedence over contracts does not indicate what the consequences are in case contracts and conduct do not match. There are two main options in that respect: (1) adjust the transfer prices so that they match the reality, or (2) disregard the transaction as it was structured by the taxpayer and replace it by what is revealed by the accurate delineation of the transaction. In theory, both options could lead to the same result since it is the actual conduct of the parties – which is an objective element, although revealed through a subjective exercise – that should guide the determination of the pricing; however, in practice, the non-recognition of a transaction and its replacement by another may lead to important transfer pricing differences, and other consequences such as the reversal of the burden of proof or additional penalties may occur. Clearly, the OECD Guidelines give preference to the first option, i.e., to adjust the transfer prices so that they match the reality,[21] without however excluding the possibility to reconstruct an arrangement and replace one transaction by another. This means that if the accurate delineation of the transaction (in particular as evidenced by the functional analysis) reveals that the transfer prices are not at arm's length, the prices or profit margins may be adjusted, but the transaction as such should be accepted by tax administrations. It is only in 'exceptional circumstances'[22] that a transaction may be disregarded and replaced by an alternative transaction. This leads to asking when such exceptional circumstances may be at hand. The Guidelines accept the non-recognition of transactions only if two conditions are fulfilled: no similar transactions exist on the open market,[23] and the behaviour of the taxpayer is not commercially rational.[24] Recharacterising transactions

20. *See* para. 6.3.3.3 of the 2021 UN Manual, where this statement is supported by an illustration: 'For example, a pharmaceutical company might commit to undertaking R&D in order to develop a potential blockbuster drug. This "D" reflects, in addition to the development functions (R&D), a commitment to contribute assets to fund the development and the assumption of potentially significant risks.'
21. *See* para. 1.141 of the 2022 OECD Guidelines: 'Every effort should be made to determine pricing for the actual transaction as accurately delineated under the arm's length principle.'
22. *See* para. 1.141 of the 2022 OECD Guidelines.
23. *See* para. 1.142 of the 2022 OECD Guidelines: 'Where the same transaction can be seen between independent parties in comparable circumstances (...) non-recognition would not apply.' At the same time, the lack of similar transactions on the open market does not automatically lead to non-recognition: 'the mere fact that the transaction may not be seen between independent parties does not mean that it should not be recognised'.
24. *See* para. 1.142 of the 2022 OECD Guidelines: 'The transaction as accurately delineated may be disregarded, and if appropriate, replaced by an alternative transaction, where the arrangements made in relation to the transaction, viewed in their totality, differ from those which would have been adopted by independent enterprises behaving in a commercially rational manner in comparable circumstances'. Commercial rationality seems to be synonymous with pursuing

to achieve commercial rationality is inevitably a subjective exercise, so the recommendation of the Guidelines is to stick as closely as possible to the facts when replacing one structure by another.[25]

5.2 THE DETERMINATION OF THE APPROPRIATE SUBSTANCE TO SUPPORT INTERCOMPANY TRANSACTIONS

5.2.1 Introduction

The second implication of the substance requirement in transfer pricing consists in determining the functions, risks, and assets that should be expected from a group company to be able to sustain a transfer pricing model. To put it in a nutshell, for a given transfer pricing model to be consistent with the arm's length principle and thus be recognised by tax administrations, it has to be supported by appropriate substance (i.e., by an adequate reality) to ensure that economic activities and transfer pricing outcomes match. The reinforcement of the connection between the taxes levied and the actual substance supporting transfer pricing models was one of the key ambitions of the BEPS project.[26]

The substance requirement is a logical consequence of the arm's length principle in the field of transfer pricing. Since independent enterprises normally make profits that result from their actual business activities, associated enterprises should also be subject to tax on the basis of their actual business activities: in an independent context, profits are also dependent on substance, especially when it comes to the importance of functions: the more important functions a company performs, the more likely it is to make profits; conversely, an empty company is not likely to make any profits. Therefore, a balance has to be struck between, on the one hand, the right of multinational enterprises to structure their business activities, and, on the other hand, the right of tax administrations to require that the substance supporting intercompany transaction matches that of comparable independent companies.

The determination of whether or not an intercompany transaction is supported by sufficient substance is a complex and highly factual matter. The difficulty of applying the substance requirement in the area of transfer pricing is mainly explained by the fact that it cannot be determined in advance what substance is expected from the parties to an intercompany transaction. Accordingly, the functions, risks, and assets that may be expected from a multinational enterprise to recognise a given intercompany transaction depend on the nature of the intercompany transaction at hand. For example, in an independent context, a principal in a contract R&D

'legitimate business transactions' (para. 1.143 of the 2022 OECD Guidelines). Two examples in paras 1.146 and 1.148 of the 2022 OECD Guidelines illustrate transactions that are deemed commercially irrational.

25. *See* para. 1.144 of the 2022 OECD Guidelines.
26. *See*, e.g., OECD, *Action Plan on Base Erosion and Profit Shifting*, 20 (2013), where BEPS Action 8 is attributed the objective to develop rules 'ensuring that profits associated with the transfer and use of intangibles are appropriately allocated in accordance with (rather than divorced from) value creation'.

arrangement would typically provide key instructions to the researcher, and thus the same expectations exist in a controlled context; at the same time, it would typically be expected from the contract R&D to actually perform the very R&D activities.

The OECD Guidelines provide some indications to help multinational enterprises and tax administrations assess the level of substance necessary to support an intercompany transaction. These indications are, however, neither binding nor sufficient, especially since the interpretation of these indications may vary from one country to another.[27] In addition, the substance-over-form principle provided in the OECD Guidelines does not prevent national or treaty-based anti-abuse provisions from being applied.

The core idea of the substance requirement from a transfer pricing perspective consists in determining which functions, risks, and assets are necessary to support a given intercompany transaction. In this respect, the OECD Guidelines provide certain proxies (especially the DEMPE concept and a description of the features expected for the control over risks) as well as examples. As with other transfer pricing issues, the primary benchmark would be the substance that is observed or that may be expected at the level of independent companies entering into comparable transactions. This may prove highly factual and subjective, as contrary to financial information or business descriptions, companies usually do not publish comprehensive information concerning the details of their organisation, i.e., which functions they perform and how important they are in relation to other functions, what competence and experience their personnel has, who controls risks, who assumes risks in case they are realised, or how IP has been developed.

In the sections below, the substance requirement is considered with respect to functions (section 5.2.2), risks (section 5.2.3), and assets (section 5.2.4).

5.2.2 The Substance Requirement Applied to Functions

As mentioned above, the successive amendments brought to the OECD Guidelines in 2010, 2017, and 2022 gave functions the highest priority (over risks and assets considered as such) for the determination of substance.[28] This is partly due to the fact that the practical operation of the arm's length principle, when interpreted on the basis of older versions of the OECD Guidelines, was deemed sometimes too formalistic, with too much emphasis on the contractual allocation of functions, assets and risks, the

27. This means that although being supported by the same substance, the pricing of an intercompany transaction may be acknowledged in certain countries while it is rejected in other countries. This may seem contrary to the neutral character of the arm's length principle, but it is at the same time difficult to avoid that a principle is interpreted differently by different countries, especially in the presence of different legal cultures and diverging interests as to how the tax base should be attributed.
28. Indeed, the attribution of risks and IP rely on the performance of appropriate functions: the attribution of IP (and thus of intangible-related returns) follows mainly the performance of DEMPE functions (*see* paras 6.32 and following of the 2022 OECD Guidelines) and the attribution of risks (and thus the reward corresponding to the assumption of risks) supposes control over risks, which is also based largely on the performance of functions (*see* para. 1.65 of the 2022 OECD Guidelines).

provision of capital, or the legal ownership of intangibles.[29] In other words, the arm's length principle has been considered 'vulnerable to manipulation'.[30] The amendments brought as part of the BEPS project aim at ensuring that profit allocation largely follows the performance of functions, as well as the importance of certain functions in relation to others.

In practical terms, a company claiming recognition of the performance of a function needs to have appropriate resources to perform it or to control it, for the prices, profits or the losses connected to this function to be attributed to this company. Having appropriate resources refers primarily to the capability to perform decision-making functions, defined mainly in terms of competence, experience, and authority to take decisions.[31] For example, if a group company claims the performance of a management function and charges other group companies for the provision of management services, this company will be expected to employ sufficiently qualified and numerous personnel to effectively be able to perform the management function; the personnel of the company should have the right to take certain decisions and effectively use this right. The company should also be able to prove that it fulfils the substance requirement, for example, by keeping notes of the meetings where management decisions were taken. Functions need to be performed by physical persons. If functions are performed remotely (e.g., a surgeon making an operation remotely), they will be considered to be performed where the person is located (the surgeon), not where the result of the function can be observed (the place of the operation). If functions are performed digitally (e.g., a software automatically analysing the stock market and buying/selling stocks), the principles enshrined in the 2022 OECD Guidelines will allocate profits to the place where the important functions related to the hardware or software are performed (especially the DEMPE functions), rather than where hardware or software is physically located.[32]

A question frequently arises as to whether the personnel performing a function must be employed by the company claiming the function, or if such personnel may be employed by another associated company to which a certain task has been outsourced. In principle, there is no requirement that all functions should be performed by personnel directly employed by a company since independent companies may purchase services from third parties.[33] Therefore, certain functions may be outsourced. Depending on the importance of the functions outsourced, more or less profits will be lost by the outsourcing company, and attributed instead to the service provider. For example, if a routine function such as contract manufacturing is outsourced by a principal, the routine profit connected to that function (e.g., a FCM covering the

29. *See* the important role of the contractual allocation of risks in the principal transfer pricing model described in Joseph Andrus and Michael Durst, *Standing on 'Principal': Risk-Limiting Transfer Pricing Structures*, 959–963 (Tax Notes International, 18 December 2006).
30. *See* OECD, *Aligning Transfer Pricing Outcomes with Value Creation, Actions 8-10: 2015 Final Reports*, 9 (2015).
31. *See* para. 1.66 of the 2022 OECD Guidelines.
32. For that reason, a server would normally attract very low, or even nil profits. Similarly with respect to servers as permanent establishments, *see* OECD, *Report on the Attribution of Profits to Permanent Establishments*, Part I, para. 66 (22 July 2010).
33. *See* para. 6.51 of the 2022 OECD Guidelines.

contract manufacturer's costs and attributing to it a profit margin) will be attributable to the service provider; the remaining profits will still be attributable to the principal. However, for outsourcing to be acknowledged for transfer pricing purposes, the outsourcing company must control[34] and assume the risks connected to such functions.[35] In other words, while the actual performance of certain functions may be outsourced, the important decisions must remain with the outsourcing company, which must also support the financial consequences of the activities that have been outsourced. Moreover, when it comes to intangibles, the 2022 OECD Guidelines contain additional requirements: if no DEMPE functions are performed, no intangible-related returns can be earned.[36] This means that DEMPE functions may not be outsourced if intangible-related returns are to be fully attributed to the company claiming the ownership of intangibles.[37]

What are 'important functions'? Although from a theoretical perspective it is not possible to tell in advance which precise functions are important, the OECD Guidelines contain as part of the DEMPE concept suggestions of functions that are typically important.[38] These functions depend on whether intangibles have been self-developed or acquired:

- For self-developed intangibles, design and control of research and marketing programmes, direction of and establishing priorities for creative undertakings including determining the course of 'blue-sky' research, control over strategic decisions regarding intangible development programmes, and management and control of budgets are considered as important.
- For all intangibles, it would normally be expected to take important decisions regarding defence and protection of intangibles, as well as ongoing quality control over functions performed by independent or associated enterprises that may have a material effect on the value of the intangible.

In case several associated enterprises share these important functions, intangible-related returns will necessarily have to be shared, and since it is unlikely that reliable comparables can be found, a transfer pricing method not based on

34. In this respect, para. 1.65 of the 2022 OECD Guidelines indicates that when 'day-to-day mitigation activities are outsourced, control of the risk would require capability to determine the objectives of the outsourced activities, to decide to hire the provider of the risk mitigation functions, to assess whether the objectives are being adequately met, and, where necessary, to decide to adapt or terminate the contract with that provider, together with the performance of such assessment and decision-making'. A similar view on the notion of control over risks when risk mitigation is outsourced is found in para. 3.4.4.33 of the 2021 UN Manual.
35. *See* paras 1.61 and following of the 2022 OECD Guidelines.
36. *See* para. 6.54 of the 2022 OECD Guidelines.
37. For a contrasting view on the importance of functions performed by a company's own employees for the attribution of profits, *see* Wolfgang Schön, *International Taxation of Risk*, 290 (Bulletin for International Taxation, July/August 2014): 'The most important argument against profit allocation based on the physical presence of people performing "significant functions" lies in the fact that people who decide on the assumption of risk do not bear these risks themselves. Therefore, any income allocation on the basis of decision-making people leads to arbitrary results. The ultimate risk-bearers in a corporation are always the shareholders of the company.'
38. *See* para. 6.56 of the 2022 OECD Guidelines.

comparables (mainly the profit split method) will need to be used. In addition to the personnel necessary to perform a given function, the recognition of the performance of a function may also require other types of resources such as premises and/or equipment in order to realistically support the performance of the function. Which resources may be expected from a company performing a given function is determined by a comparison with the resources employed by comparable independent companies.

5.2.3 The Substance Requirement Applied to Risks

The recognition of the assumption of risks, and therefore, the attribution of income connected to risks, triggers particularly difficult transfer pricing issues. Risks are an intrinsic part of any business activity and influence the level of profitability in the long run, i.e., a sufficient period of time for risks to materialise and income connected to such risks to be generated. The assumption of risks may be hard to identify and attribute with precision since risks may easily be shifted by contract.[39] Given that risks are part of the factors attributing income under the arm's length principle, risks have been the subject of tax planning strategies often consisting in choosing a low-tax jurisdiction for the location of risk-taking activities and the attribution of income connected to such risks. To mitigate the problems raised by the transfer pricing aspects of risks,[40] certain changes were brought to the Guidelines in 2010,[41] and a major review of Chapter 1 was made with the BEPS project. The main change, if one compares the 1995 and 2022 OECD Guidelines, consists in mitigating the importance of the financial assumption of risks (which can be described as the 'form') while strengthening the importance of functions necessary for the control of risks (which can be described as 'substance'): while in the past the financial assumption of risks (e.g., by assuming certain costs)[42] could – according to what the OECD describes as too formal

39. Indeed, as a consequence of certain formalistic interpretations of the 1979 and 1995 OECD guidance, the allocation of risks could mainly be a consequence of the terms of intercompany agreements; i.e., risks could be allocated by deciding so in a contract: *see* OECD, *Aligning Transfer Pricing Outcomes with Value Creation, Actions 8-10: 2015 Final Reports*, 9 (2015).
40. The BEPS project revealed a need for tax administrations to be able to rely on rules that let them look through the formal allocation of risks. For an explanation of this issue, *see Spillovers in International Corporate Taxation*, IMF Policy Paper, 32 (9 May 2014): 'A fundamental issue here is that, since a pure reallocation of risk within the group cannot affect the risk borne by the group as a whole – to the extent, at least, that it is hard for all other group members to step away from the failure of any affiliate – there is inherently no comparable price between unrelated parties on which to draw; and the bundling of such risk transfers with changes in function whose substance can be hard to judge adds further difficulty. Companies may be able to secure reduction in taxation by exploiting these difficulties of pricing.'
41. *See* among other recommendations, para. 9.32 of the 2010 OECD Guidelines, *in fine*: 'a high level of capitalisation by itself does not mean that the highly capitalised party carries risk'.
42. For example, a transfer pricing model could consist in establishing a principal in a low-tax jurisdiction and a contract R&D in a high-tax jurisdiction; the principal would not perform strategic functions but it would assume significant costs, especially the costs charged by the contract R&D. As a result of the assumption of costs, the principal may have been considered as the owner of IP, and thus be entitled to the intangible-related returns. Such transfer pricing models, with low or no substance where important profits are attributed, have been found to rely on too formalistic a reading of the previous OECD Guidelines, and were thus at the heart of

interpretations of the OECD Guidelines[43] – suffice to attribute risks (and thus profits connected to such risks) to a company, the 2022 OECD Guidelines contain recommendations that give little importance to the provision of capital or the assumption of risks that materialise.[44] The recognition of the attribution of risks is now subject to a twofold expectation: the risk should be controlled and assumed by the party to which it is attributed. Consequently, if, for example, a pharmaceutical group wishes to attribute to a certain group company the product risk (and the profits or losses associated with such a risk) in relation to a particular drug, it is necessary – for such a risk to be recognised from a transfer pricing perspective – that this risk is actually controlled (e.g., through participating in the strategic R&D decisions on the intrinsic qualities of the drug) and assumed (e.g., by being exposed to potential damages in case the product is flawed) by this entity.

The language of the 2022 OECD Guidelines uses the terms *control over risk*[45] and *financial capacity to assume the risk*;[46] these two parameters are cumulative for a risk to be attributed to a party.[47] The 2021 UN Manual also requires the cumulative exercise of control over risk and financial capacity to assume a risk in order to recognise its

---

the preoccupations of the review of the OECD Guidelines as part of the BEPS project: *see* OECD, *Aligning Transfer Pricing Outcomes with Value Creation, Actions 8-10: 2015 Final Reports*, 9 (2015).

43. *See* OECD, *Aligning Transfer Pricing Outcomes with Value Creation, Actions 8-10: 2015 Final Reports*, 9 (2015).
44. *See* para. 1.108 of the 2022 OECD Guidelines: if 'a funder lacks the capability, or does not perform the decision-making functions, to control the risk associated with investing in a financial asset, it will be entitled to no more than a risk-free return'. A risk-free return may correspond to the return of a government bond.
45. The content of the notion of 'control over risk' is defined in para. 1.65 of the 2022 OECD Guidelines: control over risk involves '(i) the capability to make decisions to take on, lay off, or decline a risk-bearing opportunity, together with the actual performance of that decision-making function and (ii) the capability to make decisions on whether and how to respond to the risks associated with the opportunity, together with the actual performance of that decision-making function'.
46. The content of the notion of 'financial capacity to assume the risk' is defined in para. 1.64 of the 2022 OECD Guidelines: 'Financial capacity to assume risk can be defined as access to funding to take on the risk or to lay off the risk, to pay for the risk mitigation functions and to bear the consequences of the risk if the risk materialises.' *See also* para. 3.4.4.36 of the 2021 UN Manual.
47. *See* para. 1.60 of the 2022 OECD Guidelines, at point 4. Here the question may be raised whether independent parties taking financial risks always control such risks; for example, on the open market, an investor may take a risk by making an investment in a company it does not control, and thus be exposed to a financial risk without control. Also, it cannot be excluded that an investor has a high risk appetite and takes risks it may not be able to assume, hoping for a significant gain. Therefore, the need to cumulate the control over risks and the financial capacity to assume risks may not always be consistent with how independent parties act. The concrete expectations expressed in the 2022 OECD Guidelines with respect to the control over risk and the financial capacity to assume risks illustrate the growing anti-abuse dimension of the arm's length principle in the Guidelines, as well as the choice, in certain cases, to introduce predetermined proxies. For an example of court case in which these two criteria were found to be cumulative, *see SAS R.K.S.*, French Supreme Administrative Court (4 October 2021, case number 443130); *SAS SKF Holding France*, French Supreme Administrative Court (4 October 2021, case number 443133).

attribution.[48] The notion of control over risk is functional (i.e., it supposes the performance of certain functions), and thus illustrates the priority given to functions over risks in the interpretation of the arm's length principle made in the 2022 OECD Guidelines. This reform mitigates the possibility to engage in tax planning strategies consisting in attributing costs to a company in the hope of a proportional profit attribution, or over-capitalising a company in order to let this company provide funding and be allocated profits.

For the purpose of testing the consistency between the formal allocation of risks and the actual assumption of risks, the 2022 OECD Guidelines contain an analytical framework with several steps that are to be followed in order to correctly identify the existence and the assumption of risks.[49] If a risk analysis carried out according to this analytical framework reveals that the party assuming a risk does not control that risk or does not have the financial capacity to assume it (i.e., contracts and conduct do not match), the risk will be partly or wholly reassigned to another party; income connected to the risk will follow the risk that is reassigned.

The need to control risks is illustrated in the example below.

Example: A risk-bearer should control risks related to a warranty

Assume that company A, resident in country A, acts as a principal towards company B, resident in country B, who acts as a contract manufacturer. Company A provides technical instructions, places orders, purchases the finished goods once they have been manufactured by company B, and assumes the warranty risks in case of claims coming from consumers. Company A may consider shifting the warranty risk to company C, resident in country C, in order to also shift certain profits to company C, as such profits would then be taxed in country C. From an operational perspective, it may be easy to shift the assumption of the warranty risk, should it materialise: it could be enough to write on the products and on the website of the group that claims relating to the warranty of the products should be placed with company C, which could effectively assume this risk and reimburse the defective products. From a transfer pricing perspective, the tax administration of country A would be keen on ensuring that company C has the necessary substance to support the warranty risk. In this example, it could be expected from company C that it employs personnel that assesses the claims of the clients and decides on potential reimbursements that would be financially assumed by the same company, or that company C pays insurance premiums and manages the contacts with insurance companies, in order for the control of the risk to be recognised by the tax administration of country A.

Finally, it should be observed that the position described in the 2022 OECD Guidelines is not uncontroversial, and that different interpretations of the arm's length principle can be made in relation to risks. For example, the possibility of controlling

48. *See* para. 3.4.4.30 of the 2021 UN Manual, where it is indicated that both control and financial capacity are necessary for one party to be treated as having assumed a particular risk; at the same time, it is emphasised that 'neither of them is by itself sufficient'.
49. *See* paras 1.60 and following of the 2022 OECD Guidelines. *See also* Figure 3.D.1 in para. 3.4.4.28 of the 2021 UN Manual for an illustration of the analytical framework for risks.

risks remotely, and thus relieve entities in a given country from certain significant risks, is subject to debate.[50]

5.2.4 The Substance Requirement Applied to Assets

A company may own different types of assets. From a transfer pricing perspective, intangible assets raise the most important issues. This is due to several reasons: intangible assets are of utmost importance for the generation of profits, they can be legally owned and sold, they may but do not need to appear on a company's balance sheet, they are mobile across borders, and suppose a combination of different - yet sometimes hard to identify - functions to maintain as well as increase their value. As risks, the transfer pricing aspects of IP have exacerbated BEPS issues, thus contributing to the need to review the OECD Guidelines. The response as part of the BEPS project has been, similarly to the guidance applicable to risks, to diminish the importance of formal factors for the attribution of IP (e.g., the legal ownership of intangible assets or their transfer by contract) and reinforce the substance necessary for the recognition of IP through determining rather precisely which functions must be performed or controlled for an entitlement to intangible-related returns.

As presented above in sections 3.3 and 5.1 of this book, the 2022 OECD Guidelines emphasise the need to perform functions related to the DEMPE functions of the intangibles, to be entitled to intangible-related returns. The Guidelines contain also a description of the functions that, in practice, are typically expected to be performed.[51] As emphasised above, the 2021 UN Manual uses the terminology 'DAEMPE' functions,[52] but this addition is solely meant to clarify that intangibles can be acquired either through development activities or by an acquisition from a third party.[53]

Both the 2022 OECD Guidelines and the 2021 UN Manual condition the attribution of intangible-related returns to the performance of DEMPE/DAEMPE functions. This means that DEMPE/DAEMPE functions may not be outsourced if intangible-related returns are to be fully attributed to the company claiming the ownership of intangibles.[54] This means also that since the recognition of DEMPE/DAEMPE functions supposes that the risks associated with these functions are

50. However, as for any recommendation under the OECD Guidelines, countries may disagree with such recommendations or interpret them differently. *See*, e.g., para. 3.4.4 of the 2021 UN Manual (Part D): 'The notion that risks can be controlled remotely by the parent company and that the Indian subsidiary engaging in core functions, such as carrying out R&D activities or providing services, is a risk-free entity has not been found acceptable.'
51. *See* para. 6.56 of the 2022 OECD Guidelines. These functions are described above in section 5.2.1 of this book.
52. *See* para. 6.3.3.1 of the 2021 UN Manual.
53. *See* para. 6.3.3.4 of the 2021 UN Manual.
54. For a contrasting view on the importance of functions performed by a company's own employees for the attribution of profits, *see* Wolfgang Schön, *International Taxation of Risk*, 290 (Bulletin for International Taxation, July/August 2014): 'The most important argument against profit allocation based on the physical presence of people performing "significant functions" lies in the fact that people who decide on the assumption of risk do not bear these risks themselves. Therefore, any income allocation on the basis of decision-making people leads to arbitrary results. The ultimate risk-bearers in a corporation are always the shareholders of the company.'

controlled by the party who claims the intangible-related returns, eventually it is the control over the risks connected to intangibles that will largely determine the profit allocation.

5.3 EXAMPLE OF THE APPLICATION OF THE SUBSTANCE REQUIREMENT TO A CROSS-BORDER BUSINESS RESTRUCTURING

The substance requirement is a particularly sensitive issue when it comes to cross-border business restructurings, when such restructurings result in moving part of the corporate tax base from one country to another. Let us illustrate this with an example.

Example: A group moves part of its marketing activities to a country with a lower corporate income tax rate

Company A (resident in State A) provides marketing services to the other companies of a multinational group. These marketing activities result in a taxable profit of 100 per year. The corporate income tax rate in State A is 30%, so the tax paid annually by the group on the marketing activities amounts to 30. However, State B offers an advantageous tax rate of 15% on profits made on marketing activities, so the same function, if it were carried out in State B, would lead to a tax burden of 15 per year instead of 30 paid in State A. Consequently, by moving the marketing activities to State B, the group will be able to save annually 15[55] of corporate income tax, although the taxable profits (100) remain unchanged.[56]

In the above example, the business restructuring (consisting in moving the marketing function from State A to State B) should in principle result in a tax saving.[57] Here, the question is whether the group should be allowed to decrease its total tax burden by moving (part of) its taxable profits from State A to State B, or if the tax administration of the State that loses tax revenues (i.e., State A) should have the right to disregard the business restructuring on the basis of a lack of substance, in order to keep taxing the group as if no change had occurred.[58] The OECD Guidelines and the UN Manual make it clear that, as long as the arm's length principle is respected, multinational enterprises may structure their operations as they see fit,[59] even if this implies a reduction in their tax burdens or if an intercompany transaction does not occur between independent enterprises. Therefore, normally a tax administration may not disregard a business restructuring per se and keep taxing a company as if no

55. 30 in taxes previously paid in State A – 15 in taxes now paid in State B = a tax saving of 15.
56. The rules for the computation of corporate income should also be taken into account, but for the sake of simplicity it is assumed in this example that the tax accounting rules in States A and B result in a similar taxable profit.
57. In this example, it is assumed that no domestic or treaty-based anti-avoidance rules apply.
58. *See* Baker & McKenzie, *Comments on the OECD Restructuring Discussion Draft*, vol. 37, issue 2, 143–146 (Intertax, 2009).
59. *See* para. 9.34 of the 2022 OECD Guidelines. *See also* paras 8.1.1.4 and 8.2.1.4 of the 2021 UN Manual.

restructuring had occurred. However, as with other intercompany transactions, if a business restructuring lacks substance, such a transaction may be subject to a transfer pricing adjustment, or even non-recognition by tax administrations. In the above example, the form refers to the apparent move of the marketing function from company A to company B, and the substance refers to the actual provision of marketing services by people employed by the multinational enterprise (the group claims the marketing function is performed by company B, and no longer by company A) so that the profits of the marketing activities are rightfully attributed to company B and taxed in State B. A lack of substance would suppose that the group declares the profits of the marketing function in its tax return in State B, while the marketing function is still performed (at least to a certain extent) in State A.

A purported lack of substance may result in an income adjustment in country A, on the basis of the fact that the marketing function is still performed (at least partly) by company A. At the same time, country B may consider that the marketing function is supported by sufficient substance, in order to find a right to tax the income attributable to the marketing function. The combination of these claims would result in double taxation, as the same item of income would be taxed by the two countries.

CHAPTER 6

The Attribution of Profits to Permanent Establishments

6.1 INTRODUCTION: WHAT IS A PERMANENT ESTABLISHMENT?

A permanent establishment corresponds to a taxable presence that a company resident in one country (the State of residence) has in another country (the State of establishment). It is a kind of threshold that, when met, gives the State of establishment a right to tax part of the profits of the non-resident company. If this threshold is not met, the State of establishment, in principle, has no right to tax the business profits of the non-resident company.[1] In contrast, other items of income, such as passive income, may be taxed outside the State of residence and despite the absence of a permanent establishment, in countries where the source of income is located.

Example: A company rents an office in another country

Company A (resident in country A) may have a permanent establishment in country B if: (i) it rents an office in country B during a sufficiently long period of time, and (ii) the business activities of company A are carried out in country B through this office. Country B would then have a taxing right on the part of the profits of company A.

1. The exclusive taxing right of the State of residence on a company's business profits, except if a company has a permanent establishment in another State, is prescribed by tax treaties drafted on the basis of Art. 7 of the OECD and the UN Model Tax Conventions. *See* the drafting of Art. 7(1) of the 2017 OECD Model Tax Convention: 'Profits of an enterprise of a Contracting State shall be taxable *only* in that State *unless* the enterprise carries on business in the other Contracting State through a permanent establishment situated therein' (emphasis added). However, Art. 7 relates only to business profits. Consequently, a company resident in one country may be subject to tax in another country if it earns other types of income in the latter country: for example, Art. 6 of the OECD and UN Model Tax Conventions provides that 'Income derived by a resident of a Contracting State from immovable property [...] situated in the other Contracting State may be taxed in that other State.'

The definition of what constitutes a permanent establishment is outside the scope of this book.[2] Here, it is simply recalled that, according to Article 5 of the 2017 OECD Model Tax Convention, an enterprise may be deemed to have a permanent establishment in the other country in two situations. On the one hand, a company may have a permanent establishment through a fixed place of business.[3] On the other hand, it may have a permanent establishment when a dependent agent has, and habitually exercises, an authority to conclude contracts in the name of the enterprise, or when the agent habitually plays the principal role leading to the conclusion of contracts that are routinely concluded without material modification by the enterprise.[4] Article 5 of the 2021 UN Model Tax Convention finds also a permanent establishment in these two situations, although the two models have different wordings. In either case, the existence of a permanent establishment supposes a physical presence, which explains the need felt by many countries to reform Articles 5, 7, and 9 of the OECD Model Tax Convention in order to be able to tax certain of the digital or remote activities of multinational enterprises.[5] In addition, paragraph 144 of the commentary to Article 5 of the 2017 OECD Model Tax Convention includes, since the 2008 update of the OECD Model, a provision for countries that are willing, in their tax treaties, to broaden the definition of a permanent establishment to companies providing services in their territory.[6] A service permanent establishment is also found in Article 5(3)(b) of the 2021 UN Model Tax Convention, the scope of which is broader than paragraph 144 of the commentary to Article 5 of the 2017 OECD Model Tax Convention.

A permanent establishment may be deemed to exist either following the spontaneous registration of a branch by a non-resident company or by the tax administration of the State of establishment if it considers that a non-resident company has a sufficient tax presence there. Once it has been determined that a non-resident company has a permanent establishment, the question is how much of its profits (or losses) should be attributed to the permanent establishment and taxed in the State of establishment. This issue is complex and has historically given rise to differences of views. Therefore, the OECD has been working on issuing recommendations on the attribution of profits to permanent establishments, improving the theoretical grounds

2. On the definition of a permanent establishment, *see* Art. 5 of the OECD and UN Model Tax Conventions, and the commentaries thereof. For a general overview, *see* Ekkehart Reimer and Alexander Rust (eds), Klaus Vogel on Double Taxation Conventions, Art. 5 (5th ed., Kluwer International Law, 2021); Arvid Skaar, *Permanent Establishment: Erosion of a Tax Treaty Principle* (2nd ed., Kluwer Law International, 2020); Jacques Sasseville and Arvid A. Skaar, General Report, Cahiers de Droit Fiscal International, *Is There a Permanent Establishment?*, vol. 94a (2009).
3. *See* Art. 5(1) of the 2017 OECD Model Tax Convention. Such a permanent establishment may be referred to as a fixed place permanent establishment.
4. *See* Art. 5(5) of the 2017 OECD Model Tax Convention. Such a permanent establishment may be referred to as a dependent agent permanent establishment.
5. This resulted in the introduction of taxes on digital services, as well as the so-called Pillar 1 reform.
6. *See* para. 144 of the commentary to Art. 5 of the 2017 OECD Model Tax Convention. Such a permanent establishment may be referred to as a service permanent establishment. For a comment on the inclusion of an alternative service permanent establishment provision in the commentary to the OECD Model Tax Convention, *see* Hans Pijl, *The OECD Services Permanent Establishment Alternative*, vol. 48, issue 9, 472–476 (European Taxation, September 2008).

for taxing the business profits of non-resident companies as well as eliminating situations of double taxation. The current position of the OECD is referred to as the *authorised OECD approach*.[7]

After presenting a background on the attribution of profits to permanent establishments together with the former principles recommended by the OECD (section 6.2), the authorised OECD approach is described (section 6.3). Given the complexity of the attribution of profits to permanent establishments, and with regard to the purpose of this book, this chapter presents only an overview of the general recommendations provided in the authorised OECD approach.[8]

6.2 BACKGROUND ON THE ATTRIBUTION OF PROFITS TO PERMANENT ESTABLISHMENTS AND FORMER PRINCIPLES RECOMMENDED BY THE OECD

A permanent establishment has certain features, especially from a civil law perspective, that explain why different countries may have diverging views on the question of the attribution of profits. This is mainly due to the fact that a permanent establishment, even if it is legally registered as a branch,[9] is not a legal subject. A permanent establishment and its head office are one and the same legal entity. As a result, a permanent establishment does not have the legal capacity to contract; it cannot be legally bound by an agreement, either with the rest of the enterprise of which it is a part or with separate enterprises. It cannot either own an asset. It is the whole company that is a legal subject and has the legal capacity to contract, own assets, and bear responsibilities. These peculiarities have consequences for the purpose of the taxation of permanent establishments.

While not having legal personality, a permanent establishment fulfils an important function in the tax field. It is the recognition from a tax perspective of the presence (and potentially the tax liability) of a foreign legal subject. Traditionally,

7. For a comprehensive description of the authorised OECD approach, *see* Art. 7 of the 2017 OECD Model Tax Convention and the commentary thereof; *see also* OECD, *Report on the Attribution of Profits to Permanent Establishments* (22 July 2010); OECD, *Additional Guidance on the Attribution of Profits to Permanent Establishments, BEPS Action 7* (2018); Ekkehart Reimer and Alexander Rust (eds), Klaus Vogel on Double Taxation Conventions, Art. 7 (5th ed., Kluwer International Law, 2022); Mary Bennett, *Article 7: New OECD Rules for Attributing Profit to Permanent Establishments*, in Dennis Weber and Stef van Weeghel (eds), The 2010 OECD Updates, 21–36 (Kluwer Law International, 2011); Jacques Malherbe and Philip Daenen, *Permanent Establishments Claim Their Share of Profits: Does the Taxman Agree?* 359–366 (Bulletin for International Fiscal Documentation, July 2010).
8. The particular recommendations of the OECD with regard to banks, enterprises carrying on global trading of financial instruments, and insurance companies are not touched upon in this book. Therefore, when referring to the OECD reports on the attribution of profits to permanent establishments, only Part I of these reports ('general considerations') is referred to, unless stated otherwise. For an explanation of some of the issues arising in the area of global trading together with an example based on the profit split method, *see* Adam M. Katz, Barry Dennis, Richard S. Collier and Stanley J. Hales, *Applying the Arm's-Length Principle to Global Interbranch Financial Dealings*, 741–748 (Tax Notes International, 25 August 2003).
9. Registration of foreign companies as branches is normally not compulsory, but it may be helpful or necessary to perform certain activities.

non-resident companies have been subject to a limited tax liability in the countries where they have a permanent establishment,[10] although to various extents. To determine such a limited tax liability, the main method consists in attributing part of the profits of the whole company to a permanent establishment, hence the expression 'attribution of profits to permanent establishments'. To that end, Article 7 of the OECD Model Tax Convention limits the taxing rights of the host country to income that is *attributable* to a permanent establishment. However, this does not answer the question of how to attribute profits, which has always been controversial.

Even if permanent establishments are not legal entities on their own, the OECD has for long recommended, as a starting point, taxing the profits attributable to permanent establishments according to the *separate entity approach*, as evidenced already in the 1963 draft model convention.[11] However, important differences existed between Articles 7 and 9, the arm's length principle being only applied to a limited extent under former recommendations. Indeed, the lack of legal personality of a permanent establishment affects the three main factors that steer profit attribution under the arm's length principle: functions are performed by people employed by the whole company, not by a permanent establishment; risks are assumed by the company, not by the permanent establishment itself;[12] assets are owned by the company, not by a permanent establishment that cannot own an asset separately from its head office. And since one and the same legal entity cannot contract with itself, the lack of legal personality may also preclude the existence of a profit element in transfers or payments between a permanent establishment and another part of the same enterprise.

The previous commentary to Article 7 of the OECD Model Tax Convention (i.e., before the adoption of the authorised OECD approach and the 2010 update) was not subject to a consensus amongst the OECD member countries. This resulted in different views on how to attribute profits to permanent establishments and, ultimately, in situations of double taxation or less than single taxation. Therefore, the OECD reexamined the attribution of profits to permanent establishments, something that resulted in new recommendations referred to as the authorised OECD approach. This

10. *See* para. 14 of the commentary to Art. 7 of the 2017 OECD Model Tax Convention: 'The purpose of paragraph 1 is to limit the right of one Contracting State to tax the business profits of enterprises of the other Contracting State.'
11. Article 7(2) of the 1963 Income and Capital Draft Model Convention issued by the OECD stated that 'Where an enterprise of a Contracting State carries on business in the other Contracting State through a permanent establishment situated therein, there shall in each Contracting State be attributed to that permanent establishment the profits which it might be expected to make if it were a distinct and separate enterprise engaged in the same or similar activities under the same or similar conditions and dealing wholly independently with the enterprise of which it is a permanent establishment.' *See also* Raffaele Russo, *Application of Arm's Length Principle to Intra-company Dealings – Back to the Origins*, vol. 12, issue 1, 7–15 (International Transfer Pricing Journal, 2005); Philip Baker and Richard S. Collier, General Report, Cahiers de Droit Fiscal International, *The Attribution of Profits to Permanent Establishments*, vol. 91b, 26 (2006).
12. As a result, the impossibility for a permanent establishment to bear a responsibility on its own can be considered as reducing the risks it assumes (because the risks are borne by the whole legal entity), thereby affecting the transfer pricing consequences of risk-taking.

approach was later supplemented with guidance specific to the changes made to Article 5 of the OECD Model Tax Convention as part of the BEPS project.[13]

Before the adoption of the authorised OECD approach, the principles recommended in the OECD Model Tax Convention for the attribution of profits to permanent establishments did not result in a full recognition of transfers or payments between a head office and its permanent establishment, and a comprehensive application of the arm's length principle for the attribution of profits to permanent establishments. In particular, the following *dealings*[14] were not (fully) recognised, and had to be priced in a way that might differ from what would be agreed between two separate legal entities:

- When services are performed by one part of an enterprise for the benefit of another part of the same enterprise, the former principles recommended by the OECD precluded that certain costs are charged with a profit mark-up,[15] unless the services performed could be charged at a standard rate that may include a profit mark-up (e.g., on the basis of the CUP method),[16] or when the main activity of a permanent establishment is to provide 'specific services to the enterprise to which it belongs and where these services provide a real advantage to the enterprise and their costs represent a significant part of the expenses of the enterprise'.[17] In contrast, management or service fees between different legal entities may be priced on the basis of the cost-plus method or the TNMM,[18] except for costs that simply flow through the invoicing company without value being added to such costs.
- Apart from banks and financial institutions,[19] the commentary on Article 7 of the OECD Model Tax Convention before the 2010 update considered that internal movements of funds (i.e., internal loans) between two parts of the same enterprise should not give rise to the deduction of internal interest expenses.[20] At the same time, intercompany loans were to be remunerated at

13. *See* OECD, *Additional Guidance on the Attribution of Profits to Permanent Establishments, BEPS Action 7* (2018).
14. The term '*dealings*' between different parts of the same enterprise is used in the context of Art. 7 of the OECD Model Tax Convention (and to a more limited extent in the UN Model Tax Convention), instead of *transactions* between different associated enterprises which is used in the context of Art. 9 of the OECD and UN Model Tax Conventions.
15. *See* para. 37 of the commentary to Art. 7 of the 2008 OECD Model Tax Convention, *in fine*. The commentary to Art. 7 before the 1994 update of the OECD Model Tax Convention clearly excluded that a profit mark-up be added to the cost base: *see* para. 20 of the commentary to Art. 7 of the 1992 OECD Model Tax Convention. On the topic of expenses of permanent establishments, *see* Kees van Raad, *Deemed Expenses of a Permanent Establishment under Article 7 of the OECD Model*, vol. 4, issue 28, 162–167 (Intertax, 2000).
16. *See* para. 35 of the commentary to Art. 7 of the 2008 OECD Model Tax Convention.
17. *See* para. 36 of the commentary to Art. 7 of the 2008 OECD Model Tax Convention.
18. *See* para. 7.31 of the 2022 OECD Guidelines: 'A cost based method would likely be the most appropriate method in the absence of a CUP where the nature of the activities involved, assets used, and risks assumed are comparable to those undertaken by independent enterprises.'
19. *See* para. 41 of the commentary to Art. 7 of the 2008 OECD Model Tax Convention.
20. *See* paras 41 and 42 of the commentary to Art. 7 of the 2008 OECD Model Tax Convention.

arm's length, which normally resulted in the borrower being charged interest by the lender.[21]

- With respect to the use by one part of an enterprise of intangibles developed by another part of the same enterprise, the former principles recommended by the OECD precluded that such use gave rise to the payment of internal royalties, because of the impossibility of allocating legal ownership of the intangibles to any particular part of the enterprise.[22] In contrast, the OECD Guidelines state that the arm's length principle should apply to intercompany transactions involving intangibles,[23] i.e., the use by one company of intangibles owned by an associated enterprise should be priced in the same way as between independent enterprises.

The OECD adopted the authorised OECD approach in 2008 in a separate report, and the commentary on Article 7 was amended to the extent of what could be implemented without modifying the text of Article 7. Article 7 of the OECD Model Tax Convention was reformed in 2010, to fully implement the authorised OECD approach. The commentary on Article 7 as well as the report on the attribution of profits to permanent establishments were updated accordingly. The authorised OECD approach implies an application of the arm's length principle to a greater extent than in the past, although differences still remain with the pricing of intercompany transactions. In addition, since Article 5 of the OECD Model Tax Convention was amended as part of the BEPS project,[24] the OECD issued specific guidance relating to the application of the authorised OECD approach in the context of these amendments.[25]

Finally, mention must be made of an approach that consists in taxing the permanent establishment on all the business profits earned by the non-resident company in the host country. Such an approach – which may be described as the principle of *force of attraction* – is rejected by the OECD Model Tax Convention,[26] but is partly implemented by the UN Model Tax Convention.[27] However, even under the UN Model Tax Convention, it is still necessary to determine how much of the profits of the enterprise should be attributed to a permanent establishment, thus limiting (albeit to a lower extent than the OECD Model) the taxing rights of the host country. Such a limitation is particular to permanent establishments, in contrast to resident companies that are most often subject to an unlimited tax liability in their country of residence.

21. *See* para. 3(a) of the commentary to Art. 9 of the 2017 OECD Model Tax Convention.
22. *See* para. 34 of the commentary to Art. 7 of the 2008 OECD Model Tax Convention.
23. *See* Chapter 6 of the 2022 OECD Guidelines.
24. The amendments to Art. 5 were implemented in the 2017 update to the OECD Model Tax Convention.
25. *See* OECD, *Additional Guidance on the Attribution of Profits to Permanent Establishments, BEPS Action 7* (2018).
26. *See* para. 12 of the commentary to Art. 7 of the 2017 OECD Model Tax Convention.
27. *See* Art. 7(1) of the 2011 UN Model Tax Convention and the commentary thereof. For a comment, *see* Amar Mehta, *The Limited Force of Attraction Rule*, vol. 21, issue 2 (Asia-Pacific Tax Bulletin, 2015), where it is argued that the purpose of the limited force of attraction rule of the UN Model Tax Convention is to constitute an anti-avoidance provision.

6.3 THE AUTHORISED OECD APPROACH

6.3.1 The Applicability of the Authorised OECD Approach

The recommendations of the OECD on the attribution of profits to permanent establishments were first published in a report issued in 2008.[28] The commentary on Article 7 was amended to the extent of what could be implemented without modifying the text of Article 7.

Article 7 of the OECD Model Tax Convention was then updated in the 2010 version of the model, together with the commentary thereof, to fully implement the authorised OECD approach.[29] The report issued in 2008 was formally updated in 2010 to be consistent with the 2010 version of the OECD Model Tax Convention, but no material changes were made between the 2008 and the 2010 reports.[30] Although the authorised OECD approach in principle reflects the views of the members of the OECD, it should be underlined that no general consensus exists on all aspects of the attribution of profits to permanent establishments.

Before exploring the authorised OECD approach, it is important to emphasise that these recommendations may not be applicable in all situations. In particular, a question that frequently arises is whether or not the authorised OECD approach may be applied to tax treaties concluded on the basis of the former Article 7 of the OECD Model Tax Convention, or on Article 7 of the UN Model Tax Convention. This is mainly an issue pertaining to the interpretation of tax treaties, and whether one should adopt a static or ambulatory approach. Since the authorised OECD approach implies certain material changes compared to previous guidance (as emphasised by the fact that the 2008 commentary could not implement the whole new approach), the most recent commentaries that may be applied to a treaty concluded before 2008 are the 2008 commentaries. Yet one cannot apply the 2008 commentary without further distinction, since in 2008 the commentary on Article 7 was updated to partly take into account the authorised OECD approach. Even if the text of Article 7 has remained unchanged before the 2010 update, the commentary on Article 7 has evolved, especially with the updates made in 1994 and 2008. Therefore, the 2008 commentary may not necessarily be applicable to a treaty that was negotiated on the basis of an older version of the OECD Model Tax Convention. Even if a dynamic interpretative approach to tax treaties is considered, in most countries that accept an ambulatory approach, later commentaries would only be taken into account if such commentaries provide clarifications, as opposed to implying material differences. Therefore, whether or not the 2008 commentary on Article 7 may be applied in a given situation supposes an

28. *See* OECD, *Report on the Attribution of Profits to Permanent Establishments* (17 July 2008).
29. *See* Art. 7 of the 2010 OECD Model Tax Convention, and the commentary thereof. The 2014 update to the OECD Model Tax Convention does not include any change with respect to Art. 7 and the commentary thereof.
30. *See* OECD, *Report on the Attribution of Profits to Permanent Establishments* (22 July 2010). The 2010 report is intended to serve as guidance on the interpretation of tax treaties that include a business profits article drafted according to the wording of Art. 7 of the 2010 OECD Model Tax Convention.

analysis of its content, in comparison with earlier commentaries. It is only if the material content has not evolved through the updates that the latest commentary may be applied.

In other words, the 2008 report cannot be applied to tax treaties concluded on the basis of a pre-2008 version of the OECD Model without determining if the report is compatible with the commentaries that were available at the time of the conclusion of the treaty. This is because the 2008 report contains certain conflicts with both the pre-2008 and the 2008 commentary on Article 7: it is emphasised in the 2008 commentary on Article 7 that the 2008 report represents internationally agreed principles and provides guidelines for the application of the arm's length principle incorporated in the article 'to the extent that it does not conflict with this Commentary'.[31]

The 2008 report does not explicitly mention which parts of the authorised OECD approach are applicable to treaties based on the pre-2010 wording of Article 7. This is why a case-by-case analysis is necessary. In this respect, there are certain parts of the 2008 report that are clearly in conflict with the commentary on Article 7, including its 2008 update. An example is the recognition of internal interest payments between a head office and its permanent establishment: whereas the 2008 report accepts that interest-bearing debt and internal interest expenses are allocated to a permanent establishment,[32] it is generally agreed in the 2008 commentary that such internal interests need not be recognised.[33] The 1977 commentary is even more restrictive in this respect.[34]

In addition, certain other aspects need to be considered when assessing the applicability of the authorised OECD approach. First, while the OECD Guidelines are often applied by countries that are not members of the OECD, the authorised OECD approach is less widely applied, even by OECD member countries.[35] It has been observed that 'A large majority of tax treaties that were signed between 2010 and 2018 did not include Article 7 of the OECD Model as modified in 2010.'[36] Differences of views on the attribution of profits to permanent establishments may even arise between OECD members, either because they accept the authorised OECD approach to different

31. *See* the last sentence of para. 7 of the commentary on Art. 7 of the 2008 OECD Model Tax Convention.
32. *See*, e.g., paras 184 and following of Part I of the 2008 OECD report on the attribution of profits to permanent establishments.
33. *See* para. 41 of the commentary on Art. 7 of the 2008 OECD Model Tax Convention.
34. *See* para. 17 of the commentary on Art. 7 of the 1977 OECD Model Tax Convention.
35. However, for the example of the US with respect to tax treaties that do not explicitly implement the authorised OECD approach, *see* Bob Stack, *US Tax Policy and Attribution of Profits to Permanent Establishments*, vol. 13, issue 3, 385–404 (World Tax Journal, 2021).
36. *See* Jacques Sasseville and Richard J. Vann, *IBFD Global Tax Treaty Commentaries, Article 7: Business Profits*, section 4.2.2.2. However, the contracting States may be willing to apply the authorised OECD approach without amending the drafting of the business profits article. For example, the United States and Canada have decided through a mutual agreement concluded between their competent authorities to fully apply the authorised OECD approach to the attribution of profits to permanent establishments: *see* Internal Revenue Bulletin 2012-34, Announcement 2012-31, 20 August 2012. On this topic *see also* Christos A. Theophilou, *Attribution of Profits to Permanent Establishments: Should the AOA Be Maintained as the OECD Standard?*, vol. 27, issue 1, 36–41 (International Transfer Pricing Journal, 2020).

extents[37] or because they have enacted domestic legislation that may not exactly implement the authorised OECD approach.[38] Second, the 2021 UN Model Tax Convention does not follow all the recommendations of the OECD when it comes to the attribution of profits to permanent establishments,[39] especially since internal royalties, services, and interests are neither deductible nor taxable for a permanent establishment. This position, comparable to the one favoured in the OECD Model Tax Convention before the 2010 update, is now different from the one suggested in the authorised OECD approach. Therefore, in a situation where a tax treaty has been concluded on the basis of the UN Model Tax Convention, the authorised OECD approach is normally not applicable.[40]

Third, the authorised OECD approach is contained in documents that are generally not considered as legally binding, something that contributes to differences of views between countries on the principles for the attribution of profits to permanent establishments. The binding effect of the commentary to the OECD Model Tax Convention and of reports published by the OECD is a matter that relates to the legal value of material relevant for the interpretation of tax treaties, and, in that respect, there is no international consensus.[41] Here, it can be argued that reports such as the 2008 and 2010 OECD reports on the attribution of profits to permanent establishments are less likely to have been taken into account by tax treaty negotiators than the commentary on the OECD or the UN Model Tax Convention, thus pointing to a lesser binding effect than the commentary. However, if a tax treaty explicitly refers to one of the OECD reports on the attribution of profits to permanent establishments, the legal value of such reports would obviously be affected.

37. In this respect, the observations and reservations made to the commentary on Art. 7 of the 2017 OECD Model Tax Convention reveal some of the differences of views between the OECD members with respect to the attribution of profits to permanent establishments. In certain cases, these statements are effectively applied in practice: *see*, e.g., Art. 23(6)(a) of the tax treaty concluded between the United Kingdom and Sweden on 26 March 2015, which excludes from the scope of mandatory arbitration 'issues concerning the attribution of capital to a permanent establishment under Article 7', although Art. 7 of this treaty is by and large drafted on the basis of Art. 7 of the 2014 OECD Model Tax Convention; this exclusion is consistent with the observation made by Sweden in para. 82 of the commentary on Art. 7 of the 2017 OECD Model Tax Convention, where it is indicated that Sweden 'does not consider that the different approaches for attributing "free" capital that are included in the Report *Attribution of Profits to Permanent Establishments* will necessarily lead to a result in accordance with the arm's length principle'.
38. *See*, e.g., the regulations published in Germany on 17 October 2014, which have been found to go 'beyond the rules that the OECD has developed in the context of the authorized OECD approach': *see* Ulf Andresen, *Regulations Provide Further Guidance on the Application of the Authorized OECD Approach to the Attribution of Profit to Permanent Establishments*, vol. 22, 84 (International Transfer Pricing Journal, March/April 2015).
39. In this respect, *see* Michael Lennard, *Update of the United Nations Model Tax Convention*, vol. 18, issue 2, 97 (Asia-Pacific Tax Bulletin, March/April 2012).
40. *See* para. 1 of the commentary on Art. 7 of the 2021 UN Model Tax Convention.
41. For a thorough study on this matter, *see* David Ward, et al., *The Interpretation of Income Tax Treaties with Particular Reference to the Commentaries on the OECD Model* (IFA/IBFD, 2005).

6.3.2 Rationale of the Authorised OECD Approach

Under the authorised OECD approach, permanent establishments are deemed as separate independent entities for income tax purposes. The aim of the authorised OECD approach is to attribute profits to permanent establishments based on the arm's length principle and the application of the OECD Guidelines by analogy.[42] The authorised OECD approach implies important changes compared to previous OECD guidance (especially the pre-2008 commentary on Article 7), in situations where transfers or payments (described as *dealings* in the authorised OECD approach) between a head office and its permanent establishment did not result in the attribution of an arm's length profit to the different parts of the same enterprise.[43]

The authorised OECD approach implies recognising dealings between a head office and its permanent establishment, and 'pricing' such dealings by attributing profits on the basis of the arm's length principle. This means that the profits attributable to a permanent establishment will not necessarily be a part of the total profits of the whole enterprise, but rather a consequence of the arm's length remuneration of the functions performed by the permanent establishment. For example, when a company is globally loss-making but when, at the same time, a permanent establishment belonging to that company performs routine functions, the authorised OECD approach may point to the need to remunerate that permanent establishment with a low profit, although the whole enterprise is loss-making.

The recognition of the dealings between the head office and the permanent establishment supposes making a fiction according to which the head office and the permanent establishment are assimilated into two separate legal entities. This is why this method is described in the work of the OECD as the *functionally separate entity approach*. The word 'functionally' indicates that it is the functions performed by the head office and the permanent establishment that will lay the ground for separating the permanent establishment from the head office from a tax perspective. The functionally separate entity approach differs from an alternative method, described by the OECD as the *relevant business activity approach*, according to which it is only the profits from a given business activity – the 'relevant business activity' – that may be shared between a head office and its permanent establishment. Accordingly, no profits should be earned on internal dealings between a head office and its permanent establishment. In other words, under the relevant business activity approach, profits are earned on transactions with other enterprises (whether associated or not), so that the profits attributed to a permanent establishment 'could not exceed the profits that the whole

42. 'Analogy' does not mean similarity. Articles 7 and 9 of the OECD Model Tax Convention have different functions, and while the authorised OECD approach largely overlaps with the OECD Guidelines, certain differences remain. On this topic, *see* Ryan Finley, *Transfer Pricing and Profit Attribution: A Strained Analogy*, 868–871 (Tax Notes International, 21 February 2022); Ryan Finley, *Profit Attribution Ain't Transfer Pricing, But Should It Be?*, 1232–1237 (Tax Notes International, 14 March 2022).

43. *See* Philip Baker and Richard S. Collier, General Report, Cahiers de Droit Fiscal International, *The Attribution of Profits to Permanent Establishments*, vol. 91b, 31, 41 (2006).

enterprise earns from the relevant business activity'.[44] The profits or losses incurred by the relevant business activity would then have to be shared between the head office and the permanent establishment. While the relevant business activity approach is not the method chosen as part of the authorised OECD approach, it is considered to have been 'largely endorsed' in the commentary until 2008.[45]

The example below illustrates the difference between the relevant business activity approach and the functionally separate entity approach.

Example: Illustration of the difference between the relevant business activity approach and the functionally separate entity approach

Assume that a company resident in State A has a permanent establishment in State B. The company is specialised in the construction of bridges and carries out a project in State B, on behalf of an independent client. It is assumed that the whole project results in a loss. Under the relevant business activity approach, since the project is carried out by the permanent establishment on behalf of another legal person, income may be attributed to the permanent establishment. The income attributed would be a share of the total income of the construction project (i.e., the relevant business activity). Consequently, a loss would be attributed to the permanent establishment since the whole project was loss-making. Under the functionally separate entity approach, one would have to attribute to the permanent establishment the profits (or losses) that would be incurred by an independent enterprise under similar circumstances, i.e., an independent enterprise having a functional profile comparable to the one of the permanent establishment. This may result in either a loss (e.g., if the permanent establishment has been actively participating in the strategic aspects of the construction project, which turned out to be a poor deal) or a profit (e.g., if the construction project was negotiated, designed, and managed by the head office, while the permanent establishment merely built the bridge under the instructions provided by the head office).

The OECD members have expressed their preference for the functionally separate entity approach over the relevant business activity approach,[46] although – as emphasised above – not all OECD members apply fully the authorised OECD approach; moreover, non-OECD members may not support the authorised OECD approach, in particular countries where permanent establishments were traditionally taxed under the relevant business activity approach or a form of profit split.

It should also be emphasised that while the authorised OECD approach attributes profits to permanent establishments based on the arm's length principle, this approach does not fully equate the tax treatment of a permanent establishment to the tax treatment of a legal entity. For example, the authorised OECD approach does not

44. *See* OECD, *Report on the Attribution of Profits to Permanent Establishments*, Part I, para. 62 (17 July 2008).
45. *See* Jonathan Schwarz, *Schwarz on Tax Treaties*, 228 (4th ed., Kluwer Law International, 2015); the same observation is made in the sixth edition of this book published in 2021.
46. *See* OECD, *Report on the Attribution of Profits to Permanent Establishments*, Part I, para. 78 (17 July 2008).

recommend granting a permanent establishment a separate credit rating,[47] while a legal entity would normally have its own credit rating.[48] Also, the authorised OECD approach does not imply the levy of withholding taxes on payments made between two parts of one and the same enterprise.[49]

The authorised OECD approach supposes to isolate the profits of the permanent establishment from those of the whole enterprise. The profits of a permanent establishment are based on all its activities, whether such profits are made with other parts of the same enterprise, associated enterprises, or independent enterprises.[50] To isolate the profits of the permanent establishment from those of the whole enterprise, a starting point may be the accounting of the permanent establishment.[51] However, dealings are recognised as a result of a functional and factual analysis, not as a result of the accounting records or other documents. Dealings may occur without an existence in the accounting, for example, if employees located in one part of the enterprise spend some time providing services to another part of the enterprise. That is, the attribution of profits to permanent establishments is subject to the principle of substance-over-form. Also, in addition to the financial statements of the permanent establishment, which are prepared under the domestic law of the host country, the authorised OECD approach supposes that one draws up a tax balance sheet particular to the permanent establishment.[52] This tax balance sheet will enable the enterprise to hypothesise assets, the economic ownership of which should be attributed to the permanent establishment. Consequently, since the income of the permanent establishment results from the accounting records issued under the domestic law of the host country, it may be significantly adjusted for taxation purposes.

The authorised OECD approach involves two steps: a functional and factual analysis (section 6.3.3), and a comparability analysis (section 6.3.4).

---

47. *See* OECD, *Report on the Attribution of Profits to Permanent Establishments*, Part I, para. 30 (22 July 2010): 'the creditworthiness of the PE is generally the same as the enterprise of which it is a part'.
48. *See* paras 7.13 and 10.19 of the 2022 OECD Guidelines.
49. *See*, e.g., OECD, *Report on the Attribution of Profits to Permanent Establishments*, Part IV, para. 166 (22 July 2010). *See also* Arts 10(4), 11(4) and 12(3) of the 2017 OECD Model Tax Convention as well as Arts 10(4), 11(4) and 12(4) of the 2021 UN Model Tax Convention, where the right of the State of source to levy a withholding tax on payments to a resident of the other contracting State may not be exercised when the income is paid to, and connected with, a permanent establishment (or a fixed base under the UN Model Tax Convention) of the beneficial owner that is located in the State of the payer.
50. *See* OECD, *Report on the Attribution of Profits to Permanent Establishments*, Part I, paras 10, 17 and 44 (22 July 2010).
51. *See* OECD, *Report on the Attribution of Profits to Permanent Establishments*, Part I, para. 177 (22 July 2010). It can be observed that many countries seem to use the accounts of a permanent establishment as a starting point to assess income attributable to it: *see* Philip Baker and Richard S. Collier, General Report, Cahiers de Droit Fiscal International, *The Attribution of Profits to Permanent Establishments*, vol. 91b, 41 (2006).
52. *See* OECD, *Report on the Attribution of Profits to Permanent Establishments*, Part I, paras 99 (22 July 2010) and following.

6.3.3 The Functional and Factual Analysis

6.3.3.1 Introduction

As with the pricing of transactions between separate legal entities, the pricing of dealings between two parts of the same enterprise involves performing a functional analysis of the two sides to the dealing. However, such a functional analysis has to be adapted to the special features of permanent establishments. Since a permanent establishment cannot enter into a legally binding agreement, it cannot formally bear risks on its own, as risks are borne by the enterprise as a whole. A permanent establishment cannot own assets by itself either, as assets are legally owned by the enterprise of which the permanent establishment is a part. Therefore, to be able to hypothesise the permanent establishment as if it were a separate legal entity for transfer pricing purposes, the authorised OECD approach recommends that the functional analysis focuses on the physical presence of persons performing functions (referred to as *significant people functions*) in the permanent establishment. It is indeed the functions performed by people in the permanent establishment that will lay the ground for making a fiction and assuming that the permanent establishment is a separate legal entity, which will eventually enable an attribution of profits in line with the functional profile of the permanent establishment. Since functions are the primary criterion for profit attribution and that risks and assets are not legally attributable to a permanent establishment, risks and assets are attributed to a permanent establishment by following the functions performed by persons physically located in the permanent establishment.

As a result, the authorised OECD approach implies that the profits or losses incurred by the company will be shared between the head office and its permanent establishment on the basis of the physical location of people performing functions. *A contrario*, a consequence of the authorised OECD approach is that in the lack of people performing functions in the permanent establishment, no risks or assets should be attributable to the permanent establishment.[53] An example of a situation combining the existence of a permanent establishment and the lack of attribution of profits is the presence of a server in a foreign country, with no personnel located there. A server may indeed be operated from abroad or locally with the help of third parties. In such a case,

53. This contrasts not only with the previous approach under Art. 7 but also with the OECD Guidelines before the BEPS amendments. Indeed, as mentioned above, with the amendments to the OECD Guidelines made in 2017, the physical performance of functions has gained priority over risks and assets (*see* section 1.4.2 of this book). This evolution has narrowed taxation under Arts 7 and 9 of the OECD Model Tax Convention, when the attribution of profits to permanent establishments is made in accordance with the authorised OECD approach. This is because the authorised OECD approach attributes profits in accordance with the exercise of significant people functions: a significant people function for the exploitation of an asset may, for example, lead to the attribution of that asset to a permanent establishment for taxation purposes, together with the income connected to it. By strengthening the role of functions for transfer pricing purposes (i.e., for the purpose of taxation under Art. 9), the BEPS changes to the OECD Guidelines have narrowed profit allocation under Art. 7 and 9 of the OECD Model Tax Convention.

the authorised OECD approach implies that no profits should be attributed to the server,[54] although it may very well constitute a permanent establishment.[55]

The functional analysis of a permanent establishment consists in analysing the functions (section 6.3.3.2), risks (section 6.3.3.3), assets (section 6.3.3.4), rights and obligations arising from transactions with separate enterprises (section 6.3.3.5), and funding (section 6.3.3.6) attributable to a permanent establishment.

6.3.3.2 Analysis of the Functions Attributable to a Permanent Establishment

The authorised OECD approach implies important changes compared to previous guidance, especially the pre-2008 commentary on Article 7. In order to tax permanent establishments on the basis of the arm's length principle, ensure taxation in line with substance, and remedy the problems implied by the lack of legal personality of a permanent establishment, the role of functions for the attribution of profits was made central in the authorised OECD approach. To that end, the concept of *significant people functions* was introduced.[56] This concept is not based on legal criteria, such as the entity that legally employs people performing functions, but on the physical place where functions are being performed. This approach, which would later influence the amendments made to Chapters 1 and 6 of the OECD Guidelines through giving a central role to the physical performance of functions (especially functions for the control of risks as well as DEMPE functions), leaves less room to tax avoidance since it is the physical reality existing within an enterprise that determines the attribution of profits to permanent establishments. To identify which significant people functions are performed and where such functions take place, the authorised OECD approach implies identifying the economically significant activities and responsibilities undertaken by the permanent establishment in the context of the enterprise taken as a whole, particularly those parts of the enterprise that enter into dealings with the permanent establishment.[57] The purpose of such an analysis is to understand the way the activities and responsibilities are shared between the different parts of the enterprise. This analysis is quite factual and takes into account aspects such as how

54. *See* OECD, *Report on the Attribution of Profits to Permanent Establishments*, Part I, para. 66 (22 July 2010): 'since a server-PE will not be carrying out any significant people functions relevant to the attribution of economic ownership of assets and/or the assumption of risks in the absence of personnel acting on behalf of the enterprise, no asset or risk could be attributed to it under the authorised OECD approach, supporting the conclusion that little or no profit would be attributed to such a PE'. For a discussion on the relevance of this solution, *see* Jérôme Monsenego, *May a Server Create a Permanent Establishment? Reflections on Certain Questions of Principle in Light of a Swedish Case*, vol. 21, issue 4, 255–257 (International Transfer Pricing Journal, July/August 2014).
55. *See* in particular paras 123 and following of the commentary on Art. 5 of the 2017 OECD Model Tax Convention.
56. In this respect it can be observed that the concept of significant people functions is not mentioned in the 2008 commentary on Art. 7, which nevertheless uses the concepts of 'functions' and 'activities'.
57. *See* OECD, *Report on the Attribution of Profits to Permanent Establishments*, Part I, para. 62 (22 July 2010).

often key employees have been physically present in different parts of the enterprise, to whom certain employees report, or where the key decisions are made.

6.3.3.3 *Analysis of the Risks Attributable to a Permanent Establishment*

When the most important functions of the permanent establishment have been identified, the functional and factual analysis attributes to the permanent establishment the risks that should follow these functions. As indicated above, it is the enterprise as a whole that legally bears risks, not the permanent establishment on its own. Therefore, the authorised OECD approach implies an assessment of the risks that follow the functions performed by the personnel of the permanent establishment. The functional and factual analysis attributes to the permanent establishment those risks for which the significant functions relevant to the assumption and/or the management of risks are performed by people in the permanent establishment. In other words, when the functions performed by the people located in the permanent establishment consist in managing or controlling certain risks, the assumption of such risks would be attributed - from a tax perspective - to the permanent establishment, something that also implies the attribution of the economic outcome (i.e., the profit or the loss) connected to the risks.

Example: Attribution of inventory risk to a permanent establishment

Assume that a company sells goods in a foreign country through a permanent establishment. It is assumed that the enterprise bears an important inventory risk because of the need to have important stock levels. It is also assumed that the significant people functions responsible for managing the stock levels and the inventory risk, such as the heads of logistics, stock planning, and sales, are working in the premises of the permanent establishment. That is, no important functions that are relevant for the assumption and the management of the inventory risk are located in the head office. According to the authorised OECD approach, the permanent establishment should assume the inventory risk that is formally borne by the enterprise, as the significant people functions relevant to the assumption and the management of the inventory risk are performed by people located in the premises of the permanent establishment. Consequently, if, e.g., write-downs on the inventory are booked in the accounts of the enterprise, such write-downs should be attributed to the permanent establishment and decrease its taxable base, as opposed to be attributable to the head office.

6.3.3.4 *Analysis of the Assets Attributable to a Permanent Establishment*

When the most important functions of the permanent establishment have been identified, the functional and factual analysis attributes to the permanent establishment the economic ownership of assets (tangible and intangible) that should follow these functions.[58] Indeed, in a permanent establishment context, it is the enterprise, of which the permanent establishment is a part, that legally owns the assets. Therefore, to enforce the separate entity approach, the OECD has developed the notion of economic ownership so as to hypothesise the assets that would be owned by the permanent establishment if it were a legal and independent entity. As a result, the authorised OECD approach supposes the determination of the extent to which the assets (tangible and intangible) of the whole enterprise are economically owned by and/or used in the functions performed by the permanent establishment. For example, depreciation, rent, or interest expenses (i.e., examples of costs related to an asset) should be attributed to a permanent establishment if such a permanent establishment is attributed the economic ownership of a tangible asset. Similarly, intangibles (and the income related to such intangibles) are attributed to a permanent establishment if there are significant people functions in the permanent establishment that are exercising active decision-making with regard to taking and managing risks related to the intangibles. In addition, the conditions of such ownership and/or use (joint or sole ownership, position as a licensee or licensor, whether the permanent establishment is a member of a CCA, etc.) are also taken into account.

Example: Attribution of an asset to a permanent establishment as a consequence of the presence of certain significant people functions relevant for marketing activities

Assume that a company resident in State A has a permanent establishment in State B. It is assumed that the marketing function is particularly important within this enterprise and consists in managing the branding strategy. It is also assumed that the management and control of the branding strategy are exclusively exercised by the personnel of the permanent establishment. Under the authorised OECD approach, the intangible asset (i.e., the brand) will be attributable to the permanent establishment. Accordingly, revenues related to the brand (e.g., licence fees) and costs connected to the branch (e.g., expenses necessary to protect the brand) should be attributed to the permanent establishment.[59]

6.3.3.5 Analysis of the Rights and Obligations Arising from Transactions with Separate Enterprises That Are Attributable to a Permanent Establishment

The authorised OECD approach implies attributing to the permanent establishment a part of the enterprise's rights and obligations that arise from transactions with separate enterprises. Profits are then attributed to the permanent establishment either directly

58. To illustrate the changes implied by the authorised OECD approach, it can be observed that while the authorised OECD approach endorses the attribution of economic ownership of intangible assets to a permanent establishment, no such necessity was expressed in the pre-2008 or even the 2008 commentary on Art. 7.

59. *See* OECD, *Report on the Attribution of Profits to Permanent Establishments*, Part I, para. 97 (22 July 2010).

(in case of transactions with independent enterprises) or through applying the OECD Guidelines (in case of transactions with associated enterprises).

Example: Attribution to a permanent establishment of a part of an enterprise's rights and obligations that arise from transactions with separate enterprises

Assume that a company resident in State A has a permanent establishment in State B. It is also assumed that the permanent establishment acts as a fully fledged manufacturer; products are manufactured by the permanent establishment without any involvement of the rest of the enterprise. Under the authorised OECD approach, the profits (or the losses) from the sale of the products manufactured by the permanent establishment to independent enterprises must be entirely attributed to the permanent establishment since there was no involvement of the head office in the manufacturing and sales processes. In other words, all significant people functions related to manufacturing and sales are performed by the permanent establishment. No adjustments to the profits are needed, as the prices of the sales hypothetically made by the permanent establishment (legally, the sales are still made by the company) are subject to the market forces, and no profit is attributable to the head office. In contrast, for sales to associated enterprises, the pricing of such transactions will follow the principles set in the OECD Guidelines, without however necessarily resulting in a different outcome if all significant people functions are exercised by the permanent establishment. Therefore, an internal CUP may very well be the most reliable method (i.e., prices of transactions with independent enterprises could be used as a benchmark for pricing the dealings entered into by the permanent establishment with the rest of the enterprise). Moreover, the risks that are assumed and managed by the significant people functions in the permanent establishment (e.g., the product risk related to the goods manufactured by the permanent establishment) should also be borne by the permanent establishment.

6.3.3.6 Analysis of the Funding Attributable to a Permanent Establishment

The funding of a permanent establishment is a complex issue that starts from the premise that a separate legal entity's funding may come from equity (i.e., contributions from shareholders and retained earnings) or debt. Payments made to holders of equity capital are usually not tax deductible, whereas deductions are often available for payments of interest to the holders of debts. The same sort of dual funding does not exist for a permanent establishment: it does not have a separate equity, there are no systematic obligations to allot capital to a permanent establishment, and a permanent establishment cannot have debts on its own. Therefore, to approximate the treatment of legal entities and permanent establishments, the authorised OECD approach implies a twofold process: the attribution of a free capital (which is meant to resemble the equity of a legal entity) and, for the financial needs that exceed the free capital, the attribution of interests-bearing debt. This approach is described below in more detail.

To start with, it is necessary to ensure an appropriate attribution of the enterprise's *free capital* to a permanent establishment. Free capital refers to 'funding that does not give rise to a tax deductible return in the nature of interest'.[60]

Only the need of funding of a permanent establishment that exceeds the free capital may give rise to interest expenses that are attributable to the permanent establishment.[61] Indeed, in the absence of regulatory requirements, there is normally no obligation for free capital to be allotted to a permanent establishment.[62] As a result, a permanent establishment may be entirely debt-funded, which would entitle a permanent establishment to the possibility to deduct interests for all its funding needs, in contrast to a legal entity.[63] This possibility is not accepted under the authorised OECD approach, which considers that a permanent establishment needs an appropriate amount of free capital to support its functions, risks, and assets, as would be the case for a separate legal entity. Consequently, the view of the OECD is that a permanent establishment should not be entirely funded by debt. Instead, a permanent establishment's funding needs first to be made up of free capital and, possibly, of interest-bearing debt. The free capital attributed to a permanent establishment must follow the functions, risks, and assets it has been attributed, in relation to those of the enterprise as a whole.[64] The more functions, risks, and assets attributable to the permanent establishment, the more free capital it needs. In other words, the functionally separate entity approach requires the attribution of free capital consistently with the outcome of the functional and factual analysis.

The OECD report on the attribution of profits to permanent establishments describes different methods for the allocation of free capital to permanent establishments.[65] These methods can be divided into two main categories. On the one hand, certain methods focus on the capital structure of the enterprise. These methods attribute a part of the actual free capital of the enterprise to the permanent establishment depending on the functions, risks, and assets attributed to the

60. *See* OECD, *Report on the Attribution of Profits to Permanent Establishments*, Part I, para. 28 and 105–106 (22 July 2010). It should be emphasised that the free capital attributed to a permanent establishment does not require, in principle, that money is actually allotted to the permanent establishment: *see* OECD, *Report on the Attribution of Profits to Permanent Establishments*, Part I, para. 116 (22 July 2010). On the determination of the free capital of a permanent establishment, *see also* Norma Kraay and Leon Bloom, *The Missing Link: Transfer Pricing and Regulatory Capital Compliance for Global Financial Institutions*, 527–531 (Tax Notes International, 13 February 2012).
61. It should be emphasised that the authorised OECD approach is without prejudice for the application of a country's domestic tax law. Therefore, even if interest expenses are attributed to a permanent establishment under the authorised OECD approach, such interest expenses may not necessarily be deductible for corporate income tax purposes. The right of deduction is ultimately up to the domestic legislation of the host country.
62. Such regulatory requirements prescribing capital that should be allotted to permanent establishments may, however, be applicable within the financial sector.
63. *See* OECD, *Report on the Attribution of Profits to Permanent Establishments*, Part I, para. 115 (22 July 2010).
64. *See* OECD, *Report on the Attribution of Profits to Permanent Establishments*, Part I, para. 107 (22 July 2010).
65. *See* OECD, *Report on the Attribution of Profits to Permanent Establishments*, Part I, paras 121–145 (22 July 2010).

permanent establishment. On the other hand, other methods focus on the capital structure of comparable independent companies, and attribute free capital to a permanent establishment in proportion to the free capital of comparable independent companies. Other methods are also described for certain situations. However, the OECD emphasises that there is no single internationally accepted approach for attributing an arm's length amount of free capital to a permanent establishment.[66]

After having determined the amount of free capital attributable to a permanent establishment, the remaining need for funding (if any) may be financed by *interest-bearing debt* and could result in interest expenses being attributed to the permanent establishment, to an extent that is 'commensurate with the functions, assets and risks attributed'.[67] The attribution of interest-bearing debt to a permanent establishment may relate to either internal or external funding:

- Interest expenses may be purely internal to the enterprise (*internal funding*). Funding is then provided by different parts of the enterprise through internal movements of funds. Such internal movements of funds may give rise to the payment of interest. However, for such interest expenses to be recognised for transfer pricing purposes (and possibly be deductible in the host country), interest expenses should be recognised as internal interest dealings.[68] This supposes that interests reward a treasury function qualifying as a significant people function,[69] which is a logical outcome given that it is the performance of functions and the assumption of risks that entitles to income under the OECD Guidelines. If there is no treasury function qualifying as a significant people function within the enterprise, the OECD report does not recognise any internal interest dealings, which means that no internal interest can be charged for tax purposes between the head office and the permanent establishment. However, in the absence of a treasury function qualifying as a significant people function, a part of the external interest expenses of the enterprise may still be allocated to the permanent establishment (external funding),[70] assuming that the permanent establishment has a financing need that exceeds the free capital that it has been allocated. For the purpose of investigating whether there is a treasury function qualifying as a significant people function within the enterprise, one has to identify the significant people functions relevant to the economic ownership of cash or financial assets; i.e., it is necessary that the enterprise employs people that actually manage the

66. *See* OECD, *Report on the Attribution of Profits to Permanent Establishments*, Part I, para. 147 (22 July 2010).
67. *See* OECD, *Report on the Attribution of Profits to Permanent Establishments*, Part I, para. 152 (22 July 2010).
68. *See* OECD, *Report on the Attribution of Profits to Permanent Establishments*, Part I, para. 151 (22 July 2010).
69. *See* OECD, *Report on the Attribution of Profits to Permanent Establishments*, Part I, para. 152 (22 July 2010).
70. *See* OECD, *Report on the Attribution of Profits to Permanent Establishments*, Part I, para. 157 (22 July 2010): 'If there are no significant people functions then only the actual external interest expense of the enterprise will be allocated amongst the various parts of the enterprise.'

internal financing.[71] Only then could internal movements of funds be recognised as treasury dealings[72] and result in the attribution of internal interest expenses to a permanent establishment. Once a treasury function has been identified, it is necessary to determine the level of interest that should be applied to the internal treasury dealing. Here, the authorised OECD approach implies charging interest that is in line with the arm's length principle. The level of interest is determined on the basis of the functional and factual analysis, in accordance with the methods provided in the OECD Guidelines.[73]

- Interest expenses may also be incurred by the enterprise through taking a loan from a third party (*external funding*). The question is then whether or not a portion of the interest expenses incurred by the enterprise as a whole should be attributed to a permanent establishment. Here, there is no need of a treasury function qualifying as a significant people function, as the funding has an origin that is external to the enterprise. However, the arm's length principle commands that the external interest expenses attributed to a permanent establishment correspond to the need of funding required to perform the functions, assume the risks, and economically own the assets that are attributed to the permanent establishment. The authorised OECD approach does not recommend a single method for determining the amount of external interest expenses attributed to a permanent establishment, but describes different methods used in different countries.[74]

As a result of the functional and factual analysis, functions, risks, assets, rights, and obligations arising from transactions with separate enterprises, as well as capital, are attributed to a permanent establishment. The pricing of the dealings between the permanent establishment and the head office is then made on the basis of a comparability analysis.

6.3.4 The Comparability Analysis

The comparability analysis helps determine the prices to be applied, or the profit margins to be aimed at, to remunerate appropriately a permanent establishment based on the outcome of the functional and factual analysis. The pricing of the dealings between the permanent establishment and the head office is made by applying the

71. *See* OECD, *Report on the Attribution of Profits to Permanent Establishments*, Part I, para. 153 (22 July 2010).
72. *See* OECD, *Report on the Attribution of Profits to Permanent Establishments*, Part I, paras 152 and 153 (22 July 2010).
73. *See* OECD, *Report on the Attribution of Profits to Permanent Establishments*, Part I, paras 159–168 (22 July 2010).
74. The OECD report identifies several methods in that respect: *see* OECD, *Report on the Attribution of Profits to Permanent Establishments*, Part I, paras 154–156 and paras 159–168 (22 July 2010).

OECD Guidelines by analogy. This implies choosing a transfer pricing method and possibly performing a benchmarking study according to the recommendations of the OECD Guidelines.[75]

75. *See* OECD, *Report on the Attribution of Profits to Permanent Establishments*, particularly in para. 10 of the preface (22 July 2010).

CHAPTER 7

Administrative Aspects: Compliance Issues and Transfer Pricing Disputes

This chapter presents two types of administrative aspects linked to transfer pricing: the need to enforce certain compliance rules (section 7.1), and the prevention as well as the resolution of cross-border transfer pricing disputes (section 7.2).

7.1 TRANSFER PRICING AND COMPLIANCE ISSUES

Compliance issues play an ever more important role in the field of transfer pricing. With the increasing role of monitoring transfer pricing for fiscal revenue purposes, the growing complexity of transfer pricing rules, the perception that these rules may be manipulated, and the emergence of transparency expectations on the tax policies of multinational enterprises, compliance has become an important part of the work of transfer pricing professionals. This section of the book touches upon the three most significant compliance issues for multinational enterprises as well as tax administrations: transfer pricing documentation (section 7.1.1), country-by-country reporting (section 7.1.2), and the mandatory disclosure of transfer pricing arrangements (section 7.1.3). Here, it can be observed that these different compliance obligations impose an important burden on both multinational enterprises and tax administrations. Hence, the access to and management of data has become a key issue, contributing to the digitalisation of the tax function.[1]

1. On this topic, and especially with respect to the use of blockchain technology, *see* Luís Flávio Neto, *The Blockchain Revolution for Transfer Pricing Documentation: If Not in 2020, Then When?*, in Pasquale Pistone and Dennis Weber (eds), Taxing the Digital Economy: The EU Proposals and Other Insights, 307–334 (IBFD, 2019).

7.1.1 Transfer Pricing Documentation

Numerous countries have implemented transfer pricing documentation requirements, and these requirements often vary from one country to another.[2] At the same time, there is a 'great benefit of having consistent documentation rules from country to country to minimize transfer pricing compliance burdens'.[3] The main purpose of transfer pricing documentation is to provide tax administrations with explanations on the transfer pricing policy applied to the intercompany transactions within a multinational enterprise. Such explanations will help tax administrations assess whether transfer prices have been set at arm's length. Paragraphs 5.5 and following of the 2022 OECD Guidelines assign three objectives to transfer pricing documentation: (i) ensure that a culture of compliance with the arm's length principle is created (i.e., the taxpayer's own assessment of its enforcement of transfer pricing rules),[4] (ii) enable tax administrations to accurately evaluate whether a taxpayer's transfer pricing arrangements create a need for a tax audit (i.e., transfer pricing risk assessment from the perspective of tax administrations),[5] and (iii) provide tax administrations with useful information to employ in conducting a thorough transfer pricing audit.[6]

All these objectives have to be balanced with the need to carefully consider the increased compliance burdens placed on taxpayers.[7] Indeed, there are often diverging interests between tax administrations and multinational enterprises. This concerns several aspects, such as the administrative burden put on multinational enterprises or the level of secrecy relating to information that is made available to tax

2. Whereas certain countries have no transfer pricing documentation requirements at all, other countries have very detailed and demanding requirements. In the countries that do have transfer pricing documentation requirements, multinational enterprises are expected to hand in the documentation to tax administrations either spontaneously (e.g., at the time of handing in the tax declaration) or upon request (e.g., within a certain delay following the start of a tax audit): *see* para. 5.29 of the 2022 OECD Guidelines. It is considered in the Guidelines that 'The best practice is to require that the local file be finalised no later than the due date for the filing of the tax return for the fiscal year in question. The master file should be reviewed and, if necessary, updated by the tax return due date for the ultimate parent of the MNE group (para. 5.30).' The country-by-country report can be submitted later, up to one year following the end of the fiscal year of the ultimate parent entity of a multinational enterprise (para. 5.31). As emphasised in the UN Manual, the recommendations included in the OECD Guidelines 'were designed by the countries involved in the BEPS Project for adoption by them in the context of their own transfer pricing legislation, priorities, capabilities and experience. It cannot automatically be assumed that these OECD/G20 guidelines should be adopted in their entirety by every developing country' (*see* para. 12.2.2.1 of the 2021 UN Manual).
3. *See* para. 12.2.2.1 of the 2021 UN Manual.
4. *See* para. 5.7 of the 2022 OECD Guidelines.
5. *See* para. 5.10 of the 2022 OECD Guidelines.
6. *See* para. 5.13 of the 2022 OECD Guidelines.
7. *See* paras 5.4 and 5.28 of the 2022 OECD Guidelines. For example, while transfer pricing documentation should in principle be updated annually (except benchmarking studies that the Guidelines find suitable to update every three years, *see* para. 5.38), it is recognised that there may not be significant changes from one year to the other (para. 5.37); similarly, it is recommended to prepare transfer pricing documentation in 'commonly used languages' (para. 5.39).

administrations.[8] On the one hand, tax administrations may need extensive information to be able to assess the correctness of transfer prices; on the other hand, preparing transfer pricing documentation is often quite burdensome, and there may be business information that is sensitive to reveal. To reach a balance and achieve a greater level of coordination between the different rules on transfer pricing documentation, the Guidelines contain a three-tiered approach to transfer pricing documentation consisting of a master file, a local file[9] and a country-by-country report:

- The master file contains high-level – i.e., not exhaustive – information relevant for all group members (or, when justified, per line of business) with respect to the group's organisational structure, business, intangibles, intercompany financial activities, and financial as well as tax positions.[10]
- The local file supplements the master file and relates to specific intercompany transactions of a specific group member in a given country.[11] Only information that is material enough (in view of the specific country's needs) should be reported;[12] no materiality thresholds are provided in the Guidelines.
- The country-by-country report contains information relating to the global allocation of the group's income and taxes paid, together with certain indicators of the location of economic activity within the group.[13] Country-by-country reporting is presented in more detail in section 7.1.2 below.

The fulfilment of transfer pricing documentation requirements does not guarantee that transfer prices are at arm's length or that no tax audit can be initiated. The Guidelines indicate also that a tax administration's access to information should

8. For an overview of some these issues *see* Patrick Boone and Madlen Haupt, *Transfer Pricing Documentation for Business Restructurings*, vol. 20, issue 3, 127–131 (International Transfer Pricing Journal, May/June 2013).
9. The master file/local file concept is inspired by the work of the JTPF, which aimed at a coordinated approach to transfer pricing documentation, the EU transfer pricing documentation. The European Commission suggested the adoption of a code of conduct on transfer pricing documentation for related parties in the EU (COM(2005) 543 final) which was eventually subject to a resolution of the council (*resolution of the council and of the representatives of the governments of the Member States on a code of conduct on transfer pricing documentation for associated enterprises in the European Union*, OJ C 176, 28.7.2006, pp. 1–7); this resolution is, however, not legally binding. Despite being inspired by the EU transfer pricing documentation, the transfer pricing documentation described in the 2022 Guidelines partly departs from it. Therefore, this section of the book focuses on the transfer pricing documentation in the OECD Guidelines, not the EU transfer pricing documentation.
10. *See* Annex 1 to Chapter 5 of the 2022 OECD Guidelines for a detailed presentation of the items of information to be included in the master file.
11. *See* Annex 2 to Chapter 5 of the 2022 OECD Guidelines for a detailed presentation of the items of information to be included in the local file.
12. *See* paras 5.22 and 5.32 of the 2022 OECD Guidelines.
13. *See* Annex 3 to Chapter 5 of the 2022 OECD Guidelines for a detailed presentation of the items of information to be included in the country-by-country report, including a model template together with accompanying instructions. Annex 4 to Chapter 5 of the 2022 OECD Guidelines contains a country-by-country reporting implementation package, consisting of model legislation as well as models for bilateral and multilateral competent authority agreements on the exchange of country-by-country reports.

not be limited to, or by, the transfer pricing documentation.[14] In other words, transfer pricing documentation is usually considered as necessary, but not always sufficient for risk assessment purposes.[15] Not complying with these requirements can have significant consequences for a multinational enterprise. If too little or incorrect information is presented to the tax administration, a reassessment may be made on the basis of the information that is available.[16] In addition, certain countries levy penalties in case transfer pricing documentation has not been prepared or is handed in too late; the non-compliance with transfer pricing documentation requirements may also shift to the taxpayer the burden of proof that the arm's length principle has been enforced. Therefore, transfer pricing documentation is particularly important to draft in relation to transactions that have an important effect on the tax base of the parties to a transaction since large transactions entail a large risk on a country's fiscal revenues; hence they are the most likely transactions to be audited by tax administrations. For that reason, several countries alleviate or even have no transfer pricing documentation requirements on transactions of a low value, or on smaller taxpayers.[17]

7.1.2 Country-by-Country Reporting

Country-by-country reporting is intended to help countries assess whether the biggest multinational enterprises (often defined as groups with total consolidated revenue equal or higher than EUR 750 million) that carry on business activities in their territories pay the right amount of taxes, in relation to their worldwide activities. The country-by-country report should only be used for high-level transfer pricing risk assessment; i.e., it does not suffice to assess compliance with the arm's length principle. In other words, a tax reassessment cannot be based solely on the country-by-country report.[18] Once filed, the report may be communicated through exchange of information to the other countries where the group has subsidiaries or permanent establishments.

The report contains a list of all the group members for which financial information should be reported. The country-by-country report shall cover a group's allocation of income, taxes, and business activities on a country-by-country basis: it includes for each tax jurisdiction information on the revenue (both towards related and

14. *See* para. 5.14 of the 2022 OECD Guidelines.
15. Transfer pricing documentation does not necessarily correctly reflect the reality existing within a group of companies, as the documentation is only a description that is made by the group. Also, several elements of the documentation are relying on judgment (e.g., characterisation following a functional analysis, or the assessment of implicit support for the pricing of intercompany loans), and thus the assessments made by the taxpayer will not necessarily be agreed to by the tax administration. Therefore, information provided in the transfer pricing documentation will in many cases need to be verified by tax administrations. This means that transfer pricing documentation may not prevent tax audits, income tax reassessments, and transfer pricing disputes.
16. For an example of court case in which the transfer pricing documentation was deemed insufficient, *see Tetra Pak Processing Systems A/S*, Højesteret (Danish Supreme Administrative Court, 26 April 2021, case number BS-19502/2020-HJR).
17. *See* paras 5.32–5.34 of the 2022 OECD Guidelines with respect to materiality.
18. *See* para. 5.25 of the 2022 OECD Guidelines.

unrelated parties), the profit before tax, the income tax paid and accrued, the stated capital, the accumulated earnings, the number of employees, and the tangible assets of the entities concerned by the report.

Country-by-country reporting is in general not available to the public, an important exception being the EU:[19] within the EU, country-by-country reporting has been made public mainly to increase transparency and enable the public to assess the impact of the activities of multinational enterprises on the real economy.[20]

7.1.3 Mandatory Disclosure

It was concluded as part of the BEPS project that tax administrations experience a lack of information on certain tax planning strategies.[21] Therefore, the report on BEPS Action 12 formulated recommendations on the design of rules for the mandatory disclosure of certain arrangements deemed abusive, the aim of which is to provide governments with early access to information and enable them to quickly respond to risks of tax avoidance. However, the recommendations included in the report on BEPS Action 12 do not represent a minimum standard, and there are no mandatory disclosure rules in force on a global level.[22] In contrast, common rules have been developed at the regional level in the EU, through the adoption of a directive providing for the mandatory disclosure and the automatic exchange of information in relation to certain reportable cross-border arrangements.[23] This directive amended the directive on administrative compliance (often referred to as the 'DAC'). The mandatory disclosure of reportable cross-border arrangements implies a reporting obligation, and applies primarily to intermediaries. Intermediaries are defined as any person that designs, markets, organises or makes available for implementation or manages the implementation of a reportable cross-border arrangement. The taxpayer may also be subject to the reporting obligation, e.g., in the lack of intermediary, when the intermediary is bound by professional privilege or secrecy rules, or if the intermediary is not located in the EU.

Cross-border arrangements that contain one or more of the 'hallmarks' described in the Directive are subject to the reporting obligation, which does not mean that such reportable arrangements are necessarily abusive. In the area of transfer pricing, three

19. *See Directive (EU) 2021/2101 of the European Parliament and of the Council of 24 November 2021 amending Directive 2013/34/EU as regards disclosure of income tax information by certain undertakings and branches*, OJ L 429 (1 December 2021), pp. 1–14. For a comment, *see* Susanne Verloove, Peter Hoving and Roberto Aviles Gutierrez, *EU Public Country-by-Country Reporting*, vol. 29, issue 3, 153–160 (International Transfer Pricing Journal, 2022); Patrick Velte, *The New European Public Country-by-Country Reporting Requirement*, 168–172 (European Taxation, 2022-4).
20. *See* point 3 of the preamble to the *Directive (EU) 2021/2101*.
21. *See* OECD, *Mandatory Disclosure Rules, Action 12: 2015 Final Report* (2015).
22. Nevertheless, mandatory disclosure rules have been implemented by different countries. For the example of Mexico, *see* para. 4.12.2 of the 2021 UN Manual (Part D).
23. *See* Council Directive (EU) 2018/822 of 25 May 2018 amending Directive 2011/16/EU as regards mandatory automatic exchange of information in the field of taxation in relation to reportable cross-border arrangements, OJ L 139, 5.6.2018, pp. 1–13.

hallmarks trigger the disclosure obligation: the use of unilateral safe harbour rules, the transfer of hard-to-value intangibles, and certain cross-border business restructurings if a drop in profits is observed after the restructuring.[24] In these situations, the reporting obligation applies irrespective of whether or not the transaction is motivated by tax reasons.

Finally, it must be emphasised that sanctions may apply when the reporting obligation is not met. However, such sanctions are not harmonised at the level of the Member States of the EU: the directive requires only that the Member States implement penalties that are 'effective, proportionate and dissuasive'. Therefore, important differences exist across the Member States with respect to the level of the sanctions.[25]

7.2 THE PREVENTION AND RESOLUTION OF TRANSFER PRICING DISPUTES

Most domestic tax laws contain an arm's length rule whereby cross-border intercompany transactions must be priced in line with the market forces. This principle is also found in a great number of tax treaties containing an article on the taxation of associated enterprises drafted on the basis of Article 9 of the OECD or the UN Model Tax Convention. In addition, multinational enterprises and tax administrations may rely on the OECD Guidelines or on the UN Manual to interpret the arm's length principle. However, despite the large reliance on the arm's length principle and the frequent use of similar interpretative sources, disputes regularly arise between multinational enterprises and tax administrations in relation to transfer pricing matters.[26] It is not particularly surprising that transfer pricing disputes often arise, given the opposite interests of tax administrations and multinational enterprises, on the one hand, and the different countries where multinational enterprises are doing business, on the other hand. Such disputes would in most cases start with a transfer pricing reassessment in one country, when that country believes that taxable profits are too low because of non-arm's length transfer prices. Indeed, when a tax administration considers that the transfer prices applied between associated enterprises are not at arm's length, it may, on the basis of its domestic arm's length provision (possibly confirmed by the applicable tax treaty), reassess such prices to arrive at – what the tax administration finds being – an arm's length transfer price or profit margin.[27] Such a

24. The mandatory disclosure applies if the projected annual earnings before interest and taxes (EBIT), during the three-year period after the transfer, of the transferor or transferors, are less than 50% of the projected annual EBIT of such transferor or transferors if the transfer had not been made: *see* the Annex IV of the directive, hallmark E, point 3.
25. On the different implementations of DAC 6, *see* Elisa Casi-Eberhard, Xiao Chen, Mark D. Orlic and Christoph Spengel, *One Directive, Several Transpositions: A Cross-Country Evaluation of the National Implementation of DAC6*, vol. 13, issue 1, 63–81 (World Tax Journal, 2021).
26. On this topic, *see* Caroline Silberztein, *Transfer Pricing Disputes and Their Causes*, vol. 16, 439–446 (Asia-Pacific Tax Bulletin, November/December 2010).
27. *See* para. 2 of the commentary to Art. 9 of the 2017 OECD Model Tax Convention: 'the taxation authorities of a Contracting State may, for the purpose of calculating tax liabilities of associated enterprises, re-write the accounts of the enterprises if, as a result of the special relations between the enterprises, the accounts do not show the true taxable profits arising in that State'. In most

reassessment is likely to increase the taxable base of the company that is subject to the reassessment. However, profits gained from the intercompany transaction may have already been taxed in the country of the counterpart to the transaction, something that would result in a double taxation of such profits: in other words, the transfer pricing reassessment leads to double taxation since the increase in taxable profits in one country is normally not automatically compensated by a decrease in taxable profits in the country of the other party to the reassessed transaction. Let us illustrate this with an example.

Example: Tax reassessment resulting in double taxation

Assume that company A (resident in country A) purchases goods manufactured by the associated company B (resident in country B). Countries A and B have a 30% corporate income tax rate. Company A purchases goods for 80; i.e., the COGS of company A is 80 while the turnover of company B is 80. It is assumed that the income statements of companies A and B are, before reassessment, as follows (Table 7.1).

Table 7.1 Situation Before Tax Reassessment

Company A – Country A		*Company B – Country B*	
Turnover	100	Turnover	80
COGS	80	COGS	65
Gross margin	**20**	**Gross margin**	**15**
OPEX	15	OPEX	7
Operating margin	**5**	**Operating margin**	**8**
Other costs	2	Other costs	3
Net profit	**3**	**Net profit**	**5**
Corporate tax	0.9	Corporate tax	1.5
Total tax burden		0.9 + 1.5 = 2.4	

It is then assumed that the tax administration of country A considers that the purchase price paid by company A (80) is too high and not at arm's length, and should instead amount to 75. Consequently, the tax administration of country A reassesses the

countries, it is the tax administration that has the burden of proof that the arm's length principle has not been upheld; for an illustration, *see*, e.g., the case *Cap Gemini*, French Supreme Administrative Court (*Conseil d'État*), case numbers 266436 and 266438 (7 November 2005). However, the burden of proof may in certain cases be easily be reversed with, as a consequence, a need for taxpayers to show that a transfer pricing reassessment was in excess of the arm's length principle. For an example of case where the taxpayer could not bring evidence that a transfer pricing reassessment was in excess of the arm's length principle, *see Chevron Australia Holdings Pty Ltd v. Commissioner of Taxation*, Federal Court of Australia (23 October 2015, case number (2015) FCA 1092). A parallel may also be made to the tax cases analysed in the light of European State aid law, e.g., the *Apple* case where the European Commission was found not to bring evidence of the attribution of profits to permanent establishments in breach of the reference system: *see Ireland and Others v. European Commission*, General Court of the European Union (15 July 2020, case numbers T-778/16 and T-892/16).

income of company A and decreases the purchase price (i.e., the COGS) accepted as a deductible expense, from 80 to 75. The income statements of companies A and B, after reassessment, are as follows (Table 7.2).

Table 7.2 Situation After Tax Reassessment (Double Taxation)

Company A – Country A		*Company B – Country B*	
Turnover	100	Turnover	80
COGS	75	COGS	65
Gross margin	**25**	**Gross margin**	**15**
OPEX	15	OPEX	7
Operating margin	**10**	**Operating margin**	**8**
Other costs	2	Other costs	3
Net profit	**8**	**Net profit**	**5**
Corporate tax	2.4	Corporate tax	1.5
Total tax burden		2.4 + 1.5 = 3.9	

As evidenced by Table 7.2, the consequence of the tax reassessment in country A is that the group is subject to double taxation since a part of the group's profits has been subject to tax in both countries. This is because the turnover of company B is still 80, while the COGS of company A that is accepted as a deductible expense in country A has been decreased to 75. Accordingly, double taxation arises on the difference between the purchasing price deducted in country A (75) and the selling price accounted for in country B (80), i.e., an amount of 5 is subject to double taxation. While the total net profits subject to tax amounted to 8 in Table 7.1 (3 + 5 = 8), the total net profits subject to tax in this second example amount to 13 (8 + 5 = 13). Accordingly, the total tax burden now amounts to 3.9, while it amounted to 2.4 before the tax reassessment. The difference between these two tax burdens (3.9–2.4 = 1.5) corresponds to the corporate income tax rate (30%) applied to the income that has been taxed twice (5 × 30% = 1.5).

There may be several methods to eliminate such a double taxation. The claim of country A could be challenged before a court in country A. However, situations of double taxation relating to transfer pricing are not always suitable to be solved by domestic courts. This is partly due to the fact that transfer pricing is largely relying on facts, which are hardly handled by courts and raise difficult issues with respect to the burden of proof.[28] In addition, the claim of the tax administration of country A may very well be justified, something that would obviously prevent a court in country A from eliminating the double taxation. If there is a tax treaty between countries A and B

28. For an example where the factual nature of transfer pricing prevented a court from fully assessing a case, *see Amazon.com, Inc. & Subsidiaries v. the Commissioner of Internal Revenue*, United States Tax Court, Tax Court Memo 2014-149 (28 July 2014, case number 31197-12), where the court found that there were 'genuine disputes of material fact that preclude partial summary judgment'. Similarly, *see Tobacco S.A.*, Portuguese Supreme Administrative Court (12 May 2021, case number 0507/17).

that contains a mechanism for corresponding adjustments,[29] the taxpayer may claim a decrease of the tax base before the competent authorities of country B. Yet country B is not bound by the decisions of the tax administration or the domestic courts of country A, and may consider that the reassessment was not justified. Therefore, domestic remedies may not be suitable to efficiently eliminate the double taxation caused by a transfer pricing adjustment, because of the unilateral character of such actions while transfer pricing is by definition bilateral.

As an alternative to court proceedings, if a tax treaty exists between the countries concerned (i.e., the country of the initial tax adjustment and the State of residence of the other party to the intercompany transaction), a MAP may be a more efficient mechanism to eliminate the double taxation. MAPs between the competent authorities[30] of countries having concluded a tax treaty provide a framework to discuss the issue and, if possible, find a way to eliminate the double taxation. Assuming that the claim of country A in the example above is justified (i.e., it is correct that the transfer price of goods between companies A and B should amount to 75, not to 80), a MAP could result in country B recognising the correctness of the adjustment made by country A. In this case, country B could tax company B on the basis of a turnover decreased from 80 to 75, to take into account the lower price for the goods sold to company A. Such an elimination of the double taxation is illustrated in Table 7.3.

Table 7.3 Situation After Tax Reassessment (Double Taxation Eliminated Following a Corresponding Adjustment in Country B)

Company A – Country A		*Company B – Country B*	
Turnover	100	Turnover	75
COGS	75	COGS	65
Gross margin	**25**	**Gross margin**	**10**
OPEX	15	OPEX	7
Operating margin	**10**	**Operating margin**	**3**
Other costs	2	Other costs	3
Net profit	**8**	**Net profit**	**0**
Corporate tax	2.4	Corporate tax	0
Total tax burden	2.4		

In Table 7.3, it is observed that, as in Table 7.1, the COGS of company A is the same as the turnover of company B (75 in both cases). The net profits subject to tax amount to 8 and are the same as in Table 7.1; i.e., double taxation is eliminated. However, the difference between the two tables consists in the shift of part of the tax

29. *See* Art. 9(2) of the 2017 OECD Model Tax Convention. For a similar mechanism relating to the attribution of profits to permanent establishments, *see* Art. 7(3) of the 2017 OECD Model Tax Convention.
30. Competent authorities refer to the representatives of a country's government that deal with matters relating to the interpretation and the application of tax treaties.

base (amounting to 5), as a consequence of the reassessment in country A and the corresponding adjustment in country B. This shift has an impact on the fiscal revenues of countries A and B, but not on the total tax burden supported by the group since it is assumed that the two countries have similar tax rates.

The above example illustrates the risk of double taxation in relation to the pricing of intercompany transactions. In order to avoid or at least mitigate double taxation – and assuming that countries apply the arm's length principle,[31] multinational enterprises are encouraged to set transfer prices at arm's length and explain such a pricing in their transfer pricing documentation. However, tax administrations may conduct a tax audit and claim that the transfer prices are not at arm's length. Tax administrations may then reassess the transfer prices applied within a multinational enterprise, even though such prices have been properly documented. Since double taxation is considered to be a hindrance to the development of international trade,[32] the OECD, the UN and the EU have been working on different tools to prevent transfer pricing disputes or to eliminate double taxation resulting from transfer pricing reassessments. First, disputes may be prevented in advance through concluding APAs (section 7.2.1). Second, when a multinational enterprise is subject to double taxation as a result of a transfer pricing reassessment, such a double taxation may be mitigated or eliminated on the basis of a MAP (section 7.2.2). Last, when double taxation remains despite a MAP, it may be possible to eliminate or mitigate such a double taxation on the basis of an arbitration procedure (section 7.2.3).

7.2.1 Advance Pricing Arrangements

After discussing the purpose of APAs (section 7.2.1.1), the different types of APAs (section 7.2.1.2) as well as the procedure to apply for an APA (section 7.2.1.3) are presented.

7.2.1.1 The Purpose of APAs

APAs are agreements concluded between the competent authorities of two or more countries, or an agreement concluded between a taxpayer and the competent authority or the tax administration of a given country, with regard to the transfer pricing methodology applied to future[33] transactions between associated enterprises.[34] An

31. When the tax law of a country deviates from the arm's length principle, the elimination of double taxation may become impossible, as a consequence of the application of two different taxation principles. For a discussion from the perspective of Brazil and the US, *see* Daniel Hora do Paço and H. David Rosenbloom, *Thoughts on the Brazil-US Tax Treaty Negotiations*, 520 (Tax Notes International, 16 November 2009).
32. *See* para. 1 of the Introduction to the 2017 OECD Model Tax Convention.
33. In certain cases, APAs may also concern previous transactions, as a way to solve a tax audit and agree on a transfer pricing methodology for the future: this is often referred to as a 'rollback'.
34. For a thorough study on APAs, *see* Michelle Markham, *Advance Pricing Agreements: Past, Present and Future* (Kluwer Law International, 2012); *see also* Piergiorgio Valente, *Advance Pricing Arrangements: Optimal Tool – Optimal Framework?*, vol. 48, issue 1, 67–73 (Intertax,

APA is normally intended to implement the arm's length principle with respect to a given intercompany transaction, but in practice it cannot be excluded that the parties (i.e., the competent authorities of the countries involved in an APA, or a company and a State) depart from the arm's length principle.

The OECD Guidelines define an APA as 'an arrangement that determines, in advance of controlled transactions, an appropriate set of criteria (e.g. method, comparables and appropriate adjustments thereto, critical assumptions as to future events) for the determination of the transfer pricing for those transactions over a fixed period of time'.[35] Accordingly, the purpose of an APA is to agree on the methodology to determine transfer prices over a certain period of time; i.e., it is normally not agreed on transfer prices or profit margins as such.[36] Indeed, it may not be possible to agree on what constitutes future arm's length prices since the facts and circumstances that are relevant to pricing an intercompany transaction may evolve over the period of time that is covered by the APA. Rather, the OECD Guidelines encourage the use of comparables, adjustments to such comparables, or profit ranges (e.g., a range of profit mark-up applied with the cost-plus method) in order to enhance the reliability of assumptions about future transactions. However, in certain cases, an APA may apply to values (i.e., not only a methodology), particularly with regard to transactions that occur only once. For example, an APA may include a value if it is concluded for the sale of an intangible.

The conclusion of an APA is not compulsory, be it for the competent authorities or for multinational enterprises. Competent authorities that conclude an APA accept the application of a transfer pricing methodology for a certain period of time, on the condition that the content of the APA is enforced by the companies benefiting from the agreement and that certain conditions are fulfilled. In addition, although APAs in most cases apply only to future tax years, certain countries accept that previous years are also covered by an APA, so as to avoid or solve previous disputes.[37] Accordingly, APAs

---

2020). Certain countries publish annual reports providing an overview of the content of the APAs that they have entered into. For example, *see* the annual report for the United States published by the IRS in relation to the year 2021: *Announcement and Report Concerning Advance Pricing Agreements*, IRS (22 March 2022) (https://www.irs.gov/pub/irs-drop/a-22-07.pdf, accessed 31 July 2022). This report indicates, among other things, the number of APAs finalised and renewed, the industry to which these APAs relate, the countries with which the United States has concluded the APAs, the types of transactions covered, the transfer pricing methods and profit level indicators used, the sources relied on for the benchmarking studies, the nature of the comparability adjustments that have been performed, the length of the APAs, or the time needed to complete an APA.

35. *See* para. 4.134 of the 2022 OECD Guidelines. In addition, para. 9 of Annex II to Chapter 4 of the 2022 OECD Guidelines indicates that 'The objectives of an APA process are to facilitate principled, practical and co-operative negotiations, to resolve transfer pricing issues expeditiously and prospectively, to use the resources of the taxpayer and the tax administration more efficiently, and to provide a measure of predictability for the taxpayer.'
36. This view is clearly expressed in the Guidelines for APAs in the EU: 'The APA should not agree precisely the actual profit which should be taxed in the future' (*see Communication from the Commission to the Council, the European Parliament and the European Economic and Social Committee on the work of the EU joint transfer pricing forum in the field of dispute avoidance and resolution procedures and on guidelines for advance pricing agreements within the European Union* (26 February 2007, COM(2007) 71 final), Annex, para. 3).
37. *See* para. 4.147 of the 2022 OECD Guidelines, and para. 69 of Annex II to Chapter 4 of the 2022 OECD Guidelines. The retroactive application of an APA is sometimes referred to as a 'rollback'.

can help avoid situations of double taxation and provide certainty, both for tax administrations and for multinational enterprises. APAs may also be an efficient way for the competent authorities to verify that intercompany transactions are conducted at arm's length, thus ensuring that a correct amount of a multinational enterprise's profits (or losses) are attributable to a given company. At the same time, APAs have also drawbacks, such as the fact that the procedure to obtain an APA is often highly time-consuming, the risk that the information provided to the competent authorities is not kept secret, or the lack of guarantee that an agreement will be reached. Therefore, while certain countries have been enthusiastic about implementing APA programmes and have entered into numerous APAs, other countries may feel reluctant about enacting an APA programme or giving priority to this issue over other issues. In addition, despite the availability of APAs, multinational enterprises are not always willing to apply for an APA.

Last, it is important to emphasise that certain countries have implemented the spontaneous exchange of information relating to advance tax rulings, which in many cases includes APAs. This concerns particularly all Member States of the EU. As a result, not only the existence of an APA but also the content of APAs may have to be communicated to other countries that are likely to be impacted by the pricing of an intercompany transaction, something that may influence the willingness of multinational enterprises and competent authorities to enter into APAs. Sharing the content of APAs serves also in order to assess the existence of harmful tax practices, and within the EU the possible existence of a State aid.

7.2.1.2 The Different Types of APAs

There are three types of APAs: unilateral, bilateral, and multilateral APAs.

Unilateral APAs are agreements that are concluded between a company and the competent authority (or a tax administration) of a given State. The legal basis for concluding a unilateral APA is the country's domestic law. A unilateral APA is comparable to an advance tax ruling, as in both cases, a decision is given by an official body in a country on the tax consequences of a transaction or a series of transactions, before such a (series of) transaction takes place. By definition, a unilateral APA will give certainty as to the method to compute transfer prices or profit margins upon a (series of) intercompany transactions only in the country that issued the unilateral APA. Accordingly, the main advantage of concluding a unilateral APA is the relative simplicity of the procedure to obtain such an APA, compared to bilateral and multilateral APAs; the main drawback is that since only one country is bound by a unilateral APA, double taxation may still occur as the tax administration of the

Element 2.7 of the BEPS Action 14 minimum standard states that jurisdictions with bilateral APA programmes should provide for the rollback of APAs in appropriate cases, subject to the applicable time limits (such as statutes of limitation for assessment) where the relevant facts and circumstances in the earlier tax years are the same and subject to the verification of these facts and circumstances on audit: *see* OECD, *Making Dispute Resolution Mechanisms More Effective, Action 14: 2015 Final Report*, para. 33 (2015).

counterpart to the intercompany transaction is not involved in such an APA. Moreover, the methodology agreed in a unilateral APA may be problematic in two respects. The first issue is related to the fact that the country that grants a unilateral APA may expect higher than arm's length prices or profit margins, in order to accept to be bound by an agreement.[38] Even in the lack of an overpriced intercompany transaction, the country of the counterpart to the transaction may suspect the country that granted the unilateral APA to tax more than an arm's length income in order to accept the conclusion of a unilateral APA. The result is an increased risk of double taxation if the second country does not accept the terms of the unilateral APA concluded with the first country. The second issue is that if the methodology agreed in the unilateral APA results in transfer prices that are below arm's length prices, the country that granted the unilateral APA may be accused of harmful tax practices. In the context of the EU, the country that issued a unilateral APA may also be found to have granted unlawful State aid, when an aid has been granted without prior notification to the European Commission.[39] Consequently, although unilateral APAs provide certainty in the countries that grant them, and may be relatively simple to obtain, there are shortcomings or risks that may deter multinational enterprises - and, to some extent, countries - from entering into unilateral APAs.

Bilateral APAs are concluded between the competent authorities of the two countries where the companies that are party to a transaction are resident. Therefore, bilateral APAs offer a completely different foreseeability and certainty than unilateral APAs, since the two countries will be bound by the agreement: both multinational enterprises and tax administrations will know what transfer pricing methodology will be applied to a given intercompany transaction during the time of the bilateral APA. The risk of harmful tax practices or State aid is lower, as each country would normally negotiate the APA in its own interest in order to ensure that the transfer pricing methodology is at arm's length. The legal basis for concluding a bilateral APA is the mutual agreement article in the tax treaty between the countries at hand,[40] although domestic rules may provide a more complete legal framework. Therefore, it is not compulsory, for a bilateral APA to be concluded, that the countries at hand have implemented domestic rules on APAs. Examples of areas that may be covered by

38. For example, if a company applying for a unilateral APA is characterised as a contract manufacturer that should in principle earn a full cost mark-up of 10%, the country where the unilateral APA is sought may require a full cost mark-up of 15%, in order to accept the request.
39. Granting unlawful State aid would normally result in an obligation for the Member State to recover the taxes that have not been levied up to a period of ten years: *see* Council Regulation (EU) 2015/1589 of 13 July 2015 laying down detailed rules for the application of Art. 108 of the Treaty on the Functioning of the European Union, OJ L 248 (24 September 2015), Arts 16 and 17. The aid to be recovered includes interest from the date on which the unlawful aid was at the disposal of the beneficiary until the date of its recovery.
40. The mutual agreement article is often drafted on the basis of Art. 25 of the OECD Model Tax Convention, which provides a legal framework for discussions as well as agreements between the competent authorities of the contracting States. Paragraph 7 of Annex II to Chapter 4 of the 2022 OECD Guidelines observes, however, that 'in some cases where a bilateral APA has been sought and the treaty is not appropriate, or where a treaty is not applicable, the competent authorities of some countries may nevertheless conclude an arrangement using the executive power conferred on the heads of tax authorities'.

domestic laws are the period covered by a bilateral APA, the fee that may have to be paid by multinational enterprises to apply for an APA, the information that has to be provided to the competent authorities when applying for an APA, as well as the different steps of the procedure.[41] The main advantage of concluding a bilateral APA is that the two competent authorities (and the two tax administrations) are bound by the APA, so in principle no double taxation may occur with respect to the relevant intercompany transaction as long as the agreement is properly enforced by the parties.[42] The two countries will also obtain certainty as to the enforcement of the arm's length principle over the period covered by the APA. The main drawback of concluding a bilateral APA is the length and costs of the procedure to obtain or renew such an APA, as well as the lack of flexibility for the multinational enterprise in case it needs to make changes to the organisation of the value chain within the group. Another drawback concerns situations where the intercompany transactions entered into as part of the value chain involve more than two countries, as the risk of double taxation remains despite a bilateral APA. This is illustrated with the below example.

Example: Risk of double taxation where the value chain implies a chain of intercompany transactions that involve more than two countries

Assume that goods are manufactured in country A and sold to a wholesaler in country B for an amount of 80. The goods are then resold to a retailer in country C for an amount of 100. Even if an APA is concluded between countries B and C for the sale of goods between the wholesaler and the retailer, such an APA does not preclude a situation of double taxation between countries A and B in relation to the sale of goods from the manufacturer to the wholesaler; the tax administration of country B could consider that the arm's length price for the goods purchased from the manufacturer should be 75, not 80. Accordingly, even if country B has concluded an APA for the sale of goods between the wholesaler and the retailer, it may still challenge the purchase price of the goods by the wholesaler from the manufacturer. To eliminate the risk of double taxation for the whole value chain, it would be necessary for countries A and B, and countries B and C to conclude two bilateral APAs that are consistent with each other, i.e., a multilateral APA.[43]

Multilateral APAs refer to a series of bilateral APAs that are concluded by the competent authorities of more than two countries. Concluding a multilateral APA is, in

41. Not all countries have implemented rules on APAs, and, for those who do, the content of the domestic rules on APAs may vary from one country to another. However, domestic rules on APAs usually share similar purposes.
42. For example, the functional analysis and the characterisation of the associated enterprises should not change during the period covered by the bilateral APA, as such changes may affect the remuneration of the intercompany transactions.
43. With respect to triangular transfer pricing disputes, *see Communication from the Commission to the European Parliament, the Council and the European Economic and Social Committee on the work of the EU Joint Transfer Pricing Forum in the period April 2009 to June 2010 and related proposals 1. Guidelines on low value adding intra-group services and 2. Potential approaches to non-EU triangular cases* (25 January 2011, COM(2011) 16 final); *see also* Hugo Vollebregt, *Triangular Double Taxation: A Fresh Approach*, vol. 19, issue 2, 103–106 (International Transfer Pricing Journal, March/April 2012).

theory, the most secure means to agree on intercompany transfer prices in a consistent manner across a value chain that is fragmented between several countries. Also, considering at the same time all – or at least several of – the intercompany transactions that contribute to the same value chain offers an opportunity for understanding how value is being generated across the value chain, and set transfer prices accordingly.[44] For example, a multilateral APA may be relevant for intercompany transactions whereby companies established in countries A and B are responsible for the R&D of a product, that is then manufactured partly in country C and partly in country D, before being transported to country E for storage purposes. The legal basis for a multilateral APA is, as with bilateral APAs, the mutual agreement article in the tax treaties concluded between the relevant countries. The main advantage of multilateral APAs is that more than two tax administrations are prevented from making a transfer pricing reassessment (as long as the conditions in the APA are enforced), thus avoiding a risk of double taxation where the value chain implies a series of intercompany transactions that involve more than two countries. A multilateral APA may also provide consistency in the transfer pricing methodology of a multinational enterprise, when the bilateral APAs have terms that are consistent with each other. This allows achieving an arm's length outcome at the level of the value chain concerned by the multilateral APA. The main drawback of a multilateral APA is the significant length and costs that may be necessary to obtain or renew such an APA. Also, a multilateral APA prevents having a flexible approach to transfer pricing since the prices of various intercompany transactions are set in relation to each other so as to achieve a consistent outcome at the level of all the intercompany transactions concerned by the multilateral APA; this makes it difficult to amend part of the value chain or some elements of the transfer pricing model. Therefore, the rigid character of a multilateral APA may be problematic, for example, if the economic circumstances change or if modifications to the operation of the value chain are needed.

7.2.1.3 The Procedure to Apply for an APA

Here a distinction should be made between unilateral APAs, on the one hand, and bilateral as well as multilateral APAs, on the other hand. Unilateral APAs are necessarily granted on the basis of the domestic law, as no tax treaty provision could provide a legal basis for a unilateral APA. In addition, since unilateral APAs do not involve other countries, the procedure to obtain a unilateral APA does not need to follow the same pattern in different countries. Therefore, the procedure to obtain a unilateral APA may greatly vary from one country to another, especially if one considers both unilateral APAs and advance tax rulings that are not specifically designed for transfer pricing purposes.

The procedure to apply for a bilateral or a multilateral APA often follows the same pattern because of the need to involve foreign competent authorities before an

44. For a presentation and discussion of a multilateral APA involving four European countries, *see* Michel Fabre and Laurence Delorme, *Airbus Insiders Comment on Groundbreaking Multilateral APA*, 925–926 (Tax Notes International, 31 May 2004).

agreement may be reached. Whether or not the countries involved have domestic provisions on the procedural aspects of APAs, in most cases, the procedure to apply for an APA is divided into the following five steps:

(1) The taxpayer contacts and possibly meets the competent authority of its State of residence to present the APA project and discuss the possibility of obtaining an APA.[45] Nothing is binding at this stage for either the competent authority or the taxpayer. However, the competent authority may provide useful guidance as to the likelihood that an APA may be concluded. In particular, the competent authority may refuse to start an APA procedure, for example, if it is believed that the intercompany transaction does not need to be supported by an APA,[46] or if the transfer pricing model does not appear to be at arm's length.[47]

(2) If the competent authority has not excluded an APA for the transaction that was presented during the first stage, the taxpayer can decide to send a formal application for an APA. This application may be quite comprehensive, so as to provide the competent authority(ies) with as much valuable information as possible. The information included in a transfer pricing documentation is often necessary, but not sufficient to let the competent authority(ies) fully assess the application for an APA.[48] In addition to what is typically included in transfer pricing documentation – e.g., a functional analysis, an industry analysis, the choice of a transfer pricing method, etc. – the application for an APA often requires information such as how the multinational enterprise considers that the business model and the industry will evolve during the period covered by the APA or the evaluation of a compensation payment in case the APA is about the sale of an asset and/or a cross-border business restructuring.

(3) After the case has been submitted, the competent authority(ies) analyse(s) the case in detail and possibly ask(s) questions or request(s) additional information from the taxpayer. The purpose of such questions, or of such information requests, is to obtain all the necessary information to assess the case. For bilateral and multilateral APAs, competent authorities communicate with each other once they have received sufficient information. Since bilateral

45. This step is sometimes referred to as a pre-meeting.
46. For example, in certain countries, APAs are available only for what is deemed to be a complex transaction, in order not to spend the resources of the competent authorities on simple transactions, transactions that involve too low amounts, or transactions that are not likely to be challenged by tax administrations: *see*, e.g., Swedish law on APAs, 2009:1289, in para. 12.
47. In this respect, the Guidelines for APAs in the EU recommend that the competent authority gives 'a clear indication as soon as possible whether a taxpayer's subsequent formal application is likely to be accepted': *see Communication from the Commission to the Council, the European Parliament and the European Economic and Social Committee on the work of the EU joint transfer pricing forum in the field of dispute avoidance and resolution procedures and on guidelines for advance pricing agreements within the EU* (26 February 2007, COM(2007) 71 final), Annex, para. 23.
48. For an overview of the information typically included in transfer pricing documentation, *see* above section 1.7 in this book.

and multilateral APAs are about agreeing on a transfer pricing methodology that will be accepted by all the countries that are parties to the agreement, countries will often negotiate in order for the terms of the APA to be advantageous, or at least not disadvantageous, to their fiscal revenues. That is, although the common goal of the parties involved and the legal framework under domestic tax laws as well as tax treaties is to implement the arm's length principle, there may not be an easy agreement on how to apply the principle to a specific case: therefore, the countries involved may need to convince their counterpart of the validity of their claims, something that may lead to a negotiation between the competent authorities. During this phase of discussions and negotiations, the multinational enterprise may be requested to provide additional information and to attend meetings with the competent authorities.

(4) After considering the case, the competent authority(ies) may accept it (possibly after certain amendments as compared to the application for an APA), or reject it. There is, indeed, no obligation for the competent authorities to agree.[49] If the competent authority(ies) accept(s) to enter into an agreement, the parties to such an agreement will vary depending on the type of APA. For bilateral and multilateral APAs, a formal agreement is concluded between the competent authorities.[50] For unilateral APAs, the position of the competent authority is presented to the taxpayer before being possibly formalised in an agreement.

(5) The taxpayer has the possibility of accepting or refusing the APA, whether it is unilateral, bilateral, or multilateral.[51] If the APA is accepted by the taxpayer, it becomes binding on the taxpayer and on the competent authority(ies).[52]

49. *See* para. 16 of Annex II to Chapter 4 of the 2022 OECD Guidelines: 'Article 25 does not oblige the competent authorities to enter into MAP APAs at the request of the taxpayer.'

50. Such an agreement is a mutual agreement in the meaning of Art. 25 of the OECD Model Tax Convention, as it binds the two competent authorities to a common position. *See* para. 66 of Annex II to Chapter 4 of the 2022 OECD Guidelines for the minimum information that should be included in the mutual agreement.

51. *See* paras 64 and 65 *in fine* of Annex II to Chapter 4 of the 2022 OECD Guidelines.

52. Although an APA that has been accepted by the taxpayer becomes binding on both the taxpayer and the competent authority(ies), the binding effect of an APA is normally subject to certain conditions such as the assumption that the information provided by the taxpayer during the procedure was accurate, or the obligation to abide by the terms of the APA once it is in force. When the terms of an APA have not been enforced by a taxpayer, the tax administration would typically not be bound by the APA. For an illustration of such a right, *see Eaton Corporation v. Commissioner of Internal Revenue*, United States Tax Court (26 June 2013, case number 5576-12); in this case, the court considered that it did have jurisdiction to review the cancellation of an APA by the tax administration of the United States, and that the tax administration had the right (in general, not in this particular case) to cancel an APA.

7.2.2 Mutual Agreement Procedures

In the lack of an APA, or if an APA is not enforced, a tax administration may challenge the transfer prices applied to intercompany transactions and reassess the income of a taxpayer, when it is considered that the transfer prices were not at arm's length. Such an income reassessment normally results in double taxation when the same item of income has already been subject to tax in the country of the counterpart to the intercompany transaction.[53] In such cases, and if the applicable tax treaty allows it, a possible remedy to the double taxation would be for the country of the other party to the intercompany transaction to grant a so-called corresponding adjustment, i.e., a downwards income adjustment that matches the primary adjustment. Corresponding adjustments may take place when a tax treaty includes a provision drafted on the basis of Article 9(2) of the OECD Model Tax Convention or Article 17 of the Multilateral Instrument (MLI).[54] Article 9(2) of the UN Model Tax Convention includes a similar provision, subject to certain limitations included in Article 9(3) of the same model.[55] Corresponding adjustments may, but do not need to, be undertaken as part of the MAP.[56]

Even when a tax treaty includes a provision on corresponding adjustments, such a provision does not oblige a country to effectively grant a corresponding adjustment and eliminate double taxation. It may particularly be argued by a country that the adjustment made initially in the other country is not in line with the arm's length principle, as a justification to deny a corresponding adjustment. Therefore, the countries involved may need to consider together the intercompany transaction, and try to agree on the right transfer prices so as to eliminate the double taxation. This is the purpose of the so-called MAP, which may help eliminate or alleviate double taxation, although it provides no certainty in that respect. The MAP is the main method to solve transfer pricing disputes, as it is considered that it succeeds in avoiding double taxation

53. For an illustration of the double taxation that occurs as a consequence of a transfer pricing reassessment in one country, *see* section 7.2 above.
54. Article 9(2) of the 2017 OECD Model Tax Convention has the following drafting: 'Where a Contracting State includes in the profits of an enterprise of that State – and taxes accordingly – profits on which an enterprise of the other Contracting State has been charged to tax in that other State [*here it is assumed that the income of an associated enterprise is increased by the tax administration of one country and taxed, while such profits have also been subject to tax in the other State*] and the profits so included are profits which would have accrued to the enterprise of the first-mentioned State if the conditions made between the two enterprises had been those which would have been made between independent enterprises [*here it is assumed that the correction of profits is in line with the arm's length principle*], then that other State shall make an appropriate adjustment to the amount of the tax charged therein on those profits [*i.e., following the increase of the tax base of an associated enterprise in one country, the competent authorities of the other country shall decrease the tax base of the other associated enterprise to eliminate the double taxation if they believe that the correction of the transfer prices was in line with the arm's length principle*]. In determining such adjustment, due regard shall be had to the other provisions of this Convention and the competent authorities of the Contracting States shall if necessary consult each other.'
55. Article 9(3) of the 2021 UN Model Tax Convention provides for an exception to Art. 9(2) if it is decided in a final ruling that 'one of the enterprises concerned is liable to penalty with respect to fraud, gross negligence or wilful default'.
56. *See* para. 4.32 of the 2022 OECD Guidelines.

in 90% to 95% of cases.[57] It is conducted by the competent authorities of the contracting States. After discussing the purpose of a MAP (section 7.2.2.1), the different steps of a MAP are presented (section 7.2.2.2).

7.2.2.1 The Purpose of a MAP

Most tax treaties contain a possibility for MAPs between the competent authorities of the contracting States in certain specific situations.[58] Such a procedure is found in Article 25 of the OECD and the UN Model Tax Conventions, as well as in Article 16 of the MLI.[59] A MAP refers to the frame that is provided to the competent authorities of tax treaty partners to discuss and possibly agree, mainly with regard to two types of issues:

(1) Competent authorities may discuss situations where a taxpayer considers that it has not been (or may not be) taxed in accordance with the provisions of the tax treaty. This possibility is offered on top of domestic legal remedies such as court litigation.[60]
(2) Competent authorities may discuss the interpretation or the application of a tax treaty as part of a MAP.

57. *See* para. 15.5.5.3 of the 2021 UN Manual.
58. The legal basis for the procedure is the mutual agreement article included in the tax treaty concluded between two countries, assuming that the treaty includes such an article. In parallel, countries may issue regulations that indicate how the procedure should be conducted: *see*, for example, the guidance published by the Austrian Ministry of Finance on 31 March 2015, BMF-010221/0172-VI/8/2015.
59. Here, it can be observed that different improvements to mutual agreement procedures have been agreed as a minimum standard by the countries participating in the BEPS project: *see* OECD, *Making Dispute Resolution Mechanisms More Effective, Action 14: 2015 Final Report* (2015). The minimum standard is meant to: (i) ensure that treaty obligations related to the mutual agreement procedure are fully implemented in good faith and that MAP cases are resolved in a timely manner; (ii) ensure the implementation of administrative processes that promote the prevention and timely resolution of treaty-related disputes; and (iii) ensure that taxpayers can access the MAP when eligible. The minimum standard is also complemented by a set of best practices. The effective implementation of minimum standards is subject to regular peer reviews coordinated by the OECD; for an evaluation of that peer-review process, *see* Michelle Markham, *Action 14 of the BEPS Project: Taking the Pulse of Tax Certainty and Determining the Effectiveness of the Peer Review Process Five Years On*, 96–107 (Bulletin for International Taxation, 2022-2). For an example of court case confirming that the access to the MAP may be denied, *see SGL Carbon Holding*, Spanish Tribunal Supremo (22 September 2021, case number 1151/2021).
60. There are diverging views on the interactions between domestic legal proceedings and mutual agreement procedures: while certain countries accept that both remedies are conducted in parallel, other countries consider that the taxpayer has to choose between a mutual agreement procedure and litigation. In any case, it is generally considered that once a final decision has been issued by a national court, the competent authority of this country cannot overrule this decision. Any remaining double taxation could only be eliminated by the other country. Therefore, taxpayers may consider suspending a court proceeding or a mutual agreement procedure instead of conducting both proceedings in parallel, depending on the domestic law at hand and the dispute resolution method that is favoured. On the interactions between domestic legal proceedings and mutual agreement procedures, *see* particularly paras 25 and following of the commentary to Art. 25 of the 2017 OECD Model Tax Convention.

Accordingly, when a tax treaty has been concluded between two countries, a MAP may be a relevant dispute resolution method for transfer pricing issues in relation to situations of taxation not in accordance with a tax treaty, which refers primarily to double taxation following a tax audit in relation to transactions between associated enterprises or dealings between a head office and a permanent establishment. Moreover, the mutual agreement article is also relevant for the prevention of such disputes, as this article is the legal basis for bilateral and multilateral APAs. Last, since the interpretation or the application of a tax treaty may also be discussed between the competent authorities as part of a MAP, such a procedure may be relevant apart from actual cases, for example, when the competent authorities decide in a competent authority agreement or in a memorandum of understanding how to interpret and apply a tax treaty. In the area of transfer pricing, it may be particularly relevant to agree on the way the business profits article should be interpreted,[61] or the procedural aspects of arbitration procedures.[62]

What is mostly interesting for the purpose of this book is how double taxation may be mitigated or eliminated, thanks to a MAP when double taxation occurs following a transfer pricing reassessment. As illustrated by the example described above in section 7.2, a transfer pricing reassessment results in double taxation to the extent of the increase of a company's taxable base when the corresponding profits have already been subject to tax in the country of the counterpart to the transaction. A MAP makes it possible for the taxpayer to ask the competent authorities of the countries concerned to discuss the case at hand and, possibly, find a way to eliminate double taxation.

7.2.2.2 The Different Steps of a MAP

There are several steps between the initiation of a MAP, and the possible mitigation or elimination of double taxation as a consequence of a transfer pricing reassessment.

The first step is the initiation of the procedure as such. Depending on the wording of the tax treaty, the case may have to be presented either to the competent authority of a company's State of residence or to one of the competent authorities concerned with the case. When initiating a MAP, the taxpayer has to provide the competent authorities with sufficient information to let them deal with the case. The initiation of a MAP in most cases includes a letter describing the tax audit and its outcome, the reason why such an outcome is not in accordance with the provisions of a tax treaty, the arguments

61. *See*, e.g., the competent authority agreement signed on 27 November 2006 regarding the application of the authorised OECD approach to Art. 7 of the tax treaty concluded between the United States and Belgium on 27 November 2006 (in this respect, *see* IRS Announcement 2013-38, United States (3 September 2013)).
62. *See*, e.g., the memorandum of understanding between the competent authorities of Germany and the United States signed on 1 June 2006 regarding the application of the arbitration procedure under paras 5 and 6 of Art. 25 of the tax treaty concluded between the United States and Germany on 29 August 1989 (as amended by later protocols).

of the taxpayer in favour of another outcome, as well as material supporting the arguments put forward by the taxpayer.[63]

In addition, a MAP has, in most cases, to be initiated within a certain delay. Even if domestic law may provide certain time limits, such time limits are often overruled by those provided in tax treaties. Article 25 of the OECD and the UN Model Tax Conventions suggest a three-year delay from the first notification of an action that may result in taxation not in accordance with the provisions of the tax treaty.[64] The starting point of the delay during which a MAP may be initiated is, for tax treaties concluded on the basis of the OECD Model Tax Convention, an official 'act of taxation' from the tax administration, such as the issuance of a notice of reassessment.[65] However, the OECD commentaries consider that a taxpayer may initiate a MAP before the beginning of the time limit, when the actions[66] of one or both of the contracting States may result in taxation not in accordance with the provisions of the tax treaty.[67] Consequently, it may be enough that the risk of taxation not in accordance with the tax treaty is 'probable' to initiate a MAP, without waiting until the actions of a contracting State have actually contravened a tax treaty.

After a MAP has been initiated, the competent authority that receives the case 'shall endeavour, if the objection appears to it to be justified and if it is not itself able to arrive at a satisfactory solution, to resolve the case by mutual agreement with the competent authority of the other Contracting State, with a view to the avoidance of taxation which is not in accordance with the Convention'.[68] The word 'endeavour' is important to emphasise, as it captures the lack of obligation to eliminate the double taxation. Accordingly, the second step of a MAP consists in discussions between the competent authorities of the relevant countries to try to resolve the case, if the competent authority that receives the case does not solve it on its own or considers that the claim is unjustified. Such discussions between the competent authorities may take place through meetings or correspondence. In principle, the taxpayer is not involved in these discussions (there is no right to participate in the process),[69] but additional information may be requested from the taxpayer. The purpose of the negotiations between the competent authorities should be to apply the tax treaty correctly and thus enforce the arm's length principle in relation to the taxation of associated enterprises,

63. This may include, depending on the circumstances of the case, a functional analysis and a comparability analysis.
64. However, the delay varies greatly between tax treaties, even if para. 20 of the commentary to Art. 25 of the 2017 OECD Model Tax Convention recommends regarding the three-year time limit as a minimum. For example, in the tax treaty concluded between France and Canada on 2 May 1975, the delay for initiation of a mutual agreement procedure was two years. In the tax treaty concluded between the United States and Switzerland on 2 October 1996, no delay at all was prescribed.
65. *See* para. 21 of the commentary to Art. 25 of the 2017 OECD Model Tax Convention.
66. Such actions may, for example, consist in a tax audit during which the tax administration has expressed doubts as to the arm's length character of certain transfer prices, so that a tax reassessment is likely to be issued at the end of the tax audit.
67. *See* para. 14 of the commentary to Art. 25 of the 2017 OECD Model Tax Convention.
68. *See* Art. 25(2) of the 2017 OECD Model Tax Convention.
69. *See* para. 4.58 of the 2022 OECD Guidelines.

so that double taxation is eliminated and taxes are levied in accordance with the provisions of the treaty.

In practice, a MAP may have four possible outcomes:

- *First possible outcome*: the competent authority of the State of residence of the taxpayer (here referred to as country A, where company A is resident) may reverse the tax reassessment originally made by the tax administration of the same State. This outcome is typically reached when the original tax reassessment (often referred to as the primary adjustment) is clearly in breach of the arm's length principle. Double taxation is then eliminated unilaterally, and the competent authority of the other State (here referred to as country B, where company B – the counterpart to the transaction – is resident) may not be involved at all. In addition, if taxes have been levied by country A on a deemed transfer of profits to a non-resident associated enterprise (often referred to as secondary adjustments),[70] such taxes may also be reversed as a result of the cancellation of the primary adjustment.[71]
- *Second possible outcome*: after the discussions between the competent authorities, the competent authority of country B may fully acknowledge the tax reassessment issued by the tax administration of country A and grant a *corresponding adjustment* that eliminates the double taxation.[72] The competent authorities then conclude an agreement that determines how the double taxation should be eliminated, and this agreement is proposed to the

70. Profits may be deemed transferred as a consequence of the excess profits resulting from the primary adjustment through, e.g., a dividend, a royalty, an equity contribution, or a loan. The non-arm's length price that triggered the primary adjustment may actually have been lowered on purpose, to minimise a withholding tax. Such a deemed transfer of profits is then seen as a secondary or constructive transaction. Secondary adjustments may trigger tax consequences such as withholding taxes, if the levy of such withholding taxes is allowed under the tax treaty existing between the countries concerned: *see* paras 8 and 9 of the commentary on Art. 9 of the 2017 OECD Model Tax Convention. *See also* paras 4.68 and following of the 2022 OECD Guidelines. For an example of a court case in which a withholding tax imposed on a deemed hidden distribution of profits was accepted, *see C. SA v. Administration Fédérale des Contributions*, Swiss Tribunal Federal (14 January 2021, case number 2C_498/2020). For a comparative study of secondary adjustments in different countries, *see* Sean Foley, Cameron Taheri and Lillie Sullivan, *Country-by-Country Survey of Global Secondary Adjustment Rules*, 29–44 (Tax Notes International, 5 July 2021).
71. For a description of secondary adjustments and the way States may eliminate the effects of such secondary adjustments, *see* OECD, *Manual on Effective Mutual Agreement Procedures*, 38 (February 2007). The same conclusion is reached in the work of the EU Joint Transfer Pricing Forum: *see Communication from the Commission to the European Parliament, the Council and the European Economic and Social Committee on the work of the EU Joint Transfer Pricing Forum in the period July 2012 to January 2014* (4 June 2014, COM(2014) 315 final), Annex 1, Report on secondary adjustments, para. 4.
72. A corresponding adjustment means that the increase of the tax base in country A is mirrored by an equally important decrease of the tax base in country B. This results in a shift of the tax base from country B to country A, since the tax base is decreased in country B in order to let country A levy tax on a higher tax base.

taxpayer as a possible way of solving the case.[73] The taxpayer is normally free to accept or reject the agreement. This outcome may be reached when the competent authorities consider that the primary adjustment made by the tax administration of country A is in line with the arm's length principle. Accordingly, the competent authority of country B would decrease the tax base of the counterpart to the transaction to an extent that is similar to the increase of the taxable base of the company resident in country A. Double taxation is then eliminated since the income that was subject to the primary adjustment is, in the end, taxed only once.[74] The taxes possibly levied by country A as a result of a secondary adjustment may also be reversed when the company that has been reassessed ultimately receives an arm's length remuneration.[75] The fact that part of the taxable base of the multinational enterprise has been moved from country A to country B may have an impact on the total tax burden of the multinational enterprise, depending on the corporate income tax rates of countries A and B.[76]

- *Third possible outcome*: the competent authorities may agree on the need to eliminate the double taxation, but the agreement between the two competent authorities may differ from the primary adjustment. For example, the tax administration of country A may have increased the tax base of company A by 100; during the negotiations between the competent authorities, it may be concluded that it was correct to increase the tax base of company A, but that the right reassessment should be 80, not 100. Consequently, since a tax reassessment of 100 has already been issued by the tax administration of country A, this country will have to decrease the tax base of company A with 20 (100–80 = 20). At the same time, the tax base of company B in country B will be decreased with an amount of 80, which corresponds to the eventual increase of the tax base of company A. In the end, double taxation is eliminated and the tax base transferred from country B to country A amounts

73. In addition to solving a case, the competent authorities may also, as part of the mutual agreement, require that the taxpayer renounces the exercise of domestic legal remedies, to prevent such remedies from contradicting the decision of the competent authorities.
74. It should be emphasised that even if double taxation is eliminated on the basis of a mutual agreement procedure, the taxpayer supports a temporary double taxation between the time of the levy of taxes as a consequence of the original tax reassessment and the actual elimination of double taxation. This implies a cash flow disadvantage since capital is bound until taxes are reimbursed by either tax administration. In principle, tax treaties do not require the contracting States to take into account the time value of money and pay interest to taxpayers who have temporarily been subject to double taxation. However, domestic provisions may provide for the payment of interest in such situations. Alternatively, States may suspend the collection of taxes, as, e.g., recommended in para. 48 of the commentary to Art. 25 of the 2017 OECD Model Tax Convention.
75. In practice, the competent authorities of the country that made the primary and secondary adjustments (in this example country A) may expect the taxpayer resident in the same country to effectively receive a transfer of funds from the non-resident associated enterprise to reverse the deemed distribution of profits: *see* OECD, *Manual on Effective Mutual Agreement Procedures*, 38 (February 2007).
76. It is indeed only the taxable base that is moved between the two countries in order to eliminate the double taxation. Each country then taxes the income of each company at its own rate.

to 80. Secondary adjustments may also be reversed, as described above under the second possible outcome.

- *Fourth possible outcome*: the competent authorities may not agree on how to fully eliminate the double taxation, either because the negotiations do not reach an end or because at the end of the negotiations the competent authorities have different views on the case at hand. The multinational enterprise will then be subject to a definitive double taxation (unless the tax treaty provides for mandatory binding arbitration), and it is possible that secondary adjustments will also become definitive. For example, if the tax administration of country A had increased the tax base of company A by 100, and assuming that the competent authority of country A finds this reassessment in line with the arm's length principle, the competent authority of country B may consider that the right reassessment is 80 and decrease the tax base of company B with an amount of 80. However, since the tax base had been increased in country A with 100, the group on a whole suffers from double taxation to the extent of the profits that have been taxed in the two countries, i.e., 20.

This last outcome illustrates the two main shortcomings of MAPs: the lack of a mandatory time frame for negotiations between the competent authorities, and the lack of obligation to fully eliminate the double taxation.[77] In relation to this last point, countries are particularly likely to refuse to eliminate double taxation as part of the MAP when the applicable tax treaty does not contain an arbitration provision since such a provision may eventually oblige them to eliminate the double taxation. Consequently, a taxpayer that has been subject to a transfer pricing reassessment may support a definitive double taxation even if a MAP has been initiated between the competent authorities of the countries concerned by the case.

If the applicable tax treaty contains an arbitration provision, the taxpayer will benefit from a greater level of protection against double taxation.

7.2.3 Arbitration

7.2.3.1 Introduction

Arbitration is a dispute resolution mechanism that may be relevant when the competent authorities do not reach an agreement after a MAP has been initiated.[78] This means that while the MAP is largely the main method to solve transfer pricing disputes,

77. With respect to the lack of obligation to fully eliminate double taxation, *see* para. 37 of the commentary to Art. 25 of the 2017 OECD Model Tax Convention: 'as far as reaching mutual agreement through the procedure is concerned, the competent authorities are under a duty merely to use their best endeavours and not to achieve a result'.
78. For studies on the topic of arbitration in tax treaties, *see* Gustaf Lindencrona and Nils Mattsson, *Arbitration in Taxation* (Kluwer Law and Taxation Publishers, 1982); Mario Züger, *Arbitration under Tax Treaties: Improving Legal Protection in International Tax Law* (IBFD, 2001); *see also* the special issue of Intertax, vol. 42, issue 3 (Intertax, 2014).

arbitration is a rather 'last resort method'.[79] It consists in letting an independent group of experts either solve a case or suggest a solution to solve a case, when double taxation has not been eliminated by the competent authorities. There are different forms for tax treaty arbitration,[80] and not all arbitration provisions provide for an obligation to submit a case to arbitration or to implement the solution chosen by the arbitrators. The inclusion of an arbitration provision in tax treaties is not a minimum standard under BEPS Action 14, which is understandable as many countries fear that arbitration may infringe on their tax sovereignty; arbitration may also be problematic for developing countries.[81]

In most cases, the submission of a case to an arbitration panel may result in an arbitration decision that eliminates or mitigates double taxation and is *binding* on the competent authorities if it is accepted by the taxpayer. In some other cases, arbitration decisions have no binding effect, although this situation is now rarely found in tax treaties. When arbitration is binding, a central question is whether or not there is an obligation to submit a case to arbitration when it is not solved by the competent authorities; if such an obligation exists, arbitration is described as *mandatory*.

Arbitration is an efficient dispute resolution mechanism when tax treaties or other instruments adopt *mandatory binding arbitration*, i.e., when the submission of a case of double taxation to an arbitration panel is mandatory and that the solution reached by the arbitration panel may be imposed on the competent authorities if the taxpayer accepts the final outcome. This may be perceived as an infringement to the tax sovereignty of the countries involved as they may not control the solution given to a case,[82] but at the same time, mandatory binding arbitration offers taxpayers a guarantee that the case will be solved when the competent authorities cannot agree.

Three main legal frames are relevant from a transfer pricing perspective: arbitration provisions included in tax treaties and in the MLI (section 7.2.3.2), the arbitration convention concluded between the Member States of the EU (section 7.2.3.3), and the European Dispute Resolution Directive (section 7.2.3.4).

79. *See* para. 15.5.5.3 of the 2021 UN Manual.
80. For an overview of the arbitration provisions included in the tax treaties concluded by the United States, *see* Jérôme Monsenego, *Designing Arbitration Provisions in Tax Treaties: Reflections Based on the US Experience*, vol. 42, issue 3, 163–168 (Intertax, 2014).
81. *See* Hugh J. Ault, *Tax Treaty Arbitration: A Reassessment*, in Georg Kofler, Ruth Mason and Alexander Rust (eds), Thinker, Teacher, Traveler: Reimagining International Tax - Essays in Honor of H. David Rosenbloom, 35–37 (IBFD, 2021).
82. For that reason 'there is no consensus on moving towards universal mandatory binding MAP arbitration': *see* OECD, *BEPS Action 14: Make Dispute Resolution Mechanisms More Effective*, 4, para. 3 (December 2014). *See also* OECD, *Making Dispute Resolution Mechanisms More Effective, Action 14: 2015 Final Report*, para. 62 (2015): 'there is no consensus among all OECD and G20 countries on the adoption of arbitration as a mechanism to ensure the resolution of MAP cases'.

7.2.3.2 *Arbitration in Tax Treaties and in the MLI*

Tax treaties[83] may provide for cases of international double taxation to be solved through arbitration when the competent authorities cannot solve a case on the basis of the MAP.[84] This possibility is usually provided as part of the mutual agreement article of a tax treaty. However, arbitration may be available even when no arbitration provision is included in a tax treaty, as long as the competent authorities are willing to have a case submitted to an arbitration panel.[85]

Depending on the wording of the arbitration provision, the submission of a case to arbitration may be mandatory or voluntary. Certain tax treaties include a voluntary arbitration provision, whereby a case may be submitted to arbitration by the competent authorities of the contracting States if they so wish.[86] Such provisions were mostly included in tax treaties concluded before mandatory binding arbitration was introduced in the OECD and the UN Model Tax Conventions. Under arbitration provisions that include a voluntary referral to arbitration, a taxpayer may ask the competent authorities to hand over a case to an arbitration panel, but the referral to arbitration eventually depends on the willingness of the competent authorities. Since 2008, the OECD Model Tax Convention includes a mandatory binding arbitration provision in Article 25(5). The UN Model Tax Convention since the 2011 update also includes an arbitration provision, but the UN is more cautious to tax treaty arbitration than the OECD since the UN considers that arbitration may not necessarily be advantageous for developing countries.[87] Therefore, the 2021 UN Model Tax Convention provides two versions of Article 25, i.e., one version without an arbitration provision,[88] and the

83. For a presentation of the evolution of arbitration in tax treaties, *see* Hugh J. Ault, *Tax Treaty Arbitration: A Reassessment*, in Georg Kofler, Ruth Mason and Alexander Rust (eds), Thinker, Teacher, Traveler: Reimagining International Tax – Essays in Honor of H. David Rosenbloom, 25–37 (IBFD, 2021).
84. However, the scope of arbitration provisions is sometimes narrowed compared to the scope of mutual agreement procedures. Article 25(5) of the 2017 OECD Model Tax Convention refers to cases brought to the competent authorities on the basis of Art. 25(1), which, e.g., excludes matters under Art. 25(3) of the model (i.e., cases related to the interpretation of a tax treaty or cases of double taxation that are not covered by a tax treaty). Also, tax treaties may limit the scope of the arbitration procedure to certain treaty articles: for example, Art. 6 of the protocol of 27 August 2009 to the tax treaty concluded between France and Switzerland on 9 September 1966 added a fifth paragraph to Art. 27 of the treaty that introduced a mandatory binding arbitration provision, that is however limited to issues related to the existence of a permanent establishment (i.e., Art. 5), the attribution of profits to permanent establishment (i.e., Art. 7), and the taxation of the income of associated enterprises (i.e., Art. 9).
85. *See* para. 69 of the commentary to Art. 25 of the 2017 OECD Model Tax Convention.
86. *See*, e.g., Art. 41(5) of the tax treaty concluded on 14 July 1992 between Germany and Sweden.
87. On the position of the UN with respect to arbitration, *see* the commentary to Art. 25(5) (alternative B) of the 2021 UN Model Tax Convention. *See also* Michael Lennard, *Transfer Pricing Arbitration as an Option for Developing Countries*, vol. 42, issue 3, 179–188 (Intertax, 2014); Michael Lennard, *Update of the United Nations Model Tax Convention*, vol. 18, issue 2, 99 (Asia-Pacific Tax Bulletin, March/April 2012); Claudine Devillet, *The Text of and the Commentary on Article 25: Round-Up of the Changes and Their Significance*, 612–617 (Bulletin for International Taxation, November, 2012).
88. *See* Art. 25 (alternative A) of the 2021 UN Model Tax Convention, which contains four paragraphs to Art. 25.

other version including an arbitration provision.[89] It should also be observed that the inclusion of arbitration provisions in tax treaties is not yet a developed practice, even amongst OECD countries, although this varies greatly between different countries.[90] It should also be observed that the MLI contains an arbitration procedure that differs from that included in the OECD Model Tax Convention; arbitration in the MLI is presented below, at the end of section 7.2.3.2.

When the mutual agreement article of a tax treaty includes a mandatory binding arbitration provision drafted on the basis of Article 25(5) of the OECD Model Tax Convention (i.e., assuming the tax treaty does not contain the arbitration procedure of the MLI), taxpayers may request the submission of the case to arbitration without the competent authorities having the right to refuse it (this is the mandatory character of arbitration), thereby offering a guarantee that the case will be able to be solved.[91] In contrast, under Article 25(5) (alternative B) of the UN Model Tax Convention, only the competent authorities have the option to submit a case to arbitration, something that mitigates the mandatory character of the procedure.

Under the OECD Model Tax Convention, mandatory arbitration may be requested when the competent authorities have not 'solved' a case within a certain period of time. This raises the question of the meaning of having 'solved' a case since it is only once the case may be deemed not to have been solved that the access to arbitration becomes a right for the taxpayer. The commentary on Article 25 of the OECD Model Tax Convention answers this question negatively, by emphasising that a case is not solved when 'there is at least one issue on which the competent authorities disagree and which, according to one of the competent authorities, indicates that there has been taxation not in accordance with the Convention'.[92] The delay for solving the case is of two years under the recommendations of the OECD.[93] If the case is not solved within this period, Article 25(5) of the OECD Model Tax Convention gives the taxpayer a right to request that an arbitration procedure be started.[94] Consequently, under such a

89. *See* Art. 25 (alternative B) of the 2021 UN Model Tax Convention, which contains five paragraphs to Art. 25, the arbitration provision being included in Art. 25(5).
90. With respect to the inclusion of an arbitration provision in the OECD Model Tax Convention, it has been observed that 'not all OECD countries involved in the development of the provision intended to adopt mandatory binding arbitration': *see* OECD, *BEPS Action 14: Make Dispute Resolution Mechanisms More Effective*, 20, para. 45 (December 2014).
91. However, in certain cases, a mutual agreement procedure may be denied (and thereby access to arbitration may also be denied) 'where serious violations of domestic laws resulting in significant penalties are involved': *see* paras 26 and 68 of the commentary to Art. 25 of the 2017 OECD Model Tax Convention.
92. *See* para. 71 of the commentary to Art. 25 of the 2017 OECD Model Tax Convention.
93. *See* para. 70 of the commentary on Art. 25 of the 2017 OECD Model Tax Convention. The starting point of the two-year period may give rise to disagreements between multinational enterprises and competent authorities. Paragraph 71 of the commentary on Art. 25 of the 2017 OECD Model Tax Convention mentions that 'For the purpose of determining the start of the two year period, a case will only be considered to have been presented to the competent authority of the other State if sufficient information has been presented to that competent authority to allow it to decide whether the objection underlying the case appears to be justified.'
94. It should nevertheless be emphasised that access to arbitration is not an absolute right for the taxpayer. Indeed, if the two competent authorities agree that taxation by both States has been levied in accordance with the tax treaty, mandatory binding arbitration can normally not be requested by a taxpayer since it is a prerequisite for the opening of a mutual agreement procedure that taxes have been levied in breach of the provisions of a tax treaty. For an explicit

mandatory binding arbitration procedure, the competent authorities are first given a chance to solve the case as part of a MAP, before possibly having to hand it over to arbitrators.

The procedure according to which arbitration may be implemented depends on several parameters such as the wording of the arbitration provision of the relevant tax treaty, protocols to the treaty, the mutual agreement concluded between the competent authorities with regard to the way they wish to interpret the arbitration provision (in case such an agreement has been concluded),[95] exchanges of letters, and the mutual agreement concluded between the competent authorities with regard to the way they wish to organise the arbitration process in the particular case.[96] Consequently, there is no uniformity in arbitration procedures on the basis of tax treaties. However, two main approaches are suggested by the commentary to Article 25 of the OECD Model Tax Convention: the independent opinion approach and the streamlined approach. The choice between these two approaches is made by the competent authorities on a case-by-case basis, unless the type of procedure has been determined in advance by the contracting States.[97]

With the *independent opinion approach*, a panel of arbitrators has to solve the case in an independent manner (i.e., without having to implement either the position of the competent authorities) and within a six-month period. The *streamlined approach* is, in contrast, an accelerated procedure where one or several arbitrator(s) solve(s) the case by choosing one of the two solutions proposed by the two competent authorities within a shorter period of time. Consequently, the streamlined approach encourages the competent authorities to adopt relatively reasonable ways of solving the case, so as to maximise the chances that it will be solved according to their proposal;[98] on the other hand, there is no guarantee that the two solutions suggested by the competent authorities under the streamlined approach are theoretically correct and completely eliminate double taxation. This shortcoming is mitigated – but not necessarily eliminated – with the independent opinion approach, as the arbitration panel is given the opportunity to consider the case independently and find a solution that deviates

example of provision allowing the competent authorities to deny access to arbitration, *see* Art. 25(6)(b) of the tax treaty between the United States and Japan, as amended by the protocol signed on 24 January 2013, where it is indicated that a case shall not be submitted to arbitration if 'the competent authorities of both Contracting States have agreed that the case is not suitable for resolution through arbitration and have notified the presenter of the case of such agreement no later than two years after the commencement date'.

95. Such an agreement may be referred to as a sample agreement. It is not specific to a particular case, but provides a general framework on the way the competent authorities wish the arbitration process to function, given the wording of the tax treaty. The commentary on Art. 25 of the 2017 OECD Model Tax Convention contains in annex an example of sample mutual agreement on arbitration.
96. Such an agreement may be referred to as the terms of reference of the case. The main purpose of the terms of reference is to set forth the questions to be resolved by the arbitrators as well as the procedural rules of the particular case.
97. *See*, e.g., the protocol concluded between the United States and Germany on 1 June 2006, Art. 16, point 22(h), where the contracting States chose the streamlined approach for arbitration procedures under this tax treaty.
98. This explains why this approach may be referred to as the 'last best offer' or 'final offer' approach. It is sometimes also referred to as 'baseball arbitration'.

from the one favoured by the competent authorities. In any case, the threat constituted by mandatory binding arbitration is likely to encourage the competent authorities to narrow their positions and reach an agreement before the time comes for submitting a case to arbitration.

Whereas the independent opinion approach is the preferred procedure in the OECD Model Tax Convention,[99] the UN Model Tax Convention favours the streamlined approach.[100] Whatever procedure is applied, the case is, in principle, solved by the arbitrators through relying on the provisions of the tax treaty (the interpretation of which is done in the light of Articles 31–33 of the Vienna Convention on the Law of Treaties),[101] the contracting States' domestic laws, and the OECD Guidelines or the UN Manual.[102]

An important difference must be emphasised between arbitration procedures in the OECD and the UN Model Tax Conventions: Article 25(5) of the OECD Model Tax Convention results in a binding decision, unless the taxpayer refuses it. This means that the competent authorities are not given a last chance to solve the case; they have to implement the decision within six months, notwithstanding any time limit in their domestic laws. Accordingly, for the competent authorities to deviate from the outcome and the time constraint of the decision of the arbitrators, it is necessary for them to obtain the taxpayer's agreement. In contrast, the binding character of the arbitration decision is not as strong under the UN Model Tax Convention, as the competent authorities are given an opportunity to agree on a different solution within six months following the decision.[103]

Finally, the MLI contains an arbitration procedure that partly deviates from that included in the OECD Model Tax Convention.[104] This procedure was influenced by the objectives of BEPS Action 14, as well as by the outcomes of the negotiations relating to the drafting of the MLI. This procedure is applicable only to the tax treaties covered by the MLI, and supposes that the two contracting States have agreed on implementing the MLI arbitration provision in their tax treaty.[105] Generally, the arbitration procedure included in the MLI is meant to be more effective than the one in the OECD Model Tax Convention. With respect to the appointment of arbitrators, the arbitration panel is made up of three individuals with no presence of the competent authorities. Each competent authority appoints one panel member, and these two panel members

---

99. *See* para. 4 of the annex to the commentary on Art. 25 of the 2017 OECD Model Tax Convention.
100. *See* para. 4 of the annex to the commentary on Art. 25(5) (alternative B) of the 2021 UN Model Tax Convention.
101. Vienna Convention on the Law of Treaties of 23 May 1969. It should be observed that not all signatories to this convention have ratified it.
102. Here, it can be observed that the example of sample mutual agreement on arbitration included in the 2017 commentary on Art. 25 of the OECD Model Tax Convention does not anymore contain a reference to the applicable principles. Such a reference was included in para. 14 of the sample mutual agreement until the 2014 version of the OECD Model Tax Convention.
103. *See* Art. 25(5) (alternative B) of the 2021 UN Model Tax Convention.
104. For an analysis of the arbitration procedure in the MLI, *see* Nathalie Bravo, *Mandatory Binding Arbitration in the BEPS Multilateral Instrument*, vol. 47, issue 8/9, 693–714 (Intertax, 2019).
105. The contracting States may also deviate from the arbitration procedure included in the MLI. However, this section of the book contains only a description of the provisions included in the MLI.

appoint a third member who serves as chair. This method of appointment of the panel members contributes to a fair procedure since each competent authority is free to choose one panel member. In addition, the MLI contains several requirements that ensure the impartiality and independence of the panel members.[106] With respect to the types of arbitration process, and assuming that the competent authorities do not agree on different rules, the procedure chosen is the last best offer approach, the main principles of which are the following: each competent authority submits a proposed resolution of the case, which shall be limited to a specific monetary amount (e.g., income or expense) in the case of transfer pricing disputes, possibly supported by a position paper; the arbitration panel then selects one of the proposed resolutions for the case, with no rationale or explanation,[107] and the decision has no precedential value.[108] A party to the MLI may, however, make a reservation to the main arbitration method, and favour the independent opinion approach; in this case, the sources of law relied upon and the reasoning which led to the result must be indicated.[109] Last, the competent authorities can deviate from the final outcome within three months after the arbitration decision has been issued:[110] in other words, a last chance is given to agree on how to solve the case.

A last and important feature of tax treaty arbitration must be emphasised: an arbitration decision may be found unenforceable by the domestic courts of the contracting States, something that results in considering that the arbitration has not taken place. This is especially likely to happen when the arbitration procedure has not been respected, but even 'any other reason' may lead to the arbitration decision being found unenforceable by a domestic court.[111] Consequently, the binding nature of tax treaty arbitration may be weakened by that possibility.

7.2.3.3 The EU Arbitration Convention

The Member States of the EU, after long negotiations,[112] have concluded a convention intended at providing an arbitration mechanism in case double taxation in transfer

106. *See* OECD, *Multilateral Convention to Implement Tax Treaty Related Measures to Prevent BEPS*, Art. 20(2)(c) (2016).
107. For an analysis of this point, and arguments in favour of providing reasons for an arbitration decision, *see* John F. Avery Jones, *Types of Arbitration Procedure*, vol. 47, issue 8/9, 674–677 (Intertax, 2019).
108. *See* OECD, *Multilateral Convention to Implement Tax Treaty Related Measures to Prevent BEPS*, Art. 23(1) (2016).
109. *See* OECD, *Multilateral Convention to Implement Tax Treaty Related Measures to Prevent BEPS*, Art. 23(2) (2016).
110. *See* OECD, *Multilateral Convention to Implement Tax Treaty Related Measures to Prevent BEPS*, Art. 24(2) (2016).
111. *See* para. 81 of the commentary on Art. 25 of the 2017 OECD Model Tax Convention as well as Art. 11 of the sample mutual agreement in the annex to that commentary.
112. For a presentation of earlier initiatives, *see* Jean-Claude Scholsem, *EC: The Proposal for a Council Directive on the Elimination of Double Taxation (Arbitration Procedure)*, vol. 10, issues 11–12, 424–435 (Intertax, 1982).

pricing matters cannot be eliminated by the competent authorities.[113] To implement the arbitration convention effectively and consistently, the Member States of the EU adopted a code of conduct that provides guidance on the application of the convention. The code of conduct is not binding though.[114]

Contrary to arbitration provisions included in tax treaties or the dispute resolution directive, the EU arbitration convention applies only to transfer pricing matters.[115] The code of conduct recommends that it also be applied to cases of thin capitalisation when adjustments are based on the arm's length principle.[116] In addition, the scope of the EU arbitration convention includes triangular cases between Member States of the EU, which may be solved either through a multilateral procedure or through several bilateral procedures conducted in parallel.[117] The Member States are, however, encouraged to solve triangular cases through multilateral procedures, rather than parallel bilateral procedures.[118] A multilateral procedure may indeed allow to eliminate double taxation in triangular cases in a consistent manner,[119] as the whole chain of transactions may be analysed in a holistic manner by the competent authorities of the Member States concerned.

While the procedural aspects of arbitration in a tax treaty context may vary from one case to another, the procedural aspects under the EU arbitration convention are regulated by the convention and the code of conduct, although the latter is not binding.

113. *Convention 90/436/EEC of 23 July 1990 on the elimination of double taxation in connection with the adjustment of profits of associated enterprises*. For comments on the functioning of the EU arbitration convention, *see* Luc Hinnekens, *European Arbitration Convention: Thoughts on Its Principles, Procedures and First Experience*, vol. 19, issue 3, 109–116 (EC Tax Review, 2010); *see also* Sven-Olof Lodin, *The Arbitration Convention in Practice: Experiences*, vol. 42, issue 3, 173–175 (Intertax, 2014).

114. *See* the *Revised Code of Conduct for the effective implementation of the Convention on the elimination of double taxation in connection with the adjustment of profits of associated enterprises*, 2009/C 322/01, Official Journal of the European Union (30 December 2009). The EU Joint Transfer Pricing Forum issued a report including additional changes aimed at improving the functioning of the arbitration convention: *see* EU Joint Transfer Pricing Forum, *Final Report on Improving the Functioning of the Arbitration Convention*, JTPF/002/2015/EN, Brussels (March 2015). Even if it were approved by the Member States, this report would still constitute soft law, not hard law.

115. Both intercompany transactions between legal entities and dealings between a head office and its permanent establishment are included in the scope of the EU arbitration convention.

116. *See* point 1.2 of the *Revised Code of Conduct for the effective implementation of the Convention on the elimination of double taxation in connection with the adjustment of profits of associated enterprises*, 2009/C 322/01, Official Journal of the European Union (30 December 2009).

117. *See* point 1.1 of the *Revised Code of Conduct for the effective implementation of the Convention on the elimination of double taxation in connection with the adjustment of profits of associated enterprises*, 2009/C 322/01, Official Journal of the European Union (30 December 2009).

118. *See* point 6.2(b) of the *Revised Code of Conduct for the effective implementation of the Convention on the elimination of double taxation in connection with the adjustment of profits of associated enterprises*, 2009/C 322/01, Official Journal of the European Union (30 December 2009).

119. In contrast, a series of bilateral mutual agreement procedures may hardly eliminate double taxation in triangular matters in a consistent manner, as no possibility is given to the countries involved to take a wholistic perspective on the chain of transactions. In this respect, *see* the example above on the risk of double taxation where the value chain implies a chain of intercompany transactions that involve more than two countries, in section 7.2.1.2 of this book.

However, there are similarities between the procedure under the EU arbitration convention and the procedure described by the commentary to Article 25(5) of the OECD Model Tax Convention, something that is encouraged by both the EU[120] and the OECD.[121] As in a tax treaty context, the case is first examined – and possibly solved – by the competent authorities as part of a MAP. Such a procedure is to be initiated within three years of the first notification of the action which results or is likely to result in double taxation, irrespective of any time limits prescribed by the domestic laws of the Member States. Once the MAP has been initiated, the competent authorities have two years to solve the case. The starting point of this two-year period has given rise to differences in interpretation, which is why the code of conduct provides guidance as to when a case should be regarded as having been submitted.[122]

If the case has not been solved during the two-year period, it becomes eligible for arbitration. In principle, the opening of an arbitration procedure under the EU arbitration convention is mandatory. However, the arbitration procedure is not initiated by the taxpayer but by the competent authorities, something that may delay its start. The code of conduct recommends that the case be handed over to the arbitrators within six months following the end of the two-year period.[123] Once the case has been handed over to the arbitrators, they have six months to deliver an independent opinion (i.e., the arbitration convention does not apply the last best offer approach), which must be based on the arm's length principle.[124] The competent authorities then have another six months from the delivery of the opinion to take a decision that eliminates the double taxation. Such a decision may deviate from the opinion of the arbitrators, but should still be based on the arm's length principle. If the competent authorities do not agree on a way to eliminate the double taxation, the opinion of the arbitrators becomes binding and has to be implemented by the competent authorities.[125] Consequently, contrary to the arbitration procedure in the OECD Model Tax Convention (according to which the arbitration decision becomes binding unless it is not accepted by the taxpayer)[126] the EU arbitration convention does not grant a binding

120. *See*, e.g., points 4 and 6.5 of the *Revised Code of Conduct for the effective implementation of the Convention on the elimination of double taxation in connection with the adjustment of profits of associated enterprises*, 2009/C 322/01, Official Journal of the European Union (30 December 2009).
121. *See*, e.g., para. 84 of the commentary to Art. 25 of the 2017 OECD Model Tax Convention, and para. 29 of the annex to the commentary to Art. 25 of the 2017 OECD Model Tax Convention.
122. *See* point 5 of the *Revised Code of Conduct for the effective implementation of the Convention on the elimination of double taxation in connection with the adjustment of profits of associated enterprises*, 2009/C 322/01, Official Journal of the European Union (30 December 2009).
123. *See* point 7.2(b) of the Revised Code of Conduct for the effective implementation of the Convention on the elimination of double taxation in connection with the adjustment of profits of associated enterprises, 2009/C 322/01, Official Journal of the European Union (30 December 2009).
124. *See* Art. 11 of the Convention 90/436/EEC of 23 July 1990 on the elimination of double taxation in connection with the adjustment of profits of associated enterprises.
125. Article 12.1 of the Convention 90/436/EEC of 23 July 1990 on the elimination of double taxation in connection with the adjustment of profits of associated enterprises.
126. *See* Art. 25(5) of the 2017 OECD Model Tax Convention: 'Unless a person directly affected by the case does not accept the mutual agreement that implements the arbitration decision, that decision shall be binding on both Contracting States.'

effect to the opinion of the arbitrators at the time it is issued, but gives the competent authorities a last chance to solve the case themselves after the opinion has been issued.[127]

Finally, it should be emphasised that Article 8.1 of the EU arbitration convention provides a possibility for the competent authorities to refuse the application of the convention where, following legal or administrative proceedings, one of the enterprises concerned is liable to a *serious penalty*.[128] This criterion should not be interpreted too broadly, as the code of conduct recommends that the benefits of the EU arbitration convention be rejected only 'in exceptional cases like fraud'.[129]

7.2.3.4 The European Dispute Resolution Directive

In 2017 a directive was enacted in the EU on the resolution of cross-border tax disputes.[130] The directive – which did not repeal the arbitration convention – covers all tax treaty issues, including those related to the taxation of business profits and associated enterprises (i.e., the attribution of profits to permanent establishments and transfer pricing). The dispute resolution directive offers greater protection to taxpayers than tax treaty arbitration, thanks to the right granted to taxpayers to refer to domestic courts (or any other body designated in the domestic law) in situations where the delays provided in the directive are not respected.[131] This comes unavoidably with a greater level of complexity.

As for tax treaty arbitration, the procedure contained in the dispute resolution directive lies in an effort to let the competent authorities agree on how to solve double taxation. It is only in situations of last resort that arbitration will become mandatory. The first phase is the complaint of the taxpayer, which is to be submitted within a three-year period.[132] While the competent authorities may reject the complaint,[133] a new right is granted to taxpayers to appeal a rejection of the complaint, either before domestic courts (if all competent authorities reject the complaint) or through the arbitration procedure (if the complaint is accepted by only one of the competent

127. This option left to the competent authorities to solve the case in a different manner than what has been suggested by the arbitration panel is similar to the recommendations under Art. 25(5) (alternative B) of the 2011 UN Model Tax Convention.
128. On the issue of serious penalties, *see* Piergiorgio Valente, *Arbitration Convention 90/436/EEC: Inapplicability in Case of Serious Penalties*, vol. 40, issue 3, 220–224 (Intertax, 2012).
129. *See* point 3 of the *Revised Code of Conduct for the effective implementation of the Convention on the elimination of double taxation in connection with the adjustment of profits of associated enterprises*, 2009/C 322/01, Official Journal of the European Union (30 December 2009).
130. *See Council Directive (EU) 2017/1852 of 10 October 2017 on tax dispute resolution mechanisms in the European Union*, OJ L 265 (14 October 2017), pp. 1–14 (the 'dispute resolution directive'). For an analysis of the directive, *see* Harm Mark Pit, *The Changed Landscape of Tax Dispute Resolution Within the EU: Consideration of the Directive on Tax Dispute Resolution Mechanisms*, vol. 47, issue 8/9, 745–759 (Intertax, 2019).
131. *See* Art. 7 of the dispute resolution directive.
132. *See* Art. 3 of the dispute resolution directive.
133. When informing the affected person about the rejection of its complaint, the competent authority shall provide 'the general reasons for its rejection': *see* Art. 5(2) of the dispute resolution directive.

authorities): whether or not the complaint should be accepted will then be decided by domestic courts or the advisory commission, without prejudice for how to eventually solve the question in dispute. If at this stage the advisory commission finds the case receivable, the competent authorities may still initiate the MAP; in case they do not, the advisory commission has normally six (up to nine) months to provide an opinion on a way to remedy the dispute. This opinion is binding only if the competent authorities do not agree on another way to solve the case. In other words, several chances are given to the competent authorities to agree on how to remedy the situation of double taxation.

After the first phase of complaint starts the MAP.[134] As with other dispute resolution mechanisms, there is no obligation on the competent authorities to solve the case: they shall only endeavour to find a solution, within a two-year period.[135] At the end of this period of two (or possibly three) years, the competent authorities inform the taxpayer of the outcome of the case. If the situation of double taxation is not solved, the taxpayer will be able to start the dispute resolution phase. An advisory commission will then provide an opinion on how to solve the dispute, which will be binding if the competent authorities do not agree on another solution. The main dispute resolution method provided in the directive is the independent opinion approach; however, alternative dispute resolution mechanisms such as baseball arbitration or mediation may be applied;[136] the directive enables also the setting up of a standing committee to solve disputes.[137]

It is important to observe that all the above steps are subject to precise delays. If the delays are not respected, the taxpayer may in certain cases refer to domestic courts in order to enforce the different steps provided in the directive in a timely manner. Last, the opinions issued by the advisory commission do not constitute precedents[138] but should be published (or at least an abstract thereof should be published),[139] something that may contribute to the constitution of an implicit body of precedents.

134. *See* Art. 4 of the dispute resolution directive.
135. This two-year period can be prolonged with up to one year, if a written justification is brought.
136. *See* Art. 10 of the dispute resolution directive.
137. On this topic, *see* Sophia Piotrowski, et al., *Towards a Standing Committee Pursuant to Article 10 of the EU Tax Dispute Resolution Directive: A Proposal for Implementation*, vol. 47, issue 8/9, 678–692 (Intertax, 2019).
138. *See* Art. 15(4) of the dispute resolution directive.
139. *See* Art. 18 of the dispute resolution directive.

Bibliography

Books, Articles, Papers, Databases

Richard T. Ainsworth and Andrew B. Shact, *Transfer Pricing: Case Studies of the CUP Method*, 465–484 (Tax Notes International, 30 April 2012).

Ulf Andresen, *Regulations Provide Further Guidance on the Application of the Authorized OECD Approach to the Attribution of Profit to Permanent Establishments*, vol. 22, 77–84 (International Transfer Pricing Journal, March/April 2015).

Matt Andrew and Richard S. Collier, *COVID-19 Challenges for the Arm's-Length Principle*, 1363–1368 (Tax Notes International, 22 June 2020).

Joseph Andrus and Michael Durst, *Standing on 'Principal': Risk-Limiting Transfer Pricing Structures*, 959–963 (Tax Notes International, 18 December 2006).

Joseph Andrus and Stig Sollund, *Improving the Transfer Pricing System: Simpler, Clearer, Faster*, 79–85 (Tax Notes International, 1 October 2012).

Masatsugu Asakawa, *Transfer Pricing in the New Global Landscape: The OECD's Engagement Beyond Its Borders*, 209–213 (Tax Notes International, 17 October 2011).

Hugh J. Ault and Brian J. Arnold, *Comparative Income Taxation: A Structural Analysis* (3rd ed., Kluwer Law International, 2010).

Hugh J. Ault, *Tax Treaty Arbitration: A Reassessment*, in Georg Kofler, Ruth Mason and Alexander Rust (eds), Thinker, Teacher, Traveler: Reimagining International Tax - Essays in Honor of H. David Rosenbloom, 25–37 (IBFD, 2021).

John F. Avery Jones, *Types of Arbitration Procedure*, vol. 47, issue 8/9, 674–677 (Intertax, 2019).

Reuven S. Avi-Yonah, Kimberly A. Clausing and Michael C. Durst, *Allocating Business Profits for Tax Purposes: A Proposal to Adopt a Formulary Profit Split*, vol. 9, 497–553 (Florida Tax Review, 2009).

Reuven S. Avi-Yonah, *Between Formulary Apportionment and the OECD Guidelines: A Proposal for Reconciliation*, vol. 2, issue 1, 3–18 (World Tax Journal, February 2010).

Reuven S. Avi-Yonah and Ilan Benshalom, *Formulary Apportionment: Myths and Prospects – Promoting Better International Tax Policies by Utilizing the Misunderstood and Under-Theorized Formulary Alternative*, vol. 3, issue 3, 371–398 (World Tax Journal, October 2011).

Baker & McKenzie, *Comments on the OECD Restructuring Discussion Draft*, vol. 37, issue 2, 143–146 (Intertax, 2009).

Philip Baker and Richard S. Collier, General Report, Cahiers de Droit Fiscal International, *The Attribution of Profits to Permanent Establishments*, vol. 91b (2006).

Anuschka J. Bakker (ed.), *Transfer Pricing and Business Restructurings: Streamlining All the Way* (IBFD, 2009).

Anuschka Bakker and Belema Obuoforibo (eds), *Transfer Pricing and Customs Valuation: Two Worlds to Tax as One* (IBFD, 2009).

Anuschka J. Bakker, *Transfer Pricing and Intra-Group Financing: Low-Hanging Fruit?*, vol. 15, issue 2, 27–33 (Derivatives and Financial Instruments, March/April 2013).

Sven-Eric Bärsch and Christian Engelen, *German Federal Tax Court Rules in Favour of Taxpayer in Transfer Pricing Cases on Intercompany Financing Transactions*, vol. 29, issue 1, 19–23 (International Transfer Pricing Journal, 2022).

Andrew Barton, Vinu Subramaniam and Paola Marino, *Impact of COVID-19 and Transfer Pricing: Approaches for Comparability Adjustments*, vol. 69, issue 3, 981–1001 (Canadian Tax Journal, 2021).

Mary Bennett, *Article 7: New OECD Rules for Attributing Profit to Permanent Establishments*, in Dennis Weber and Stef van Weeghel (eds), The 2010 OECD Updates, 21–36 (Kluwer Law International, 2011).

Thomas Bittner and Anna-Katharina Jann, *Capital Adjustments in Transfer Pricing Analysis: OECD Example of Working Capital Adjustments*, vol. 18, issue 1, 14–16 (International Transfer Pricing Journal, January/February 2011).

Nikolaj Bjørnholm and Bodil Tolstrup, *Denmark: Danish Supreme Court Rules Against the Taxpayer in Its Third Transfer Pricing Case*, vol. 28, issue 5, 333–337 (International Transfer Pricing Journal, 2021).

Patrick Boone and Madlen Haupt, *Transfer Pricing Documentation for Business Restructurings*, vol. 20, issue 3, 127–131 (International Transfer Pricing Journal, May/June 2013).

Yariv Brauner, *Value in the Eye of the Beholder: The Valuation of Intangibles for Transfer Pricing Purposes*, vol. 28, 100–101 (Virginia Tax Review, 2008).

Yariv Brauner, *Formula Based Transfer Pricing*, vol. 42, issue 10, 615–631 (Intertax, 2014).

Yariv Brauner, *Transfer Pricing in BEPS: First Round – Business Interests Win (But, Not in Knock-Out)*, vol. 42, issue 1, 72–84 (Intertax, 2015).

Nathalie Bravo, *Mandatory Binding Arbitration in the BEPS Multilateral Instrument*, vol. 47, issue 8/9, 693–714 (Intertax, 2019).

Patricia Brown, General Report, Cahiers de Droit Fiscal International, *The Debt-Equity Conundrum*, vol. 97b (2012).

Andreas Bullen, *Arm's Length Transaction Structures: Recognizing and Restructuring Controlled Transactions in Transfer Pricing* (IBFD Doctoral Series, 2011).

Michael Butler and Jessica Pengelly, *Commissioner Loses Transfer Pricing Appeal in SNF Case*, vol. 18, issue 5, 362–365 (International Transfer Pricing Journal, September/October 2011).

Jose Calderón, *The OECD Guidelines as a Source of Tax Law*, vol. 37, issue 1, 4–29 (Intertax, 2007).

Elisa Casi-Eberhard, Xiao Chen, Mark D. Orlic and Christoph Spengel, *One Directive, Several Transpositions: A Cross-Country Evaluation of the National Implementation of DAC6*, vol. 13, issue 1, 63–81 (World Tax Journal, 2021).

Andrew Casley, Kevin Norton and Michael Krhoda, *The OECD's New Transfer Pricing Documentation Standard: An Overview and Possible UK Implementation*, vol. 22, issue 1, 3–10 (International Transfer Pricing Journal, January/February 2015).

Richard Collier and Joseph L Andrus, *Transfer Pricing and the Arm's Length Principle after BEPS* (Oxford University Press, 2017).

Richard S. Collier and Ian F. Dykes, *The Virus in the ALP: Critique of the Transfer Pricing Guidance on Risk and Capital in the Light of the COVID-19 Pandemic*, 702–720 (Bulletin for International Taxation, 2020-12).

Richard S. Collier and Ian F. Dykes, *On the Apparent Widespread Misapplication of the OECD Guidelines: Risk and Post-BEPS Problems for the Arm's Length Principle*, 20–43 (Bulletin for International Taxation, 2022-1).

Luis Coronado, Patrick Cheung and Justin Kyle, *An Overview of Arm's Length Approaches to Thin Capitalization*, vol. 17, issue 4, 270–275 (International Transfer Pricing Journal, July/August 2010).

Glenn DeSouza, *What the UN Manual Really Means for China?*, vol. 41, issue 5, 331–338 (Intertax, 2013).

Pinakin Desai and Shefali Goradia, Cahiers de Droit Fiscal International, *Cross-Border Outsourcing: Issues, Strategies and Solutions*, vol. 99A (2014).

Pierre-Jean Douvier and Saro Gocer, *Profit Shifting and Comparability: The French Supreme Administrative Court Provides Useful Clarification on Functional Analysis and the Concept of Routine Entity*, vol. 29, issue 2, 106–110 (International Transfer Pricing Journal, 2022).

Claudine Devillet, *The Text of and the Commentary on Article 25: Round-Up of the Changes and Their Significance*, 612–617 (Bulletin for International Taxation, November 2012).

Irina Diakonova, Steef Huibregtse and Gesa Körner, *Where Do Financial Services Meet Transfer Pricing?*, vol. 2, issue 2, 55–73 (Derivatives and Financial Instruments, March/April 2000).

Michael C. Durst, *It's Not Just Academic: The OECD Should Reevaluate Transfer Pricing Laws*, 247–256 (Tax Notes International, 18 January 2010).

Michael C. Durst, *Pragmatic Transfer Pricing for Developing Countries*, 279–285 (Tax Notes International, 23 January 2012).

Michael C. Durst, *Fixing Double Nontaxation under the Transfer Pricing Guidelines*, 839–842 (Tax Notes International, 28 May 2012).

Michael C. Durst, *Beyond BEPS: A Tax Policy Agenda for Developing Countries* (ICTD Working Paper 18, June 2014).

Michael C. Durst, *It's Time to Reform Transfer Pricing Benchmarking*, 1271–1278 (Tax Notes International, 6 June 2022).

Ramon S.J. Dwarkasing, *The Concept of Associated Enterprises*, vol. 41, issue 8/9, 412–429 (Intertax, 2013).

Michel Fabre and Laurence Delorme, *Airbus Insiders Comment on Groundbreaking Multilateral APA*, 925–926 (Tax Notes International, 31 May 2004).

Ryan Finley, *BEPS 5 Years Later: Still No Convergence on Transfer Pricing*, 26–29 (Tax Notes International, 5 October 2020).

Ryan Finley, *After Coca-Cola, Practitioners See DEMPE as Part of U.S. Law*, 1133–1134 (Tax Notes International, 24 May 2021).

Ryan Finley, *Transfer Pricing and Profit Attribution: A Strained Analogy*, 868–871 (Tax Notes International, 21 February 2022).

Ryan Finley, *Profit Attribution Ain't Transfer Pricing, But Should It Be?*, 1232–1237 (Tax Notes International, 14 March 2022).

Chris Finnerty, Paulus Merks, Mario Petriccione and Raffaele Russo, *Fundamentals of International Tax Planning* (IBFD, 2007).

Luís Flávio Neto, *The Blockchain Revolution for Transfer Pricing Documentation: If Not in 2020, Then When?*, in Pasquale Pistone and Dennis Weber (eds), Taxing the Digital Economy: The EU Proposals and Other Insights, 307–334 (IBFD, 2019).

Sean Foley, Cameron Taheri and Lillie Sullivan, *Country-by-Country Survey of Global Secondary Adjustment Rules*, 29–44 (Tax Notes International, 5 July 2021).

David L.P. Francescucci, *The Arm's Length Principle and Group Dynamics: Part 1 – The Conceptual Shortcomings*, vol. 11, issue 2, 55–75 (International Transfer Pricing Journal, March/April 2004).

Moritz Glahe, *Transfer Pricing and EU Fundamental Freedoms*, vol. 22, issue 5, 222–232 (EC Tax Review, 2013).

Eyal Gonen, Leonid Karasik and Michael McDonald, *Control over Risk, DEMPE Functions, and the Remuneration of R&D Service Providers*, 1615–1630 (Tax Notes International, 21 June 2021).

Bruno Gouthière, *Zimmer: 'Commissionaire' Agent Is Not a Permanent Establishment*, vol. 50, issue 8, 350–358 (European Taxation, August 2010).

Vesela Grozeva, Chris Schulman, Jessie Coleman and Pravin Ugalat, *Why Operationalizing Transfer Pricing Is More Important Than Ever*, 373–382 (Tax Notes International, 18 April 2022).

Hubert Hamaekers, *Arm's Length: How Long?*, in Paul Kirchhof, Moris Lehner, Kees van Raad, Arndt Raupach and Michael Rodi (eds) International and Comparative Taxation – Essays in Honour of Klaus Vogel, 29–52 (Kluwer Law International, 2002).

Björn Heidecke, *Germany: New Circular on the Application of the Arm's Length Principle Issued by the Federal Ministry of Finance – Commitment to OECD Guidelines*, 375–380 (International Transfer Pricing Journal, 2021-6).

Marjaana Helminen, *Determining the Arm's Length Interest Rate of an Intra-Group Loan*, 153–155 (European Taxation, April 2011).

Luc Hinnekens, *European Arbitration Convention: Thoughts on Its Principles, Procedures and First Experience*, vol. 19, issue 3, 109–116 (EC Tax Review, 2010).

Daniel Hora do Paço and H. David Rosenbloom, *Thoughts on the Brazil-U.S. Tax Treaty Negotiations*, 517–522 (Tax Notes International, 16 November 2009).

Andrew Hughes, *Transfer Pricing Benchmark: North American Healthcare Distribution*, 1407–1410 (Tax Notes International, 13 June 2022).

Pankaj Jain and Vikram Chand, *Location Savings: International and Indian Perspective*, vol. 43, issue 2, 192–198 (Intertax, 2015).

Anton Joseph, *Xilinx: The Unfinished Business*, vol. 17, issue 4, 283–286 (International Transfer Pricing Journal, July/August 2010).

Adam M. Katz, Barry Dennis, Richard S. Collier and Stanley J. Hales, *Applying the Arm's-Length Principle to Global Interbranch Financial Dealings*, 741–748 (Tax Notes International, 25 August 2003).

Nancy H. Kaufman, *Fairness and the Taxation of International Income*, 145–203 (Law & Policy in International Business, 1998).

Sunny Kishore Bilaney, *Operational Transfer Pricing: Transfer Pricing, Finance, and IT Functions Converge*, 1029–1032 (Tax Notes International, 23 May 2022).

Han Kogels, *Tax Systems Twenty-Five Years from Now*, vol. 22, issue 6, 266–267 (EC Tax Review, 2013).

Norma Kraay and Leon Bloom, *The Missing Link: Transfer Pricing and Regulatory Capital Compliance for Global Financial Institutions*, 527–531 (Tax Notes International, 13 February 2012).

Heinz-Klaus Kroppen and José Carlos Silva, General Report, Cahiers de Droit Fiscal International, *Cross-Border Business Restructuring*, vol. 96a (2011).

Paul B.W.L. Lamberts, *Fair Taxation: Truth Is in the Eye of the Beholder*, vol. 45, issue 1, 49–53 (Intertax, 2017).

Michael Lang, *Introduction to the Law of Double Taxation Conventions* (3rd ed., Linde/IBFD, 2021).

Stanley I. Langbein, *U.S. Transfer Pricing and the Outsourcing Problem*, 1065–1092 (Tax Notes International, 21 March 2005).

Armando Lara Yaffar and Michael Lennard, *An Introduction to the Updated UN Model (2011)*, 590–597 (Bulletin for International Taxation, November 2012).

Martin Lehner, *Article 9: Associated Companies*, in Thomas Ecker and Gernot Ressler (eds), History of Tax Treaties: The Relevance of the OECD Documents for the Interpretation of Tax Treaties, 389–409 (Linde, 2012).

Michael Lennard, *Update of the United Nations Model Tax Convention*, vol. 18, issue 2, 96–100 (Asia-Pacific Tax Bulletin, March/April 2012).

Michael Lennard, *Transfer Pricing Arbitration as an Option for Developing Countries*, vol. 42, issue 3, 179–188 (Intertax, 2014).

Gustaf Lindencrona and Nils Mattsson, *Arbitration in Taxation* (Kluwer Law and Taxation Publishers, 1982).

Emmanuel Llinares and Ralph Meghames, *Value Chain Analysis: An Analytical Tool to Evaluate Economic Contribution in the Overall Framework of Value Creation*, in Werner Haslehner and Marie Lamensch (eds), Taxation and Value Creation, 185–198 (IBFD EATLP International Tax Series 2021).

Sven-Olof Lodin, *The Arbitration Convention in Practice: Experiences*, vol. 42, issue 3, 173–175 (Intertax, 2014).

Jacques Malherbe and Philip Daenen, *Permanent Establishments Claim Their Share of Profits: Does the Taxman Agree?*, 359–366 (Bulletin for International Fiscal Documentation, July 2010).

Michelle Markham, *Advance Pricing Agreements: Past, Present and Future* (Kluwer Law International, 2012).

Michelle Markham, *Action 14 of the BEPS Project: Taking the Pulse of Tax Certainty and Determining the Effectiveness of the Peer Review Process Five Years On*, 96–107 (Bulletin for International Taxation, 2022-2).

Peter Mason, *The Greatest Profit Shifter: The Dividend*, 693–697 (Tax Notes International, 7 February 2022).

Stefan Mayer, *Formulary Apportionment for the Internal Market* (IBFD Doctoral Series, 2009).

Amparo Mercader and Horacio Peña, *'Sixth Method' Raises Transfer Pricing Concerns in Developing Countries*, vol. 69, 691–693 (Tax Notes International, 18 February 2013).

Amar Mehta, *The Limited Force of Attraction Rule*, vol. 21, issue 2, (Asia-Pacific Tax Bulletin, 2015).

Toshio Miyatake, General Report, Cahiers de Droit Fiscal International, *Transfer Pricing and Intangibles*, vol. 92a (2007).

Jérôme Monsenego, *The Substance Requirement in the OECD Guidelines: What Is the Substance of the Substance Requirement?*, vol. 21, issue 1, 9–23 (International Transfer Pricing Journal, January/February 2014).

Jérôme Monsenego, *Designing Arbitration Provisions in Tax Treaties: Reflections Based on the US Experience*, vol. 42, issue 3, 163–168 (Intertax, 2014).

Jérôme Monsenego, *May a Server Create a Permanent Establishment? Reflections on Certain Questions of Principle in Light of a Swedish Case*, vol. 21, issue 4, 247–257 (International Transfer Pricing Journal, July/August 2014).

Jérôme Monsenego, *Selectivity in State Aid Law and the Methods for the Allocation of the Corporate Tax Base* (Kluwer Law International, 2018).

Jérôme Monsenego, *The Independent Agent Exception and Group Membership*, vol 46, issue 12, 944–959 (Intertax, 2018).

Jérôme Monsenego, *Transfer Pricing in the European Union*, in Raffaele Petruzzi, Giammarco Cottani and Michael Lang (eds), Fundamentals of Transfer Pricing: Industries, Regions, New Technologies, and Other Topics, 333–367 (Kluwer Law International, 2022).

Jérôme Monsenego, *Transfer Pricing and Value Creation*, in Werner Haslehner and Marie Lamensch (eds), Taxation and Value Creation, 107–129 (IBFD EATLP International Tax Series 2021).

Jérôme Monsenego, *Nexus for Transfer Pricing Purposes Before and After BEPS 2.0: From Form to Substance, and Back to Form?*, in Edoardo Traversa (ed.), Nexus and Jurisdiction in International and EU Tax Law (IBFD GREIT Series, 2022).

Oscar Montero, *Forecasting Interest Rates for Future Intercompany Loan Planning: An Alternative Approach*, vol. 49, 313–317 (International Transfer Pricing Journal, September/October 2009).

Aitor Navarro, *Spain: Contractual Allocation of Risks and Substance: The Acer Case*, vol. 28, issue 3, 203–209 (International Transfer Pricing Journal, 2021).

Danny Oosterhoff and Bo Wingerter, *The New OECD Guidelines: The Good, the Bad and the Ugly*, vol. 18, issue 2, 103–113 (International Transfer Pricing Journal, March/April 2011).

Katriina Pankakoski, *Finland: Amendment Transfer Pricing Adjustment Provision Announcement 9 December 2021*, vol. 29, issue 3, 207–211 (International Transfer Pricing Journal, 2022).

Kristen A. Parillo, *Tax Analysts Interview: OECD's Mary Bennett*, 230–232 (Tax Notes International, 25 July 2011).

Neil Pereira, *Intangibles: The New Frontier*, 45–53 (Tax Notes International, 3 January 2022).

Hans Pijl, *The OECD Services Permanent Establishment Alternative*, vol. 48, issue 9, 472–476 (European Taxation, September 2008).

Alice Pirlot, *The Vagueness of Tax Fairness: A Discursive Analysis of the Commission's 'Fair Tax Agenda'*, vol. 48, issue 4, 402–415 (Intertax 2020).

Sophia Piotrowski, et al., *Towards a Standing Committee Pursuant to Article 10 of the EU Tax Dispute Resolution Directive: A Proposal for Implementation*, vol. 47, issue 8/9, 678–692 (Intertax 2019).

Harm Mark Pit, *The Changed Landscape of Tax Dispute Resolution Within the EU: Consideration of the Directive on Tax Dispute Resolution Mechanisms*, vol. 47, issue 8/9, 745–759 (Intertax, 2019).

Domenico Ponticelli and Sabrina Tronci, *The Non-unique Notion of 'Control' in Transfer Pricing: Interpretation, Legislative Developments and Problematic Aspects from an Italian and International Perspective*, vol. 28, issue 4, 291–298 (International Transfer Pricing Journal, 2021).

Kees van Raad, *Deemed Expenses of a Permanent Establishment under Article 7 of the OECD Model*, vol. 4, issue 28, 162–167 (Intertax, 2000).

Kees van Raad, *'Enterprise' and 'Enterprise of a Contracting State': Towards a Century of Confusion Regarding the Term 'Enterprise' in the Model Double Taxation Conventions*, in Guglielmo Maisto (ed.), The Meaning of 'Enterprise', 'Business' and 'Business Profits' under Tax Treaties and EU Tax Law, vol. 7, 61–83 (IBFD, EC and International Tax Law Series, 2011).

Merja Raunio, *Supreme Administrative Court Ruling on Interest Rate Reflecting Creditworthiness of Individual Companies*, vol. 18, issue 4, 296–301 (International Transfer Pricing Journal, July/August 2011).

Merja Raunio, *Landmark Case on the Ability of Tax Authorities to Disregard and Recharacterize Transactions*, vol. 22, issue 1, 28–32 (International Transfer Pricing Journal, January/February 2015).

Merja Raunio and Matti Urpilainen, *Finland: Case SAC 2020:35 – Supreme Administrative Court Reasserts the Prohibition to Recharacterize Transactions,*

Now in a Case That Deals with Group Internal Financing, vol. 27, issue 5, 379–383 (International Transfer Pricing Journal, 2020).

Merja Raunio and Matti Urpilainen, *Case SAC 2021:66 on Group Internal Financing: Supreme Administrative Court Provides Lessons on How the OECD Guidelines Should and Should Not Be Used*, vol. 28, issue 5, 338–341 (International Transfer Pricing Journal, 2021).

Andreas Riedl and Tyll Stechmann, *Germany: Valuation of Business Restructurings in Germany – Part I: Economic Life of Businesses*, vol. 29, issue 3, 161–172 (International Transfer Pricing Journal, 2022).

Andreas Riedl and Tyll Stechmann, *Germany: Valuation of Business Restructurings in Germany – Part II: Economic Life of Intangible Assets*, vol. 29, issue 4, 247–252 (International Transfer Pricing Journal, 2022).

Ekkehart Reimer and Alexander Rust (eds), *Klaus Vogel on Double Taxation Conventions* (5th ed., Kluwer International Law, 2021).

Ekkehart Reimer, Stefan Schmid and Marianne Orell (eds), *Permanent Establishments: A Domestic Taxation, Bilateral Tax Treaty and OECD Perspective* (3rd ed., Kluwer Law International, 2014).

James R. Repetti, Diane M. Ring and Paul McDaniel, *Introduction to United States International Taxation* (6th ed., Kluwer Law International, 2014).

João Marcus de Melo Rigoni, *A Brazilian View on Base Erosion and Profit Shifting: An Alternative Path*, vol. 42, issue 11, 732–742 (Intertax, 2014).

João Dácio Rolim, *Proportionality and Fair Taxation* (Kluwer Law International, Series on International Taxation, 2014).

H. David Rosenbloom, *Angels on a Pin: Arm's Length in the World*, 523–530 (Tax Notes International, 9 May 2005).

Raffaele Russo, *Application of Arm's Length Principle to Intra-company Dealings: Back to the Origins*, vol. 12, issue 1, 7–15 (International Transfer Pricing Journal, 2005).

Alexander Rust and Claire Micheau (eds), *State Aid and Tax Law* (Kluwer Law International, 2013).

Jacques Sasseville and Arvid A. Skaar, General Report, Cahiers de Droit Fiscal International, *Is There a Permanent Establishment?*, vol. 94a (2009).

Jacques Sasseville, *'Enterprise', 'Business' and 'Business Profits': From the League of Nations to the Current OECD Model Tax Convention*, in Guglielmo Maisto (ed.), The Meaning of 'Enterprise', 'Business' and 'Business Profits' under Tax Treaties and EU Tax Law, vol. 7, 41–58 (IBFD, EC and International Tax Law Series, 2011).

Jacques Sasseville and Richard J. Vann, *IBFD Global Tax Treaty Commentaries, Article 7: Business Profits*.

Jean-Claude Scholsem, *EC: The Proposal for a Council Directive on the Elimination of Double Taxation (Arbitration Procedure)*, vol. 10, issues 11–12, 424–435 (Intertax, 1982).

Wolfgang Schön, *The Distinct Equity of the Debt-Equity Distinction*, 490–502 (Bulletin for International Taxation, September 2012).

Wolfgang Schön, *International Taxation of Risk*, 280–294 (Bulletin for International Taxation, July/August 2014).

Caroline Silberztein, *Transfer Pricing Disputes and Their Causes*, vol. 16, 439–446 (Asia-Pacific Tax Bulletin, November/December 2010).

Caroline Silberztein, *The 2010 Update to the OECD Guidelines*, in Dennis Weber and Stef van Weeghel (eds), The 2010 OECD Updates, 147–160 (Kluwer Law International, 2011).

Caroline Silberztein, Mary C. Bennett and Gregg D. Lemein, *The OECD Discussion Draft on the Transfer of Intangibles (Revision of Chapter VI of the OECD Guidelines): Main Comments*, vol. 41, issue 2, 60–65 (Intertax, 2013).

Caroline Silberztein, Mary C. Bennett and Gregg D. Lemein, *The OECD Discussion Draft on the Transfer of Intangibles (Revision of Chapter VI of the OECD Guidelines): Detailed Comments*, vol. 41, issue 2, 66–81 (Intertax, 2013).

Arvid Skaar, *Permanent Establishment: Erosion of a Tax Treaty Principle* (2nd ed., Kluwer Law International, 2020).

Stig Sollund and Marcos Aurélio Pereira Valadão, *The Commentary on Article 9: The Changes and Their Significance and the Ongoing Work on the UN Transfer Pricing Manual*, 608–611 (Bulletin for International Taxation, November 2012).

Bob Stack, *US Tax Policy and Attribution of Profits to Permanent Establishments*, vol. 13, issue 3, 385–404 (World Tax Journal, 2021).

Christopher J. Steeves, *General Electric Capital Canada Inc. v. The Queen: Guarantee Fees and the Arm's Length Standard*, 131–136 (Derivatives & Financial Instruments, May/June 2011).

David D. Stewart, *Tax Analysts Interview: OECD's Caroline Silberztein*, 417 (Tax Notes International, 8 August 2011).

Christos A. Theophilou, *Attribution of Profits to Permanent Establishments: Should the AOA Be Maintained as the OECD Standard?*, vol. 27, issue 1, 36–41 (International Transfer Pricing Journal, 2020).

Piergiorgio Valente, *Arbitration Convention 90/436/EEC: Inapplicability in Case of Serious Penalties*, vol. 40, issue 3, 220–224 (Intertax, 2012).

Piergiorgio Valente, *Advance Pricing Arrangements: Optimal Tool – Optimal Framework?*, vol. 48, issue 1, 67–73 (Intertax, 2020).

Jefferson VanderWolk, *The Arm's-Length Standard Enters Its Second Century*, 961–968 (Tax Notes International, 4 March 2019).

Francisco Antonio Vaquer Ferrer, *The Concept of 'Permanent Establishment' at the Spanish Courts: Special Reference to the Roche and Dell Cases*, vol. 44, issue 8&9, 673–683 (Intertax, 2016).

Roberto P. Vasconcellos and H. David Rosenbloom, *Measuring a Foreign Tax Credit Generator Transaction Against the Codified Economic Substance Doctrine*, 119–125 (Tax Notes International, 11 October 2010).

Fernando Velayos and Alberto Barreix, *Towards a New Form of International Taxation: The View from Latin America and the Caribbean*, vol. 41, issue 3, 128–139 (Intertax, 2013).

Patrick Velte, *The New European Public Country-by-Country Reporting Requirement*, 168–172 (European Taxation, 2022-4).

Isabel Verlinden and Yoko Mondelaers, *Transfer Pricing Aspects of Intangibles: At the Crossroads Between Legal, Valuation and Transfer Pricing Issues*, vol. 17, issue 1 (International Transfer Pricing Journal, January/February 2010).

Isabel Verlinden, *The Value of a Principle … the Arm's Length Principle*, vol. 49, issue 3, 206–209 (Intertax, 2021).

Susanne Verloove, Peter Hoving and Roberto Aviles Gutierrez, *EU Public Country-by-Country Reporting*, vol. 29, issue 3, 153–160 (International Transfer Pricing Journal, 2022).

Hugo Vollebregt, *Triangular Double Taxation: A Fresh Approach*, vol. 19, issue 2, 103–106 (International Transfer Pricing Journal, March/April 2012).

David Ward, et al., *The Interpretation of Income Tax Treaties with Particular Reference to the Commentaries on the OECD Model* (IFA/IBFD, 2005).

Joann M. Weiner, *Using the Experience in the U.S. States to Evaluate Issues in Implementing Formula Apportionment at the International Level* (OTA Paper 83, April 1999).

Bertil Wiman and Mattias Dahlberg, General Report, Cahiers de Droit Fiscal International, *The Taxation of Foreign Passive Income for Groups of Companies*, vol. 98A, 25–47 (2013).

Bertil Wiman, *Equalising the Tax Burden in a Group of Companies*, in Gustaf Lindencrona, Sven-Olof Lodin and Bertil Wiman (eds), International Studies in Taxation: Law and Economics, Liber Amicorum Leif Mutén, 363–378 (Kluwer Law International, 1999).

Jens Wittendorff, *Transfer Pricing and the Arm's Length Principle in International Tax Law*, 84–111 (Kluwer Law International, 2010).

Jens Wittendorff, *Valuation of Intangibles under Income-Based Methods: Part I*, vol. 17, issue 5, 323–335 (International Transfer Pricing Journal, September/October 2010).

Jens Wittendorff, *Valuation of Intangibles under Income-Based Methods: Part II*, vol. 17, issue 6, 383–401 (International Transfer Pricing Journal, November/December 2010).

Jens Wittendorff, *U.N. Transfer Pricing Manual: The Choice Between International Consistency and Conflict*, 569–576 (Tax Notes International, 5 November 2012).

Jens Wittendorff, *Transfer Pricing Oddity: The OECD's New Guidelines on Financial Transactions*, 723–739 (Tax Notes International, 10 August 2020).

Jens Wittendorff, *Denmark's Supreme Court Accepts CUP in Royalty Case*, 911–915 (Tax Notes International, 17 August 2020).

Rainer Zielke, *Commissionaire Structure as an Agency Permanent Establishment (PE): Low Risk for Foreign Principals Constituting a PE in Norway – Dell Products v. Government of Norway, Decision of the Norwegian Supreme Court of 2 December 2011*, vol. 40, issue 8/9, 494–496 (Intertax, 2012).

Fredrik Zimmer, General Report, Cahiers de Droit Fiscal International, *Form and Substance in Tax Law*, vol. 87a (2002).

Theresa Zinn, Nadine Riedel and Christoph Spengel, *The Increasing Importance of Transfer Pricing Regulations: A Worldwide Overview*, vol. 42, issue 6/7, 352–404 (Intertax, 2014).

Mario Züger, *Arbitration under Tax Treaties: Improving Legal Protection in International Tax Law* (IBFD, 2001).

Table of Cases

Cap Gemini, French Supreme Administrative Court (Conseil d'État) (7 November 2005, case numbers 266436 and 266438), **193**

Kingdom of Belgium (C-182/03) and Forum 187 ASBL (C-217/03) v. Commission of the European Communities, CJEU (22 June 2006, joined cases C-182/03 and C-217/03), **125**

DSG Retail Ltd v. Her Majesty's Revenue and Customs, Commissioners for Her Majesty's Revenue and Customs (31 March 2009, case number TC 00001), **44**

Refrescos y Envasados S.A. v. Administración General del Estado, Supreme Court of Spain (*Tribunal Supremo*) (30 November 2009, case number 3582/2003), **3**

Société de Gestion Industrielle (SGI) v. Belgian State, CJEU (21 January 2010, case number C-311/08), **19**

Xilinx, Inc., and Consolidated Subsidiaries v. Commissioner of Internal Revenue, United States Court of Appeals for the Ninth Circuit (22 March 2010, case numbers 06-74246 and 06-74269), **122**

Zimmer, French Supreme Administrative Court (Conseil d'État) (31 March 2010, case number 304715), **104**

General Electric Capital Canada Inc. v. Her Majesty the Queen, Canadian Federal Court of Appeal (15 December 2010, case number 2010 FCA 344), **112, 117, 118, 120**

Toyota Argentina S.A. v. Administración Federal de Ingresos Públicos, Federal Tax Court of Argentina (*Tribunal Fiscal de la Nación*) (28 April 2011, case number 26-860), **43**

Commissioner of Taxation v. SNF Australia Pty Ltd, Federal Court of Australia (1 June 2011, case number (2011) FCAFC 74), **44, 55**

Dell products, Norwegian Supreme Court (2 December 2011, case number 2011-1581), **105**

GlaxoSmithKline Inc. v. Her Majesty the Queen, Supreme Court of Canada (18 October 2012, case number 33874), **97**

Eaton Corporation v. Commissioner of Internal Revenue, United States Tax Court (26 June 2013, case number 5576-12), **203**

Table of Legislation

Documents Published by the European Commission

Directives, Regulations, Resolutions, Conclusions, Press Releases and other documents Issued by the Council of the EU

Documents Published by the OECD

Other Documents and Sources

Index

T